MICROSOFT® EXCEL FOR WINDOWS® 95 BY PICTORIAL

VERSION 7.0

PicTorial Series

Dennis P. Curtin, Series Editor

Titles Available for Windows® 95

Windows® 95 by PicTorial

Microsoft® Word for Windows® 95 (Version 7.0) by PicTorial

Microsoft® Excel for Windows® 95 (Version 7.0) by PicTorial

Microsoft Access® for Windows® 95 (Version 7.0) by PicTorial

Titles Available for Windows® 3.1

Microsoft® Word 6.0 for Windows® by PicTorial

WordPerfect® 6.0 for Windows® by PicTorial

Microsoft® Excel 5.0 by PicTorial

Microsoft Access® 2.0 by PicTorial

Windows® 3.1 by PicTorial

Essentials of Windows® 3.1 by PicTorial

MICROSOFT® EXCEL FOR WINDOWS® 95 BY PICTORIAL

VERSION 7.0

Dennis P. Curtin

Prentice Hall, Upper Saddle River, New Jersey 07458

Library of Congress Cataloging-in-Publication Data:
Curtin, Dennis P.
Microsoft Excel for Windows 95 (version 7.0) by PicTorial / Dennis P. Curtin
p. cm. — (PicTorial series)
Includes index.
ISBN 0-13-238379-9 (pbk.)
1. Microsoft Excel for Windows. 2. Business—Computer programs.
3. Electronic spreadsheets. I. Title. II. Series: Curtin, Dennis P., PicTorial series.
HF5548.4.M523C874 1996 96-4038
005.369—dc20 CIP

Acquisitions editor: Carolyn Henderson
Marketing manager: Nancy Evans
Director of production and manufacturing: Joanne Jay
Production manager: Lorraine Patsco
Illustrator: Warren Fischbach
Design director: Patricia Wosczyk
Cover designer: Suzanne Behnke
Manufacturing buyer: Paul Smolenski
Editorial assistant: Audrey Regan
Production assistant: Renée Peletier
Development editor and project manager: Cecil Yarbrough

Interior design by Kenny Beck
Additional design by Christy Mahon
Cover art by Marjory Dressler
Screen shots and electronic composition by Cathleen Morin

ISBN 0-13-238379-9

Printed in the United States of America
9 8 7 6 5 4 3 2 1

Prentice-Hall International (UK) Limited, *London*
Prentice-Hall of Australia Pty. Limited, *Sydney*
Prentice-Hall of Canada Inc., *Toronto*
Prentice-Hall Hispanoamericana, S.A., *Mexico*
Prentice-Hall of India Private Limited, *New Delhi*
Simon & Schuster Asia Ptd. Ltd., *Singapore*
Editora Prentice-Hall do Brasil, Ltda., *Rio de Janeiro*

CONTENTS

PicTorial 5

Exploring Workbooks, Charts, and Macros *189*

PicTorial 6

Managing Lists *233*

QUICKSTEPS BOXES

PREFACE

This text is an introduction to Microsoft Excel for Windows 95 (Version 7.0), one of the leading spreadsheet programs. Spreadsheets are one of the most common programs used on computers because they allow you to calculate numbers quickly and easily. The applications of a program such as Excel are almost endless, ranging from tasks that can be done just as easily on a calculator, such as adding a column of numbers, to those that aren't anywhere near as easy without the power of a computer. For example, you can prepare a single column showing a budget for the month of January and then, just by dragging that column, copy it to calculate the budget for February through December. As powerful as these features are, they pale in comparison to the speed with which you can explore changes. Change a single number anywhere in a budget such as this and instantly, all other numbers that depend on that number also change. For example, you can see how profits are affected if sales or costs rise or fall. Or, if analyzing a home loan, you can instantly see how an increase in interest rates affects the monthly payment.

This text assumes only basic Windows experience such as pointing, clicking, and dragging. Everything else you need to know to become a proficient Excel user is presented here.

PICTORIALS

This text is organized into pictorial tutorials, called PicTorials. Each PicTorial has the following structure and features:

- Each PicTorial begins with objectives that guide you in understanding what you are about to learn.
- A brief introduction to the PicTorial follows the objectives.
- Following the introduction is a series of sections. Each section covers a single procedure or a few closely related topics. The concept behind each procedure is first discussed and then a *tutorial* guides you in exploring the concept hands-on at the computer.
- At the end of each PicTorial is a series of true-false, multiple choice, and fill-in-the-blank questions that test your understanding of the material you have covered.

EXCEL FOR WINDOWS 95—FIVE STEPS TO MASTERY

Learning application programs such as Excel takes time and practice. There really aren't any shortcuts. This text recognizes that no one masters procedures the first time through. It takes repetition and practice—and, yes, even mistakes. Our approach uses five steps to mastery: concepts, tutorials, drills, exercises, and projects.

- Concepts introduce procedures and discuss why you would use them and how they work. Many of these sections also include QuickSteps boxes that list the steps you follow. These QuickSteps boxes give you an understanding of how to complete procedures and are also useful reference tools when you want to look up something you may have forgotten.

- Tutorials provide you with step-by-step guidance as you explore a procedure for the first time. If you follow the steps, you can't go wrong.
- Drills, which you complete after finishing a matching tutorial, provide repetitive practice. For example, you may format five worksheet models instead of just the one you formatted in the tutorial. This repetition is designed to help you master a procedure.
- Exercises, which you complete after the drills, are designed to make you think. Procedures are not spelled out for you. You either have to recall them or look them up. These activities are much like the real world, where you are told what to do, but not how to do it.
- Projects, which you complete after exercises, give you an assignment and then leave you on your own. They are easy to complete if you have first completed the previous levels but there are times when you may have to look things up.

PAL—PROGRAM-ASSISTED LEARNING

If you were able to travel in time and visit a classroom not too many years in the future, you'd find most students studying all kinds of subjects using computer-based interactive multimedia programs. For students of Excel and other Windows-based applications, this future is here now because an interactive multimedia version of this text is available. This multimedia edition, called *PAL (Program-Assisted Learning)*, is designed to use your own computer to guide you through learning Excel. PAL teaches you how to use Excel features while using the actual program—not simulations of the program. It does this by displaying interactive animations, movies, graphics, and step-by-step instructions on top of the Excel screen display. PAL is an intuitive, easy-to-use system that makes learning Excel not only more efficient, but more enjoyable.

KEY FEATURES

Excel is a visually oriented program, so this text uses a visual approach. It contains a number of other features designed to make it a better learning tool.

- *Object linking and embedding* (OLE) makes computing more document-centric. It's now easy to include memos, illustrations, and databases tables in Excel workbooks. And once these object are included in a workbook, OLE it makes it easy to edit them without leaving Excel. An entire PicTorial is devoted to this important new topic.
- *QuickSteps boxes* summarize the steps you use for each procedure. These highlighted boxes are easy to find in each concepts section and make the text an ideal reference manual as well as a teaching tool.
- *Pausing for Practice boxes* appear periodically in tutorials when important procedures have been introduced. They encourage you to stop at key points and practice these procedures until they become second nature.
- *Common Wrong Turns boxes* alert you to where many people make mistakes and show you how to avoid them.
- *Tips boxes* point out shortcuts and other interesting features about many procedures.
- *Looking Back* and *Looking Ahead boxes* are used as reminders of important material covered earlier and as pointers to material to be covered later in greater detail.

SUPPLEMENTS

The following supplements to this text have been made available by the publisher:

- The *Excel Student Resource Disk* contains all of the files needed to complete the computer activities in this text.
- An *Instructor's Manual with Tests* contains suggested course outlines for a variety of course lengths and formats, teaching tips and a list of competencies to be attained for each PicTorial, solutions and answers to review questions and all computer activities, and a complete test bank of over 200 questions.
- A Windows-based computerized testing program, *Prentice Hall Custom Test*, features user-friendly test creation as well as the ability to administer tests traditionally or on-line, evaluate and track students' results, and analyze the success of each exam—all with a simple click of the mouse.

SENDING YOUR OPINIONS AND FEEDBACK

I am always happy to hear from users or potential users of my textbooks; it's through such exchanges that improvements are made. If you have any comments or questions, send them to me by e-mail on the Internet at Dennis_Curtin@msn.com. (You can use this address when sending e-mail from CompuServe, America Online, or any of the popular commercial services and it will get to me.)

ACKNOWLEDGMENTS

Working on this text has been an unusually enjoyable experience, and I owe thanks to the many people who have helped produce the final product.

At the publisher's end Cecil Yarbrough continued with his efforts to improve my texts. His guidance and leadership are always most welcome. Supporting the production at the publisher have been Suzanne Behnke, Warren Fischbach, Joanne Jay, Christina Mahon, John Nestor, Lorraine Patsco, Paul Smolenski, and Patricia Wosczyk. And thanks to Cathy Morin, who did the screen illustrations in the book and tested the materials over and over, and then turned a manuscript into the final four-color book.

All of these people, each and every one, took a personal interest in this text, and that interest shows in the work you are now holding. Any shortcomings that remain are my responsibility.

DENNIS P. CURTIN
Marblehead, Massachusetts

DEDICATION

This book is dedicated to John Davis, the editor who first put me on the path that I have followed throughout my career. His honesty and kindness have been characteristics I have tried my best to emulate in my own career. His wisdom is something I can only aspire to.

PicTorial ONE

A VISUAL INTRODUCTION

After completing this PicTorial, you will be able to:

- **Define the terms *spreadsheet program, worksheet, workbook, model,* and *template***
- **Start and close Excel**
- **Open and close workbooks**
- **Describe the Excel screen display and parts of the program**
- **Move around a worksheet and enter data**
- **Print a worksheet**
- **Use Excel's on-line Help system to get help on procedures**

THE programs you use on a computer to do your work are called application programs. Different kinds of application programs do different kinds of tasks. For example, you use spreadsheet application programs such as Excel to work with numbers and word processing application programs such as Word for Windows to work with text.

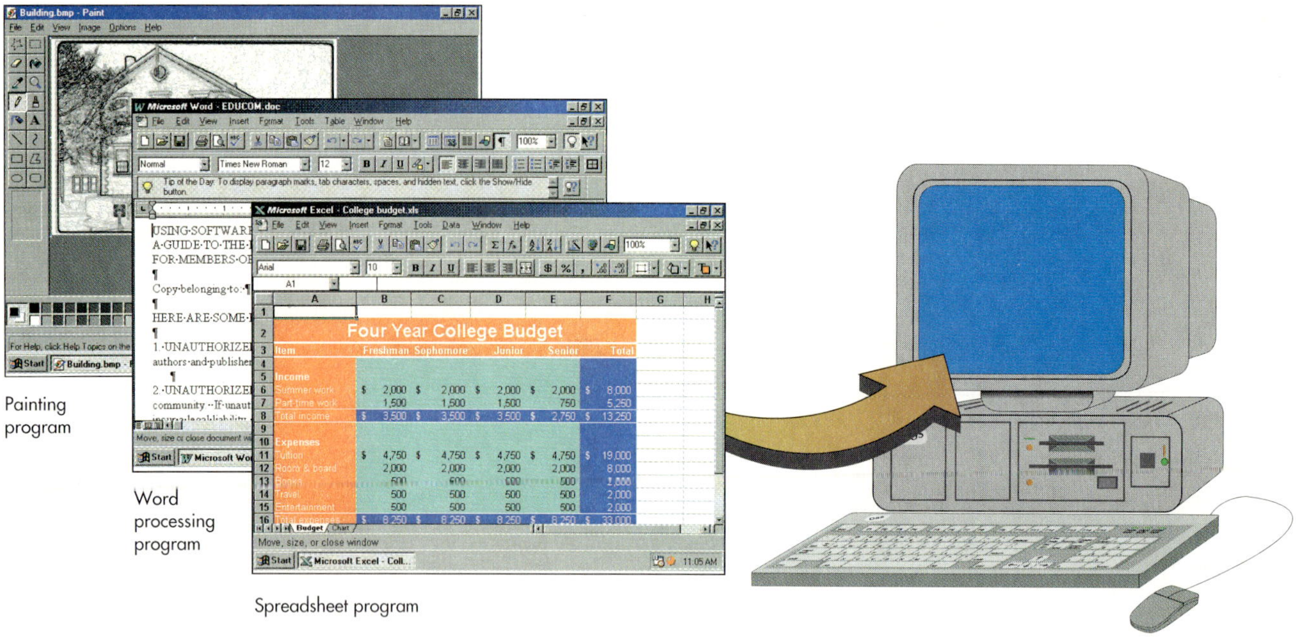

Spreadsheets, one of the most popular types of application programs, are used to solve and analyze almost any type of problem that involves numbers and calculations. In business, they are used to analyze the performance of products, salespeople, or dealers. They are used to compare costs, prices, and gross margins on individual products in a product line. They are also used to calculate prices, forecast and budget sales, predict expenses and profits, and make cash-flow projections. In the sciences and social sciences they are used to analyze research data. Even in such fields as sports, they are used to analyze performance. Their major advantage is that they allow you to explore a number of alternatives quickly and easily.

One of the primary uses of spreadsheets is to build models to analyze numerical situations and to explore the effects that changes in any assumptions have on their outcome. You use models to simulate real-world situations. Just as a model airplane is tested in a wind tunnel to determine how changing the shape of a wing will affect the airplane's performance, so a model of a situation involving numbers can be tested in a spreadsheet program to determine how changing a part can affect the outcome.

UNDERSTANDING
Spreadsheet Terminology

When using a spreadsheet, you should understand five basic terms: *spreadsheet program*, *worksheet* or *sheet*, *workbook*, *model*, and *template*.

A *spreadsheet program* such as Excel is the computer program that you use for financial or other numeric analysis.

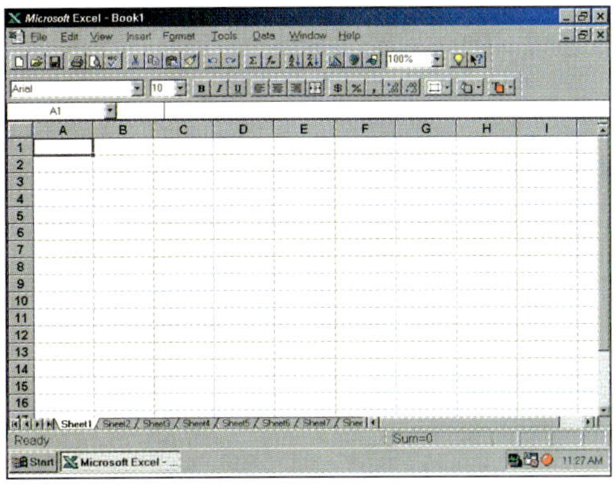

The Excel spreadsheet program's opening screen

A *worksheet* or *sheet* is the arrangement of horizontal rows and vertical columns that appears on the screen. At the intersection of each row and column is a cell into which you can enter text, numbers, or formulas.

A worksheet

A *workbook* is a collection of worksheets saved together as a single file. When you start Excel or open a new workbook, the workbook contains 16 worksheets.

A *model* is a representation of a real or hypothetical situation that you create on a worksheet to solve a problem or perform an analysis. To create a model, you use three basic types of entries: text, numbers, and formulas.

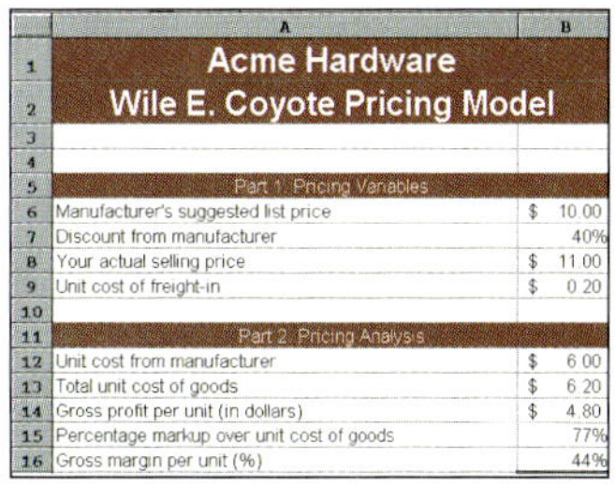

A model

A *template* is a model from which some or all the numbers specific to a situation have been removed, leaving just the descriptive text and formulas. Anyone can then enter new numbers in the labeled cells to get an answer to a problem. In many firms, templates are developed by experts and then distributed to others. For example, the accounting department might develop a template that calculates the price of an item when you know its cost. People who set prices then use the template to calculate them. Excel even comes with a number of templates built in.

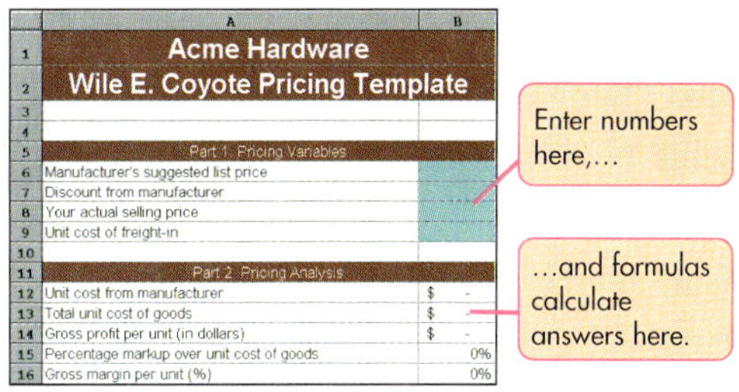

A template

Learning how to use a new application program is much like learning how to drive. To drive well, you have to learn the rules of the road and how the car should be maintained for safety and reliability, but you can't wait to get behind the wheel. Once you have taken at least a spin around the block, you have a feel for driving that makes you want to learn more. In this PicTorial, you take Excel for a spin around the block. Just as an experienced driver sat next to you and told you everything to do on your first drive, we'll sit beside you and guide you through this first lesson. The goal here is to master some of Excel's most basic features—starting and exiting Excel; opening, saving, and closing documents (called workbooks); getting around a workbook; printing a worksheet; and using Help. You should relax as you explore these procedures and get a feeling for the program.

1-1 STARTING AND CLOSING EXCEL

To use an application program such as Excel, you must first know how to start it—variously called *starting, opening, running,* or *launching it*—and how to exit it.

Starting Application Programs

There are a number of ways to start Windows 95 programs, but the most common is using the Start menu. When you use the mouse to click the **Start** button on the taskbar at the bottom of the Windows 95 screen, the *Start menu* appears. When you highlight any name on this menu that has a triangle (▶) next to it and pause or click, a submenu cascades out from the first menu. Once you locate the icon and name of the program you want to run, you click it to start it.

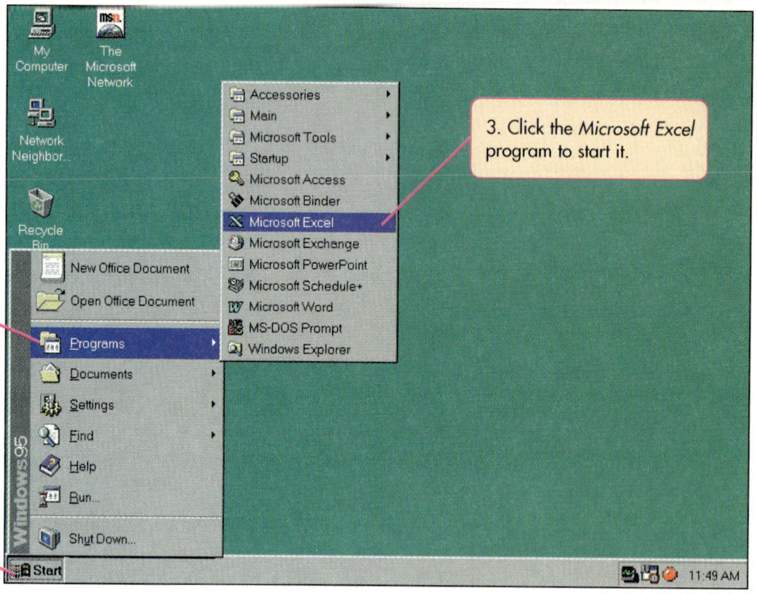

When you start a program, its button is displayed on the taskbar. When more than one program is running at the same time, you can quickly switch between them by clicking the taskbar button of the one you want to use.

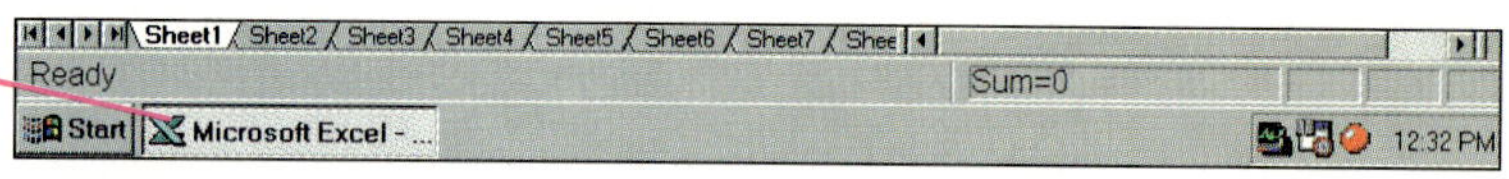

TIP
QuickSteps Boxes

QuickSteps boxes summarize the steps you follow to complete Excel procedures. These boxes can be found throughout this text and serve two purposes:

- On your first pass through a section, they give you an advance look at the steps you must follow to complete the procedure. Don't actually execute the commands this time around. If you do so, you may not know how to recover from any mistakes you might make.
- Later on, when you want to refresh your memory about a procedure, they make it easy to find and review the steps you must follow. At this stage, you can use them as a quick reference guide.

QUICKSTEPS

Starting Excel

1. Click Windows' **Start** button to display the Start menu.
2. Point to the **Programs** folder on the Start menu to cascade the menu.
3. Click the **Microsoft Excel** program name or icon to start it.

Closing Application Programs

When you are finished with a program such as Excel, you exit or close it. This removes it from the computer's memory and removes its window from the desktop and its button from the taskbar.

It is important to quit Excel using the commands designed for this purpose. Excel creates temporary files on the disk while you are working, and these are deleted only if you exit correctly. If you quit incorrectly, your workbook may be left damaged.

You can close almost any window simply by clicking the **Close** button at the far right of the title bar. This and other methods are described in the QuickSteps box "Closing Excel."

QUICKSTEPS

Closing Excel

To close Excel:

- Click the **Close** button at the far right of the title bar. (If a workbook is open, there are two **Close** buttons. Clicking the upper one closes Excel; clicking the lower one closes the workbook.)

However, you can also use these procedures:

- Pull down Excel's **File** menu and click the **Exit** command.
- Right-click Excel's button on the taskbar, and click the shortcut menu's **Close** command.
- Double-click Excel's icon at the left of the title bar, or click the icon to display a shortcut menu, and then click the **Close** command.
- Right-click Excel's title bar, then click the shortcut menu's **Close** command.
- Hold down Alt and press F4 when Excel is the active window.

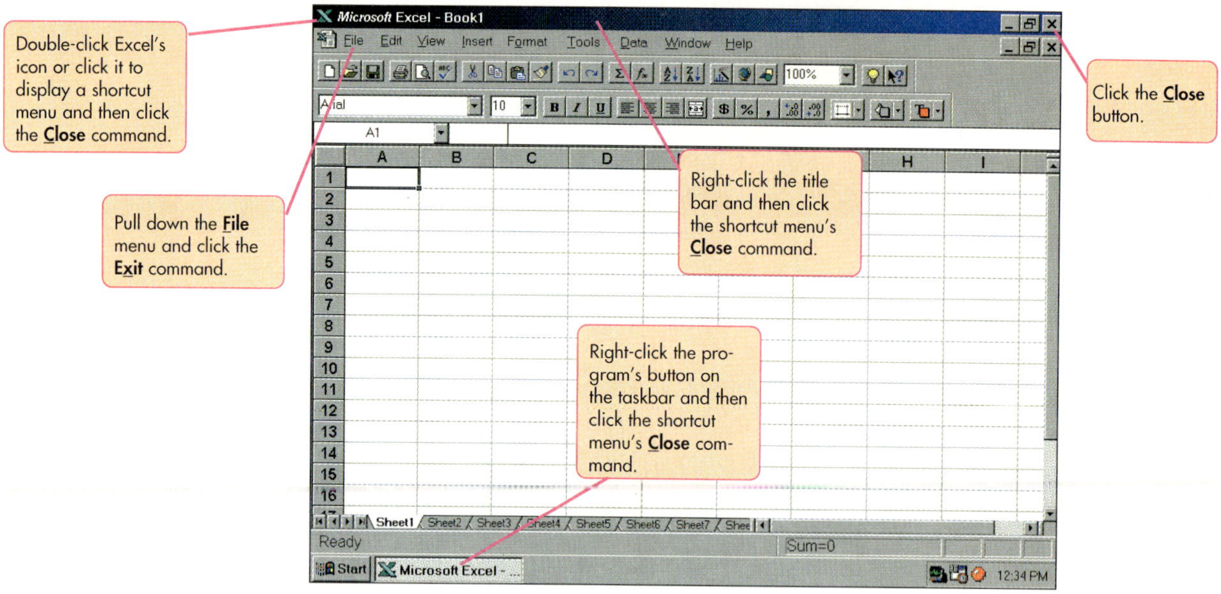

COMMON WRONG TURNS

Not Saving Workbooks

If you close Excel without saving changes to any open workbooks, a dialog box asks if you want to save the current changes.

- To save the workbook, click the **Yes** button.
- To abandon the workbook, click the **No** button.
- To cancel the command and return to the workbook instead of closing it, click the **Cancel** command button.

TUTORIAL

In this tutorial you explore starting and closing Excel using the **Start** button on the taskbar. Two things may confuse you on some systems, a moved taskbar or a hidden taskbar.

- The taskbar is normally located along the bottom of the screen, but you can drag it to any one of the other three sides and drop it there.
- If the taskbar is hidden, you have to point to one of the borders of the screen to display it. You can show the taskbar by right-clicking a clear area on the taskbar and then clicking the **Properties** command. Click the **Auto hide** check box to turn it off, then click the **OK** button to close the dialog box.

Getting Ready

1. Turn on the computer and start Windows. (This step will be assumed for all tutorials from here on.)

Starting Excel

2. Click the **Start** button at the far left of the taskbar on the Windows desktop to display the Start menu.

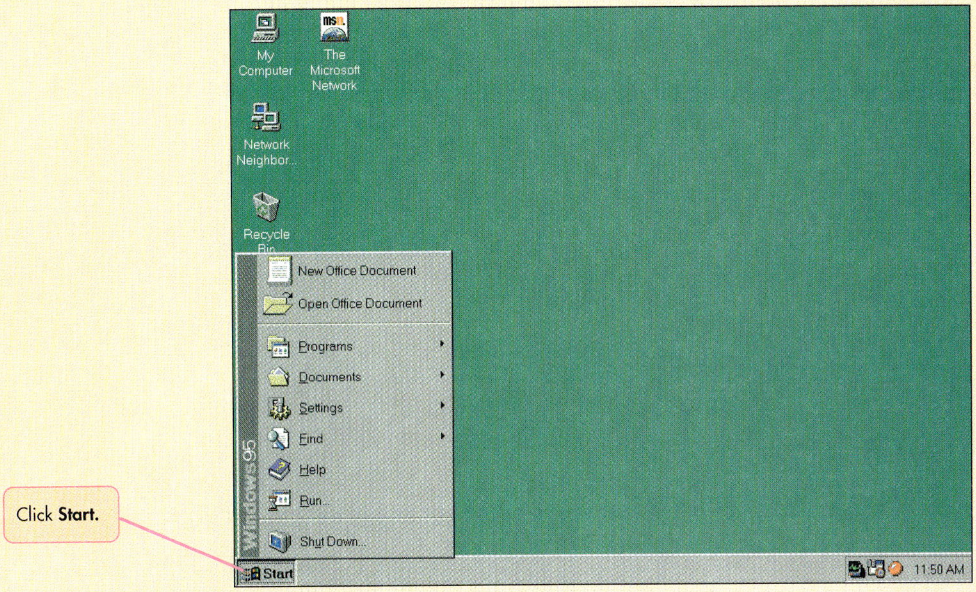

3. Point to the **Programs** folder to cascade a menu.

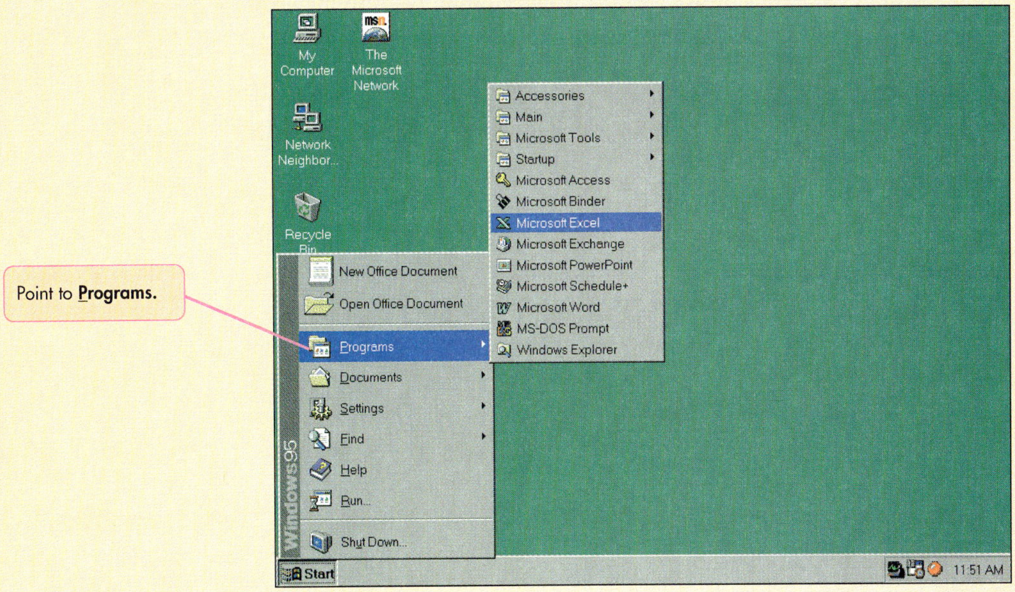

4. Click the **Microsoft Excel** program name or icon to start it and the program's window is displayed. Notice how a button for Microsoft Excel appears on the taskbar.

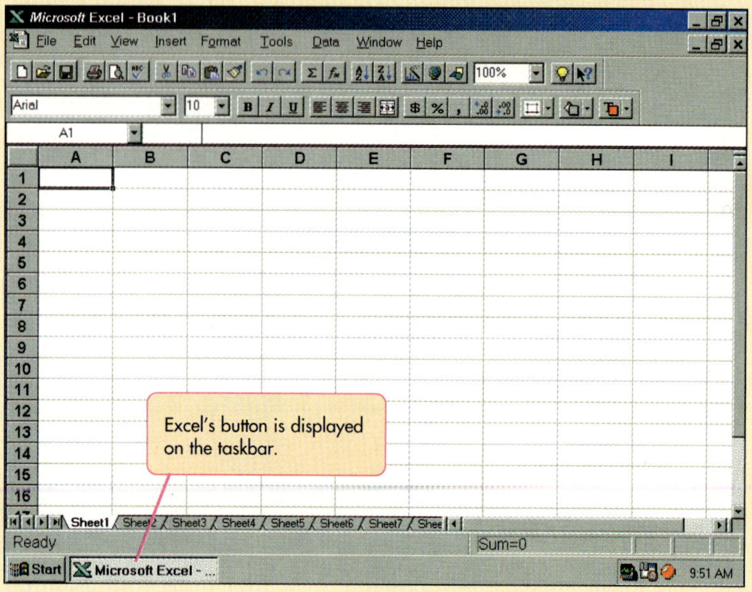

Closing Excel

5. Click the **Close** button at the far right of Excel's title bar to close the program. (Clicking the lower **Close** button closes the workbook, not the application.)

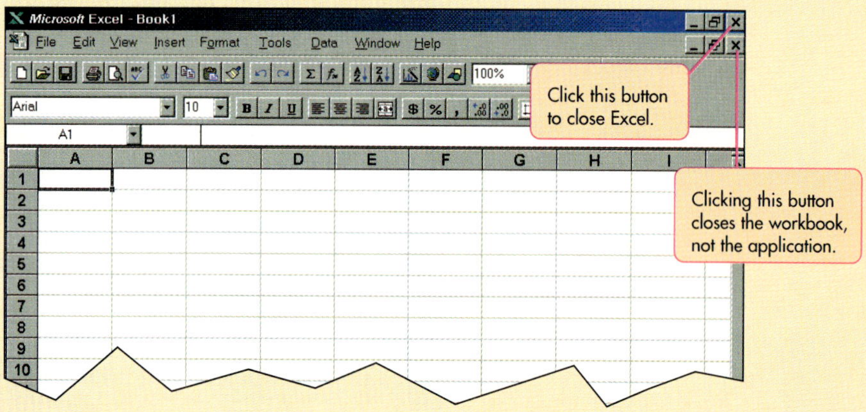

Finishing Up

6. Repeat Steps 2 through 4 to restart Excel and continue to the next section, or shut down your system. (To shut down the system, click the **Start** button on Windows' taskbar, click the **Shut Down** command, and follow the instructions that appear on the screen.)

1-2 EXPLORING EXCEL'S WINDOW

To use Excel, you should be familiar with both its application window and the worksheet within it where you enter data.

The Application's Window

When you start Excel, its window displays a number of elements that make the program fast and efficient to work with. You should become familiar with the names of these elements, many of which are common to all Windows applications.

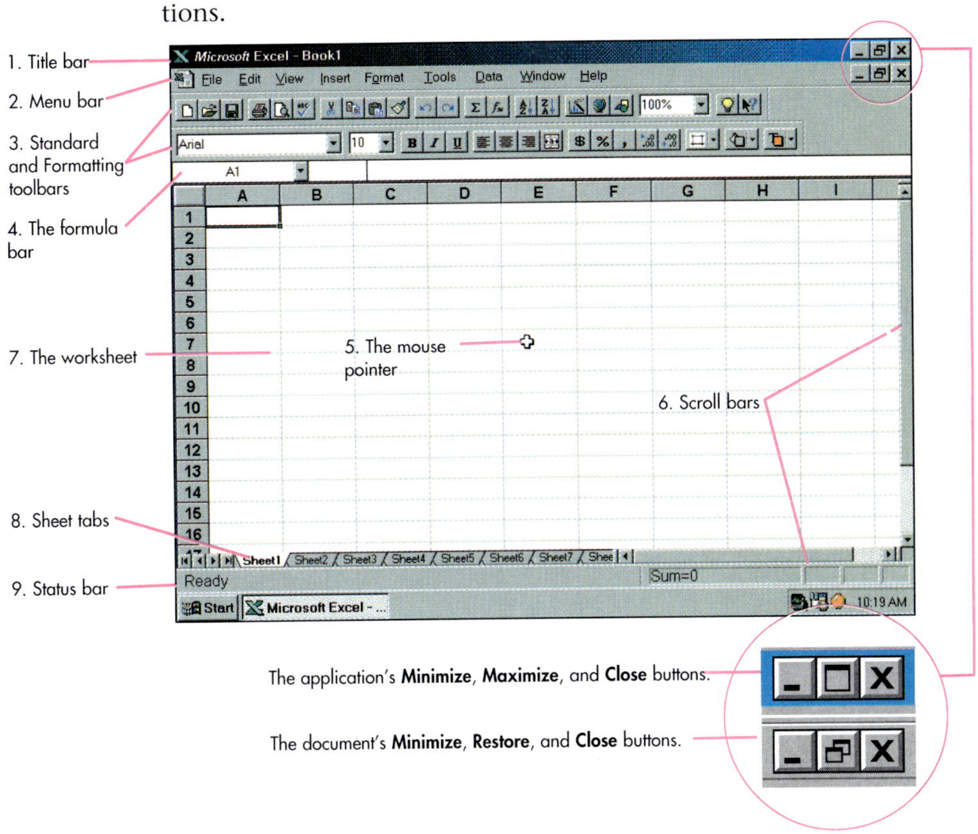

1. The *title bar* lists the name of the application and any open workbook. It also displays an icon at the left end that you can click to display a menu, or double-click to close the application. At the right end are the **Minimize**, **Maximize** or **Restore**, and **Close** buttons that affect the size of Excel's window or close the application.
2. The *menu bar* lists the names of menus that you can pull down. Each menu contains a list of commands from which you can choose.
3. The *Standard* (upper) and *Formatting* (lower) *toolbars* contain buttons you can click to execute the most frequently used commands. To see the name of any button, point to it with the mouse pointer, and a box called a ToolTip is displayed. A description of the button's function is also displayed on the status bar.
4. The *formula bar* is used to navigate on the sheet and to see and edit cell contents. This bar is described in detail in the box "Understanding the Formula Bar."
5. The *mouse pointer* takes on the shape of a cross in the worksheet area, but its shape changes when pointing to other areas of the screen. Some of the shapes it can take are described in the box "Understanding the Mouse Pointer."
6. *Scroll bars* are on the right and bottom sides of the window.

7. The *sheet* or *worksheet* contains rows and columns that divide it into cells where you enter data and create your models.
8. The *sheet tabs* at the bottom of the worksheet are used to move from one sheet to another. Sixteen worksheets are open when you start Excel, but how many tabs are displayed depends on your system.
9. The *status bar* at the bottom of the Excel window displays information on the current status of your system. At the left it displays information about a highlighted command or a command in progress. For example, if you point to a button on the toolbar, a description of the button is displayed. The right side indicates the status of keys. For example, when you press NumLock or CapsLock (or Insert in certain situations) to engage them, *NUM* and *CAPS* (or OVR for overtype) are displayed at the right end of the status bar.

UNDERSTANDING
The Formula Bar

The formula bar is displayed between the toolbar and the sheet's column headings. It serves a number of functions.

When Not Entering Data

When not entering data, the Name box displays the address of the active cell (the cell with the thick border), and its contents (if any) is displayed to the right. You can type a cell's address into the Name box and press Enter↵ to jump to that cell. Or, if you have assigned a name to cells (as you will see later), you can click the Name box's drop-down arrow (▾) to display a list of the names you can jump to.

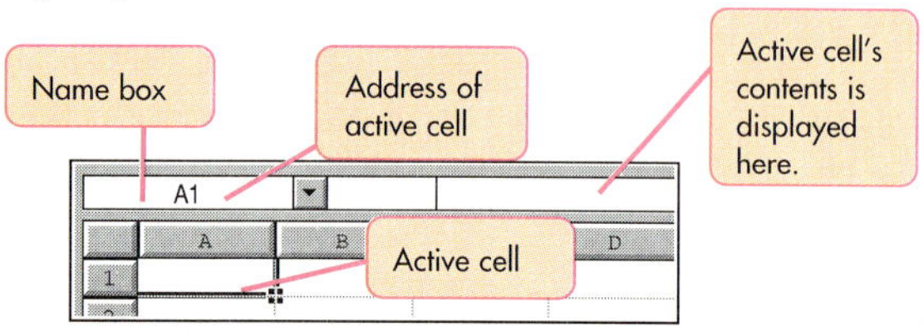

When Entering Data

As soon as you type a character, three new boxes appear on the formula bar. Clicking the Enter box (☑) enters the data into the cell. It's just like pressing Enter↵. Clicking the Cancel box (☒) cancels the entry. Clicking the Function Wizard box displays dialog boxes that guide you through the process of entering functions.

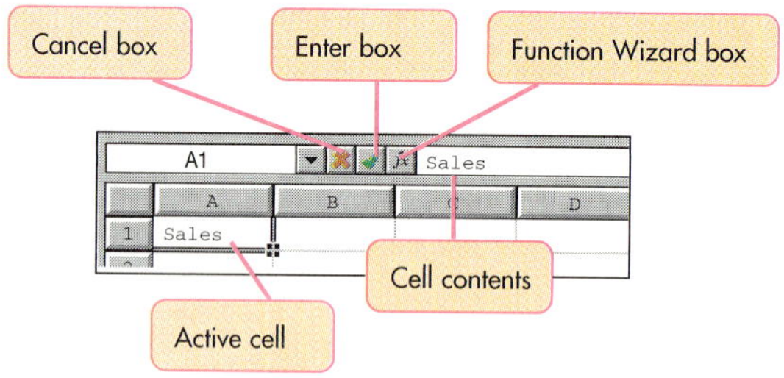

The Worksheet

The worksheet is where you enter data in the spreadsheet. It has a number of parts with which you should be familiar.

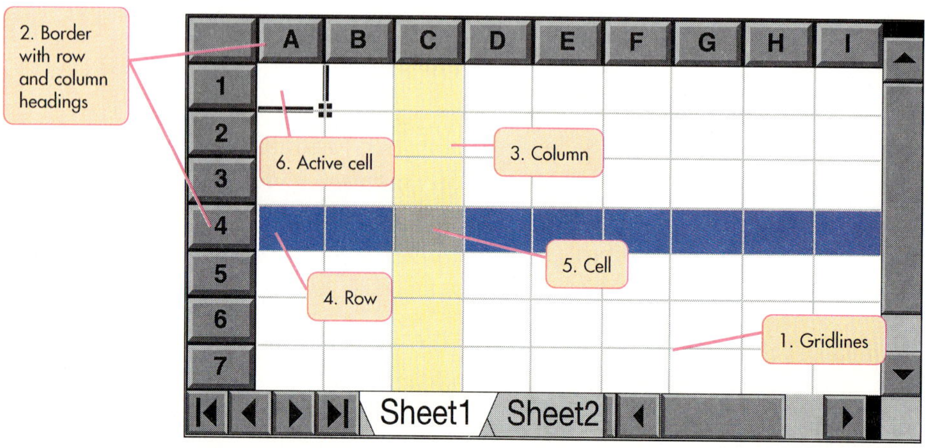

1. *Gridlines* divide the worksheet into rows, columns, and cells.
2. The sheet border contains column headings across the top and row headings down the left side.
3. Columns run vertically down the worksheet and have lettered headings. The first twenty-six columns have the headings A to Z, the next twenty-six AA to AZ, the next twenty-six BA to BZ, and so on up to column IV, the 256th column.
4. Rows run horizontally across the worksheet and have numbered headings. The headings start with row 1 at the top of the worksheet and end at row 16,384 at the bottom.
5. *Cells,* into which you enter data, fall at the intersection of each column and row. Cells are referred to by their coordinates, called their *cell reference* or *address*. The reference is given as the column letter followed by the row number. For example, the cell at the intersection of column C and row 4 is cell C4.
6. The *active cell* is outlined with a heavier border that you can move to another cell by clicking with the mouse or pressing arrow keys. It's into this cell that you enter data when you type on the keyboard. The address of the active cell is always displayed in the Name box at the left end of the formula bar.

UNDERSTANDING
Cell Entries

As you progress through this text, here are some of the things you'll see how to enter into the active cell:

- *Numbers* can be calculated when referred to by formulas. For example, the principal on a loan may be entered as 10,000 and the interest rate as 10%.
- *Dates* and *times* are special kinds of numbers that can also be used in calculations.
- *Formulas* calculate numbers entered either into the formulas themselves or into other cells that the formulas refer to. One special type of formula, called a *function*, automatically performs complicated calculations such as mortgage payments.
- *Text* is anything you enter that isn't in a form Excel recognizes as a number, date, time, or formula. It is commonly used for titles and as labels for other parts of the worksheet. For example, if a worksheet is used to calculate a loan, it may have a title that reads *Loan Payment Calculator*. Various rows may then have descriptive labels such as *principal, interest, term,* and *monthly payments*.
- *Formats* control the way numbers are displayed on the screen and the way text is aligned in a cell. For example, a number entered as 10000 may be formatted so it's displayed as 10,000, $10,000, or $10,000.00.

TUTORIAL

In this tutorial you explore moving the mouse pointer, displaying names of toolbar buttons, and selecting cells.

Getting Ready

1. Start Excel if it isn't on the screen.

Exploring the Mouse Pointer

2. Move the mouse pointer around the screen to see how it takes on one of the shapes shown in the box "Understanding the Mouse Pointer."

UNDERSTANDING
The Mouse Pointer

The mouse pointer changes shape when you point to various elements on the screen.

It is shaped like an arrow (⇖) when pointing to the title bar, toolbar, or menu bar so you can click buttons, menu names, or menu commands to choose them.

It is shaped like an I-beam (I) when inside one of the text boxes on the Formatting toolbar or formula bar. When it has this shape, you can click in the text box to move the insertion point there to type a new entry, or to select the current entry so you can edit or replace it.

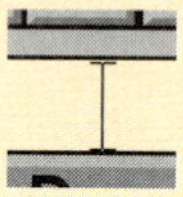

It is shaped like a large outlined plus sign when in the worksheet area. When it has this shape, you can click cells to select them.

It is shaped like a split double arrow when positioned on the border between column or row headings. When it has this shape, you can drag the mouse to widen or narrow columns and rows.

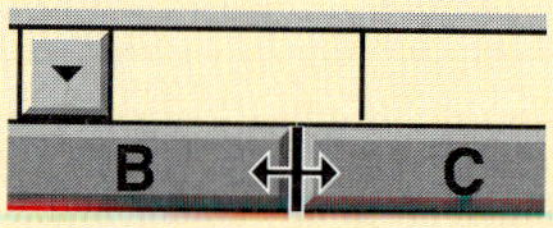

It is shaped like a small plus sign (+) when pointing to the small square (called the *fill handle*) in the lower-right corner of the active cell. When it has this shape, you can drag the active cell's outline to copy the contents of the cell to adjoining cells.

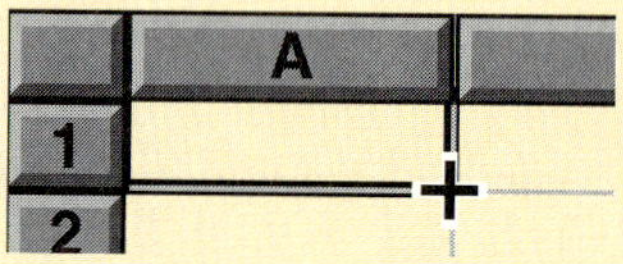

3. Point to any button on the toolbar, and you'll see its name displayed in a small yellow box called a Tooltip below the mouse pointer. A description of what the button does is displayed on the status bar at the bottom of the screen.

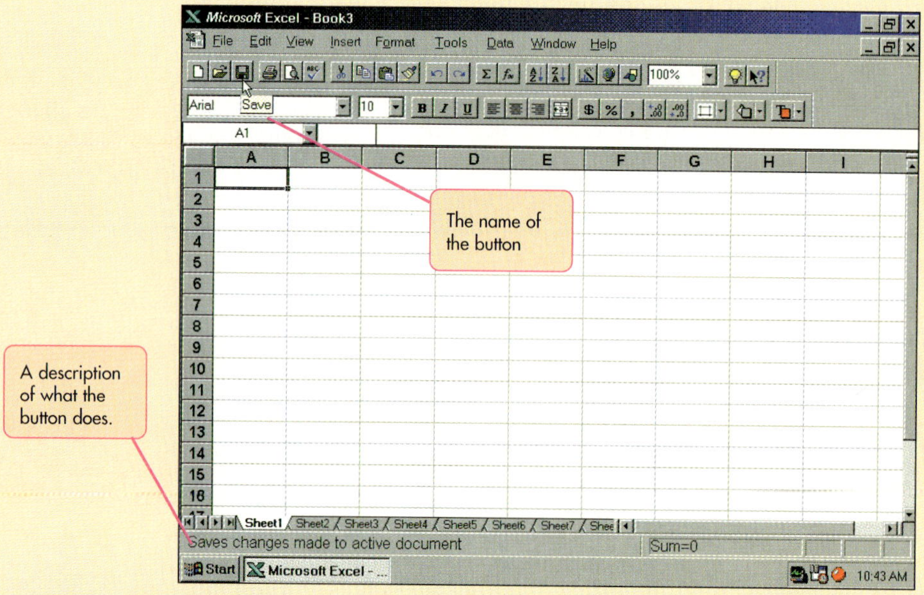

Exploring Cells

4. Notice which cell is outlined with the heavy border. This is the active cell. Read up the column to find the column letter. Read across the row to find

the row number. When combined, these two elements give you the cell's address—for instance, cell A1.

5. Press ←, →, ↑, and ↓ to move the active cell, and watch as its address changes in the Name box at the left end of the formula bar. (If any cell had any contents—such as text, a number, or formula—that too would be displayed on the formula bar.)

Finishing Up

6. Click Excel's **Close** button to close the program, or continue to the next section.

1-3 OPENING AND CLOSING WORKBOOKS

To use Excel or any other Windows program you must know how to open and close documents or files—which Excel calls workbooks. You open a workbook just as you open documents in all Windows programs. When you first start Excel, a new workbook is automatically opened containing only the cell pointer that marks the cell where any typed data will go.

Opening Existing Workbooks

To open an existing workbook—Excel's name for a document or file—you have to know three things about it: the drive it is on, the folder it is in, and its name. When you use the Open command, the Open dialog box appears so you can use this information to locate the workbook.

Opening Documents
To open a workbook, you need to specify the drive it's on, the folder it's in, and its name.

1. Clicking the **Look in** drop-down arrow (▾) displays a list of the items on your system. Clicking *My Computer* on the drop-down list displays the drives on your system in the window below.

2. Double-clicking a drive opens it to display folders, applications, or workbooks.

3. Double-clicking a folder opens it to display folders, applications, or workbooks. Double-clicking a workbook's name opens it. You can also click the name and then click the **Open** button to open it.

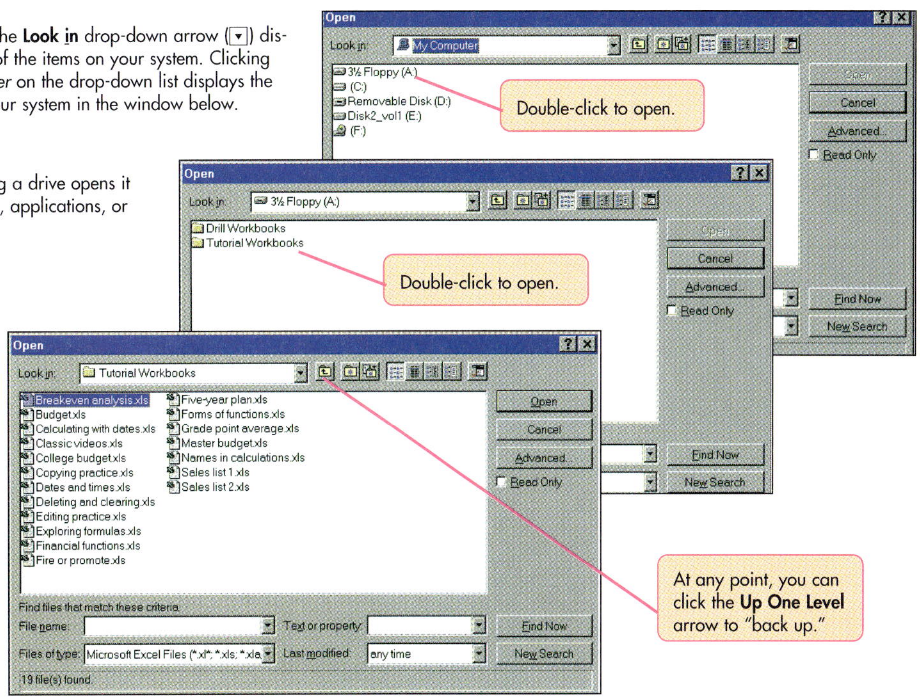

To locate a workbook, you have to open the folder in which it is stored. Dividing a disk into folders helps you organize your files better. A disk is like an empty drawer in a new filing cabinet: It provides storage space but no organization. To make it easier to find items in a file drawer, you divide it into categories with hanging folders. You can file materials directly into the hanging folders, or you can divide the hanging folders into finer categories with manila folders. A folder on a drive is like either a hanging folder or a manila folder within a hanging folder. A workbook or file within a folder is like a letter, report, or other document in a filing cabinet.

A new hard disk is like an empty file drawer. It has lots of room for files but no organization.

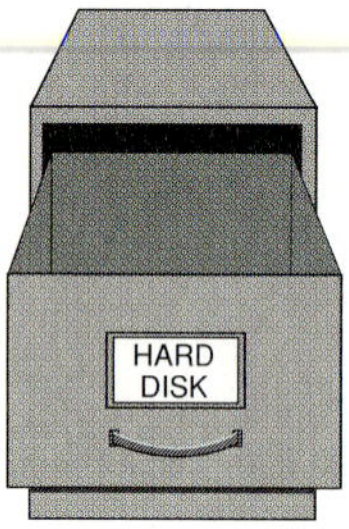

You can divide the hard disk into folders, which is like dividing the file drawer with hanging folders.

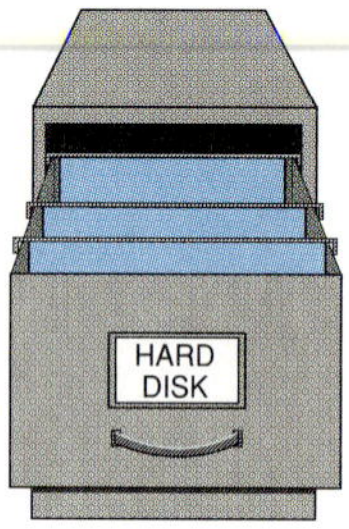

If you want, you can then subdivide the folders into smaller subfolders, which is like dividing the hanging folders with manila folders.

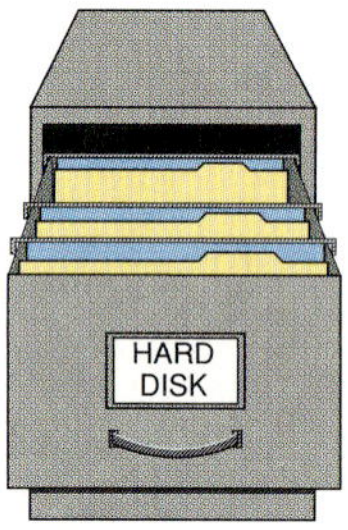

You can save files in any of these folders or subfolders the same way you would file a document in one of the hanging or manila folders.

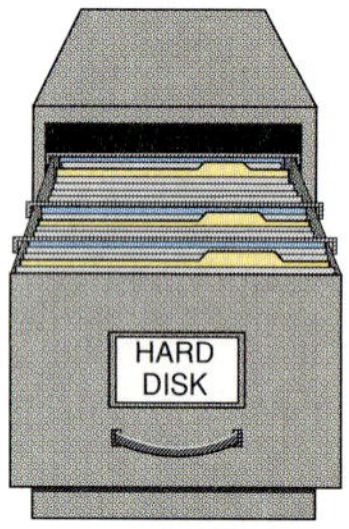

Folders are organized in a hierarchy called a tree. The main folder, the one that isn't contained in any other folder, contains other folders, and those may contain still other subfolders. Any of these folders can also contain programs, workbooks, or other documents. To move down the tree to see what a folder contains, double-click any folder you want to open. To move back up the tree, click the **Up One Level** button on the toolbar.

Moving Up and Down a Tree
To move down a tree, you double-click folders to open them. When some folders are opened, they contain subfolders which you can also open.

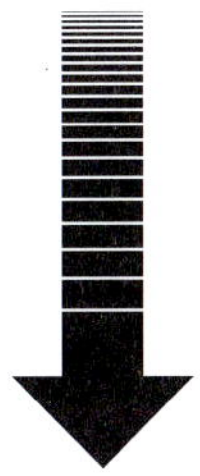

To move down to the *John's Expenses folder* on drive B, you would double-click each of these icons or folders in the order shown.

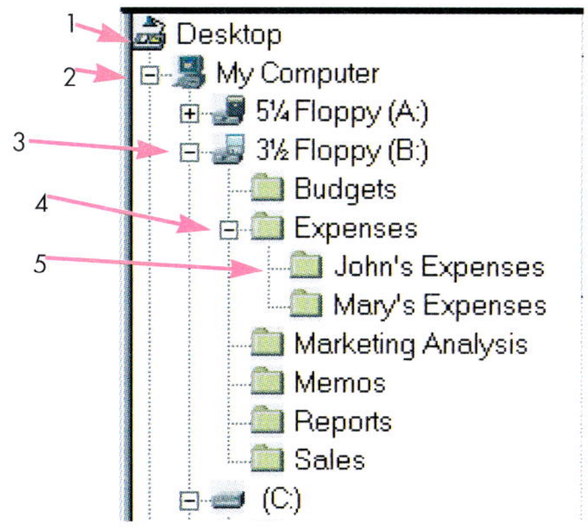

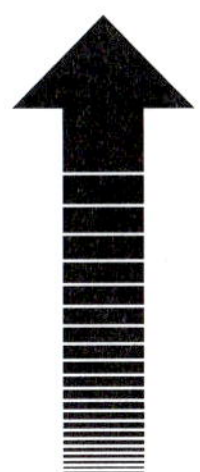

To move back up to the desktop, you would click the **Up One Level** button four times to return to each of the folders or other objects in the order shown

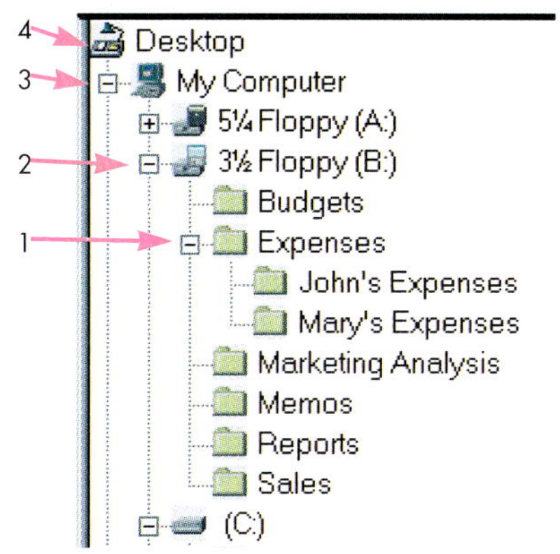

The **Open** button

QUICKSTEPS

Opening Existing Workbooks

1. Click the **Open** button on the Standard toolbar, or pull down the **File** menu and click the **Open** command to display the Open dialog box.
2. To specify the drive the workbook is on, click the **Look in** drop-down arrow (▾) and select the drive from the list that appears. A list of folders on that drive appears in the dialog box window—how it looks and what is shown depends on whether the **List**, **Details**, or **Properties** button on the toolbar is on.
3. The name of the open folder is displayed in the **Look in** box and a list of the documents it contains appear in the box below. To open the folder the document is to be saved in:
   - To move down the tree, double-click a folder you want to open.
   - To move up the tree, click the **Up One Level** button on the toolbar.
4. To open the workbook once you locate it, click its name or icon and then click the **Open** button. You can also double-click the workbook's name to open it without clicking the **Open** button. To see what's in the selected workbook before you open it, click the **Preview** button on the toolbar.

When the Open dialog box is displayed, you can click buttons on its toolbar to change the way workbook names are displayed.

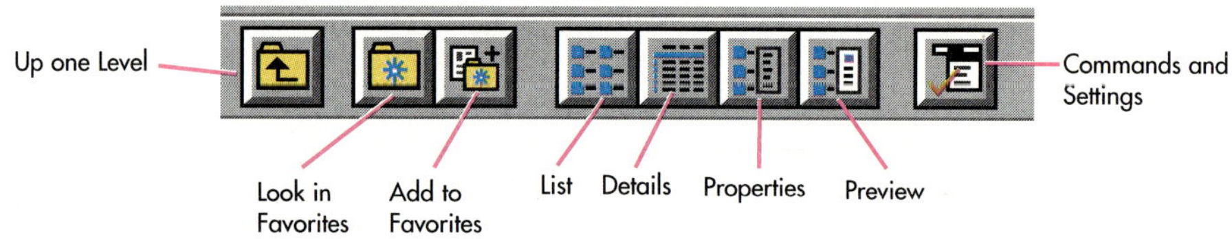

- **Up One Level** moves you up the tree.
- **Look in Favorites** displays a list of workbooks that you have designated as favorites with the **Add to Favorites button** (see below).
- **Add to Favorites** adds any selected workbooks to your list of favorite workbooks when you click it. This is a shortcut you can use to quickly locate workbooks you work on frequently.
- **List** displays just icons and the names of folders or workbooks.
- **Details** displays information about workbooks including their size, type, and date last modified.
- **Properties** displays information about any highlighted workbook including the name of its creator and its size in bytes.
- **Preview** displays a small image of the workbook so you can check that it's the one you want before opening it.
- **Commands and Settings** displays a menu you can use to print selected workbooks, sort the list of workbooks, and perform other procedures.

When the Open dialog box is displayed, you can also enter the name of a workbook you want to find in the **File name** text box and click the **Find Now** button to search for it. It will search the drive or folder listed in the **Look In** text box.

Opening a Recently Opened Workbook

After you've opened and then closed a workbook, there may be a shortcut to opening it again. The four most recently opened workbooks are listed on Excel's **File** menu. (Four is the default number but you can change it.) The fifteen most recently opened documents of any type are listed on Windows' Start menu in the **Documents** folder.

QUICKSTEPS

Opening a Recently Opened Workbook

- If Excel is already running, pull down Excel's **File** menu and click one of the four most recently listed workbooks at the bottom of the menu.
- If Excel is running or even if it isn't, click the **Start** button on the Windows taskbar to display the Start menu, and point to the **Documents** folder to cascade the menu and display the fifteen most recently opened documents of all kinds. Click the name of the workbook you want to open. If Excel isn't already running, Windows will start it for you.

COMMON WRONG TURNS

Removing a Floppy Disk Too Soon

When you work on Excel workbooks, Windows creates temporary files on the disk. When saving a workbook to and opening a workbook from a floppy disk, do not remove the disk from the drive until you have quit Excel. If you do, you may see a message telling you that there is a disk error. If this message appears, reinsert the disk and click the **OK** button.

Opening New Workbooks

When you start Excel, it opens a new workbook automatically. But if you are already working in Excel and want to create another new workbook, you will need to open it. The title bar of each new workbook that you open reads *Bookx*, where x stands for the number of new workbooks you have opened in the current session. This automatically assigned name is replaced with the name you give to the workbook when you save it.

You can open a new workbook by clicking the **New Workbook** button on the Standard toolbar, or by pulling down the **File** menu and clicking the **New** command. When you use the menu command, a tabbed dialog box lists available templates. Templates are simply stored formulas, text, formats, or other elements that make using Excel easier because they automate common tasks. For example, you can use invoice or purchase order templates to create those documents and the data is automatically stored in a special file called a database. The dialog box has two tabs: *General* and *Spreadsheet Solutions*. Normally you use the workbook template listed on the *General* tab but you can click the *Spreadsheet Solutions* and select a template designed for home or business.

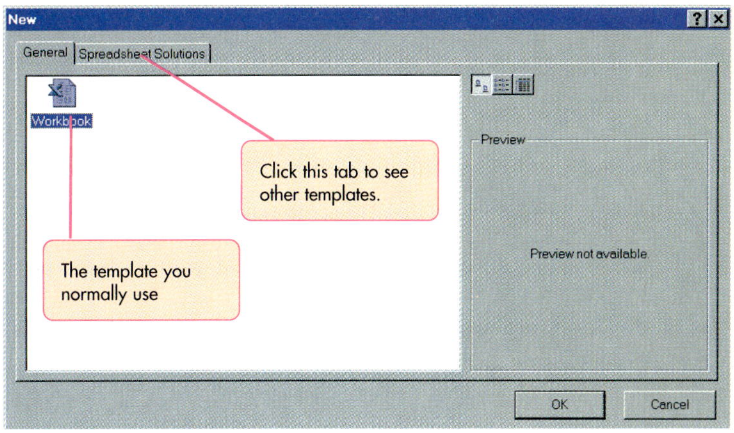

QUICKSTEPS
Opening a New Workbook

To open a new workbook, do any of the following:

- Click the **New Workbook** button on the Standard toolbar.
- Pull down the **File** menu and click the **New** command to display the New dialog box. The *General* tab and the *Workbook* template should already be selected. Click the **OK** button and the new workbook appears on the screen.
- Right-click Windows' desktop to display a shortcut menu. Point to or click the **New** command to cascade the menu and list things you can create. Click *Microsoft Excel Worksheet* to place an icon on the desktop. Type its name and press Enter. To open the workbook, double-click it. (Workbooks created in this way are actually saved in the *Desktop* subfolder located in the *Windows* folder.)

Closing Workbooks

When you are finished with a workbook, you close it. This removes it from the computer's memory and removes its window from Excel's window.

QUICKSTEPS
Closing a Workbook

Do any of the following:

- Click the workbook's **Close** button. It's at the far right of the title bar when the workbook is displayed restored and at the far right of the menu bar when it's displayed maximized. (When a workbook is open, there are two **Close** buttons. Clicking the upper one closes Excel; clicking the lower one closes the open workbook.)
- Pull down the **File** menu and click the **Close** command.
- Double-click the Excel workbook icon, or click it to display a shortcut menu, and click the **Close** command. It's at the far left of the workbook's title bar when the workbook is displayed restored and at the far left of the menu bar when it's displayed maximized.

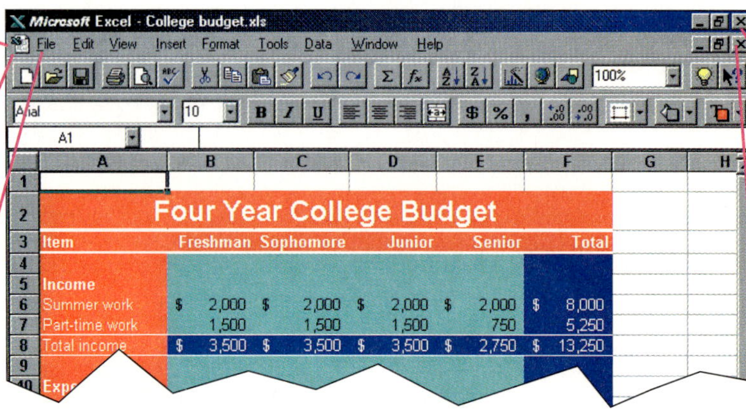

In this tutorial you open an existing workbook supplied to you on the *Excel Student Resource Disk* designed to be used with this text. This disk contains all of the workbooks on which you work while completing the lab activities in this text and instructions for copying its folders onto two floppy disks. If you do not have a copy of this disk, ask your instructor how you can obtain one. The workbook you open calculates a budget for four years at an Ivy League university such as Harvard. Although the numbers may be depressing, the budget is typical of those you would use in business to forecast the relationship between income and expenses over a period of time.

Getting Ready

1. Start Excel if it isn't on the screen. (This step will be assumed for all tutorials from here on.)
2. Insert your *Excel Student Resource Disk* with the *Tutorial Documents* folder into the floppy disk drive you use to open and save workbooks.

Opening an Existing Workbook

3. Click the **Open** button on the Standard toolbar to display the Open dialog box.

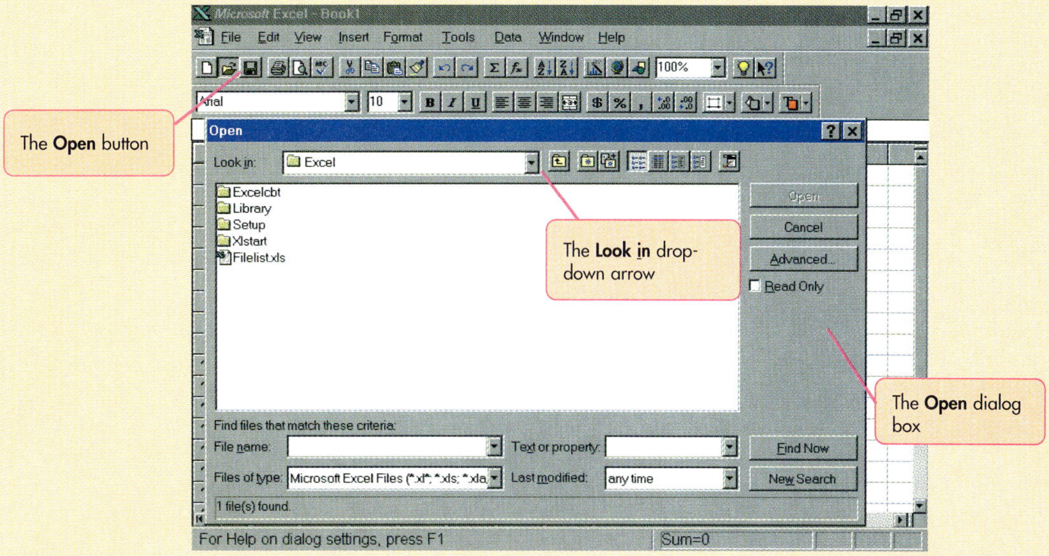

4. Click the **Look in** drop-down arrow ([▾]) and click the name of the drive you inserted the *Excel Student Resource Disk* in to display the folders on that disk. (If your list of folders looks different, click the **List** button on the dialog box's toolbar.)

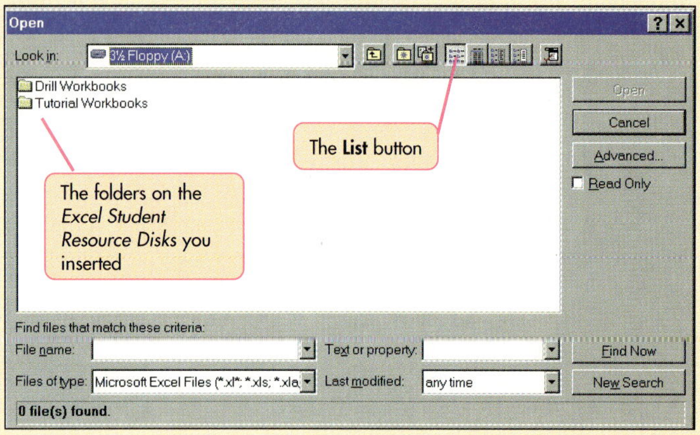

5. Double-click the *Tutorial Workbooks* folder name or icon to open it and display the workbooks in that folder.

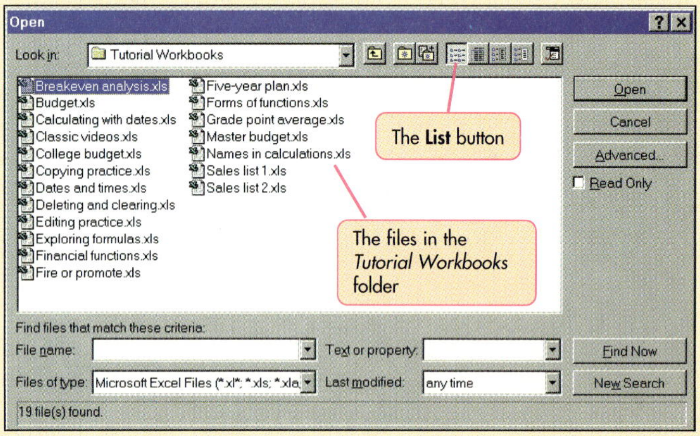

6. Click the **Details** button on the toolbar to see the way the list of workbooks changes. Then click the **List** button again.

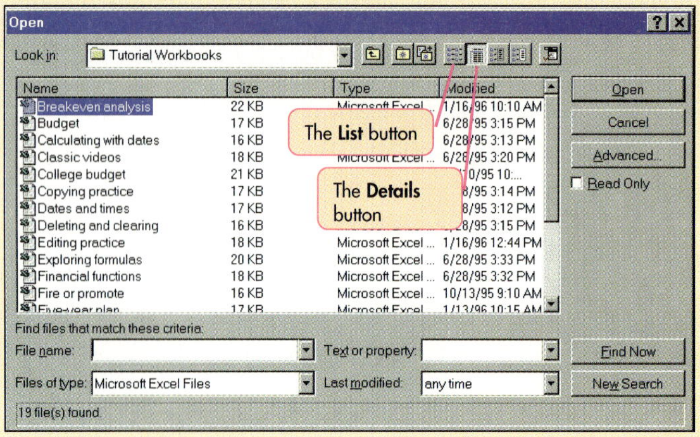

7. Click the *College budget* workbook to select it. (If you click it a second time, a box appears around it so you can change its name. If this happens, just ignore it.)

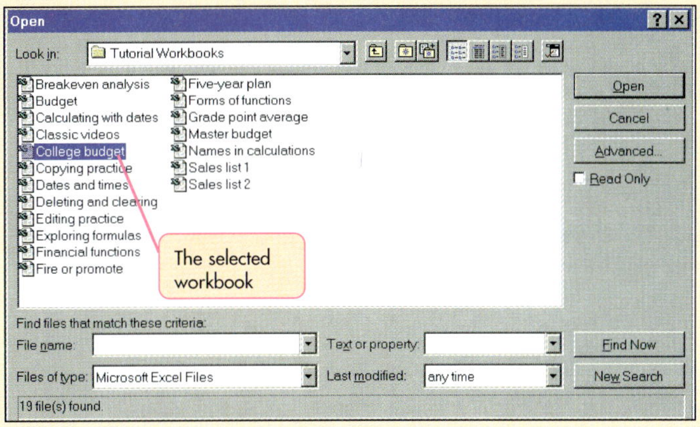

8. Click the **Preview** button on the dialog box's toolbar to see what the workbook looks like.

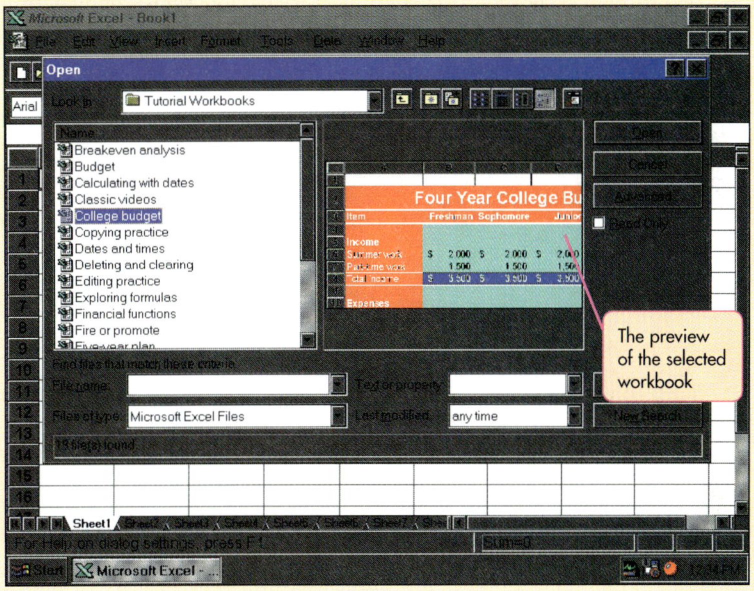

9. Click the **Open** button to open the workbook.

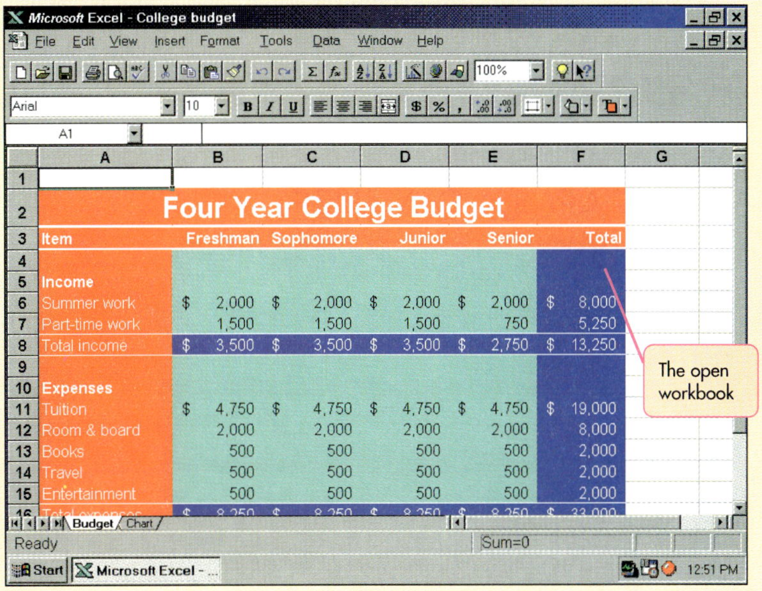

Closing the Workbook

10. Pull down the **File** menu and click the **Close** command to close the workbook. (If a dialog box asks if you want to save your changes, click the **No** button. This message is an example of a bug in the program, since you haven't made any changes.)

11. Pull down the **File** menu and you will see the name of the workbook listed at the bottom of the menu. Excel remembers the last four workbooks that you opened.

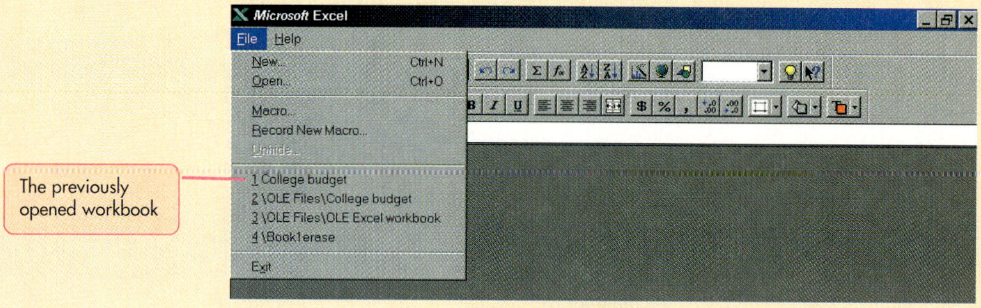

12. Click the name *1 College budget* to open the workbook.

Finishing Up

13. Click the workbook's **Close** button on the menu bar to close the workbook. (Clicking the upper **Close** button on the title bar closes Excel.) If a dialog box asks if you want to save your changes, click the **No** button.

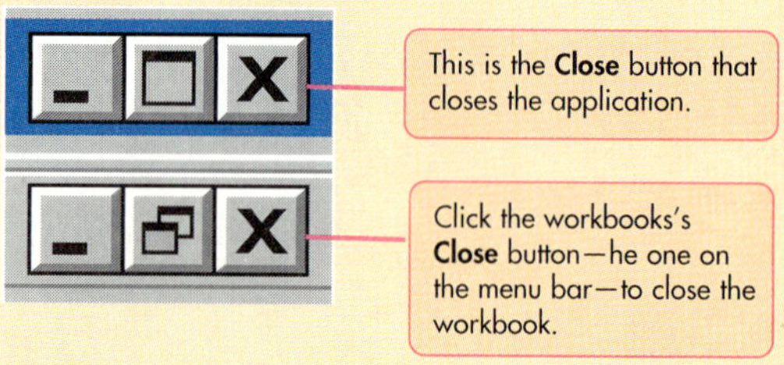

14. Click Excel's **Close** button on the title bar to close the program, or continue to the next section. If you quit, be sure to take your floppy disk out of the system's drive.

1-4. MOVING AROUND A SHEET

When you open Excel, you open a *workbook* that originally contains sixteen sheets—much like pages in a three-ring binder. Each of these sheets has its own tab at the bottom of the screen that you can click to display it. These sheets always remain together when you save and open the workbook—they are all part of the same workbook or file. This makes workbooks an ideal way to store related information together.

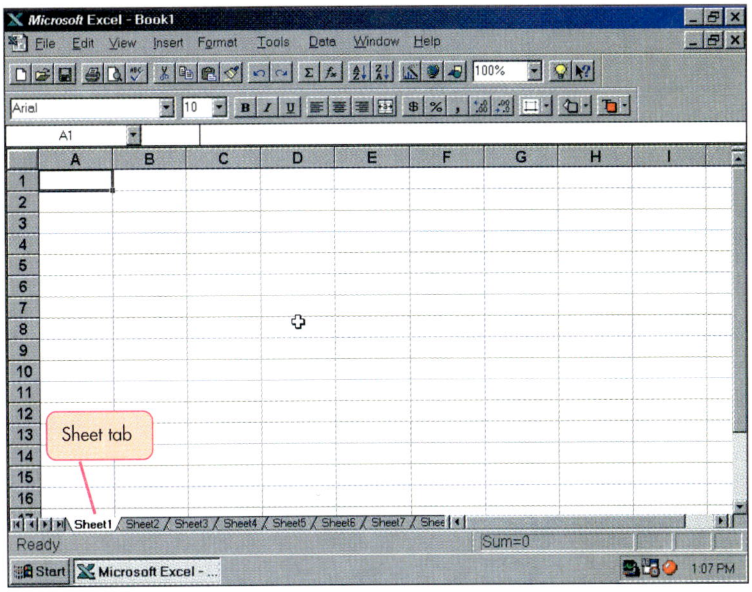

Although a workbook has many sheets, only one is active at a time. When you open a workbook, the display screen shows you a small portion of one worksheet. Normally, only one cell is selected—outlined by a heavy border. This is the *active cell*, and any data that you type is entered into it. The fastest and easiest way to select another cell is to click it to make it active. However, you can also use keyboard commands, scroll bars, the Name box on the formula bar, or the Go To command to move about the worksheet.

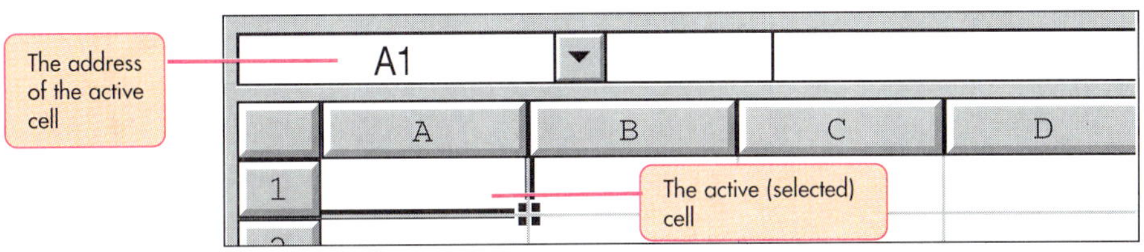

Keyboard Commands

When entering or editing data, it's often faster to change the active cell or scroll the screen from the keyboard than to reach for the mouse. Some keyboard commands move you slowly over short distances, and some move you quickly over long distances. In that respect, these commands are much like the gas pedal in your car. You may want to crawl down the driveway, but you'll want to fly on the freeway. The QuickSteps box "Moving Around a Worksheet with the Keyboard" and the box "Understanding the End key" list some of Excel's keyboard commands.

UNDERSTANDING

Understanding the End Key

The End key is very useful for moving around the worksheet. Using it in combination with other keys allows you to select the first or last cell in a block of data—that is, the cell preceded or followed by a blank cell.

- If the worksheet contains data, pressing End (the status bar reads *END*) and then one of the arrow keys selects the next cell followed or preceded by a blank cell. If the sheet contains no data in the direction of the arrow key you press, it selects the first or last cell in the row or column.
- If the worksheet contains data, pressing End and then Home selects the cell in the lower-right corner of the working area of the model. If the sheet contains no data, it selects cell A1.

QUICKSTEPS

Moving Around a Worksheet with the Keyboard

Crawling Along

Previous or next cell on row	← or →
Previous or next cell in column	↑ or ↓

Stepping On It

Up or down one window	Page Up or PageDown
Beginning of row	Home

Putting the Pedal to the Metal

Beginning of sheet (usually cell A1)	Ctrl+Home
Last cell containing data (lower right)	Ctrl+End

Using Scroll Bars

You can also move the screen, but not change the active cell, with the *scroll bars* on the right and bottom sides of the window.

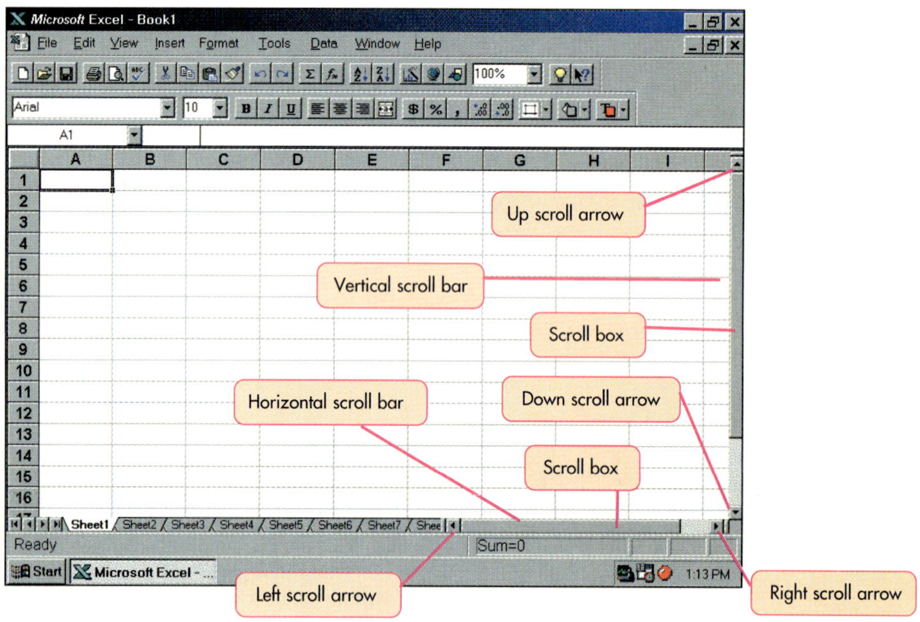

The scroll bar you use to move the sheet up and down is called the vertical scroll bar. The one you use to move the sheet side to side is called the *horizontal* scroll bar.

- The vertical scroll bar contains three basic elements: the *up scroll arrow* (▲), the down scroll arrow (▼), and the scroll box (☐).
- The horizontal scroll bar also contains three basic elements: the *left scroll arrow*, the *right scroll arrow*, and the *scroll box*.

You scroll through a sheet by clicking the scroll arrows or by dragging the scroll box. The scroll box serves three functions:

- When you drag it up or down the vertical scroll bar with the mouse, you move quickly to any point in a sheet. As you drag it, the topmost row or leftmost column that will be displayed when you release the mouse button is indicated in a small box called a ScrollTip to the left of or above the scroll bar you are using.

- The scroll box also indicates where you are in a sheet. If it is at the top of the scroll bar, you are at the top of the sheet. If it is at the bottom of the scroll bar, you are at the bottom of the sheet. If it is halfway between the top and bottom of the scroll bar, you are at the middle of the sheet.
- The size of the scroll box varies to reflect the difference between what is visible in the window and the entire content of the sheet. For example, it is small when only a small portion of the sheet can be displayed at one time, and large when a large portion can be displayed. Basically, the larger the area of the sheet covered with data, the smaller the scroll box.

QUICKSTEPS

Moving Around a Worksheet with the Scroll Bars

- To move the worksheet up or down one row, click the up (▲) or down scroll arrow (▼).
- To move the worksheet left or right one column, click the left or right scroll arrow.
- To scroll the worksheet continuously, point to any scroll arrow and hold down the mouse button.
- To scroll the worksheet a screen at a time, click above or below the vertical scroll box (□) or to the left or right of the horizontal scroll box.
- To scroll to a specific point in a sheet, drag the scroll box (□) and release it. As you do so, a ScrollTip indicates the row or column you will move to.

Using the Name Box

The Name box at the left end of the formula bar always displays the address of the active cell. To jump to a specific cell, click the Name box to select the current address listed there, type a new cell address (for example, C10 or F54), and press Enter↵.

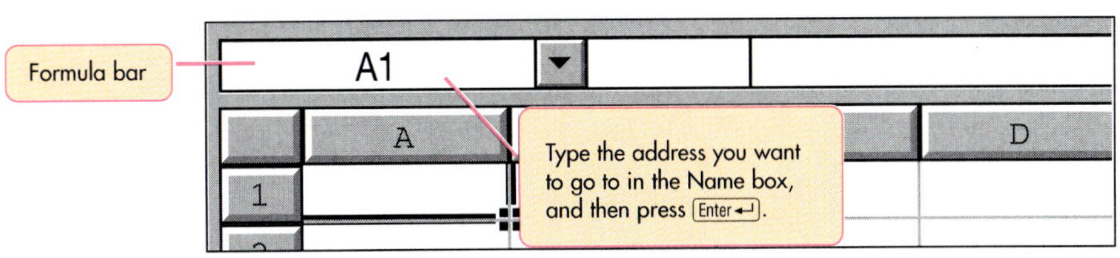

Using the Go To Command

To jump to a specific cell, pull down the **Edit** menu and click the **Go To** command (you can also press F5, or hold down Ctrl and press G) to display the Go To dialog box. Type the address of the cell that you want to jump to into the **Reference** text box, and then click the **OK** command button.

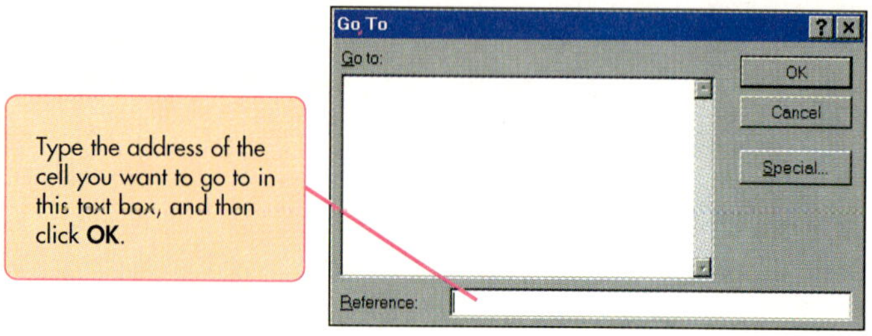

You can quickly move to the end of a row or column of data. To do so, select a cell in the row or column of data and double-click the side of the cell facing the direction you want to move.

TUTORIAL

In this tutorial you explore selecting cells, scrolling the worksheet, and displaying other worksheets.

Getting Ready

1. Open the *College budget* workbook stored in the *Tutorial Workbooks* folder of the *Excel Student Resource Disk*. (If you can't remember how, refer to Steps 3 through 9 in the tutorial in Section 1-3.)

Selecting by Clicking

2. Click one of the red cells with white text in it (other than the centered heading on the second row—only one of its cells has contents) to select the cell and display its contents on the formula bar. Many of these cells contain text.
3. Click one of the light blue cells to select it and display its contents on the formula bar. Many of these cells contain numbers.
4. Click one of the dark blue cells with white text to select it and display its contents on the formula bar. Many of these cells contain formulas. For example, if you click cell B8, you'll see the formula *=B7+B6* on the formula bar. This formula adds the number in cell B7 to the one in cell B6. Some of these cells contain a special type of formula called a function. For example, if you click cell B16, you'll see the function *=SUM(B11:B15)* on the formula bar. This function adds (sums) the contents of all cells between cells B11 and B15.

LOOKING AHEAD
The Sum Function

Spreadsheets are widely used because you can enter formulas in them that calculate numbers entered into other cells. You can also enter functions—think of them as condensed formulas. For example, in this model, there is a SUM function in cell B16 that adds, or sums, all of the cells to which it refers. In this case the *=SUM(B11:B15)* function adds cells B11 and B15 and all of those between them. Entering this function is faster and easier than entering the equivalent formula, =B11+B12+B13+B14+B15. You'll see more SUM functions as you progress through this text, so just remember that they add the cells specified in parentheses. The colon that separates the cell references is Excel's way of saying *through*, as in *"B11 through B15."*

Using Keyboard Commands

5. Use the commands described in the QuickSteps box "Moving Around a Worksheet with the Keyboard" to move around the worksheet. (Keys connected with plus signs (+) are to be pressed together. For example, to use the Ctrl+Home command, hold down Ctrl and then press Home as if you were typing a character.)

Using the Name Box

6. Click the Name box on the formula bar and the current entry is highlighted. Type **T50** and press Enter to jump to that cell.

Clicking the Name box selects the current entry.

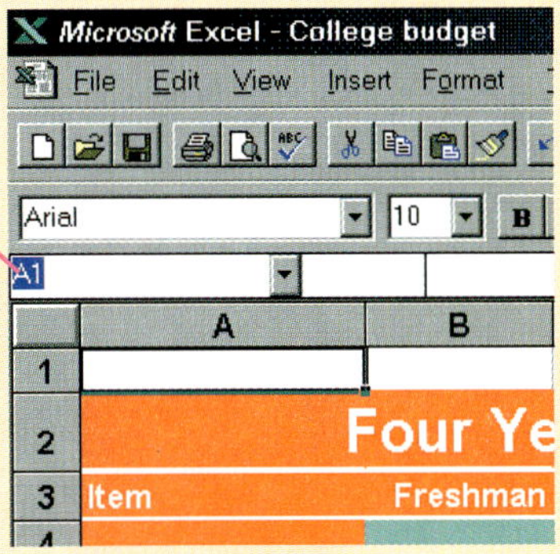

7. Click the Name box, type **A1** and press Enter to jump to that cell.

Using the End Key

8. With cell A1 still selected, press End, then press → to select cell IV1—the last cell on the row.
9. Press End, then press ↓ to move to the cell in the lower-right corner of the sheet.
10. Press End, then press ← to move to the last cell in the first column of the sheet.
11. Press End, then press ↑ to move to the first cell encountered in column A that contains data.

Using the Scroll Bar

12. Point to the up scroll arrow (▲) on the vertical scroll bar and hold down the left mouse button until the scroll box reaches the top of the scroll bar. This indicates that you are at the beginning of the sheet.
13. Point to the scroll box on the vertical scroll bar, hold down the left mouse button, and drag the scroll box to the bottom of the scroll bar. (A ScrollTip showing the topmost row that will be displayed when you release the mouse button is displayed to the left of the scroll bar.) Release the mouse button to move to the end of the area of the worksheet with data in it.
14. Practice scrolling the worksheet contents up and down a line at a time by clicking the up (▲) and down (▼) scroll arrows on the vertical scroll bar.
15. Practice clicking the scroll bar above and below the scroll box to scroll the worksheet a screen at a time.

Displaying Another Sheet

16. Click the sheet tab at the bottom of the worksheet labeled *Chart* to display a chart created from the data on the first sheet.

17. To improve the view of the chart, do the following:

- Pull down the **View** menu and click the **Sized with Window** command to turn it on.
- Pull down the **View** menu and click the **Full Screen** command to turn it on.

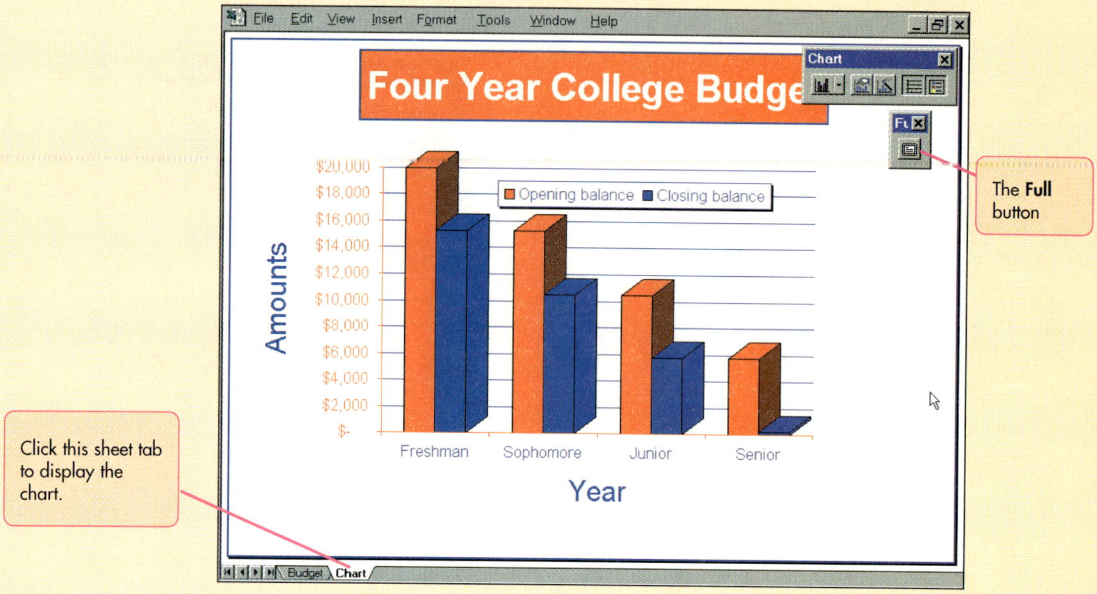

18. Click the sheet tab labeled Budget to return to the first sheet. There is a **Full** button displayed on the screen since you turned the **Full Screen** command on. Click the **Full** button to return the display to normal.

PAUSING FOR PRACTICE

Practice using the scroll bar until you have mastered the three basic procedures: clicking the arrows and the scroll bar, pointing to the arrows and holding down the left button, and dragging the scroll box.

Finishing Up

19. Click the workbook's **Close** button on the menu bar to close the workbook. (If a dialog box asks if you want to save your changes, click the **No** button.)

20. Click Excel's **Close** button on the title bar to close the program, or continue to the next section. If you quit, be sure to take your floppy disk out of the system's drive.

1-5 ENTERING AND VIEWING DATA

To create models, you have to enter data such as text, numbers, and formulas. While doing so, you can also change the way it is displayed.

Entering Data

You enter data on a worksheet by selecting a cell and typing it in. The data is displayed on the formula bar as you type it. You complete the entry by pressing [Enter ←] or by clicking the Enter box (☑) on the formula bar.

- Pressing [Enter ←] completes the entry and automatically selects the cell below.
- Clicking the Enter box (☑) completes the entry and leaves the same cell selected.

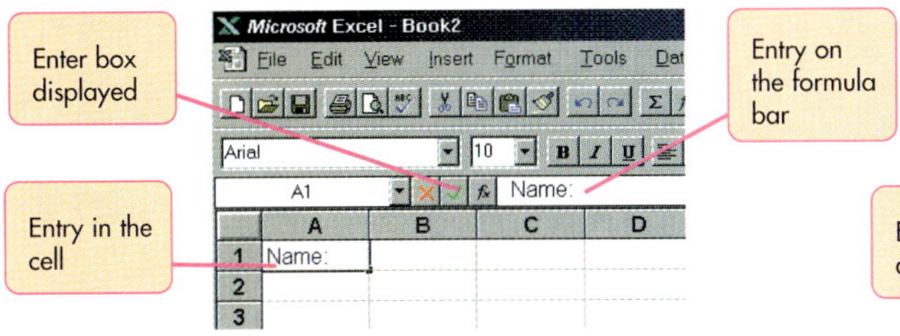

The worksheet as you enter data

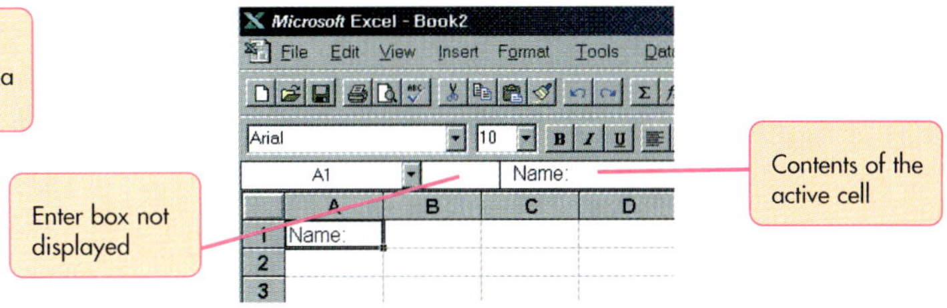

After you complete the entry

If the cell already contains an entry, typing a new entry over it and then pressing [Enter ←] or clicking the Enter box (☑) on the formula bar replaces the original entry.

Viewing Data

Once a workbook has been created or opened, you can zoom it to make it bigger or smaller on the screen or display it full screen.

QUICKSTEPS

Changing Zooms or Views

- To change the size of the worksheet displayed on the screen, click the **Zoom Control** drop-down arrow (▾) on the Standard toolbar to display a list of zooms, and click the zoom you want to use. You can also pull down the **View** menu, click the **Zoom** command, then click the option button to turn on (◉) the zoom you want to use.
- To zoom a part of the worksheet so it fills the screen, select the section, click the **Zoom Control** drop-down arrow (▾) on the Standard toolbar, and click *Selection*.
- To devote more of the screen to the worksheet by hiding the toolbar and formula bar, pull down the **View** menu and click the **Full Screen** command to turn it on. Use the same command to return to normal view (or click the **Full** button that is only displayed when you are in this view) so you can see the toolbars, formula bar, and status bar.

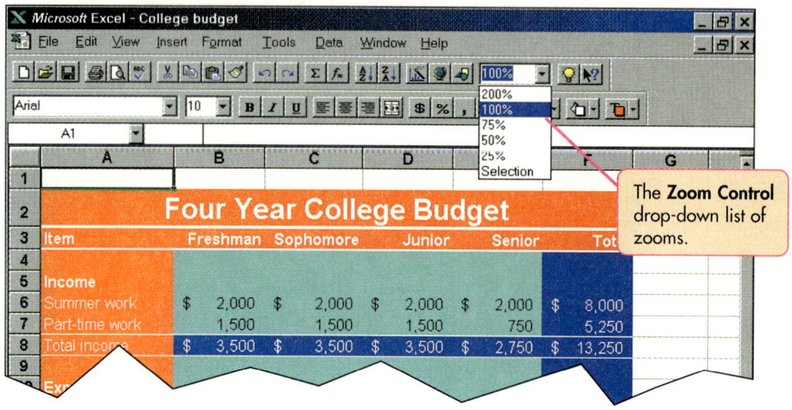

TUTORIAL

In this tutorial you enter data into a worksheet. You also explore the true power of a spreadsheet program by changing numbers and seeing new results calculated instantly, a feature called *what-if* or *sensitivity analysis*.

COMMON WRONG TURNS
Mistakes While Typing

If you notice a mistake while typing an entry, press [←Bksp] to delete it. You can also press [F2], then use [←] and [→] to move the insertion point through the entry to the spot where you want to insert or delete characters. Once you have completed the entry by pressing [Enter←] or by clicking the Enter box (☑) on the formula bar, you have to edit the cell's contents in a different way, as described in Section 2-3.

Getting Ready

1. Open the *College budget* workbook stored in the *Tutorial Workbooks* folder of the *Excel Student Resource Disk*. (If you can't remember how, refer to Steps 3 through 9 in the tutorial in Section 1-3.)

Entering Your Name

2. Click cell A1 to make it the active cell, type **Name:** and press [Spacebar], and then type your name. As you do so, the text you type appears both in cell A1 and on the formula bar. (If your text is longer than the cell, it extends into the next cell to the right. This wouldn't happen if that cell contained data.)

3. Press [Enter←] to complete the entry and automatically select cell A2.

Entering the Date

4. Click cell F1 to make it the active cell and type today's date in the format 1/15/97. As you do so, it appears both in cell F1 and on the formula bar. Click the Enter box (☑) on the formula bar to complete the entry.

Saving your Changes

5. Click the **Save** button on the Standard toolbar to save your changes.

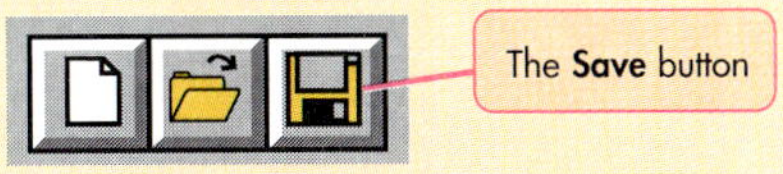

Exploring What Ifs

6. Click cell B6 to make it the active cell, then type **1000** and press Enter. The *Total income and Closing Balance* for the freshman year change and those changes ripple to the following year's opening and closing balances.

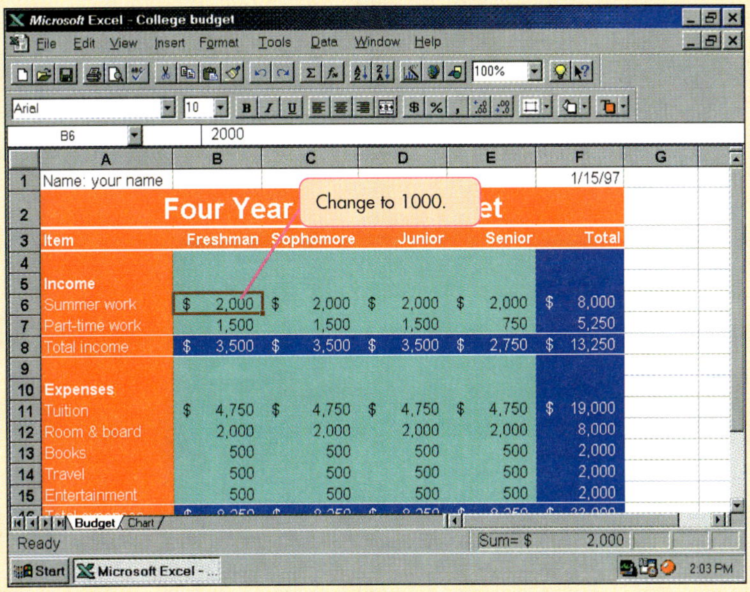

7. With cell B19 the active cell, type **10000** and press Enter. This reduces the opening cash balance, and the closing cash balance below begins to show negative values before college is completed.

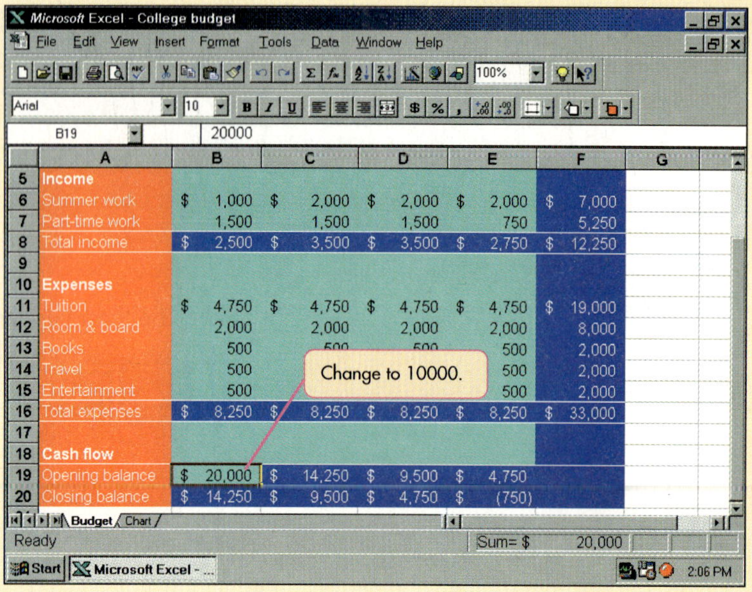

8. Click the tab labeled *Chart*, and you'll see a chart illustrating the opening and closing cash balances for each of the four years of college. Ideally, all of these should be positive numbers. To see the chart better, pull down the **View** menu and click the **Full Screen** command to turn it on. Then pull down the **View** menu again and click the **Sized with Window** command.

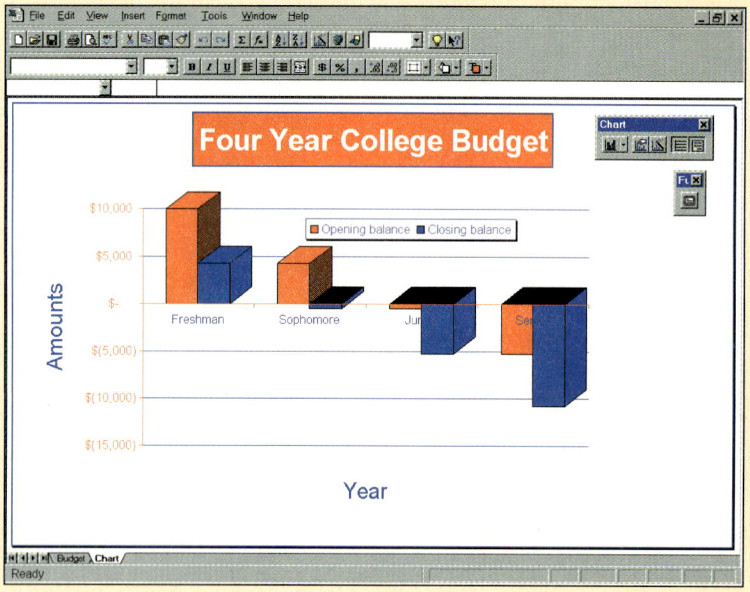

9. Click the tab labeled *Budget* to return to the first sheet. To see the toolbars, formula bar, and status bar, pull down the **View menu** and click the **Full Screen** command to turn it off.

10. Continue entering numbers in any of the light blue cells that already have numbers to see how easy it is to explore a budget. Try to find a set of numbers that keep the cash flow positive for all four years when the tuition is the same as yours. (If you try to enter numbers in any but the right cells, a message will tell you *Locked cells cannot be changed*. If this appears, just click the **OK** button to continue.)

Zooming the Workbook

11. Click the **Zoom Control** drop-down arrow (▾) to display a list of zooms you can use.

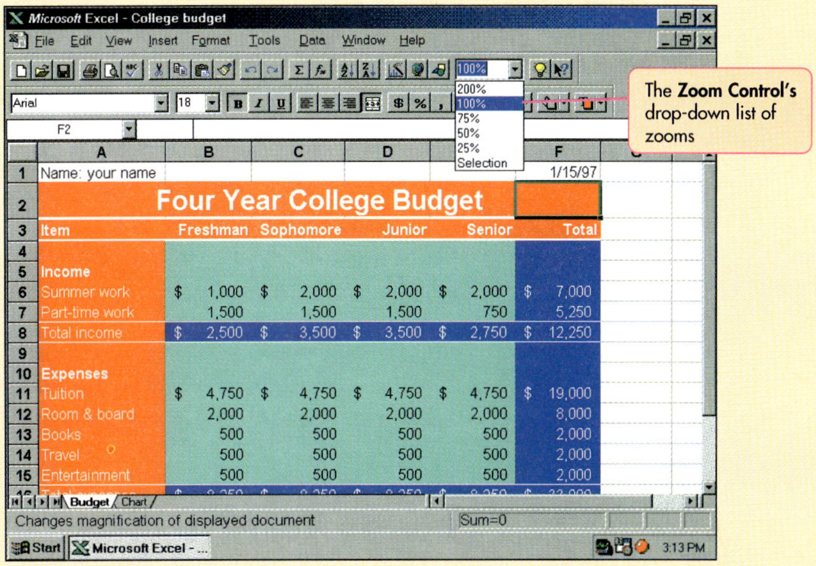

12. Click the 75% command and the worksheet is reduced in size. The text may be unreadable at this zoom, but you can see the layout. The percentage in the **Zoom Control** text box changes to 75%.

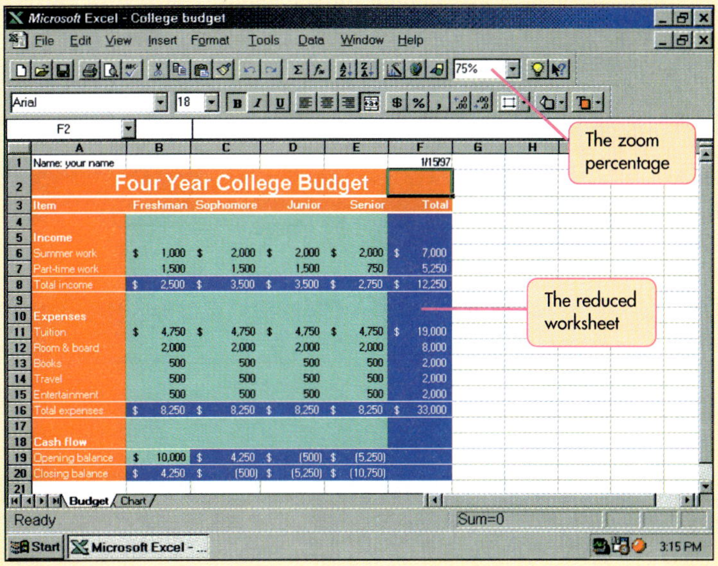

13. Click the **Zoom Control** drop-down arrow (▾) and click the 100% command to return the sheet to its original size.

Finishing Up

14. Click the workbook's **Close** button on the menu bar to close the workbook. (If a dialog box asks if you want to save your changes, click the **No** button.)

15. Click Excel's **Close** button on the title bar to close the program, or continue to the next section. If you quit, be sure to take your floppy disk out of the system's drive.

1-6 SAVING WORKBOOKS

You should frequently save the workbook you are working on. If you turn off the computer, experience a power failure, encounter hardware problems, or make a mistake, you may lose workbooks that are in the computer's memory. Your workbooks are not safe from these disasters until you save them onto a disk. You should always save a workbook:

- Before experimenting with unfamiliar commands
- Before making major revisions
- Before printing it (in case something goes wrong during the process)
- Before closing it or exiting Excel

On many systems, you save your workbooks onto a hard disk. On others, especially those you share with other students in a computer lab, you save them onto a floppy disk (usually in drive A or B) so that you can take them with you.

Saving Workbooks the First Time

Just as when opening workbooks, you have to decide three things when saving a workbook the first time: the drive to save it on, the folder to save it in, and its name. When you use a Save command the first time, the Save As dialog box appears so you can specify this information. Once a workbook has been saved, you can save it again after making any changes just by clicking the **Save** button on the Standard toolbar.

Saving Workbooks
To save a workbook, you need to specify the drive to save it on, the folder to save it in, and the name to save it under.

1. Clicking the **Save in** drop-down arrow (▾) displays a list of the drives on your system. Selecting *My Computer* from the list displays the drives on your system in the window below.

2. Double-clicking a drive opens it to display folders, applications, or workbooks.

3. Double-clicking a folder opens it to display folders, applications, or workbooks. Usually, only the workbooks with the same format are displayed. Type the name of the workbook in the **File name** text box and then click the **Save** button to save it.

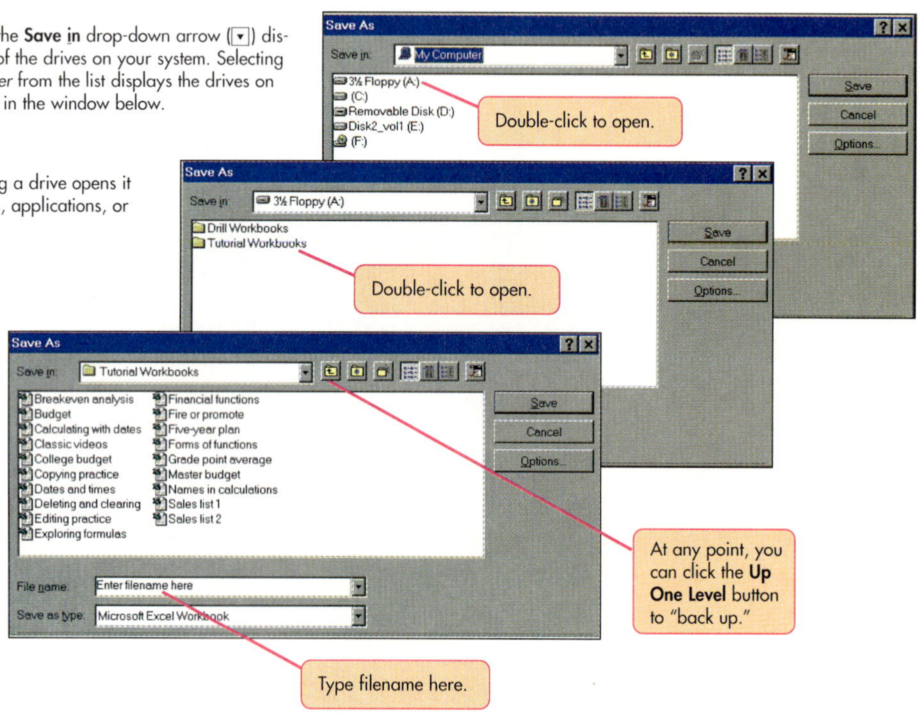

There are certain rules to keep in mind when naming workbooks:

- Filenames can be up to 255 characters long.
- Filenames can include spaces and as many periods as you want.
- Filenames cannot include the characters \ / : * ? " < > or |. If you use any of these characters, a message box appears and lists them for you so you can change the name.
- Each filename should be unique. If you assign a workbook the same name as a file that is already on the disk in the same folder, the new file can overwrite the previous file and erase it (although you will be warned first).
- Filenames retain the capitalization you use to enter them. For example, you could type a filename as *filename*, *Filename*, *FileName*, or *FILENAME*.

QUICKSTEPS

Saving Workbooks for the First Time

1. Click the **Save** button on the Standard toolbar, or pull down the **File** menu and click the **Save** command to display the Save As dialog box. (You can also right-click the menu bar.)
2. To specify the drive to save the workbook on, click the **Save in** drop-down arrow and select the drive from the list that appears.
3. To open the folder the workbook is to be saved in:
   - To move down the tree, double-click a folder you want to open.
   - To move up the tree, click the **Up One Level** button on the toolbar.
4. The default name *Bookx* is listed in the **File name** text box. (If the default name isn't highlighted, double-click it to select it.) Type the name you want to use and the first character you type deletes the existing entry.
5. Press Enter or click the **Save** button.

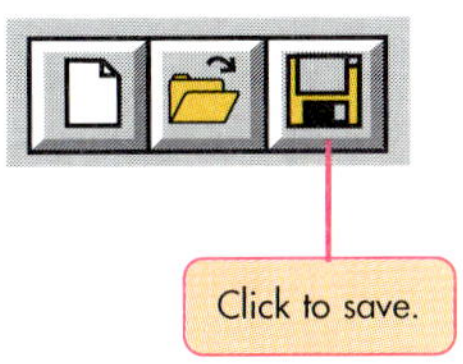

When the Save As dialog box is displayed, you can click buttons on its *toolbar* to change the way workbooks are displayed.

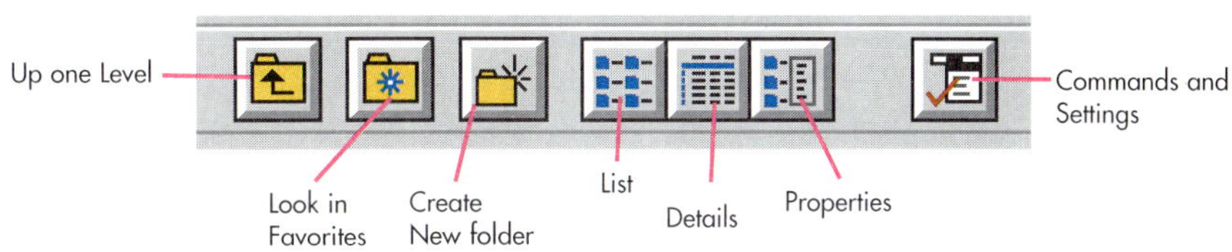

- **Up One Level** moves you up the tree.
- **Look in Favorites** displays a list of workbooks that you have added to your list of favorite workbooks using the Open dialog box.
- **Create New Folder** creates a new folder in which to save workbooks.
- **List** displays just icons and the names of folders or workbooks.
- **Details** displays information about workbooks including their size, type, and date last modified.
- **Properties** displays information about the highlighted workbook including the name of its creator, the number of times it's been revised, and its size in pages, words, characters, and bytes.
- **Commands and Settings** displays a menu you can use to sort the list of workbooks or perform other procedures.

Saving a Workbook Under a New Name

There are times when you want to save a workbook under a new name. You may have made a mistake and don't want to overwrite the version on the disk with the new version until you are certain it's OK to do so. Or you may have opened an existing workbook that you want to revise into a new and different one. To save an already saved workbook under a new name, you use the **Save As** command on the **File** menu.

QUICKSTEPS

Saving a Workbook Under a New Name

1. Pull down the **File** menu and click the **Save As** command instead of the Save command.
2. Type a new filename into the **File name** text box or edit the one that is there and click the **Save** button. (You can also specify a new drive and folder before clicking **Save**.)

TUTORIAL

In this tutorial you save a workbook by clicking a button. This saves the workbook under the same name and in the same folder from which you opened it or in which you previously saved it. You then use the **Save As** command to save the workbook under a new name. Finally, you save a new workbook the first time and assign it a name.

Getting Ready

1. Open the *College budget* workbook stored in the Tutorial Workbooks folder of the *Excel Student Resource Disk*. (If you can't remember how, refer to Steps 3 through 9 in the tutorial in Section 1-3.)

Saving a Previously Saved Workbook Under the Original Name

2. Click the **Save** button on the Standard toolbar. (If you don't know which it is, you can point to any button to display its name.) As the workbook is saved, an hourglass (⌛) is displayed, and the status bar keeps you informed of the command's progress.

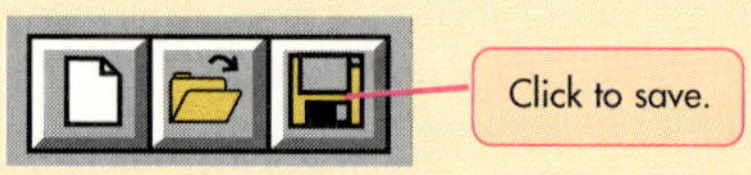

Saving a Previously Saved Workbook Under a New Name

3. Pull down the **File** menu and click the **Save As** command to display the Save As dialog box. The workbook's name is highlighted in the **File name** text box. The drive should be set to the one containing your disk and the *Tutorial Workbooks* folder should be open.
4. Click to the right of the filename in the **File name** text box (or to the left of the period in *.xls* if that file extension is displayed), press Spacebar, type **copy** (the new filename should read *College budget copy*), and click the dialog box's

Save button to save the workbook under that name. You now have two copies of the same workbook, one named *College budget* and one named *College budget copy*.

Type **copy** at the end of the workbook's name.

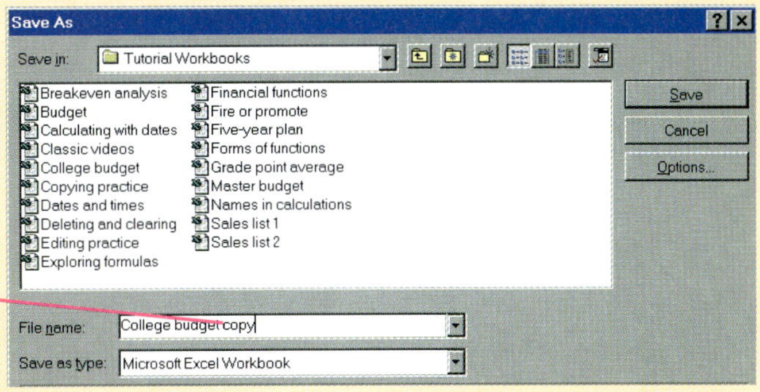

5. Click the workbook's **Close** button on the menu bar to close the workbook.

Saving a New Workbook for the First Time

6. Click the **New Workbook** button on the Standard toolbar to open a new workbook.
7. Type your name into cell A1 and press Enter↵.
8. Click the **Save** button on the Standard toolbar to display the Save As dialog box. The *Tutorial Workbooks* folder is open.
9. To move up the tree, click the **Up One Level** button on the toolbar. This displays all of the folders on the disk.
10. Double-click the *Drill Workbooks* folder to open it.
11. The default filename *Bookx* (where *x* is a number) is listed in the **File name** text box. To use it as this file's name, click the dialog box's **Save** button.

Finishing Up

12. Click the workbook's **Close** button on the menu bar to close the workbook.
13. Click Excel's **Close** button on the title bar to close the program, or continue to the next section. If you quit, be sure to take your floppy disk out of the system's drive.

1-7 PRINTING A SHEET

When you want to share a worksheet with others or file a copy for future reference, you usually make a printout. Before you do so, you can preview how the workbook will look when printed. If you find that you need to make adjustments, you can do so without wasting a sheet of paper.

QUICKSTEPS

Previewing and Printing the Active Sheet

1. Click the **Print Preview** button on the Standard toolbar to display the worksheet on the screen just the way it will look when printed. A row of command buttons appears at the top of the window.
2. Click the **Next** or **Previous** command button to page through the workbook, or click **Zoom** to enlarge or reduce it (**Setup** and **Margins** are discussed in Section 3-6, "Printing and Page Setup").
3. Click the **Print** command button to print the sheet or click **Close** to return to the workbook.

TUTORIAL

IN this tutorial you print the worksheet on which you have been working. Before you begin, be sure there is a printer connected to your system and that it is on and has paper in it.

Getting Ready

1. Open the *College budget* workbook stored in the *Tutorial Workbooks* folder of the *Excel Student Resource Disk*. (If you can't remember how, refer to Steps 3 through 9 in the tutorial in Section 1-3.)

Previewing and Printing a Worksheet

2. Click the **Print Preview** button on the Standard toolbar to preview how your model will look when printed. (This can take a while on some systems.)

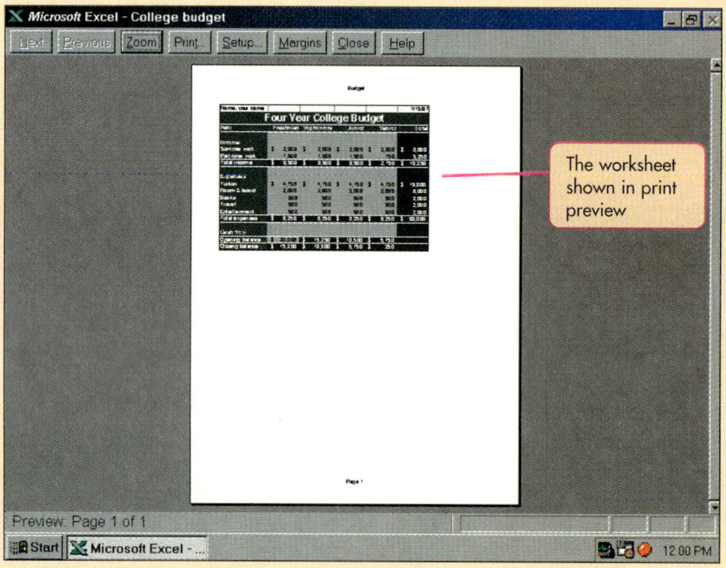

3. Click various parts of the model with the magnifying mouse pointer to enlarge it and then with the regular mouse pointer to shrink it.
4. Click the **Close** command button on the toolbar to return to the sheet on which you have been working.

5. Make sure your printer is on, is connected, and has paper in it.
6. Click the **Print** button on the Standard toolbar to print the sheet displayed on the screen.

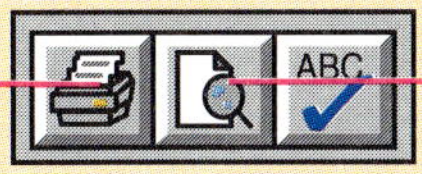

TIP

Printing Charts and Waiting

You can display the chart sheet on the screen and repeat Step 6 to print it. However, when you print a sheet containing a graphic, it can take some time, especially if others in the class are also sending their worksheets to the same printer. Before printing this chart, you might ask the lab instructor or other students what to expect.

Finishing Up

7. Click the workbook's **Close** button on the menu bar to close the workbook. (If a dialog box asks if you want to save your changes, click the **No** button.)
8. Click Excel's **Close** button on the title bar to close the program, or continue to the next section. If you quit, be sure to take your floppy disk out of the system's drive.

1-8 USING ON-LINE HELP

When you are using Excel, you can have tips automatically displayed as you go about your usual tasks, or you can ask for detailed help whenever you want information on a specific procedure.

The TipWizard

Excel's TipWizard watches how you perform a procedure, and if there is a faster or more efficient way to do it, the **TipWizard** button on the Standard toolbar lights up by changing from white to yellow. To see the suggestion it has to offer, click the button to display the current tip in the TipWizard box just below the toolbar. If the tip involves the use of a button, a copy of the button appears to the right of the tip. You can click the up and down scroll arrows (⬍) at the right end of the TipWizard box to scroll through all tips offered so far in a session. To hide the TipWizard box, just click the **TipWizard** button again. The TipWizard does not repeat a suggestion it has already made unless you reset it. To do so, hold down Ctrl and click the **TipWizard** button.

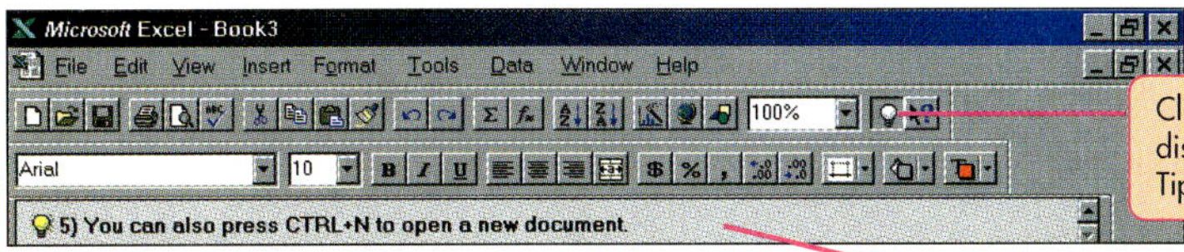

ScreenTips

If you click the **Help** button on the Standard toolbar, it adds a question mark to the mouse pointer. You can then click buttons or areas of the screen to display a pop-up description called a ScreenTip. To close the ScreenTip, click it. Also, many Help windows and dialog boxes have a question mark button on their title bar that works the same way. You can use ScreenTips to learn about parts of the Help window or dialog box.

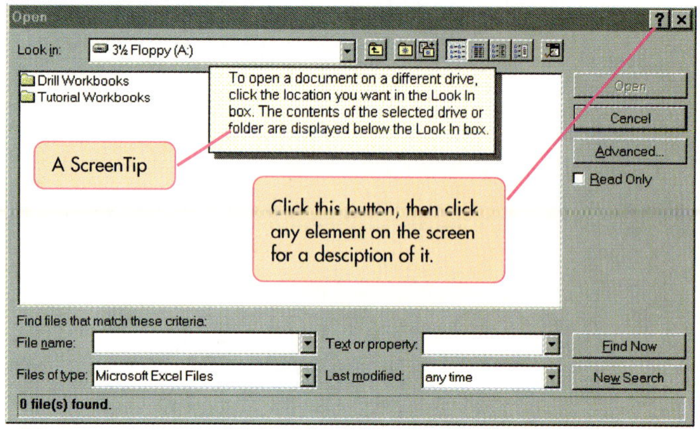

The Help System

Windows has extensive *on-line help* available from almost anywhere in any program such as Excel. When you call up Help, you'll find that it is organized into topics, much like sections in a book. To find help on a specific topic, you click one of the four tabs in the Help Topics window: *Contents*, *Index*, *Find*, and *Answer Wizard*. Each tab uses a different method of locating help.

HELP—THE CONTENTS TAB

The *Contents* tab lists topics group by subject much as the table of contents in a book.

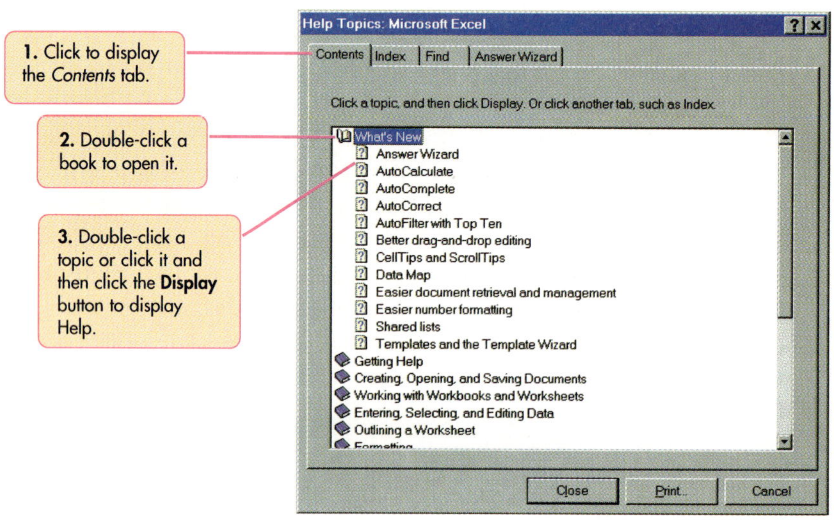

HELP—THE INDEX TAB

The *Index* tab lets you look up topics much as you would in the index of a book.

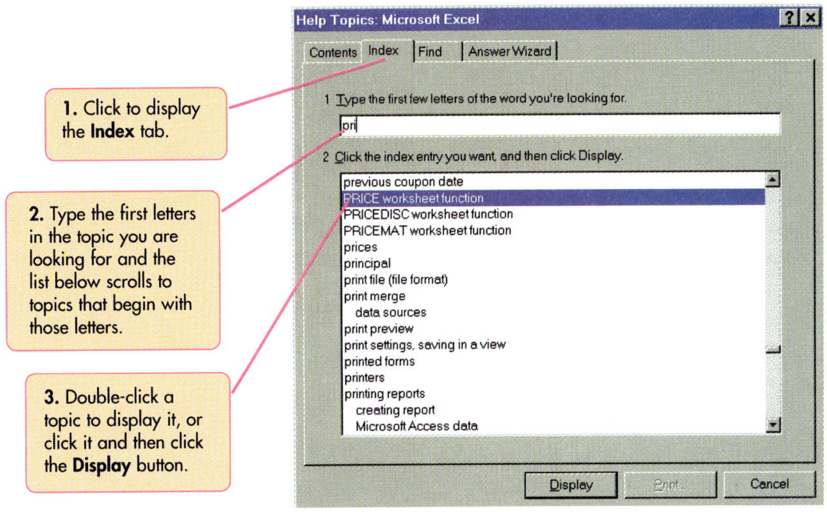

HELP—THE FIND TAB

The *Find* tab lets you search for words or phrases that might appear in a Help topic's title.

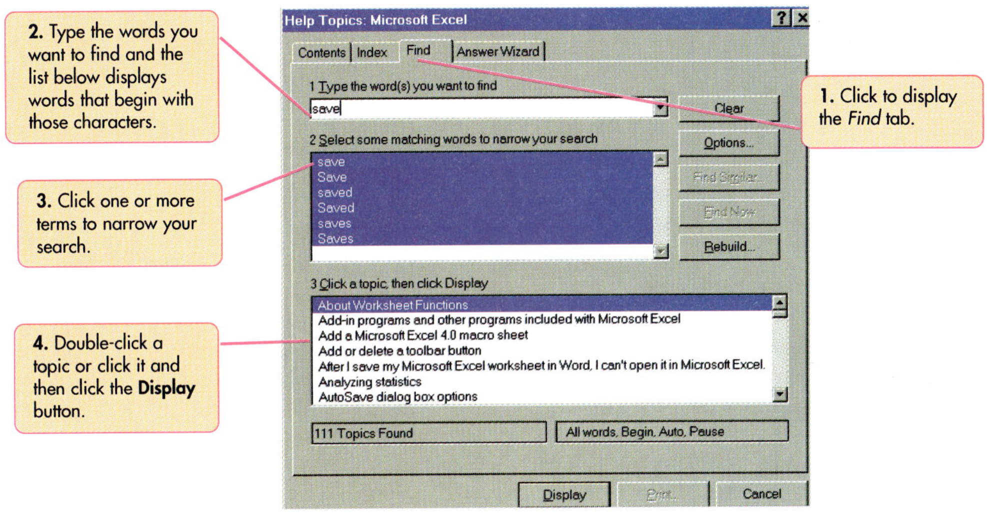

HELP—THE ANSWER WIZARD TAB

The *Answer Wizard* not only gives you help; it also guides you through many procedures step by step. Unlike other sections of Help that give only procedures, the Answer Wizard also provides you with background information. When you ask for help on a topic, a heading reads *Tell Me About*. Double-clicking any topic under this heading displays a description and not procedural steps.

Step-by-step answers

Explanations and visual answers

Programming and language reference—beyond the scope of this text

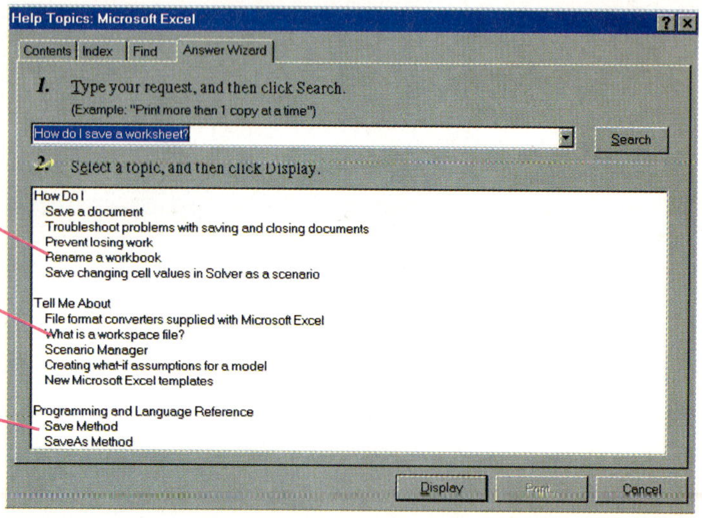

QUICKSTEPS

Displaying Help

1. Double-click the **Help** button on the Standard toolbar, or pull down the **Help** menu and click the **Microsoft Excel Help Topics** command to display the Help Topics dialog box.
2. Locate Help using the tabs *Contents*, *Index*, *Find*, or *Answer Wizard* as shown in the illustrations in the section "The Help System." You may see hypertext links within the Help windows that take you directly to other places. *Hypertext links* are simply "hot spots" you click to jump to another location. (You know you are pointing to a hypertext link when the mouse pointer turns into a pointing finger.) Sometimes these open other windows or display pop-ups. Click in a pop-up or any area but a button or menu command to close it.
3. After locating and reading Help, do one of the following:
   - Pull down the **Options** menu and click the **Print Topic** command.
   - Click the **Help Topics** button to return to the Help Topics dialog box.
   - Click the Help window's **Minimize** button to display it as a button on the taskbar.
   - Click the Help window's **Close** button to close it.

When the mouse pointer takes the shape of a pointing finger, clicking jumps you to a new topic.

TUTORIAL

In this tutorial you practice using Excel's on-line Help to locate information on some of the topics you have explored in this PicTorial.

Getting Ready

1. Double-click the **Help** button on the Standard toolbar to display the Help Topics window. It has four tabs: *Contents*, *Index*, *Find*, and *Answer Wizard*.

The TipWizard button

The Help button

Exploring ScreenTips

2. Click the *Contents* tab to display it.

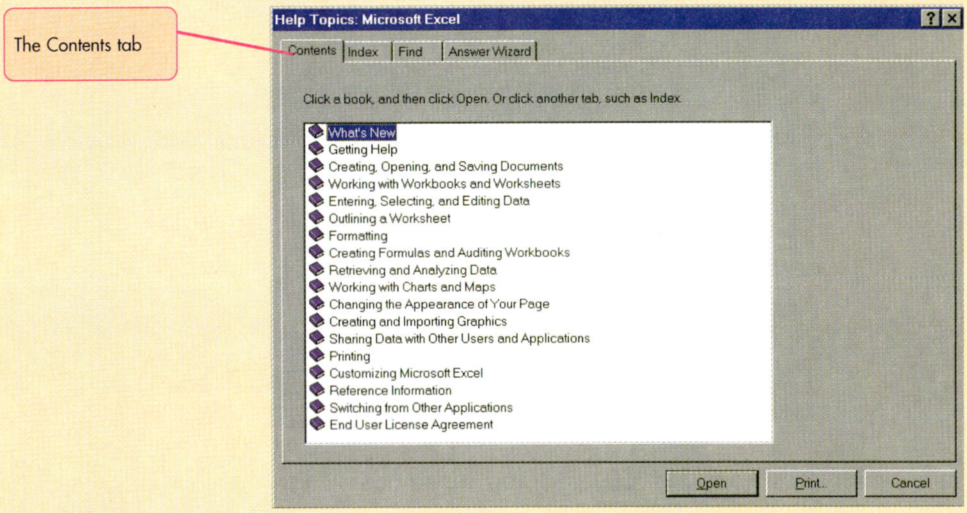

3. Click the question mark button on the Help window's title bar to add a question mark to the mouse pointer.
4. Click the window listing Help books to display a pop-up describing it.
5. Click inside the pop-up to close it. (You can also close it by clicking outside of it, but may inadvertently execute some other command if you aren't careful.)

Exploring the Contents Tab

6. Double-click the *Getting Help* book to display a list of its contents.

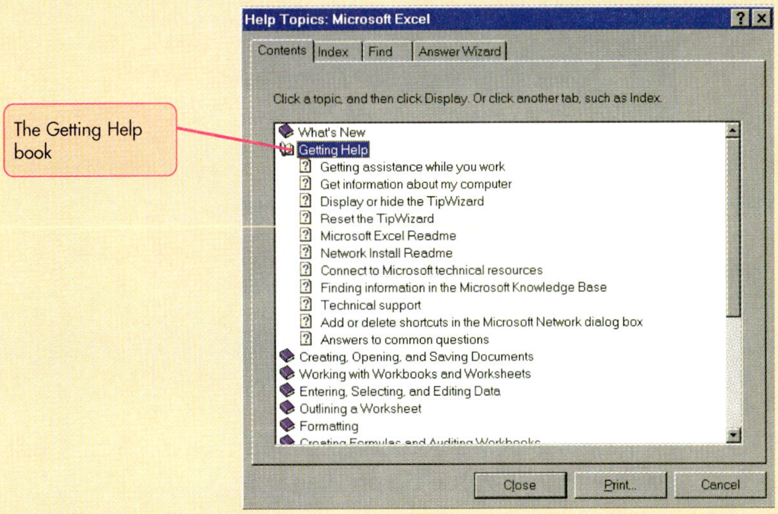

7. Double-click the *Getting assistance while you work* topic to display a screen with labels in boxes. When you point to a label box, its red bar brightens to indicate it's a hot spot.
8. Click each label box to display a pop-up on that topic. If the pop-up covers another label, you can click it to close it.
9. Click the **Help Topics** button in the lower-right corner of the Help window to return to the Help Topics window.

1-9 MANAGING WORKBOOKS

What if you want to copy, move, delete, rename, or explore workbooks or folders? You can do so from within Excel without opening Windows' My Computer or Windows Explorer. To do so, you right-click a workbook or folder displayed in the Open or Save As dialog boxes, and a shortcut menu appears. Which menu appears depends on whether you right-click a workbook, a folder, or anywhere in the box except on a folder or workbook. The commands listed on the menus are described below, although not all of these commands appear on the same menu.

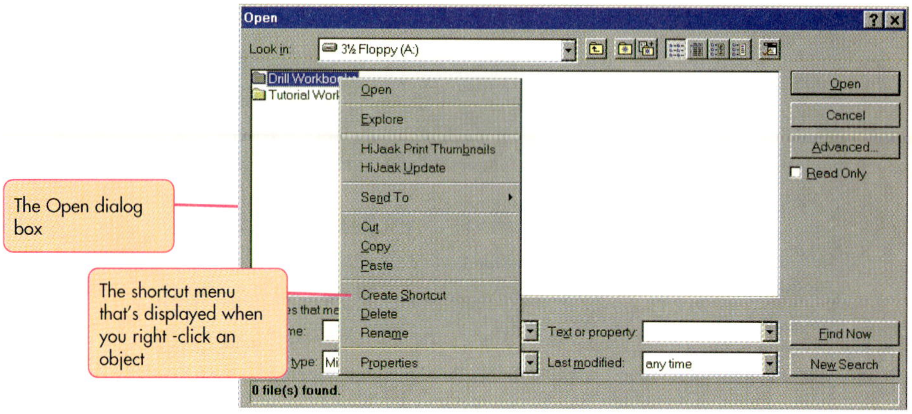

- **Open** opens the selected object in the dialog box.
- **Open Read Only** opens the workbook so you can read it but not change it.
- **Explore** opens the selected folder and displays it in Windows Explorer.
- **Print** prints the selected workbook.
- **Save** saves the workbook using the selected filename.
- **Quick View** displays the contents of the selected workbook.
- **Send To** sends the selected workbook or folder to a floppy disk, or to a fax or e-mail recipient.
- **Cut** moves the selected folder or workbook to the Clipboard.
- **Copy** copies the selected folder or workbook to the Clipboard.
- **Paste** pastes the cut or copied workbook or folder into the current folder.
- **Create Shortcut** creates a shortcut to the selected folder or workbook in the same location. You can then drag or move this shortcut to another folder or to the desktop.
- **Delete** deletes the selected folder or workbook to the Recycle Bin.
- **Rename** highlights the name of the selected folder or workbook so you can type a new one.
- **Properties** displays the properties of the selected folder or workbook.

QUICKSTEPS

Managing Workbooks

1. To manage your workbooks, do one of the following:
   - Click the **Open** button on the Standard toolbar, or pull down the **File** menu and click the **Open** command to display the Open dialog box.
   - Click the **Save** button on the Standard toolbar, or pull down the **File** menu and click the **Save** or **Save As** command to display the Save As dialog box.
2. Do one of the following:
   - Right-click a folder or workbook to manage it.
   - Select a number of folders or workbooks to manage, then right-click any of them.
   - Right-click in the list box, but not on a specific folder or workbook, to display a shortcut menu with choices that apply to the open folder (or if it's a floppy disk, to the disk as a whole).
3. Click any of the shortcut menu commands described in the text.

TUTORIAL

In this tutorial you use the Open dialog box to manage a few workbooks. Although you normally use this dialog box to open workbooks, you can also use it to move, copy, rename, or delete files.

Getting Ready

1. Insert your *Excel Student Resource Disk* containing the *Tutorial Documents* folder into the floppy disk drive you use to open and save workbooks.

Opening an Existing Workbook

2. Click the **Open** button on the Standard toolbar to display the Open dialog box.
3. Click the **Look in** drop-down arrow (▾) and click the name of the drive you inserted the *Excel Student Resource Disk* in to display the folders on that disk.

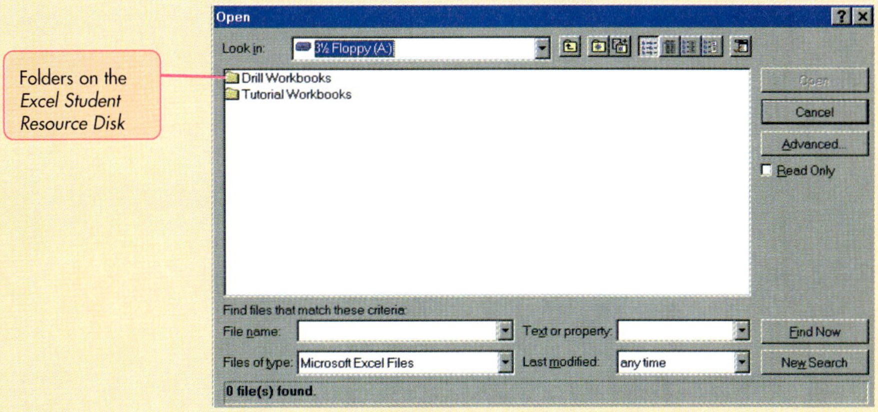

4. Double-click the *Tutorial Workbooks* folder name or icon to open it and display the workbooks in that folder. (If your list of folders looks different, click the **List** button on the dialog box's toolbar.)

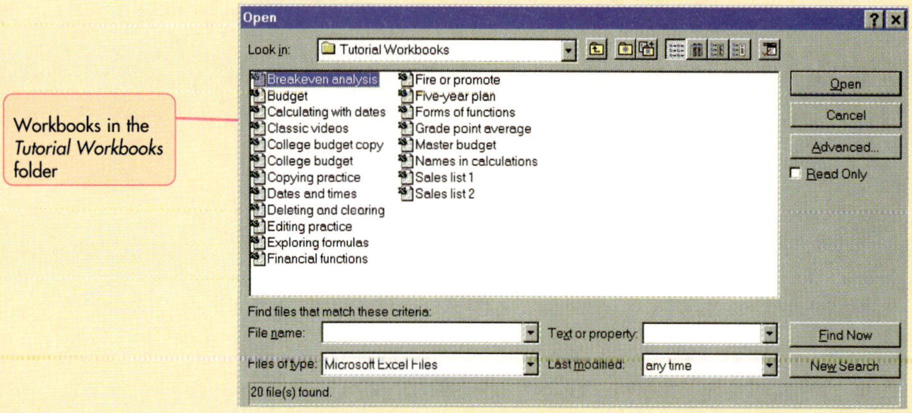

Copying a Workbook

5. Right-click the *Budget* workbook, then click the shortcut menu's **Copy** command.

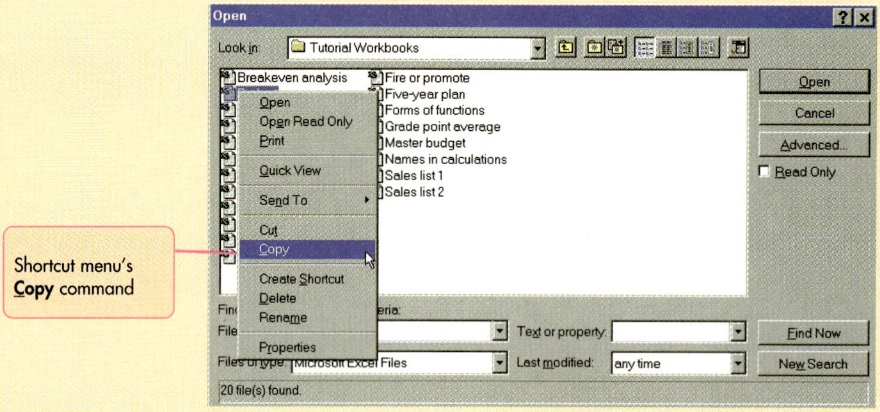

6. Click the **Up One Level** button on the toolbar, then double-click the *Drill Workbooks* folder to open it.

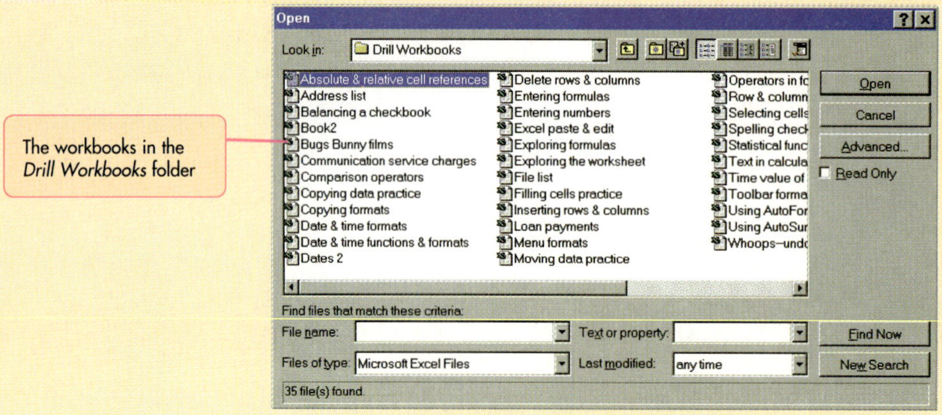

7. Right-click in a clear area (not on a file name or icon), then click the shortcut menu's **Paste** command. The *Budget* workbook is listed because there is now a copy of it in this folder.

Deleting a Workbook

8. Right-click the *Budget* workbook, then click the shortcut menu's **Delete** command. When prompted *Are you sure you want to delete 'Budget'?* click the **Yes** button.

Finishing Up

9. Click the Open dialog box's **Cancel** button.
10. Click Excel's **Close** button to close the program or continue to the drills, exercises, and projects. If you quit, be sure to take your floppy disk out of the system's drive.

PicTorial 1

REVIEW QUESTIONS

TRUE-FALSE

T F 1. A spreadsheet model simulates situations involving numbers.

T F 2. Templates are designed to be used again and again by anyone who knows how to enter the numbers to be analyzed.

T F 3. To start Microsoft Excel, you begin by clicking the **Start** button on Windows taskbar.

T F 4. The **Restore** button is displayed only after you have clicked the **Minimize** button.

T F 5. To open an existing workbook, you need to know what folder it is in.

T F 6. Sheet tabs are clicked to display other sheets.

T F 7. The scroll bar's scroll box is always the same size so it's easy to identify.

T F 8. If you type data into a cell that already contains data, the new data is rejected.

T F 9. You can press Enter← or click the Enter box on the formula bar to complete the entry in a cell.

T F 10. To print a workbook, you just click the **Print** button on the Standard toolbar.

MULTIPLE CHOICE

1. To open an application program once you have located it on the Start menu, you ___.
   a. Click its name or icon
   b. Click its icon and then pull down the **File** menu and click the **Run** command

c. Double-click its icon

d. Click its icon and then pull down the **File** menu and click the **Open** command

2. To close or exit an application properly, you ___.

a. Click its **Minimize** button
b. Click its **Close** button
c. Turn off the computer
d. None of the above

3. A _________ is the arrangement of horizontal rows and vertical columns that appears on the screen.

a. Worksheet
b. Spreadsheet
c. Workbook
d. Template

4. The Excel screen usually displays the ___.

a. Formatting and Standard toolbars
b. Menu bar
c. Formula bar
d. All of the above

5. A _________ is the intersection of a column and a row.

a. Model
b. Prism
c. Range
d. Cell

6. The active cell is the one _________.

a. With its address in the Name box
b. Outlined with a heavy border
c. Into which data you type is entered
d. All of the above

7. A _____ is a stored workbook layout with preset margins and other formats.

a. File
b. Template
c. Macro
d. Document

8. The scroll box can _________.

a. Indicate where you are in a worksheet
b. Be dragged up and down or side to side to scroll the worksheet
c. Indicate the size of the worksheet containing data
d. All of the above

9. The Zoom Control affects _________.

a. Calculation speed
b. Scrolling rate
c. Size of worksheet on the screen
d. None of the above

10. When saving a workbook for the first time, you must specify a ________.

a. Filename
b. Folder
c. Drive
d. All of the above

FILL IN THE BLANK

1. The first step in starting an application is to click the ________________ button to display the ________________ menu.
2. To quickly close an application, you click its ________________.
3. A worksheet is divided into _________ and _________.
4. The _________ cell is always outlined with a heavy border.
5. By default, the _____ most recent files are listed on the bottom of the File menu when you pull it down.
6. To clear a worksheet from the screen, choose the File, __________ command.
7. The shape of the mouse pointer appears like a _________ when positioned on the border between column or row headings.
8. To quickly position the active cell in the cell where the lowest row and rightmost column containing data intersect, press ________.
9. If you notice a mistake while typing an entry, press ________ to move the insertion point to the left to delete it.
10. To edit an entry, you can press function key ________.

PICTORIAL 1

LAB ACTIVITIES

DRILLS

1-1 Starting and Exiting Excel

To do any useful work on a computer you have to first start an application program. In this drill you practice that procedure.

1. Click the **Start** button on the taskbar to display the Start menu, then click **Programs**, **Microsoft Excel** to open that application.
2. Click the **Close** button to close Excel.
3. Start Excel again, right-click its button on the taskbar, and click the shortcut menu's **Close** command to close the application.
4. Start Excel again, right-click its title bar, and click the shortcut menu's **Close** command to close the application.

1-2 Exploring Excel's Window

All application windows have buttons you can click to change their size. In this drill you practice using these buttons.

1. Click the **Start** button on the taskbar to display the Start menu, then click **Programs**, **Microsoft Excel** to open that application.
2. Click the **Minimize** button and then the Microsoft Excel button on the taskbar to minimize and restore the application's window. Do this a few times until you are familiar with the results of clicking each button.

3. Click the **Restore** and **Maximize** buttons to restore and maximize the application's window (one of them is always displayed). Do this a few times until you are familiar with the results of clicking each button.
4. Click Excel's **Close** button on the title bar to close the application.

1-3 Opening and Closing Workbooks

One of the most basic skills you need to master is opening and closing workbooks. In this drill, you practice opening workbooks stored in folders on your *Excel Student Resource Disks*. As you complete this drill, and others in this text, you will have to insert the correct disk.

1. Insert the *Excel Student Resource Disk* containing the *Tutorial Workbook* folder into the floppy disk drive you use to open and save workbooks.
2. Use the **Open** button on the Standard toolbar or the **Open** command on the **File** menu to open each of workbooks listed in the table "Workbooks to Open and Close." Each workbook is in the indicated folder and you may have to swap disks to access some folders. Write down a brief description of each workbook, and then close each workbook by clicking its **Close** button—the one on the menu bar. To open a workbook, you only need these three procedures after you display the Open dialog box:
   - To select a drive, use the **Look in** drop-down arrow.
   - To open a folder, double-click it.
   - To move back up one level, click the **Up One Level** button

TIP

Save Changes?

When you close some workbooks, a dialog box asks if you want to save your changes—even when you have made no changes. In some cases this is caused by a date function in the workbook's heading that automatically calculates the date from the system clock and then updates it in the workbook. In other cases it's an unexplainable bug.

Workbooks to Open and Close

Done	Folder	Filename
❑	*Tutorial Workbooks*	*Classic videos*
❑	*Tutorial Workbooks*	*Exploring formulas*
❑	*Drill Workbooks*	*Bugs Bunny films*
❑	*Drill Workbooks*	*Communication service charges*
❑	*Exercise Workbooks*	*Members of 103rd Congress*
❑	*Exercise Workbooks*	*Exchange rates*

1-4 Moving Around a Sheet

Moving around the worksheet is simple, but moving quickly to places takes some practice. In this drill you practice using the End key to quickly move to the four corners of the worksheet.

1. Open the *Exploring the worksheet* workbook stored in the *Drill Workbooks* folder on the *Excel Student Resource Disk.*
2. Use the End key to quickly move to the four corners of the worksheet, and

write down the words you find in each cell in the table "Exploring the Worksheet."

3. Use the Name box on the formula bar to quickly jump to cell CC100, and write down the words you find in the cell in the table "Exploring the Worksheet."
4. Practice using the commands described in the QuickSteps box "Moving Around a Worksheet with the Keyboard" to move around the worksheet.
5. Practice using the commands described in the QuickSteps box "Moving Around a Worksheet with the Scroll Bars" to move around the worksheet.
6. Click the workbook's **Close** button on the menu bar to close the workbook.

Exploring the Worksheet

Cell	Words in Cell
A1	____________
A16384	____________
IV16384	____________
IV1	____________
CC100	____________

1-5 Entering and Viewing Data

In this drill you enter a simple model that calculates the total number of cells in the Excel worksheet.

	A	B
1	Name: your name	
2	Filename: fearless	
3	Date: today's date	
4		
5	Number of cells	
6	Width	256
7	Depth	16384
8	Total	4194304

=B7*B6

1. Use the **New Workbook** button on the Standard toolbar to open a new workbook and then enter the model shown here. All of the entries are numbers or text except for the formula in cell B8. The asterisk in the formula is Excel's multiplication sign. Just as you might write out 256 × 16384, in Excel you enter the formula as =B6*B7. How large would a worksheet be if it were entirely printed out with each cell 1 inch wide and/inch deep? The size may surprise you. Since each sheet has 256 columns and 16,384 rows, for a total of 4,194,304 cells, its printout would be over 21 feet wide by 341 feet long! Try studying a printout of that in the car on the way to work in the morning.
2. Use the **Zoom Control** drop-down arrow (▼) on the Standard toolbar to display the workbook in each of the available zooms. When finished, set the **Zoom Control** to 100%.
3. Click the workbook's **Close** button on the menu bar to close the workbook. When asked if you want to save your changes, click the **No** button.

1-6 Saving Workbooks

In this drill you create a new workbook, enter your name into it, and then save it under a specific filename in a folder on the *Excel Student Resource Disk*.

1. Insert your *Excel Student Resource Disk* with the *Drill Workbooks* folder into the floppy disk drive you use to open and save workbooks.
2. Click the **New Workbook** button on the Standard toolbar to open a new workbook.
3. With cell A1 selected, type your name and press Enter↵.
4. Save the workbook as *Only my name 1* in the *Drill Workbooks* folder.
5. Click the workbook's **Close** button on the menu bar to close the workbook.
6. Repeat Steps 2 through 5 for three other new workbooks, but change the

number at the end of each filename to 2, 3, and 4 and save each in the folder described in the table "Saving My Name" on the appropriate disk.

Saving My Name	
Filename	**Folder**
Only my name 1	*Drill Workbooks*
Only my name 2	*Tutorial Workbooks*
Only my name 3	*Exercise Workbooks*
Only my name 4	*Project Workbooks*

1-7 Printing a Sheet

Printing a worksheet is as simple as clicking a button on the toolbar. In this drill you print a worksheet that lists all of the files on your *Excel Student Resource Disk*.

1. Open the *File list* workbook stored in the *Drill Workbooks* folder on the *Excel Student Resource Disk* and enter your name into cell A1.
2. Use the **Print** button on the Standard toolbar to print the worksheet, and file the printout where you can easily find it, because you may want to refer to it at some point. It lists all of the workbooks that you work with throughout this text.
3. Click the workbook's **Close** button on the menu bar to close the workbook.

1-8 Using On-line Help

The best thing about Excel's on-line Help is that it's always available, even long after you've lost the manual. In this drill you use Help to idenfiy items on the screen and get help on procedures.

1. Click the **New Workbook** button on the Standard toolbar to open a new workbook.
2. Click the **Help** button on the Standard toolbar to add a question mark to the mouse pointer. Then click each part of the screen shown here to display a pop-up. Summarize the description in the space provided, click the pop-up to close it, then repeat the procedure for the next item.

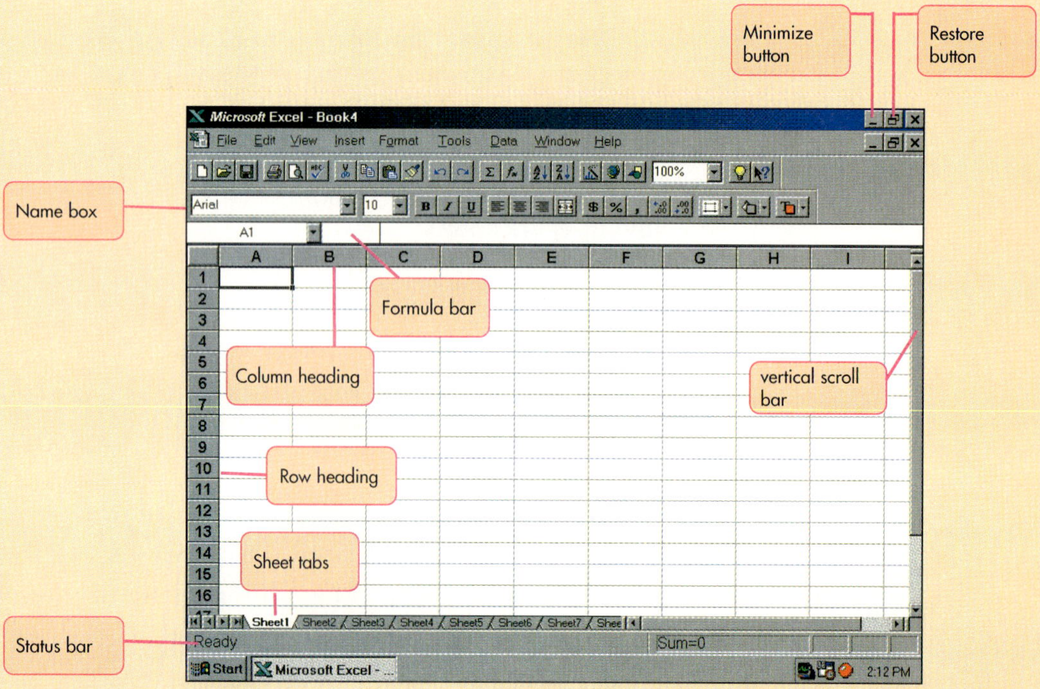

- ❑ Name box ____________________
- ❑ Formula bar ____________________
- ❑ Column heading ____________________
- ❑ Row heading ____________________
- ❑ Minimize button ____________________
- ❑ Restore button ____________________
- ❑ Vertical scroll bar ____________________
- ❑ Any sheet tab ____________________
- ❑ Status bar ____________________

3. Double-click the **Help** button on the Standard toolbar to display the Help Topics window.
4. Use the *Contents* tab to locate help on *Printing Your Work* in the *Printing* book and then display the topic *Preview a document before printing.*
5. Display the Help Topics window again, and use the *Index* tab to locate help on *Help* and then select the subtopic *available help and how to use it.* Click each of the labels marked with a red tab. Click the **Help Topics** button to return to the Help Topics window.
6. Use the *Find* tab to search for *closing* and then display the topic *Troubleshooting problems with saving and closing documents.* Click the **Help Topics** button to return to the Help Topics window.
7. Use the *AnswerWizard* tab to search for *opening a document* and then display *Finding, opening, and managing documents* under the *Tell Me About* heading. Close any open Help windows by clicking their **Close** button.

1-9 Managing Documents

In this drill you practice managing documents when the Open dialog box is displayed.

1. Click the **Open** button on the Standard toolbar to display the Open dialog box.
2. Open the *Drill Workbooks* folder on the *Excel Student Resource Disk.*
3. Right-click the *Address list* workbook and then click the shortcut menu's **Copy** command.
4. Click the **Up One Level** button on the toolbar, right-click a clear area of the box, then click the shortcut menu's **Paste** command. A copy of the workbook appears along with the folders.
5. Right-click the new *Address List* workbook and then click the shortcut menu's **Quick View** command to see the workbook's contents. (If this command isn't on your menu, Quick View has not been installed on your system. Click anywhere but the menu to close it.) Close the Quick View window.
6. Right-click the new *Address List* workbook and then click the shortcut menu's **Properties** command. Click each of the dialog box's tabs to see the workbook's properties. Close the Properties window.
7. Right-click the new *Address List* workbook and then click the shortcut menu's **Delete** command. When asked *Are you sure you want to delete 'Address List'?,* click the **Yes** button.
8. Click the dialog box's **Cancel** or **Close** buttons to close it.

EXERCISES

1-1 Exploring the Standard Toolbar

Click the **Help** button on the Standard toolbar, then click each of the other buttons on that toolbar to display a description. Write down the name of each button and summarize its function on the list below.

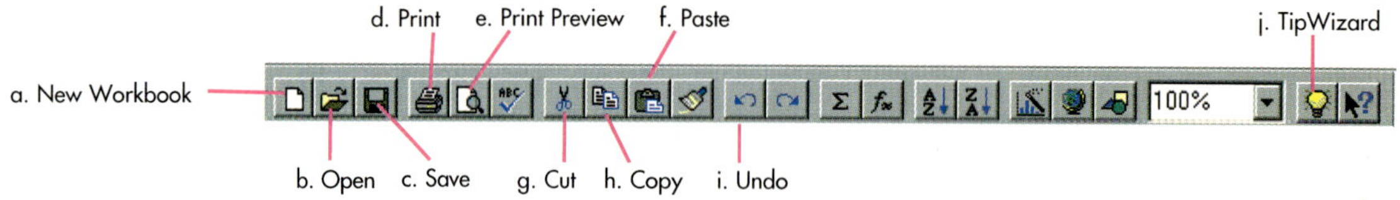

a.________________ b.________________

c.________________ d.________________

e.________________ f.________________

g.________________ h.________________

i. ________________ j.________________

1-2 Creating and Saving Workbooks

In this exercise you practice many of the procedures you learned in this PicTorial.

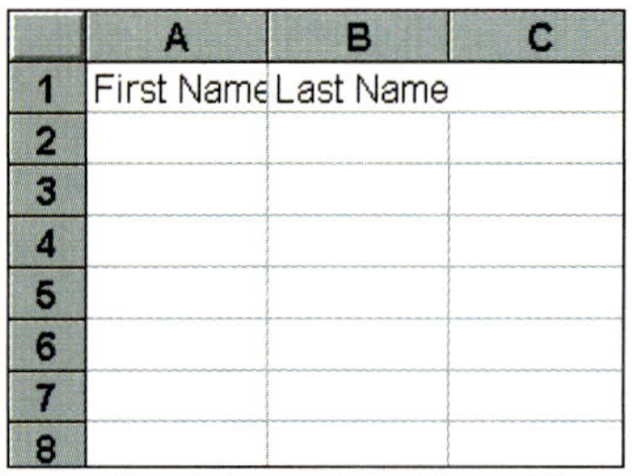

The Name List Workbook

1. Open a new workbook.
2. Type in the headings shown in the figure "The Name List Workbook." Then type in the first and last names of some of your family or friends. To do so, just click the cell, type the name, and press Enter↵. As you type entries in cells, some may be so long that they overflow into the cell to their right. You'll see later how to widen columns so full names can be displayed.
3. Save the workbook as *My first exercise workbook* in the *Project Workbooks* folder on the *Excel Student Resource Disk.*
4. Close the workbook.
5. Use the Open dialog box display the *My first exercise workbook,* then use right-clicking to cut the workbook from the *Project Workbooks* folder and paste it into the *Exercise Workbooks* folder.
6. Right-click the *My first exercise workbook* workbook and use the shortcut menu's **Rename** command to change its name to *Moved and renamed name list.* (If Windows Explorer is set to display extensions, the filename will end with *.xls.* If this extension is there, don't delete it, or if you do, type it back in. Otherwise, the file will be stored improperly.)
7. Close the workbook and Excel.

PICTORIAL

TWO

MASTERING THE BASICS

After completing this PicTorial, you will be able to:

- **Open, save, and close workbooks to any drive or folder**
- **Enter text, numbers, and formulas to create models**
- **Edit cell contents and undo mistakes**
- **Select ranges of cells**
- **Copy the data in cells to other cells**
- **Explain the difference between absolute and relative cell refer ences**
- **Adjust column widths and row heights**

THERE are only a few procedures that you absolutely must know to get value from a program such as Excel, and they are covered in this PicTorial. These procedures include opening and saving workbooks; entering text, numbers, and formulas; editing or undoing mistakes; and copying data.

2-1 ENTERING TEXT AND NUMBERS INTO CELLS

One of the most basic steps in using a spreadsheet is entering text and numbers—often called data. This is a straightforward process, but there are variations and shortcuts that you should be aware of.

Entering Data

You enter data by selecting a cell and typing. (Up to 255 characters are allowed in a cell). As you type, the data is displayed in the cell and on the formula bar. There are three ways to complete an entry:

- Press Enter↵ to remove the data from the formula bar and automatically select the cell below (the program assumes you are entering data down a column unless a setting has been changed).
- Click another cell, or press any of the keys that change the active cell. For example, press ↑, ↓, ←, or → to complete the entry and select the next cell in the direction of the arrow you press. When making several entries along a row or up a column, entering data using the appropriate arrow keys saves you a keystroke each time.
- Click the Enter box (☑) that appears on the formula bar when you begin entering data in a cell. When you click this box, the active cell doesn't change. (The formula bar is discussed in detail in the box "Understanding the Formula Bar" in Section 1-2.)

The Undo button

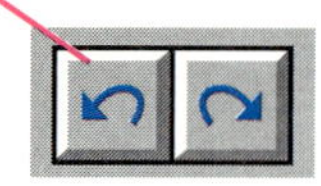

Canceling Entries

When entering data, you can cancel the entry before or after you complete it.

- To cancel the entry before you complete it, press Esc, click the Cancel box (☒) on the formula bar, or pull down the **Edit** menu and click the **Undo Typing** command.
- To cancel the entry after you have completed it, click the **Undo** button on the Standard toolbar, or pull down the **Edit** menu and click the **Undo Entry** command.

Long text with data in the next cell

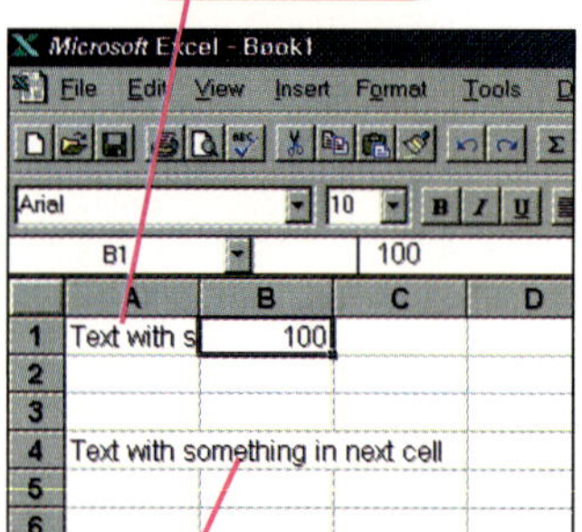

Long text without data in the next cell

Text too long to fit in a cell

Entering Text

Text is just like the text in this book or other documents. It can consist of any combination of letters, numbers, or other characters. To enter text, just select the cell, type it in, and press Enter↵. Even if the entry has a number in it (for example, *45 Elm Street*), Excel accepts it as text. If you enter just numbers in a cell and want them treated as text—for example, serial numbers or ZIP codes—precede them with an apostrophe. Once a number is entered as text, it cannot be used in normal mathematical operations.

If your text is longer than its cell is wide, it overflows into the next cell to the right if that cell is empty. If that cell is not empty, only the characters that fit in the cell being typed in are displayed.

To display all of the text, you can widen the column. The quickest way to do so is to point to the right border of the column heading at the top of the worksheet (the mouse pointer turns into a split double arrow) and double-click.

Double-click when the mouse pointer looks like this to widen the column to the left.

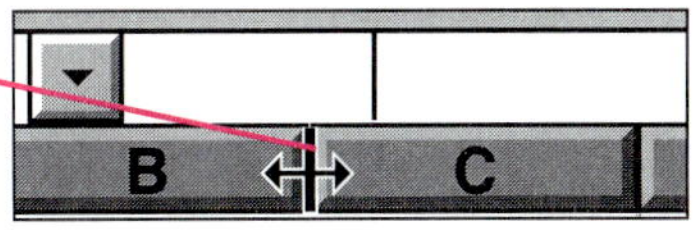

A feature called *AutoComplete* simplifies data entry in certain situations. When you type data into a cell, Excel compares the first letter with any other data already entered in that column or row. If it finds an existing entry with the same character, it completes the entry in the current cell for you.

- To accept the entry, just press Enter↵ or click the Enter box on the formula bar.
- To reject the automatically added portion, continue typing (the next character you type deletes it) or press Delete to delete it.

You can also pick a cell entry from a list of things you have already entered in a column. To do so, right-click the cell, and click the shortcut menu's **Pick from list** command to display a list of words or phrases you have entered into the column. Click one of them to enter it into the cell.

Another feature, called *AutoCorrect*, will fix some of the typing errors that you make. To see what changes are made, and to turn options on and off, pull down the **Tools** menu and click the **AutoCorrect** command. You can add words to be replaced when the dialog box is displayed. You can also add them during a spell check.

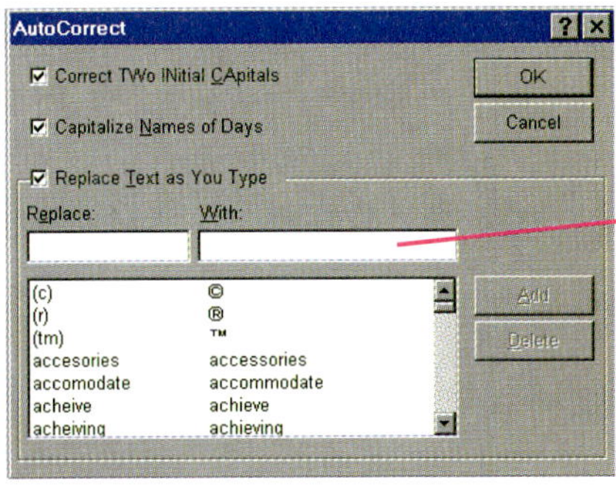

Enter a word or phrase you want replaced and the word or phrase you want to replace it with in these spaces, and then click the **Add** button.

Entering Numbers

To enter numbers into a cell, just type them in. They will automatically align with the right edge of the cell. Characters Excel recognizes as numbers include the digits 0 through 9 plus a variety of other characters (see the box "Characters You Can Use in Numbers and Formulas" in Section 2-5, "Entering Formulas.")

When entering numbers, keep these points in mind:

- To enter fractions, precede them with a zero and a space so Excel doesn't consider them to be dates. (Excel treats dates and times in a special way, described in Section 4-5.) For example, if you type 1/2 into a cell, Excel displays it as *2-Jan* since it assumes it's a date. However, if you enter it as **0 1/2** (the space following the 0 is essential), it is displayed as *1/2* in the cell and 0.5 on the formula bar.
- Enter percentages either as decimals or with a percent sign. For example, enter 20 percent either as .2 or 20%.
- Numbers can have only one period (decimal point). If you enter more than one period in a cell, the entry is treated as text.
- Precede negative numbers with a minus sign, as in **–10**, or enclose them in parentheses, as in **(10)**.

- When NumLock is engaged, you can enter numbers by typing them on the numeric keypad. When NumLock is engaged, the status bar displays the NUM indicator.

TIP

Leading Zeros Disappear

You enter a ZIP code such as 01945 and it is displayed as 1945. This is because Excel treats it as a number and therefore drops any beginning zeros. To enter a number as text, type an apostrophe (') as the first character.

TIP

Converting from Scientific Notation

When a number is too long to be displayed in full, Excel displays it in scientific notation. Scientific notation is based on powers of 10. The number 1,250,000 can also be expressed as 1.25×10^6. In an Excel cell, this appears as 1.25E+06, where the E separates the exponent (6) from the base (1.25). If the cell is too narrow to show the number even in scientific notation, Excel will fill the cell with a row of number signs (######). In either case, the original number you entered, or which has been calculated by a formula, is shown on the formula bar.

Shortcuts

When you enter a number into a cell, the cell is automatically formatted with the General number format which displays numbers as precisely as possible. However, you can display a number differently by changing its format. Although formatting numbers is discussed in detail later in this text, there are a few formats you can enter as you enter numbers. For example:

- To format the cell using the Currency format ($10.00), enter a dollar sign in front of the number.
- To format the cell using the Comma format (1,000), use commas in the number to separate thousands.
- To format a number as a percentage, enter the number followed by a percent sign. For example, instead of entering .2, enter 20%. When you enter a percentage as a whole number followed by a percent sign, the program automatically formats the cells using the Percentage format and converts the number in front of the percent sign into a decimal by dividing the number by 100. For example, entering a percentage as 20% is the same as entering it as 0.2 or 20/100.

TUTORIAL

In this tutorial you begin to create a 2-year budget by entering text and numbers. When you have finished this tutorial, your model will look like the one shown in the figure "The Budget—Labels and Numbers."

1. Enter text shown here in cells with light yellow background.

	A	B	C	D	E
1	Type **Name: your name** into cell A1 and press **Enter**				
2	Filename: Budget				
3	Mar-96				
4					
5	2-Year Budget				
6	INCOME	FALL	SPRING	FALL	SPRING
7	Bank balance	3,000			
8	Income during semester	1,250	1,250	1,250	1,250
9	College loans	1,000	1,000	1,000	1,000
10	Total				
11					
12	EXPENSES				
13	Tuition	1,000	1,000	1,000	1,000
14	Room & board	1,000	1,000	1,000	1,000
15	Books	200	200	200	200
16	Entertainment	300	300	300	300
17	Travel	500	500	500	500
18	Misc.	200	200	200	200
19	Total				
20					
21	Balance				

2. Enter numbers shown here in cells with light blue background.

The Budget—Labels and Numbers

Getting Ready

1. Open the *Budget* workbook stored in the *Tutorial Workbooks* folder on the *Excel Student Resource Disk* and enter your name into cell A1.

Entering Text

2. Enter the text shown in the light yellow cells in the figure "The Budget—Labels and Numbers." Before typing **Total** in cell A10 and cell A19, press Spacebar twice to indent the word.

Entering Numbers

3. Enter all of the numbers shown in the light blue cells in the figure "The Budget—Labels and Numbers." When typing numbers with commas between thousands, type the commas in the numbers exactly as shown. This will format the cell to match the entry.

Finishing Up

4. Save, print, and close the workbook.

2-2 EDITING CELL CONTENTS

When you enter data into a cell, it is displayed on the formula bar and you can press ←Bksp to delete characters. Once you have completed the entry, you can edit it either in the cell or on the formula bar.

QUICKSTEPS
Editing Cell Contents

1. Select the cell to be edited and then do one of the following:
   - Click the formula bar to move the insertion point there so you can edit the entry on the formula bar.
   - Press F2 or double-click the cell to move the insertion point there so you can edit the entry right in the cell.
2. Edit the entry using the commands described in the box "Understanding Editing Commands."
3. Press Enter↵ or click the Enter box (☑) on the formula bar to complete the edit.

UNDERSTANDING
Editing Commands

- To move the insertion point through the entry, press ← or →. Press Home or End to move it to the beginning or end of the entry. Press Ctrl+← or Ctrl+→ to move it to the beginning of the previous or next word.
- To insert characters at the insertion point, type them in.
- To delete characters, press ←Bksp to delete those to the left of the insertion point and Delete to delete those to the right. Hold either of these keys down to delete one character after another.
- To switch between insert and overtype modes, press Insert. In *insert mode* (the default mode), if you type a character into an existing line of characters, the characters to the right move over to make room for the new character. In *overtype mode* (the status bar reads *OVR* when in this mode), any character that you type replaces any character the edit cursor is highlighting.

TUTORIAL

In this tutorial, you open the *Editing practice* workbook and edit the misspelled entries in column A—some on the formula bar and some in the cell itself.

Getting Ready

1. Open the *Editing practice* workbook stored in the *Tutorial Workbooks* folder on the *Excel Student Resource Disk*.

Correcting a Mistake While Entering

2. With cell A1 selected, type **Naame:** just as shown here, with an extra *a*.
3. Press ←Bksp four times so that the line reads *Na*.
4. Type **me:** and press Spacebar, then type your name and press Enter↵ to enter the new revised label.

Editing Cell Contents on the Formula Bar

5. Correct just the misspelled words or incorrect phrases in the cells with the light yellow background color (see the list "Editing on the Formula Bar"). To do so:
   - Click the cell to display its contents on the formula bar.

- Click the entry on the formula bar to move the insertion point into it.
- Use the arrow keys to move the insertion point through the entry, and insert new characters as needed.
- Use ←Bksp and Delete to delete unwanted characters.
- When finished, press Enter↵ or click the Enter box (☑) on the formula bar to enter the revised entry into the cell.

Edit the cells with the light yellow background on the formula bar.

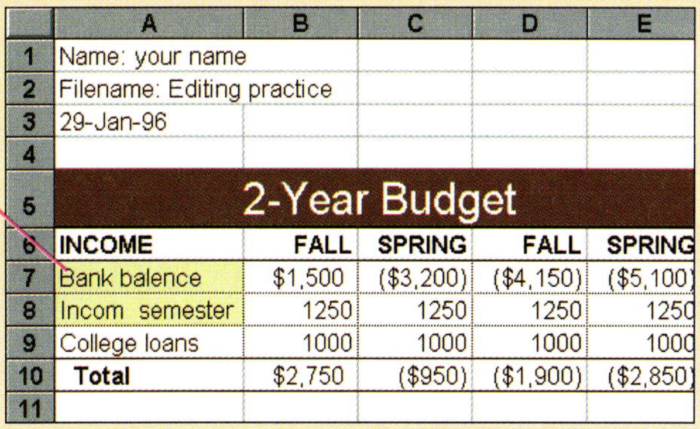

	A	B	C	D	E
1	Name: your name				
2	Filename: Editing practice				
3	29-Jan-96				
4					
5	2-Year Budget				
6	INCOME	FALL	SPRING	FALL	SPRING
7	Bank balence	$1,500	($3,200)	($4,150)	($5,100)
8	Incom semester	1250	1250	1250	1250
9	College loans	1000	1000	1000	1000
10	Total	$2,750	($950)	($1,900)	($2,850)
11					

The Unedited Model—Part 1

Editing on the Formula Bar	
Current Form	**Corrected Form**
balence	balance
Incom semester	Income during semester

Editing Cell Contents in the Cell

6. Now correct the misspelled text in the cells with the light blue background color (see the list "Editing in the Cell"). To do so:
   - Double-click the cell to move the insertion point there.
   - Use the arrow keys to move the insertion point through the entry in the cell (not on the formula bar), and insert new characters as needed.
   - Use ←Bksp and Delete to delete unwanted characters.
   - When finished, press Enter↵ or click the Enter box (☑) on the formula bar to enter the revised entry into the cell.

Edit the cells with the light blue background in the cell.

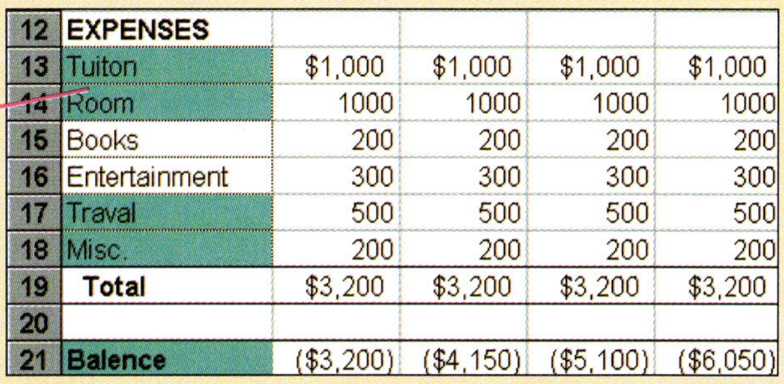

12	EXPENSES				
13	Tuiton	$1,000	$1,000	$1,000	$1,000
14	Room	1000	1000	1000	1000
15	Books	200	200	200	200
16	Entertainment	300	300	300	300
17	Traval	500	500	500	500
18	Misc.	200	200	200	200
19	Total	$3,200	$3,200	$3,200	$3,200
20					
21	Balence	($3,200)	($4,150)	($5,100)	($6,050)

The Unedited Model—Part 2

Editing in the Cell	
Current Form	**Corrected Form**
Tuiton	Tuition
Room	Room & board
Traval	Travel
Misc.	Miscellaneous
Balence	Balance

Finishing Up

7. Save, print, and close the workbook.

2-3 UNDOING MISTAKES

If you make a mistake when working with Excel, you can reverse it if you notice it before you have gone further. Only the last command or data entry you have made can be undone. You can undo all kinds of actions including entering, editing, formatting, and deleting data.

The Undo button

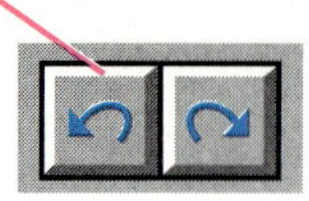

QUICKSTEPS

Undoing Mistakes

To undo the effect of the last command, click the **Undo** button on the Standard toolbar, or pull down the **Edit** menu and click the **Undo** command (the most recent command that can be undone is listed following the Undo part of the command).

TUTORIAL

In this tutorial you make a number of deliberate mistakes so you can see how easy it is to undo them.

Getting Ready

1. Open the *Editing practice* workbook stored in the *Tutorial Workbooks* folder on the *Excel Student Resource Disk*.

Undoing and Redoing Data Entry With the Menu

2. Click cell A1 to select it, type **Oh no, why did I do this?** and press Enter to replace the current entry.
3. Pull down the **Edit** menu and click the **Undo Entry** command to restore the original cell contents.
4. Pull down the **Edit** menu and click the **Redo (u) Entry** command to replace the original cell contents with the second entry.
5. Pull down the **Edit** menu and click the **Undo Entry** command to restore the original cell contents.

Undoing and Redoing Data Entry with the Toolbar

6. With cell A1 selected, type **Oh no, why did I do this again?** and press Enter to complete the entry.
7. Click the **Undo** button on the Standard toolbar and the original cell contents are restored.
8. Click the **Undo** button on the Standard toolbar again to replace the original cell contents with the second entry.

9. Click the **Undo** button on the Standard toolbar a third time to restore the original contents again.

Undoing a Deletion with the Menu

10. Click the heading for column A to select the entire column (the heading is the box with the letter A in it.)

Click the column heading to select the entire column.

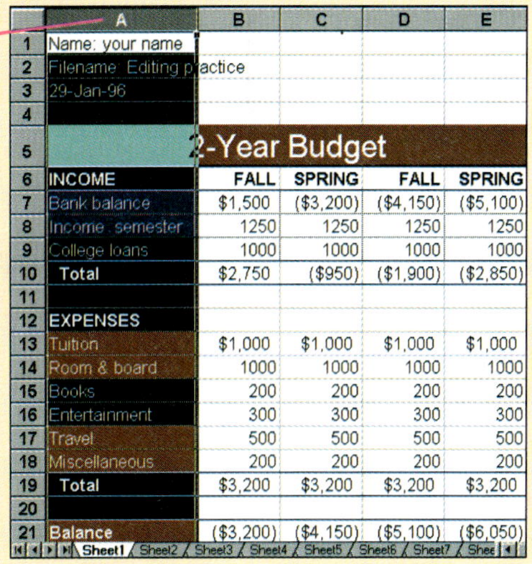

11. Pull down the **Edit** menu and click the **Delete** command to delete the column.
12. Pull down the **Edit** menu and click the **Undo Delete** command to restore the deleted column.

Undoing a Deletion with the Toolbar

13. With column A still selected, pull down the **Edit** menu and click the **Redo (u) Delete** command to delete the column again.
14. Click the **Undo** button on the Standard toolbar to restore the deleted column.

Finishing Up

15. Close the workbook without saving your changes.

2-4 UNDERSTANDING FORMULAS

Very few people would use spreadsheet programs if all you could enter were text and numbers. What makes spreadsheets so popular is the ability to enter formulas. The formulas can calculate numbers entered in other cells on the worksheet, on other worksheets, or even other workbooks. This ability makes the spreadsheet a very useful and powerful tool for anyone who works with numbers of any kind.

You can enter formulas into worksheet cells that either calculate numbers directly or refer to cells elsewhere on the worksheet into which you enter numbers or other formulas. The basic rule is that all Excel formulas begin with an equal sign (=).

TIP

Exceptions to the Rule That Formulas Must Begin with an Equal Sign

You can begin a formula with a plus or minus sign, but Excel will add a beginning equal sign when you complete the entry.

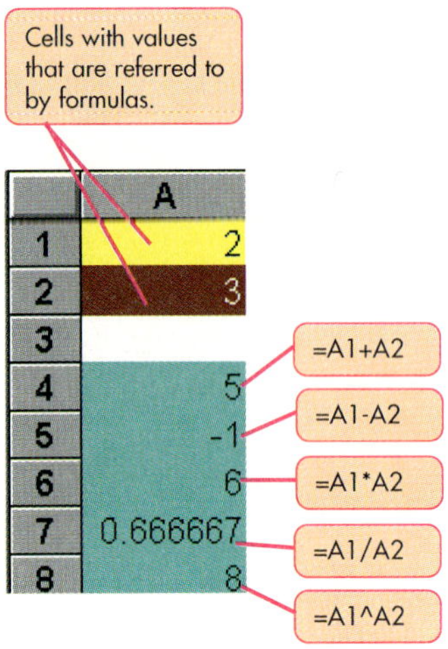

Operators in Formulas

Operators—The Basic Building Blocks

When you enter formulas, certain symbols, called operators, tell the program what calculations to perform. These operators are used in conjunction with numbers or cell references to create formulas. The table "Excel Operators" lists some of Excel's operators, and the figure "Operators in Formulas" illustrates some of them.

Excel Operators

Operator	Use
+	Performs addition
–	Performs subtraction
*	Performs multiplication
/	Performs division
%	Percent (when placed after a value, as in 20%)
^	Raises a number to a specified power

The Order of Operations

When you enter formulas that contain more than one operator, the order in which they are evaluated becomes important. Each operator is assigned a priority that determines the sequence in which it is calculated. The table "Order of Operations" shows these priorities.

- Operators with a higher priority are performed first. For example, if you enter the formula =4*2+3, it contains two operators: + (addition) and * (multiplication). Since multiplication has a higher priority, it is performed first, so 4*2 = 8; then addition is performed, so 8+3 = 11.
- Operators with the same level of priority are calculated in the order they appear in the formula from left to right. For example, if you enter the formula =5*4/2, it has two operators: * (multiplication) and / (division), which have the same priority. Since calculations are performed from left to right, the answer is 10. First multiplication is performed, so 5*4 = 20; then division is performed, so 20/2 = 10.

You can enter formulas so that calculations occur in the desired sequence, but it is usually easier to use parentheses to control the order of calculations regardless of the priorities assigned to the operators. For example, entering a formula as =4*2+3 calculates an answer of 11. However, the formula =4*(2+3) calculates a different answer since the operations within the parentheses are always performed first. Hence, 2+3 = 5, which is then multiplied by 4 to give 20. If parentheses are nested—for example, 1+(1/(1/2))—the operations are performed from the innermost parentheses outward; in this formula, the answer would be 3. You can use up to 32 sets of parentheses in any formula.

Order of Operations		
Operator	**Description**	**Priority**
–	Negation (as in –10)	Highest
%	Percent	
^	Exponentiation	
* and /	Multiplication and division	
+ and –	Addition and subtraction	Lowest

Numbers and Cell References

When you enter formulas, you can use numbers and/or references to other cells. For example, entering the formula =5+10 into a cell displays 15 in the cell because that is the value of 5 and 10 added together. You could also enter the number 5 into cell A1 and the number 10 into cell A2. You can then enter a formula in a third cell that refers to those two cells. For example, the formula =A1+A2 would display 15 because it adds the values in the two cells that it refers to. The formula calculates the values just as if they were entered directly into the formula.

Let's look at an example. Your boss tells you that sales and costs for the month are as follows and asks you to calculate the monthly profit.

A Formula with Only Numbers

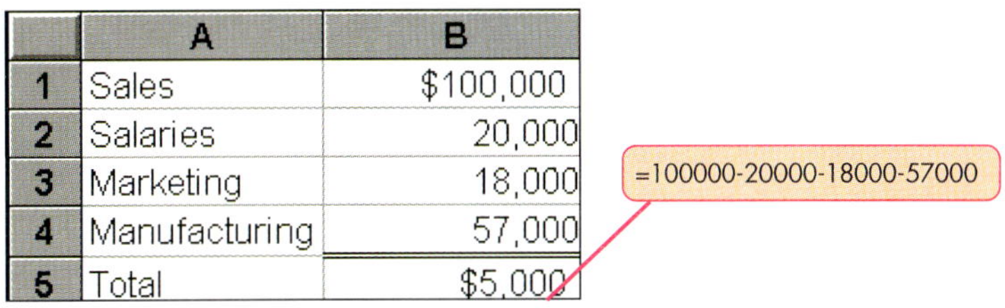

	A	B
1	Sales	$100,000
2	Salaries	20,000
3	Marketing	18,000
4	Manufacturing	57,000
5	Total	$5,000

Using only numbers, you can enter the formula =100000–20000–18000–57000 into cell B5 and get the answer 5000.

Or, using cell references, you can enter the formula =B1-B2-B3-B4 into cell B5 and get the same answer, 5000.

A Formula with Cell References

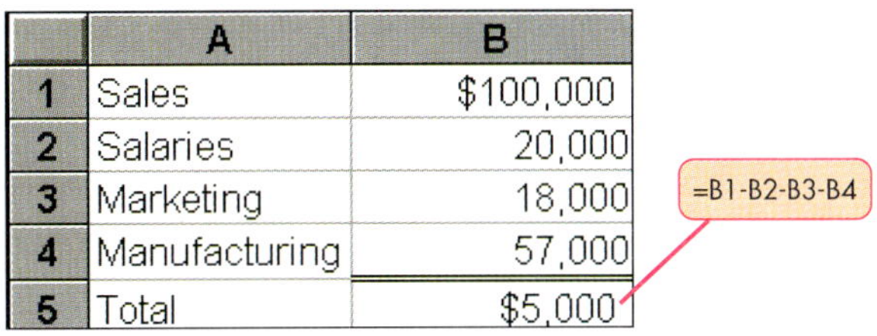

	A	B
1	Sales	$100,000
2	Salaries	20,000
3	Marketing	18,000
4	Manufacturing	57,000
5	Total	$5,000

Just as you finish, your boss comes in and tells you he has some updates for the figures he gave you. Sales are only $99,000 and marketing costs are $18,500. To recalculate using a formula containing numbers, you have to reenter, or edit, the entire formula so it reads =99000-20000-18500-57000. Using the formula containing cell references, you just type in new numbers for sales and marketing, and the formula automatically calculates the new result.

TIP
Why No Formula Should Contain Numbers

A strong case can be made for never including numbers in formulas. Here are some of the reasons:

- Embedding a number in a formula is making an assumption either that it should not or cannot be changed or that changes in it are unimportant to the outcome of the analysis. When exploring the model, you may find it is very sensitive to changes in that number—a phenomenon you would never discover if the number were embedded in a formula.
- The next time you use the model, you may forget there is a number embedded in a formula and not take it into consideration.
- When you print a sheet, only the displayed values are normally printed, not the formulas behind them. Anyone else trying to follow your analysis might get lost if numbers are embedded in formulas rather than shown on the printout.

Displaying Formulas in Their Cells

If you press Ctrl+` Excel displays formulas and full values of numbers in your worksheet. Press it again to return to the normal display. (The ` character is the left single quotation mark located on the key to the left of the 1 key on the alphanumeric keyboard.)

TIP
Stored and Displayed Values

Excel stores values calculated by formulas with up to 15 digits of accuracy. However, you can change the way they are displayed by formatting the cells that contain them (formatting is discussed in Sections 3-2 through 3-4). For example, you can calculate pi as 3.14159265358979 and format it to be displayed as 3, 3.1, 3.14, 3.141 and so on. Regardless of how it is formatted, it will be calculated by other formulas using the full value.

TUTORIAL

IN this tutorial you are introduced to formulas by looking at various types in a typical model—shown in the figure "Understanding Formulas." There are formulas that use each of the five most commonly used operators.

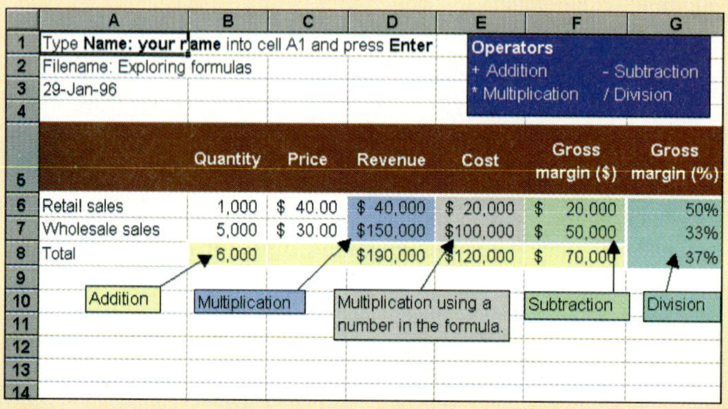

Understanding Formulas

Getting Ready

1. Open the *Exploring formulas* workbook stored in the *Tutorial Workbooks* folder on the *Excel Student Resource Disk* and enter your name into cell A1.

Exploring Formulas

2. Select a cell on row 8 that contains a number (except the percentage) to display the cell's formula on the formula bar. These formulas use the addition operator to add the values in the two cells above them.
3. Select cells D6 or D7, and you'll see that these formulas use the multiplication operator to multiply the values in the two cells to their left on the same row (price × quantity).
4. Select cells E6 or E7, and you'll see multiplication using a number (a constant) embedded in a formula. These formulas multiply 20 times the quantity sold in column B on the same row.
5. Select cells F6 or F7, and you'll see subtraction operators in action. These formulas subtract cost from revenue to calculate gross margin in dollars.
6. Select cells G6, G7, or G8, and you'll see division in action. These formulas divide the gross margin by the sales revenues to calculate gross margins in percentages.

Displaying Formulas

7. Press Ctrl+` to display formulas in the cells instead of their calculated values. You'll notice that columns widen so formulas can be displayed in their entirety. Scroll the screen to see how all of the formulas work.

Pressing Ctrl+` displays formulas in their cells.

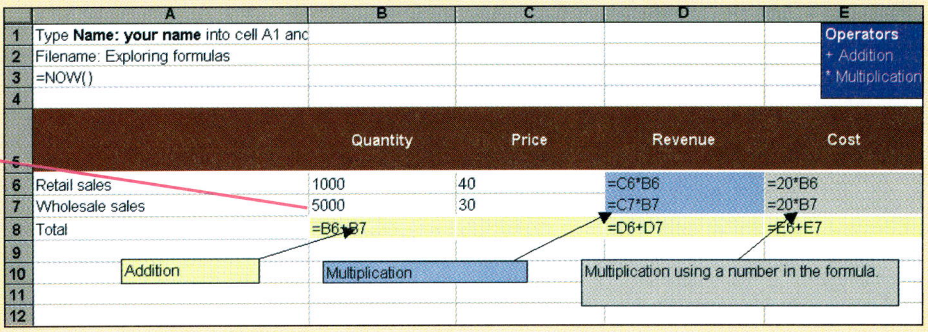

8. Press Ctrl+` again to return to displaying calculated values.

Finishing Up

9. Close the workbook without saving it.

TIP

Closing Workbooks

When you close many of the workbooks that accompany this text, a dialog box asks if you want to save your changes even when you haven't made any. This is because these worksheets contain a function in cell A3 that calculates today's date. When you open the workbook, Excel recalculates that function and considers that updating to be a change. Just click the No button when the dialog box appears.

2-5 ENTERING FORMULAS

There are two ways to enter formulas: by typing them in or, if they refer to other cells, by selecting the cells they refer to. For a summary of the characters you can use when entering formulas, see the table "Characters You Can Use in Numbers and Formulas."

Characters You Can Use in Numbers and Formulas

Character	Examples	Description
Digits	0–9	Used for the numbers themselves. For example, to enter 100, type 100.
Plus sign	+	Used to indicate a positive value. Since this is the default you needn't enter it when entering numbers. (In formulas, it is used to indicate addition, as in =2+2, which calculates 4.)
Minus sign	-	Used to indicate a negative value. In formulas it is used to indicate subtraction, as in 3–2.
Parentheses	( )	Used to enclose formulas within formulas, as in =1+(1/2), which calculates 1.5.
Comma	,	Used to format an entry so commas are displayed between thousands.
Asterisk	*	Used to indicate multiplication in a formula, as in 3*2, which calculates 6.
Slash	/	Used to indicate division in a formula, as in 1/2, which calculates .5.
Dollar sign	$	Used to format an entry so dollar signs and commas between thousands are displayed.
Percent sign	%	Used to format an entry as a percentage. For example, entering 20% is the same as entering .2. However, when entered as 20% it is displayed as 20% and not as .2.
Period	.	Used as a decimal point, as in 3.14.
Upper- and lowercase E	E	Used to indicate scientific notation (powers of 10), as in 3e2, which is the same as 300.

Typing Formulas

You can type in a formula that refers to another cell, for example, A1*A2. But this formula begins with a letter, so if you type that letter first, the program assumes you are entering text. To enter the formula, you first press = (the equal sign) to enter the formula as =A1*A2.

TIP

Using Excel as a Calculator

When working with Excel, you can use it as a calculator. Type any formula such as =.5*24.95 but do not press Enter↵. Instead, press F9, and the result of the formula is displayed on the formula bar and in the cell. You can then press Esc or click the Cancel box (☒) to clear it, or press Enter↵ to enter the calculated value into the work-

COMMON WRONG TURNS

This Isn't What I'd Hoped For!

When you enter a formula, you may get an error value in the cell rather than the calculated result you expected. Sometimes these error values cascade throughout a worksheet because any cell that refers to a cell with an error value also displays an error value. Error messages in cells always begin with a number sign (#) and end with an exclamation point (!). For example, you might see *#NUM!*, *#REF!*, or *#VALUE!*. If you get one of these error messages, use Excel's Help command to search the Index for topics that begin with #.

Selecting Cells to Build Formulas

You can create a formula by selecting the cells referred to in it whenever the formula bar is active. For example, you could enter a formula into cell A3 that subtracts the value in cell A2 from the value in cell A1 as shown in the illustration "Entering a Formula by Pointing and Clicking."

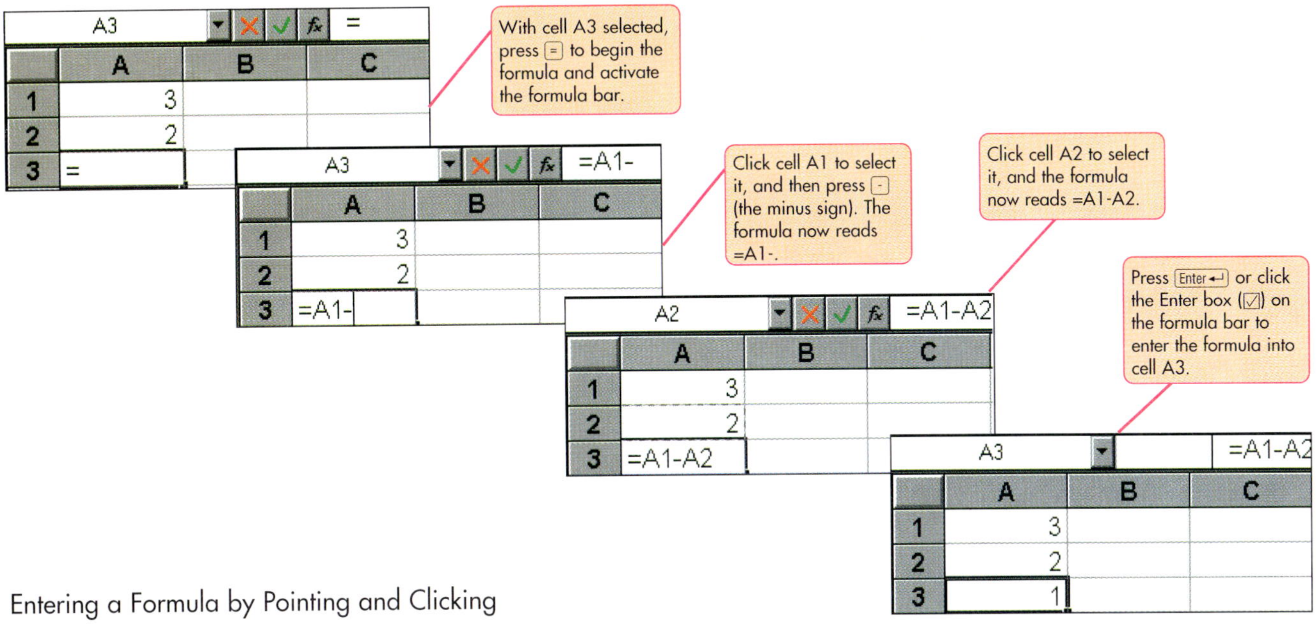

Entering a Formula by Pointing and Clicking

Selecting cells is especially useful when working on larger models where the cells you want to refer to are not displayed on the screen. Experienced users almost always build formulas by selecting cells because it is faster, more accurate, and easier than typing.

Editing Formulas

You edit formulas just as you edit text. How you do so depends on whether you want to edit before or after you have clicked the Enter box (☑) on the formula bar or pressed Enter to complete the entry.

- If you notice a mistake before you complete the entry, press F2 to edit the entry or press Esc and begin over.
- If you notice a mistake after you have completed the entry, select the cell to display the formula on the formula bar and edit it there.

You can also edit a formula in its cell. To do so, double-click the cell or select it and press F2 to display the formula in the cell rather than its calculated result. After editing the formula in the cell, press Enter or click the Enter box (☑) on the formula bar to complete the entry

TUTORIAL

In this tutorial, you enter formulas into the budget model on which you have been working. You do so by typing them in and by selecting cells to create them. When finished, your model will look like the figure "The Budget—The Formulas."

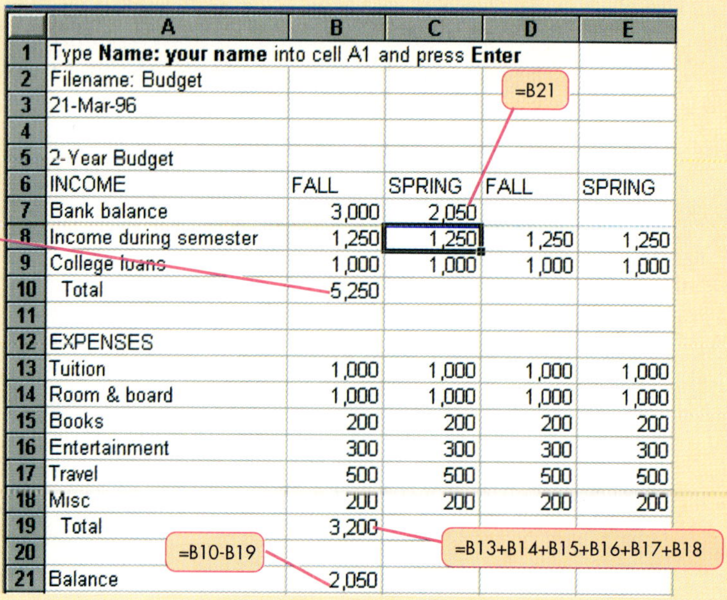

	A	B	C	D	E
1	Type **Name: your name** into cell A1 and press **Enter**				
2	Filename: Budget				
3	21-Mar-96				
4					
5	2-Year Budget				
6	INCOME	FALL	SPRING	FALL	SPRING
7	Bank balance	3,000	2,050		
8	Income during semester	1,250	1,250	1,250	1,250
9	College loans	1,000	1,000	1,000	1,000
10	Total	5,250			
11					
12	EXPENSES				
13	Tuition	1,000	1,000	1,000	1,000
14	Room & board	1,000	1,000	1,000	1,000
15	Books	200	200	200	200
16	Entertainment	300	300	300	300
17	Travel	500	500	500	500
18	Misc	200	200	200	200
19	Total	3,200			
20					
21	Balance	2,050			

The Budget—The Formulas

Getting Ready

1. Open the *Budget* workbook stored in the *Tutorial Workbooks* folder on the *Excel Student Resource Disk*.

Entering a Formula by Selecting Cells

2. Click cell B10 to select it, and then press [=] to begin a formula. The entry is displayed in the cell and on the formula bar.
3. Click cell B7, and both the cell and the formula bar display *=B7*.
4. Press [+] (you may have to hold down [Shift]), and both the cell and the formula bar display =B7+.
5. Click cell B8, and both the cell and the formula bar display *=B7+B8*.
6. Press [+], and both the cell and the formula bar display *=B7+B8+*.
7. Click cell B9, and both the cell and the formula bar display *=B7+B8+B9*.
8. Click the Enter box (☑) on the formula bar to enter the formula, and the three cells are added. The formula is displayed on the formula bar when cell B10 is the active cell.

Entering a Formula by Typing

9. Click cell B19 to select it, and then type **=b13+b14+b15+b16+b17+b18** and press [Enter ↵]. The formula adds the numbers in the column between cells B13 and B18.

Entering a Formula by Selecting Cells

10. Click cell B21 to select it, and then press [=] to begin a formula. The entry is displayed on the formula bar.
11. Click cell B10, and both the cell and the formula bar display *=B10*.
12. Press [-], and both the cell and the formula bar display *=B10-*.
13. Click cell B19, and both the cell and the formula bar display *=B10-B19*.

14. Click the Enter box (☑) on the formula bar to enter the formula, and the number in cell B19 is subtracted from the number in cell B10. The formula is displayed on the formula when cell B21 is the active cell.

Entering a Formula by Selecting Cells

15. Click cell C7 to select it, press (=), click cell B21, and then click the Enter box (☑) on the formula bar. The cell reference carries the value in cell B21 to cell C7. This makes the new month's beginning bank balance the same as the previous month's ending balance.

Finishing Up

16. Save, print, and close the workbook.

2-6 SELECTING RANGES OF CELLS

To work with formulas (and use many other procedures), you have to know how to select the cells you want to refer to. Normally, only one cell—the active cell—is selected. As you've seen, you can select another cell by clicking it with the mouse or by pressing the arrow keys to move the heavy border to it.

Although you normally enter data into a single cell, many commands can be applied to a number of cells at once. To do so, you extend the selection. When you then execute a command, it affects all of the selected cells.

One way to extend a selection is to point to a cell, hold down the left mouse button, and drag the mouse to highlight adjoining cells.

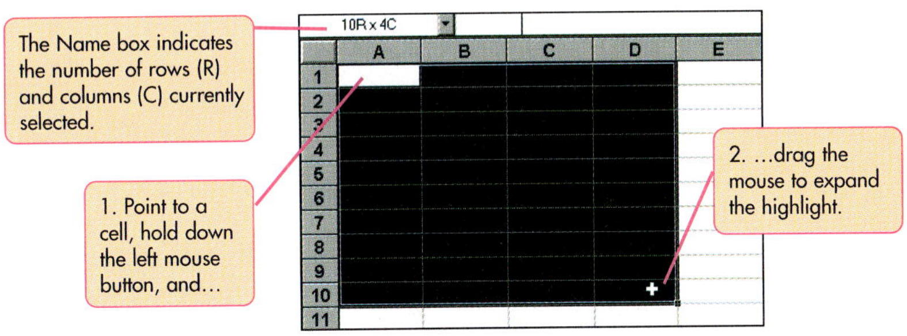

TIP

AutoCalculate

When you select a range of cells containing values, the sum of those values is displayed on the status bar. If you right-click that area of the status bar you can choose from the shortcut menu's commands that average or count the range or find the largest (Max) or smallest (Min) number in it.

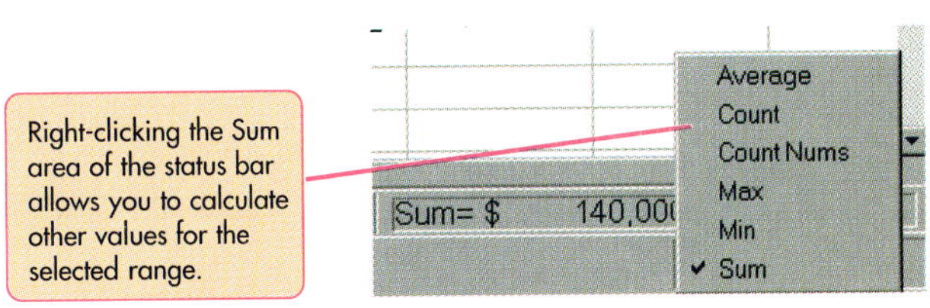

Another way to extend a selection is to click on row or column headings. Clicking a row heading selects the entire row. Clicking a column heading selects the entire column. Clicking the **Select All** button, the gray rectangle in the upper-left corner of the worksheet, selects the entire worksheet.

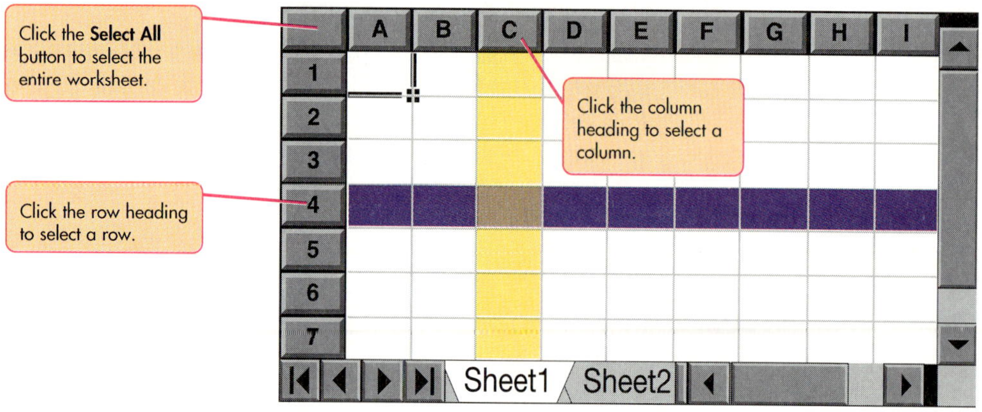

If you point to a row or column heading, hold down the left mouse button, and drag the mouse pointer, you can select adjacent rows or columns.

You can also use the arrow keys to expand the highlight. One way is to hold down [Shift] while you press the arrow keys (or other keys that move the selected cell). Another way is to press [F8] so the status bar displays *EXT*. Then press the arrow keys (or other keys that move the selected cell) or click anywhere in the sheet to extend the highlight. Press [F8] again to turn *EXT* off.

To select nonadjacent areas, select the first area as you would normally. Then hold down [Ctrl] while you select one or more other areas.

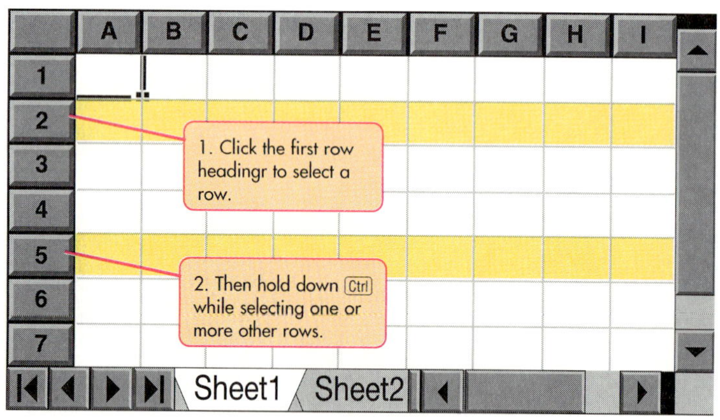

TIP

Entering the Same Data into Several Cells

To enter the same data into several cells, select the cells, type the data, and then press [Ctrl]+[Enter].

QUICKSTEPS

Selecting Cells, Rows, and Columns

Selecting Cells, Rows, or Columns

- Click a cell to select it.
- Click a row or column heading to select the entire row or column.
- Click the **Select All** button at the intersection of the row and column headings to select all cells on the worksheet.

Extending a Selection to Other Cells, Rows, or Columns

To extend a selection, do any of the following:

- Point to a cell, row heading, or column heading; hold down the left mouse button and drag the highlight to select adjacent cells, rows, or columns. Release the mouse button, and the selected area remains highlighted.
- Click one cell, row heading, or column heading to select it. Then hold down [Shift] and click another cell, row heading, or column heading.
- Hold down [Shift] while you press the arrow keys (or other keys that move the selected cell).
- Press [F8], then press the arrow keys (or other keys that move the selected cell) or click anywhere in the sheet to extend the highlight. Press [F8] again to turn *EXT* off and leave the selection highlighted.

Selecting Nonadjacent Areas

- Select the first cell, row heading, or column heading as you normally would, then hold down [Ctrl] while you select each of the others.

TUTORIAL

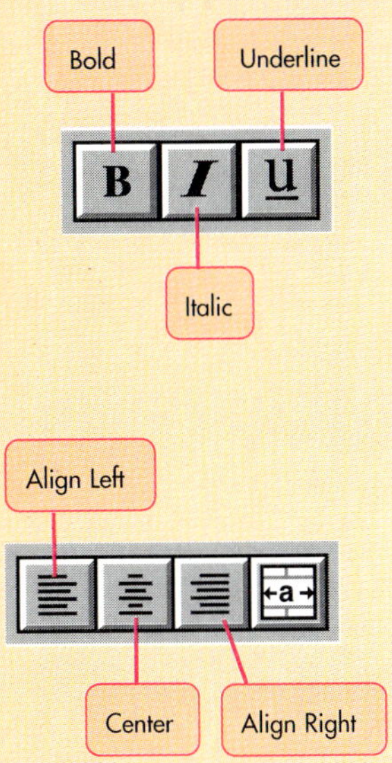

The Formatting Buttons

In this tutorial you are introduced to selecting cells, rows, columns, and the entire sheet listing well-known movies now on video. After selecting various areas, you then format them by clicking buttons on the toolbar. Since these buttons are not discussed until later, they are illustrated in the figure "The Formatting Buttons."

Getting Ready

1. Open the *Classic videos* workbook stored in the *Tutorial Workbooks* folder on the *Excel Student Resource Disk.*

Extending the Selection by Dragging

2. Click cell A5 to select it. Then hold down the left mouse button and drag the highlight to cell E5 and release it. The cells you highlighted remain selected. Notice how the address of the leftmost cell in the range (A5) is listed on the formula bar and that cell is highlighted differently than the other selected cells. This tells you that the cell is the active cell.

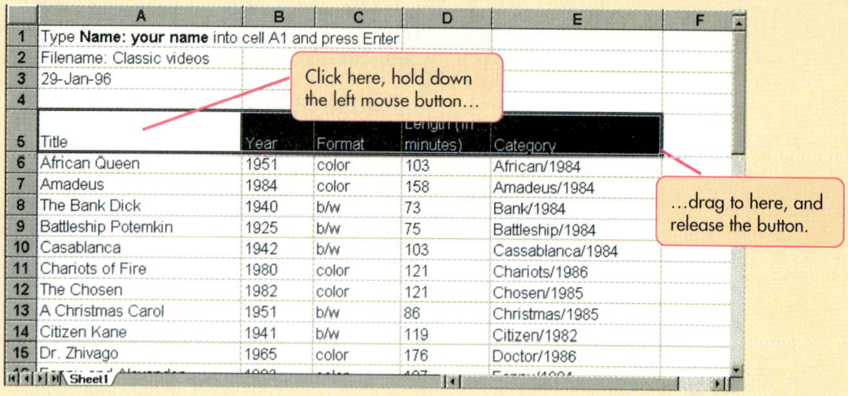

3. Click the **Bold** button on the Formatting toolbar to boldface the selected area.
4. Click the **Italic** button on the Formatting toolbar to also italicize the selected area, then click any cell to remove the highlight.

Selecting Columns

5. Click column heading B on the border to select that entire column.

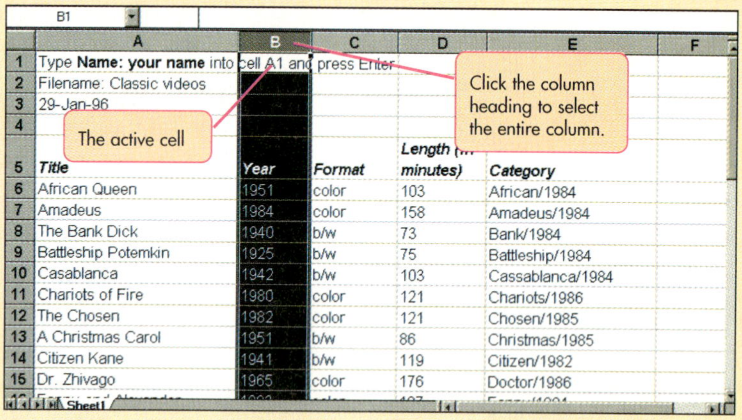

6. Click the **Italic** button on the Formatting toolbar to italicize text in the column.
7. Click the **Center** button on the Formatting toolbar to center text and numbers in the column, then click any cell to remove the highlight.
8. Click column C's heading on the border to select the column, then hold down the mouse button, and, without releasing it, drag the highlight to the right to also select column D, then release the mouse button.

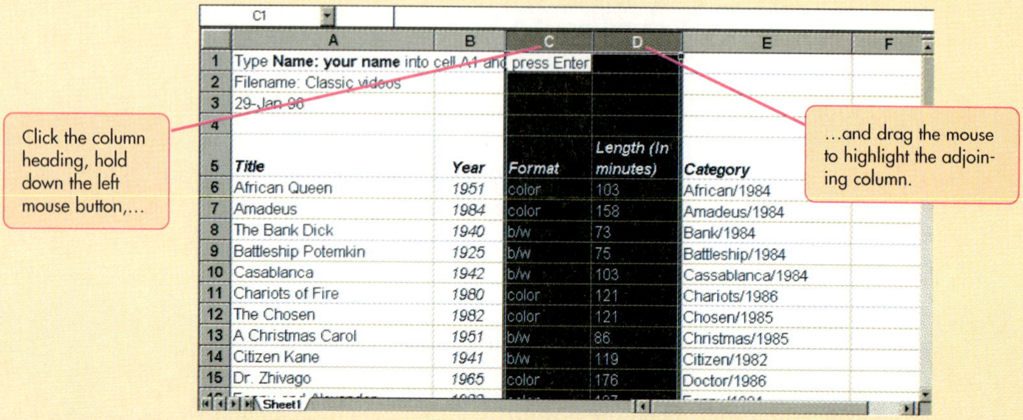

9. Click the **Center** button on the Formatting toolbar to center the column entries, then click any cell to remove the highlight.

10. Click column E's heading on the border, then click the **Align Right** button on the Formatting toolbar to align the text with the right edge of the cells. Click any cell to remove the highlight.

Selecting the Entire Worksheet

11. Click the **Select All** button in the upper-left corner of the border to select the entire worksheet. Notice how cell A1 is listed on the formula bar and that cell is highlighted differently than the other cells. This tells you that cell A1 is the active cell.

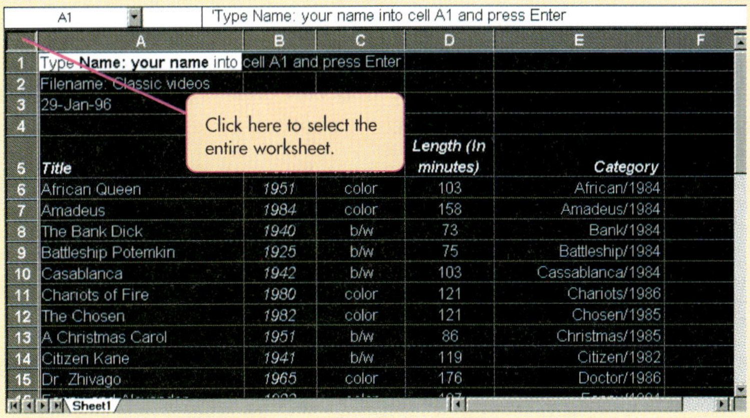

12. Click any cell to remove the highlight.

PAUSING FOR PRACTICE

Selecting cells is one of the basic skills you must master to use Excel. Pause here to practice until you have mastered this basic skill.

Finishing Up

13. Close the workbook without saving your changes.

2-7 FILLING ADJACENT CELLS

Filling copies the contents of selected cells to adjoining cells. This saves you time because you can enter a formula or other data once and then copy it as needed. For example, you can create a monthly budget by entering the necessary formulas in the first monthly column and then copying them to the other monthly columns. To copy data in one cell to adjacent cells, you select the cell or cells that you want to copy and then drag the fill handle, the small square in the lower-right corner of the selected cells. As you do so, an outline highlights the cells that the data will be copied to. When you release the mouse button, the outlined cells are filled with the copied data.

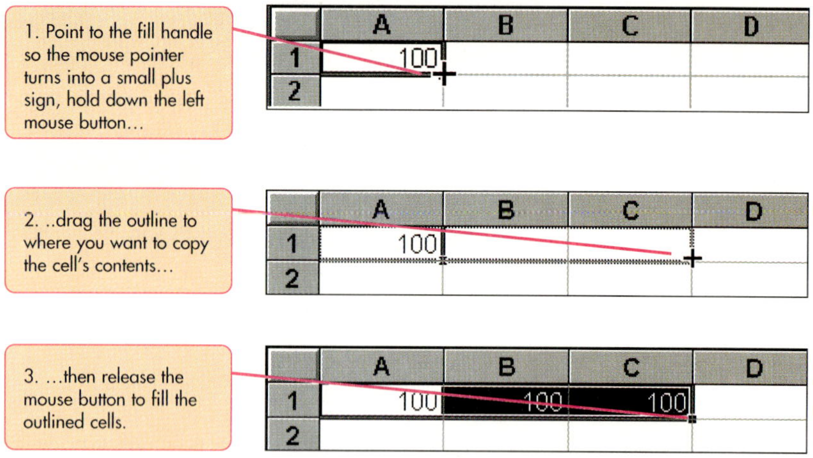

The results you obtain by filling like this depend on what was in the original selected cell or cells.

- If the data are formulas, the formulas are copied to the new positions, and any cell references in them adjust automatically.
- If the data you copy are values that Excel recognizes as a series of sequential numbers, the series will increment in the range you copy to. For example, copying 1 and 2 in adjoining cells will extend the series to 1, 2, 3, 4, 5. Mon will be extended as Tue, Wed, Thu, and so on. Some examples of what happens when you extend various series are listed in the table "Examples of Extending Series." (AutoFill, discussed in PicTorial 4, also allows you to extend dates and other series of numbers.) To copy values such as these without incrementing them, hold down Ctrl while you drag the fill handle.

Examples of Extending Series

Contents of Selected Cell	Extended Series
6:00	7:00, 8:00
Mon	Tue, Wed
Jan	Feb, Mar
Jan-96, Feb-96	Mar-96, Apr-96, May-96
1996, 1997	1998, 1999
1, 2	3, 4, 5
100, 90	80, 70, 60

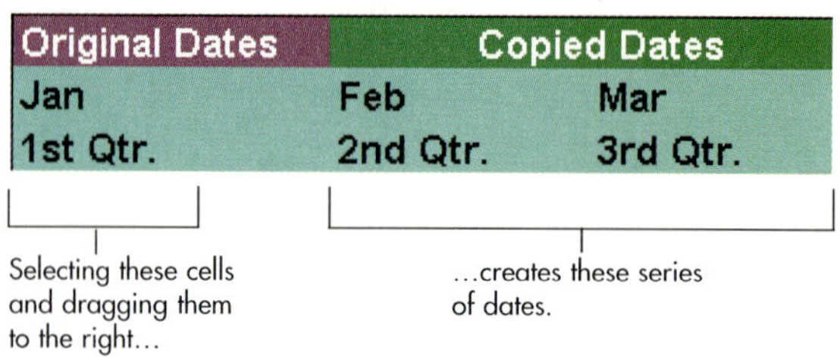

- If the data is a single value, such as 1, 10, or 100, it copies as 1, 10, or 100. To have it increment by 1, hold down Ctrl while you drag the fill handle.
- If you select two cells that already contain an increment, that increment will be repeated. For example, copying cells containing 0 and 10 will create a series 20, 30, 40, and so on.

Original Amounts		Copied Amounts	
0	10	20	30
1	2	3	4
5	10	15	20

Selecting these cells and dragging them to the right…

…creates these number series.

TIP
Filling an Adjacent Range

To fill an adjacent range without dragging the fill handle, select the range of cells you want to copy and the range you want to fill, then pull down the **Edit** menu and point to the **Fill** command to cascade the menu. Select a command that fills down, right, up, or left. If you select the **Series** command from the menu, you can specify different types of series.

TUTORIAL

In this tutorial you drag the fill handle on cells to copy formulas to adjacent cells. When you have finished, your model will look like the illustration shown here.

	A	B	C	D	E
1	Type **Name: your name** into cell A1 and press **Enter**				
2	Filename: Budget				
3	21-Mar-96				
4					
5	2-Year Budget				
6	INCOME	FALL	SPRING	FALL	SPRING
7	Bank balance	3,000	2,050	1,100	150
8	Income during semester	1,250	1,250	1,250	1,250
9	College loans	1,000	1,000	1,000	1,000
10	Total	5,250	4,300	3,350	2,400
11					
12	EXPENSES				
13	Tuition	1,000	1,000	1,000	1,000
14	Room & board	1,000	1,000	1,000	1,000
15	Books	200	200	200	200
16	Entertainment	300	300	300	300
17	Travel	500	500	500	500
18	Misc	200	200	200	200
19	Total	3,200	3,200	3,200	3,200
20					
21	Balance	2,050	1,100	150	-800

Select each cell shown here in red and drag its fill handle to highlight the cells shown here in yellow.

Getting Ready

1. Open the *Budget* workbook stored in the *Tutorial Workbooks* folder on the *Excel Student Resource Disk*.

Filling Adjacent Cells

2. Click cell C7 to select it, then point to the fill handle on the cell border so the mouse pointer turns into a small plus sign (+). Hold down the left mouse button, drag the fill handle and outline to cell E7, and release the mouse button. The formula in cell C7 is copied to each of the cells you dragged the outline over. (For now they display zeros.)

3. Select cell B10 and point to the fill handle on the cell border so the mouse pointer turns into a small plus sign (+). Hold down the left mouse button, drag the fill handle and outline to cell E10, and release the mouse button. The formula is copied to each of the cells you dragged the outline over.
4. Select cells B19 through B21.
5. Point to the fill handle on the cell border so the mouse pointer turns into a small plus sign (+). Hold down the left mouse button, drag the fill handle and outline to column E, and release the mouse button. The formulas are copied to each of the columns you dragged the outline over. The formula in each column adjusts to total the cells in the column it is copied to.
6. Press Ctrl+` to display formulas in the cells and see how they adjusted when you copied them. Press Ctrl+` to return to the display of calculated values.

Finishing Up

7. Save, print, and close the workbook.

2-8 COPYING DATA

Excel lets you copy data from one location to another in two basic ways. You can drag cells with the mouse, or you can copy data to Windows' Clipboard and then paste it into another location. Using the Clipboard is more flexible than dragging, but dragging is quicker for shorter moves.

Copying with the Clipboard

To begin copying, you first select the cells you want to copy. You then copy the content of the selected cells to Windows' Clipboard. While the cell content is stored on the Clipboard, you can paste it anywhere in the workbook you copied it from. (You can also paste it into another workbook, or even into another application's document.) When you copy and paste, you choose among menu commands, toolbar buttons, shortcut menu commands, or keyboard shortcuts as the means you use.

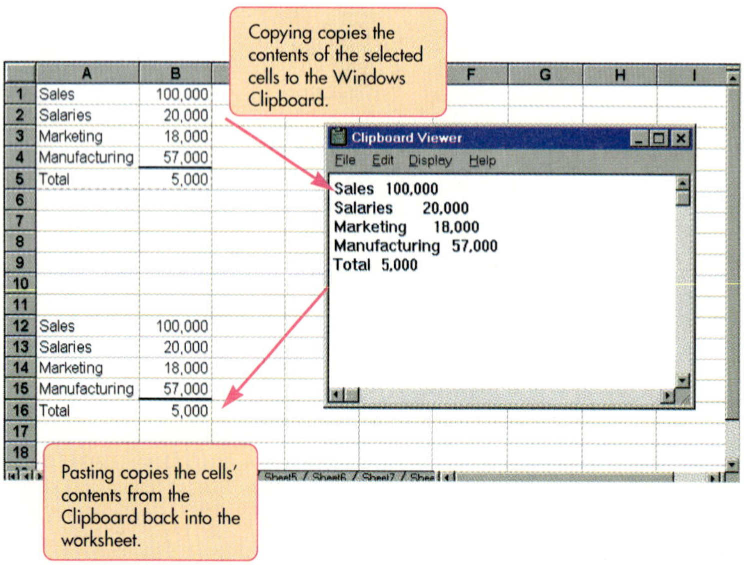

When you copy a range of cells, its content and formats are copied from the original cells to a new location. The data in the cells you copy from is left unchanged. If any cells in the range you copy to contain data, it is overwritten by the copied data.

QUICKSTEPS

Copying Using the Clipboard

1. Select the cells to be copied.
2. To copy the data to the Clipboard, click the **Copy** button on the Standard toolbar or do any of the following:
   - Right-click the selected cells and click the shortcut menu's **Copy** command.
   - Pull down the **Edit** menu and click the **Copy** command.
   - Press Ctrl+Insert.

   The selected cells are highlighted by a moving border and the status line reads *Select destination and press ENTER or choose Paste.*
3. Select the cell that will be in the upper-left corner of the range of cells to be pasted in.
4. To paste in the data from the Clipboard, click the **Paste** button on the Standard toolbar or do any of the following:
   - Right-click the cell that will be in the upper-left corner of the range of cells to be pasted in and click the shortcut menu's **Paste** command.
   - Pull down the **Edit** menu and click the **Paste** command.
   - Press Enter.
   - Press Shift+Insert.

   The cells highlighted by the moving border are copied to the new location. (The moving border around the selected cells disappears if you pressed Enter, or when you type any data.)

TIP

Pasting in More than One Location

When copying, if you use the **Paste** button on the Standard toolbar or the **Paste** command on the **Edit** menu to paste the data, it remains on the Clipboard so you can paste it into a number of locations. If you paste the contents by pressing Enter, you clear the Clipboard and cannot paste the cells in another location.

Copying by Dragging and Dropping

To begin copying with dragging and dropping, you first select the cells you want to copy. You then drag a copy of the selected cells to a new position.

To insert copied cells among existing cells so the existing cells move aside to make room for them, right-drag them. When you release them, a shortcut menu appears that lets you choose in which direction the existing cells shift. You can also hold down both Ctrl+Shift while you drag and release them. When you point to the area where you want to insert the dragged cells, the mouse pointer turns into a horizontal or vertical I-beam shape (I). When vertical, the cells to the right move to the right to make room for the dragged cells. When horizontal, the cells below move down to make room.

QUICKSTEPS

Copying by Dragging and Dropping

1. Select the cells to be copied.
2. Point to the heavy border around the selected cells, and the mouse pointer turns into an arrow.
3. Do one of the following:
   - Right-drag the outline of the cells to where you want them copied, and release the mouse button. Choose one of the commands from the shortcut menu that appears.
   - Hold down Ctrl and the left mouse button (a plus sign appears above the mouse pointer), drag the outline of the cells to where you want them copied, and release the mouse button.
   - To drag the cells to another sheet in the workbook, hold down Alt and drag the outline to that sheet's tab. This opens the second sheet. Continue to drag the outline to the spot where you want to copy the cells.

TUTORIAL

In this tutorial you are introduced to copying data using menu commands, toolbar buttons, and the shortcut menu.

Getting Ready

1. Open the *Copying practice* workbook stored in the *Tutorial Workbooks* folder on the *Excel Student Resource Disk* and enter your name into cell A1.

Copying a Range with Menu Commands

2. Select the range of cells from A5 to D10, pull down the **Edit** menu, and click the **Copy** command.
3. Select cell A12, pull down the **Edit** menu, and click the **Paste** command.

Copying a Range with Toolbar Buttons

4. Select the range of cells from A5 to D17 and click the **Copy** button on the Standard toolbar.

5. Select cell A19 and click the **Paste** button on the Standard toolbar.

Copying a Range with the Shortcut Menu

6. Select the range of cells from A5 to D10. Then point to the selected area, click the right mouse button to display the shortcut menu, and click the **Copy** command.

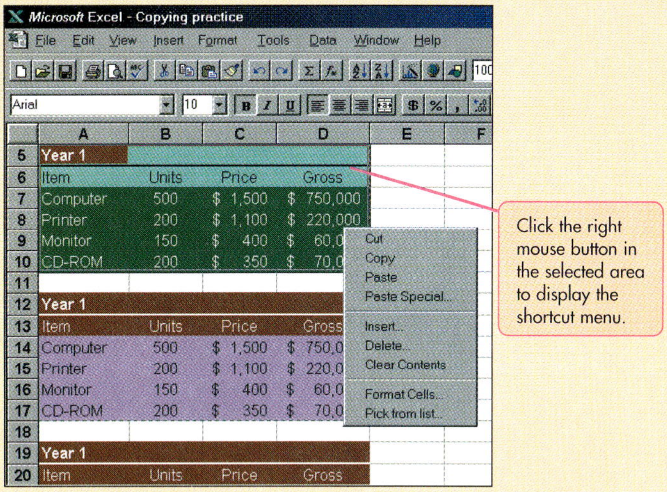

7. Right-click cell A33 to display the shortcut menu again, and click the **Paste** command.

Finishing Up

8. Edit the headings for the five copies so you have models for Years 1 through 5.
9. Save, print, and close the workbook.

2-9 SPECIFYING ABSOLUTE CELL REFERENCES

If you typed in every formula and function that you needed, you would not have to be concerned about relative and absolute cell references. But they become very important when you enter a formula in one cell and then copy it to others to save time.

When you create formulas, they often refer to other cells in the worksheet. The program does not automatically "remember" the actual cell address that the formula refers to; instead, it remembers the position relative to the cell the formula is entered in—for example, one column to the left and two rows up. No matter where you copy the formula to, it always refers not to the original cell but to whatever cell is one column to the left and two rows up from the cell you copied it to.

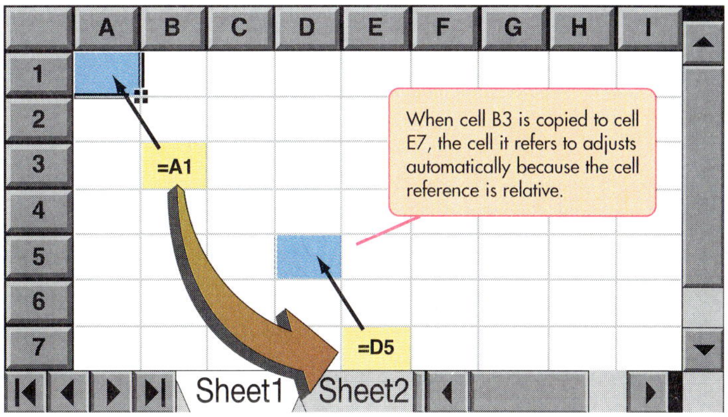

This automatic adjustment occurs because the reference to the cell is a relative reference; that is, the position of the cell referred to is relative to the position of the formula. All formulas you enter have relative references unless you specify otherwise.

You do not have to keep references to cells relative. You can make them absolute references so that a formula refers to the same cell wherever it is copied on the worksheet. For example, an absolute reference to cell A1 will continue to refer to that cell regardless of where you copy or move it to.

You can also use mixed references, which keep the reference to the row or column relative while making the other reference absolute.

Column and row references are both relative. If the reference is to a cell one column over and two rows up, the copied cell reference will also refer to a cell one column over and two rows up.

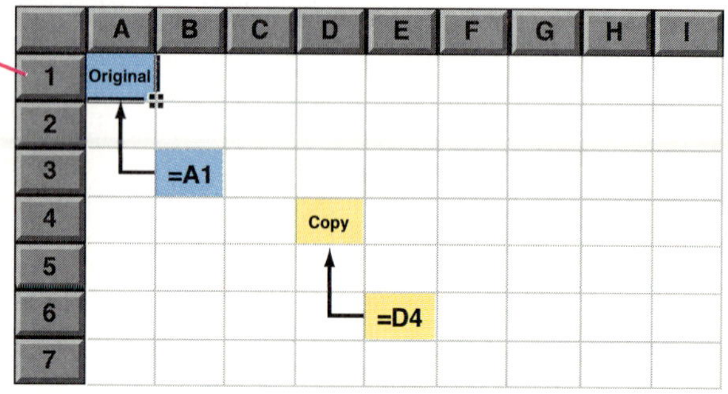

Column and row references are both absolute. No matter where the cell reference is copied, it will always refer to the same cell.

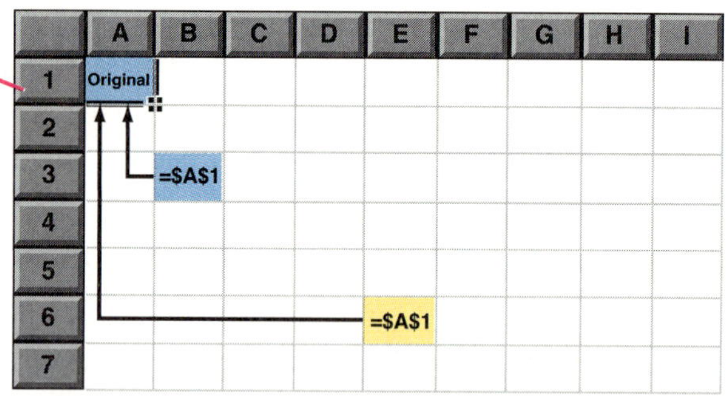

Column reference is absolute but row reference is relative. The copied cell reference will always refer to the same column. However, if the original reference was to a cell two rows up, the copied reference will refer to a cell two rows up.

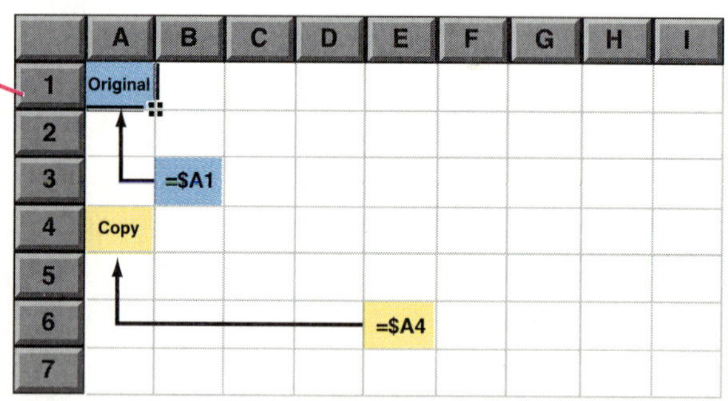

Column reference is relative but row reference is absolute. The copied cell reference will always refer to the same row. However, if the original reference was to a column one column to the left, the copied reference will refer to a column one column to the left.

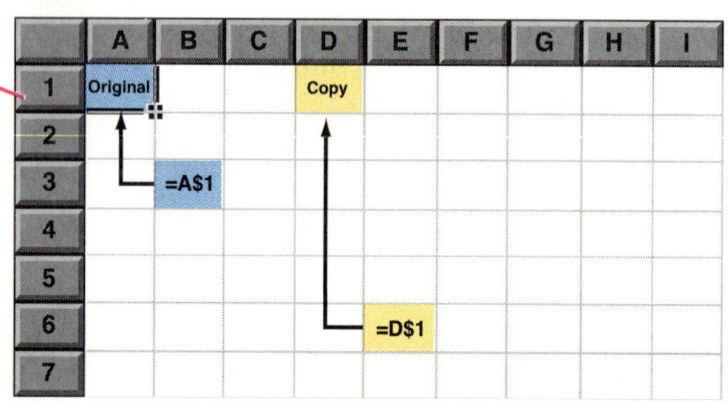

You specify absolute references by typing dollar signs ($) in front of the column or row references.

Absolute and Relative Cell References		
Cell Reference	**Column**	**Row**
A1	Relative	Relative
$A1	Absolute	Relative
A$1	Relative	Absolute
A1	Absolute	Absolute

TIP
Editing Absolute and Relative Cell References

When the cell reference is the last one on the formula bar, you can press the F4 key to cycle through the four possible reference combinations. The table "Absolute and Relative Cell References" describes the sequence of choices. Pressing F4 also works when the formula is displayed on the formula bar for editing (after you press F2 or click the formula bar). Move the insertion point into the cell reference that you want to change, and press F4 to cycle the cell reference through the four possible combinations.

TUTORIAL

In this tutorial you use absolute and relative references to copy formulas so they continue to refer to the correct cells in their new locations. The model you use is a five-year plan that is used for forecast profits given certain sales and expense estimates. The finished model is shown in the figure "The Five-Year Plan."

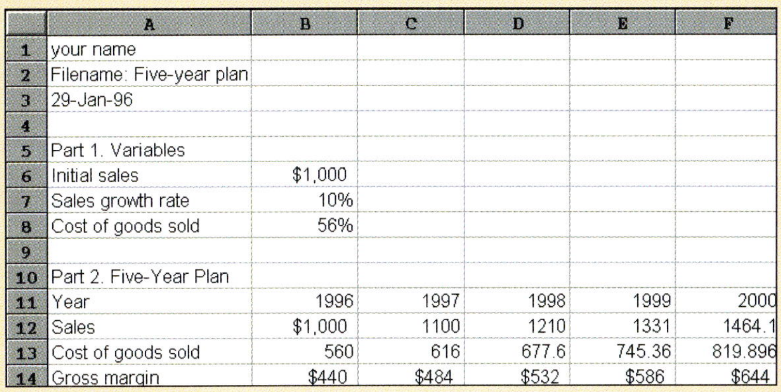

	A	B	C	D	E	F
1	your name					
2	Filename: Five-year plan					
3	29-Jan-96					
4						
5	Part 1. Variables					
6	Initial sales	$1,000				
7	Sales growth rate	10%				
8	Cost of goods sold	56%				
9						
10	Part 2. Five-Year Plan					
11	Year	1996	1997	1998	1999	2000
12	Sales	$1,000	1100	1210	1331	1464.1
13	Cost of goods sold	560	616	677.6	745.36	819.896
14	Gross margin	$440	$484	$532	$586	$644

The Five-Year Plan

Getting Ready

1. Open the *Five-year plan* workbook stored in the *Tutorial Workbooks* folder on the *Excel Student Resource Disk* and enter your name into cell A1.
2. Enter the numbers in cells B6 through B8. One of them is currency, so enter it as **$1,000**. Two of the numbers are percentages. To enter them, type **10%** and **56%** so they are displayed as percentages.

Entering Formulas

3. In cell B12, enter the formula **=B6** and press Enter↵ to carry down opening sales from cell B6 in Part 1 of the model.
4. In cell B13, enter the formula **=$B8*B12** and press Enter↵. The formula multiples the cost of goods percentage in cell B8 times the sales in cell B12. The result is the cost of goods in dollars.
5. In cell B14, enter the formula **=B12-B13** and press Enter↵ to subtract cost of goods from sales.
6. In cell C12, enter the formula **=B12+($B7*B12)** and press Enter↵ to calculate sales by adding last year's sales to 10% of last year's sales for a 10% sales increase. The dollar sign in front of the B7 cell reference will keep the column absolute when the formula is copied.

Copying Formulas

7. Select cells B13 and B14 and drag the fill handle to copy the formulas to column C.
8. Select cells C12 through C14 and drag the fill handle to copy the formula to the next three columns.

Looking at the Copied Formulas

9. Press Ctrl+` to display formulas in the cells, then scroll the screen to see what happened when formulas with absolute references were copied. All formulas that refer to cells in Part 1 of the plan continue to refer to the same cells after being copied because they had absolute references to column B. All other references to cells refer to the column to their left because they were relative references.

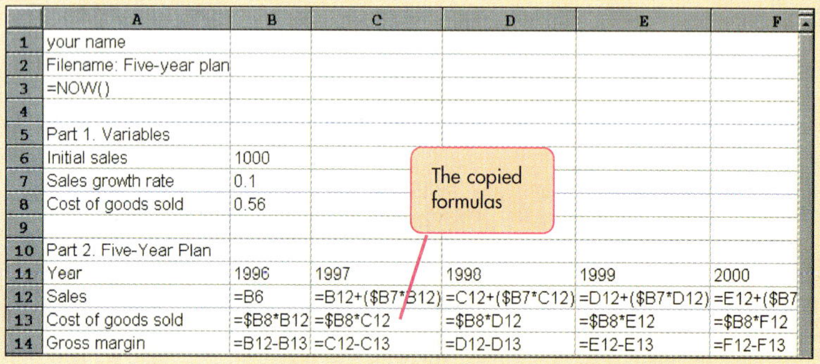

	A	B	C	D	E	F
1	your name					
2	Filename: Five-year plan					
3	=NOW()					
4						
5	Part 1. Variables					
6	Initial sales	1000				
7	Sales growth rate	0.1				
8	Cost of goods sold	0.56				
9						
10	Part 2. Five-Year Plan					
11	Year	1996	1997	1998	1999	2000
12	Sales	=B6	=B12+($B7*B12)	=C12+($B7*C12)	=D12+($B7*D12)	=E12+($B7
13	Cost of goods sold	=$B8*B12	=$B8*C12	=$B8*D12	=$B8*E12	=$B8*F12
14	Gross margin	=B12-B13	=C12-C13	=D12-D13	=E12-E13	=F12-F13

10. Press Ctrl+` again to return to displaying calculated values.

Saving the Workbook

11. Click the **Save** button on the Standard toolbar to save the workbook. You are about to make changes in it that you won't want to save.
12. Click the **Print** button on the Standard toolbar to print out the worksheet.

Exploring What-Ifs

13. Change the sales growth rate in cell B7 from 10 to 15 percent (type it as 15% or .15). If you compare the screen with the figure at the beginning of this tutorial, you'll see that sales now increase in all but the first year by 15 percent instead of the original 10 percent. Cost of goods also increases but

remains a constant 56 percent of sales. Gross margins increase because sales are increasing faster than cost of goods.

14. Change the cost of goods percentage in cell B8 from 56 to 60 percent (type it as 60% or .60). Sales stay the same as in the previous what-if but are still higher than in the original example in all but the opening year, where they remain unchanged. Cost of goods also increases and is higher than the original example because it is now 60 percent of sales instead of 56 percent. Gross margins are lower than in the previous what-if but are higher than in the original example. If your goal was to obtain higher gross margins despite increases in cost of goods (perhaps because of increased prices), you have discovered how you can achieve this—increase sales sufficiently to achieve the increase in gross margins despite the increased cost of goods.

Finishing Up

15. Close the workbook without saving your what-if changes.

2-10 ADJUSTING COLUMN WIDTHS AND ROW HEIGHTS

When you first open a workbook, all columns and rows are set to standard widths and heights. However, you can easily change these if you want to. For example, there are times when you may want to widen a column. If you enter text that is longer than the column is wide, all of the text is displayed only if the cell to its right is empty. If the adjoining cell contains data, any text that overflows into that cell is not displayed. The width of columns also affects whether numbers or values calculated by formulas are displayed correctly. If a number is too large to be displayed in a cell, Excel will either:

- Display it in scientific notation—for example, display 100,000 as 1.00E+5; or, if the cell is too narrow for that
- Fill the cell with number signs (#######).

The width of a column determines how many characters can be displayed in cells within it. Narrow columns let you display more columns on the screen and squeeze more into a printout, so there is an advantage to making columns as narrow as possible. Since column width is always set for an entire column, a column must be set to the width required by the longest entry in the column.

In addition to adjusting column widths and row heights, you can also hide rows and columns so their letters or numbers and their contents are not displayed on the screen or printed out. This is useful when you just want to show summaries of your worksheet ands hide details. It's also useful when there are some entries on the worksheet that you don't want others to see.

QUICKSTEPS

Adjusting Column Widths and Row Heights

Clicking

1. Point to the right column heading border or the lower row heading border, and the mouse pointer turns into a split double arrow. (You can also select more than one column or row, and point to any of their borders.)
2. Double-click to set the width of the columns or height of the rows so they automatically adjust to the size of the entry (or to reset a column or row to the default width or height.)

Dragging

1. Point to any row or column heading border, and the mouse pointer turns into a split double arrow. (You can also select more than one column or row, and point to any of their borders.)
2. Hold down the left mouse button, drag the columns or rows wider or narrower, and then release the mouse button.

Menus

1. Select any range of cells spanning the rows or columns to be changed, or use the row or column headings to select the entire rows or columns.
2. Pull down the **Format** menu and point to the **Row** or **Column** command to cascade the menu.
3. Choose any of the settings described in the box "Understanding Row and Column Menu Selections."

Shortcut Menus

1. Use the row or column headings to select the entire rows or columns.
2. Right-click the selection, and then click the shortcut menu's **Column Width** or **Row Height** command.
3. Enter a column width or row height and click the **OK** button.

TIP

Wrapping Text Instead of Widening Columns

To fully display text in cells, you can widen a column. However, you can also wrap long text into two or more lines in the same cell. To do so, select the cell, pull down the **Format** menu, and click the **Cells** command to display the Format Cells dialog box. Click the *Alignment* tab, click the **Wrap Text** check box to turn it on (☑), and then click the **OK** command button.

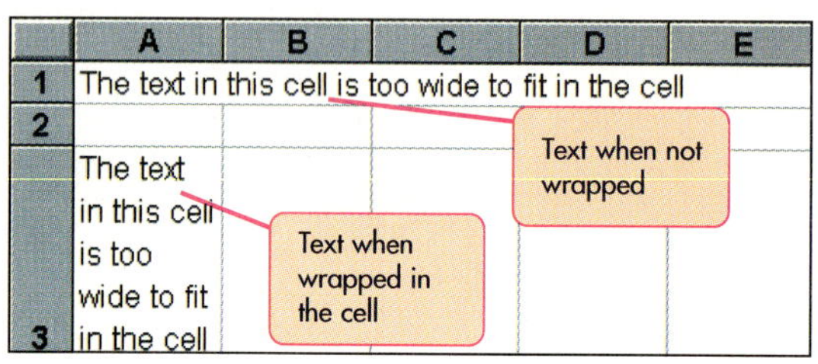

UNDERSTANDING
Row and Column Menu Selections

When you pull down the **Format** menu and point to the **Row** or **Column** command to cascade the menu you have the following choices:

Row Commands

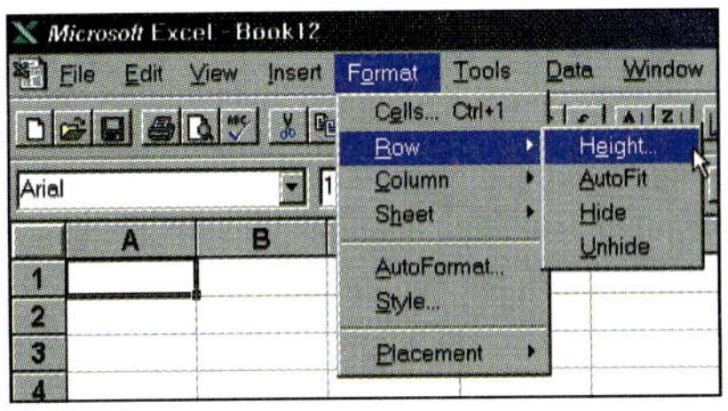

Height displays a dialog box into which you can type a row height in points (each point is 1/72 of an inch, and you can enter a number from 0 to 409—0 will hide the row).

AutoFit adjusts the height of selected rows to a size related to that of the largest type size used on the rows.

Hide hides the selected row(s) and removes its number from the border.

Unhide unhides any hidden rows in the selected range. To use this command, select the rows on both sides of the hidden rows.

Column Commands

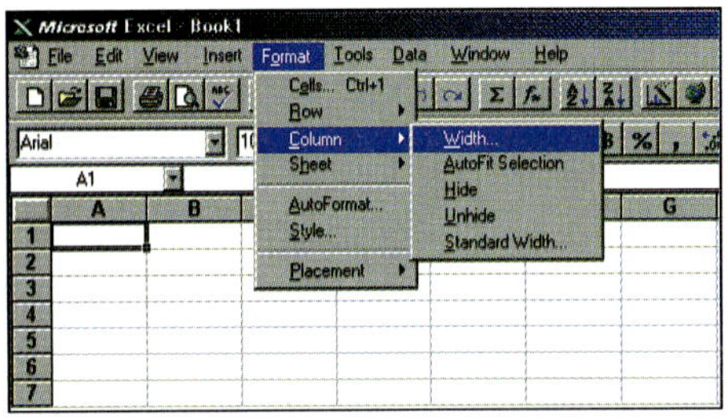

Width displays a dialog box into which you can type a column width in characters (from 0 to 255).

AutoFit Selection adjusts the width of selected columns to display the longest entry currently in the column.

Hide hides the selected column(s) and removes its number from the border.

Unhide unhides any hidden columns in the selected range. To use this command, select the columns on both sides of the hidden columns.

Standard Width displays the Standard Width dialog box so you can either:

- Click the **OK** command button to return selected columns to the standard width.
- Enter a column width (0 to 255—0 will hide the column) and click the **OK** command button to change the width of all columns on the worksheet that you have not previously adjusted.

TUTORIAL

In this tutorial you are introduced to changing column widths using the menu and by dragging their borders. You then see how to hide and unhide cell contents. The worksheet you use contains a model that calculates grade point averages. (Ignore the misspellings in the model for now; you'll fix those in a later PicTorial with Excel's built-in spelling checker.)

Getting Ready

1. Open the *Grade point average* workbook stored in the *Tutorial Workbooks* folder on the *Excel Student Resource Disk*. Do not enter your name in cell A1 yet.

Changing Column Widths with Menu Commands

2. Select columns A through E by dragging the mouse pointer over the column headings to select the entire columns.
3. Pull down the **Format** menu, point to the **Column** command to cascade the menu, and then click the **AutoFit Selection** command. This adjusts all column widths to fit their contents. Notice how column A is now much too wide because the entry in cell A1 is long and its length was used to calculate

the width of the column. Since the text in the heading will flow over into the next column, column A can be made narrower.

4. Select any cell in column A, pull down the **Format** menu, point to the **Column** command to cascade the menu, and then click the **Width** command to display the Column Width dialog box.

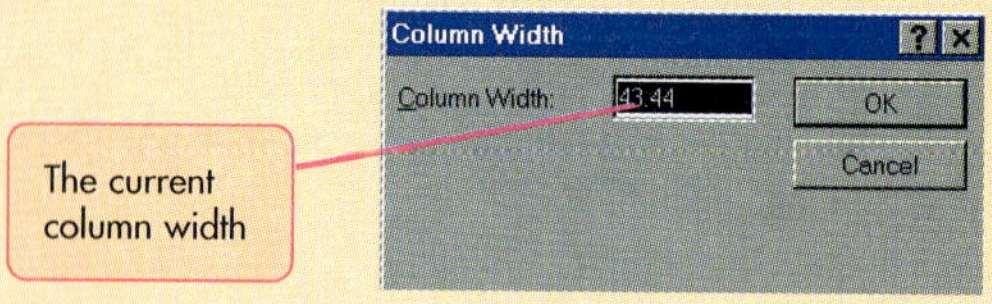

5. Type 25 in the **Column Width** text box, and then click the **OK** command button.

Changing Column Widths by Dragging

6. Select columns B through E by using the headings to select the entire columns.

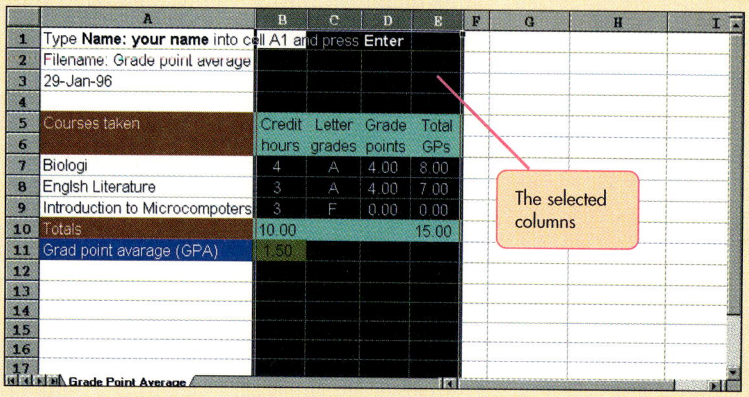

7. Point to the border between the column B and column C heading, and the mouse pointer turns into a split double arrow.

8. Hold down the left mouse button and drag the dotted line until it's in the middle of column C, then release the mouse button to change the widths of all selected columns at one time.

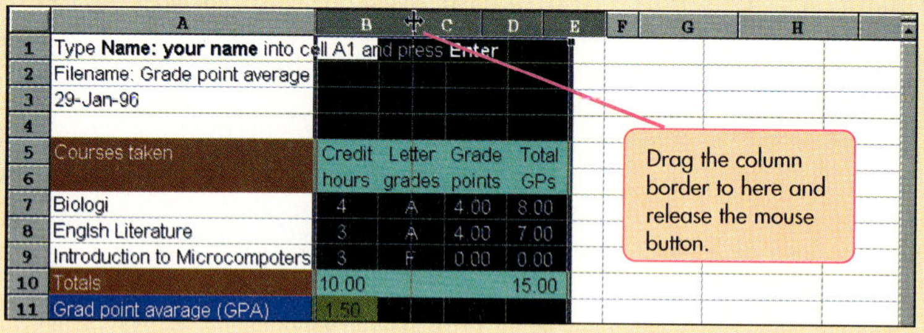

Hiding and Unhiding Rows

9. Select any cell on row 11, pull down the **Format** menu, point to the Row command to cascade the menu, and then click the **Hide** command. Row 11 is now hidden from view. (It also wouldn't print if you printed at this point.)

10. Select any cells on rows 10 and 12, pull down the **Format** menu, point to the **Row** command to cascade the menu, and then click the **Unhide** command.

Finishing Up

11. Enter your name in cell A1 and then save, print, and close the workbook.

REVIEW QUESTIONS

TRUE-FALSE

T F **1.** Numbers automatically align with the left edge of the cell.

T F **2.** The **Undo** command will usually undo the effect of the last command executed.

T F **3.** Mathematical operators with a higher priority are performed first.

T F **4.** You can press Enter to remove data from the formula bar and insert it into the selected cell.

T F **5.** Clicking a row heading selects the entire row.

T F **6.** Copying leaves intact the data in the cells you copied from.

T F **7.** Mathematical operators with the same level of priority are calculated in the order they appear in the formula from left to right.

T F **8.** Up to 265 characters can be typed in a cell.

T F **9.** Quotation marks are used to enclose formulas within formulas.

T F **10.** When creating a formula, pressing F9 will calculate the result before you press Enter.

MULTIPLE CHOICE

1. All Excel formulas begin with _________.

a. Hyphens
b. Dashes
c. Equal signs
d. Apostrophes

2. You specify absolute references by adding _______ signs in front of the column or row references.

a. #
b. @
c. $
d. *

3. When the cell reference is the last one on the formula bar, press _________ to cycle through the four possible combinations of cell referencing.

a. F5
b. Ctrl+F8
c. F8
d. F4

4. To display the formulas used in cells instead of their calculated values, press _________.

a. Ctrl+Alt
b. Ctrl+Shift
c. Ctrl+`
d. Ctrl+^

5. If you do not wish a cell reference to change when copied or moved to another location, use a(n) ________ cell reference.

a. Relative
b. Absolute
c. Mixed
d. Partial

6. The results of the formula =4*(2+3) would be ________.

a. 10 b. 9

c. 20 d. 11

7. To control the order of mathematical operations, use ________.

a. Parentheses b. Colons

c. Asterisks d. Commas

8. To enter numbers as text, type a(n) ________ as the first character.

a. Apostrophe b. Quotation mark

c. Period d. Exclamation point

9. The function key to use to activate the Extend feature is ________.

a. F2 b. F11

c. F8 d. F5

10. Which of the following is an example of an absolute cell reference:

a. A1 b. $$A$1

c. $A1 d. A1

FILL IN THE BLANK

1. As you type data into a cell, it is displayed on the ________ until you press ________, ________, or ________.
2. As you type data into a cell, you can cancel the entry before you complete it by pressing ________ or by clicking the ________ on the formula bar.
3. After entering data, you can cancel the entry by clicking the ________ button on the Standard toolbar.
4. To edit an entry in the active cell, press ________ or ________ the cell to move the insertion point there so you can edit the entry right in the cell.
5. To undo the effect of the last command, click the ________ button on the Standard toolbar.
6. You can enter formulas into worksheet cells provided they begin with a(n) ________.
7. In formulas, the symbols +, –, *, and / are called ________.
8. One way to extend a selection is to point to a cell, hold down the ________ mouse button, and ________ the mouse to highlight adjoining cells.
9. Clicking a row or column heading selects the ________ row or column.
10. Clicking the ________ button, the gray rectangle in the upper-left corner of the worksheet, selects the entire worksheet.
11. To select nonadjacent areas, select the first area as you would normally. Then hold down ________ while you select one or more other areas.
12. To copy data in one cell to adjacent cells, you select the cell or cells that you want to copy and then drag the ________, the small square in the lower-right corner of the selected cells.
13. To copy cells you first select them then copy them to Windows' ________.
14. In the cell reference A$1, the ________ is absolute.
15. To automatically adjust a column's width to the longest entry in the column, double-click its ________.

LAB ACTIVITIES

DRILLS

2-1A Entering Text and Numbers into Cells

As you've seen, templates are frequently used in business. These templates have been designed so anyone can enter data into them and the formulas will calculate the correct answers. (You can specify that a workbook be saved as a template on which to base other models by choosing **Template** in the Save As dialog box's **Save as type** box. Then, when you use it, you save your version so the template isn't overwritten.) Here you use a checkbook-balancing template to practice entering text and numbers. When finished, your model should look like the one in the figure "The Balancing a Checkbook Model."

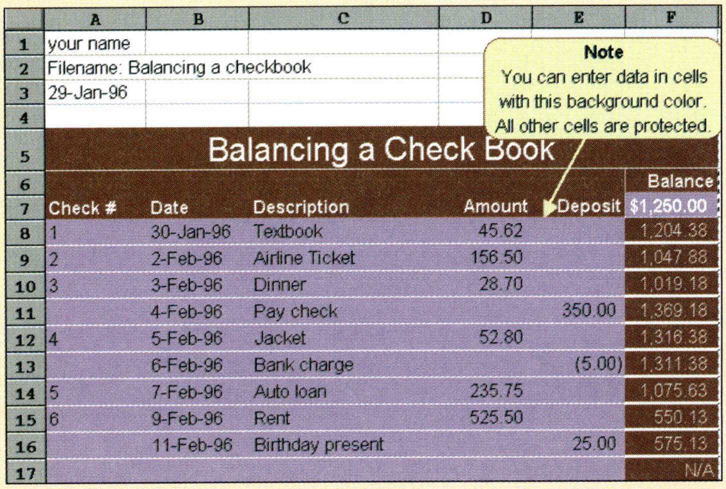

	A	B	C	D	E	F
1	your name					
2	Filename: Balancing a checkbook					
3	29-Jan-96					
4						
5	Balancing a Check Book					
6						Balance
7	Check #	Date	Description	Amount	Deposit	$1,250.00
8	1	30-Jan-96	Textbook	45.62		1,204.38
9	2	2-Feb-96	Airline Ticket	156.50		1,047.88
10	3	3-Feb-96	Dinner	28.70		1,019.18
11		4-Feb-96	Pay check		350.00	1,369.18
12	4	5-Feb-96	Jacket	52.80		1,316.38
13		6-Feb-96	Bank charge		(5.00)	1,311.38
14	5	7-Feb-96	Auto loan	235.75		1,075.63
15	6	9-Feb-96	Rent	525.50		550.13
16		11-Feb-96	Birthday present		25.00	575.13
17						N/A

The Balancing a Checkbook Model

1. Open the *Balancing a checkbook* workbook stored in the *Drill Workbooks* folder on the *Excel Student Resource Disk* and enter your name into cell A1.
2. Enter the text and numbers shown in the lighter colored cells of the template. All other cells are protected so you cannot enter data into them. As you enter numbers in columns D and E, notice how the balance automatically changes in column F.
   - To enter the numbers in column A as text, type an apostrophe first. This enters the number as text instead of as a value.
   - Enter the bank charge as -5 or (5).
3. Save your changes, make a printout, and then close the workbook.

2-1B Entering Text and Numbers into Cells

In this drill you practice entering numbers in different formats to see how they appear on the worksheet.

1. Open the *Entering numbers* workbook stored in the *Drill Workbooks* folder on the *Excel Student Resource Disk* and enter your name.

2. Enter data shown in column A on the same row in column B just as shown and read the description of the results you get in column C.
3. Save your changes, make a printout, and then close the workbook.

2-2 Editing Cell Contents

In this drill you edit text in one column of a worksheet so it matches text in another column.

1. Open the *Whoops—undoing mistakes* workbook stored in the *Drill Workbooks* folder on the *Excel Student Resource Disk* and enter your name into cell A1.
2. Correct the words in column A on rows 7 through 11 so they match the spelling on the same rows in column C.
3. Save your changes, make a printout, and then close the workbook.

2-3 Undoing Mistakes

In this drill you delete the contents of cells and then undo the deletion to restore the cells to their original state.

1. Open the *Whoops—undoing mistakes* workbook stored in the *Drill Workbooks* folder on the *Excel Student Resource Disk*.
2. Select any cell in the "Undoing" section that contains a number and press Delete to delete it. Then immediately click the **Undo** button on the toolbar to undo the deletion. Repeat with other cells until you are comfortable with the procedure.
3. Close the workbook without saving your changes.

2-4 Understanding Formulas

To calculate the net price of a product when you know the list price and discount, you use the formula (100% – discount × list price). In this drill you retrieve a workbook designed to demonstrate the principles of numbers and cell references in formulas and order of operations.

1. Open the *Exploring formulas* workbook stored in the *Drill Workbooks* folder on the *Excel Student Resource Disk*.
2. In the three-part section on numbers and cell references, select each of the following cells to display its formula on the formula bar:
   A. *All Numbers.* In cell B9, the formula **=(1-.2)*10** contains only numbers. Because the numbers are part of the formula, you cannot easily change the discount or price to calculate a new result.
   B. *Part Numbers/Part Cell References.* In cell B14, the formula **=(1-B13)*B12** contains both numbers and cell references. The formula subtracts the value in cell B13 from 1 (100%) and multiplies the result times the price in cell B12. The numbers in cells B12 and B13 are both variables that you can change to explore outcomes.
   C. *All Cell References.* In cell B19, the formula **=B18*B17** contains only references to cells and calculates the discount in dollars. In cell B20, the formula **=B17-B19** uses cell references to subtract the discount from the list price to calculate the net price.
3. Close the workbook without saving any changes you may have made.

2-5A Entering Formulas

In this drill you enter formulas using various operators described in the worksheet itself. As you do so, you immediately see the results of the calculations.

1. Open the *Operators in formulas workbook* stored in the *Drill Workbooks* folder on the *Excel Student Resource Disk* and enter your name into cell A1.
2. Enter each formula described in column A on the same row in column B and read the description of the formula in column C. For example, type **=10+10** in cell B9.
3. Change the numbers in cells B5 and B6 and watch the formulas that refer to these cells calculate new results. The formulas that contain only constants don't change.
4. Save, print, and close the workbook.

2-5B Entering Formulas

In this drill you enter formulas using numbers, references to other cells containing numbers, and a combination of numbers and cell references. As you do so, you immediately see the results of the calculations.

1. Open the *Entering formulas* workbook stored in the *Drill Workbooks* folder on the *Excel Student Resource Disk* and enter your name into cell A1.
2. Enter each of the formulas shown on the worksheet. When finished, your results should match those in the *Exploring Formulas* workbook of Drill 2-4.
3. Save, print, and close the workbook.

2-6 Selecting Ranges of Cells

In this drill you practice selecting columns and rows and rectangular ranges. As you do so, you practice dragging with the mouse to extend the selection.

1. Open the *Selecting cells practice* workbook stored in the *Drill Workbooks* folder on the *Excel Student Resource Disk* and enter your name into cell A1.
2. Follow each of the instructions on the screen to select various parts of each of the three worksheets. To cancel the selection, click any cell. Notice that the workbook contains three worksheets. To move to any of the three, click its tab. (You may have to click a tab scroll button to see the tabs at times.)
3. Repeat each of the steps in this drill until you have mastered selecting ranges, then close the workbook without saving any changes you may have made.

2-7 Filling Adjacent Cells

The easiest way to copy text, numbers, or formulas is to select the cell or cells you want to copy and then drag the highlight to the cells where you want them copied. In this drill, you practice this important procedure.

1. Open the *Filling cells practice* workbook stored in the *Drill Workbooks* folder on the *Excel Student Resource Disk* and enter your name into cell A1.
2. Select cells A8 through G8, then drag the fill handle down to row 16 and release it. Notice how the entries are each incremented by one month, number, or day.
3. Select cells A23 through G24, then drag the fill handle down to row 34 and release it. Notice how the entries are each incremented by the same amount as the first two entries were. For example, January and April in column A is incremented so there is a three-month interval between all of the copied months.
4. Save, print, and close the workbook.

2-8 Copying Data

In this drill you practice copying data, first by dragging and dropping and then using the buttons on the Standard toolbar.

1. Open the *Copying data practice* workbook stored in the *Drill Workbooks* folder on the *Excel Student Resource Disk* and enter your name into cell A1.
2. Click the sheet tab at the bottom of the sheet labeled *Dragging & Dropping* to make it the active sheet if it isn't already. There are four ranges of cells you will copy; a cell, column, row, and block. These ranges are yellow with red borders and you will copy them to the ranges shown in red with yellow borders. To do so:
   - Select the range to be copied (yellow cells with red borders).
   - Point to the range border so the mouse pointer is an arrow.
   - Right-drag the range to the range you are copying it to. When the range's outline is superimposed over the range you are copying to (red cells with yellow borders), release the mouse button and click the shortcut menu's **Copy** command.
3. Compare the cell references in the original cells with those in the copied cells to see how they have automatically adjusted the cells they refer to.
4. Click the **Print** button on the toolbar to print the worksheet.
5. Click the tab at the bottom of the sheet labeled *Copying & Pasting* to make it the active sheet.
6. Use the **Copy** and **Paste** buttons on the Standard toolbar to copy data from the "Copy From" section to the "Copy To" section.
   - In the "Copy To" section, the cells you select before pasting are highlighted with hatch marks.
   - Remember that when you use the buttons (and the Clipboard), you can copy once and paste as many times as you like until you copy another cell or cells.
7. Compare the cell references in the original cells with those in the copied cells to see how they have automatically adjusted the cells they refer to.
8. Click the **Print** button on the Standard toolbar to print the worksheet and then close it without saving your changes.

2-9A Specifying Absolute Cell References

In this drill you use a specially formatted model to see how cell references change when you copy them to a new location on the worksheet.

1. Open the *Absolute & relative cell references* workbook stored in the *Drill Workbooks* folder on the *Excel Student Resource Disk* and enter your name into cell A1.
2. Use the **Copy** and **Paste** buttons on the Standard toolbar to copy each of the red cells with the yellow border to the yellow cell with the red border in the same section. As you do so, select first the cell you copy from and then the cell you copy to and notice how the cell references change or doesn't change when copied, depending on which part of the reference is relative and which is absolute. To help you see the results better, the cell referred to by the original formula is shown in dark blue and the one it refers to after being copied is shown in light blue. (Note that when you copy a cell, the moving border around the source cell remains flashing until you copy the next cell.)

3. Click the **Print** button on the toolbar to print the worksheet, and then close it without saving your changes.

2-9B Specifying Absolute Cell References

One common use of mixed cell references is in the preparation of tables that show a range of possible outcomes. Here you create a table that compares two subscription plans from a major telecommunication provider. One plan has a lower monthly fee but a higher hourly rate than the other. The model will tell you how many hours you must use the service to benefit from paying the higher monthly fee to get the lower hourly rate. When finished, the first few rows of your model should look like the figure "The Communication Service Model".

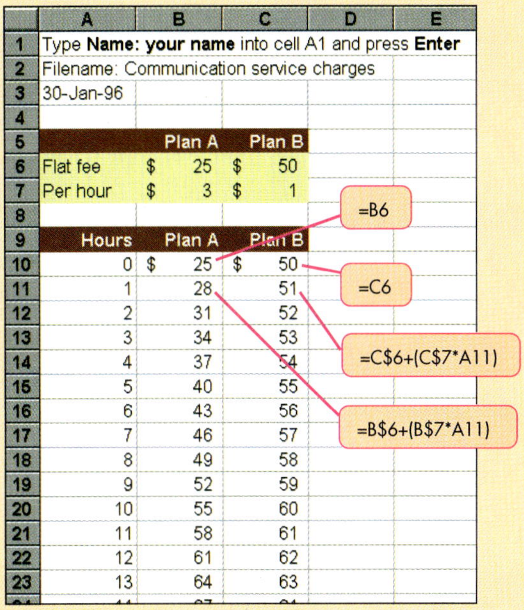

The Communication Service Model

1. Open the *Communication service charges* workbook stored in the *Drill Workbooks* folder on the *Excel Student Resource Disk* and enter your name into cell A1.
2. Enter the formulas shown in the figure "The Communication Service Model" in cells B10, C10, B11, and C11.
3. Select cells B11 and C11 and use the fill handle to copy them to all adjacent rows down to row 37. Read down the columns to see where Plan A becomes more expensive than Plan B. Up until that point, Plan A would be the better plan. After that point, Plan B would be.
4. Press Ctrl+` to display formulas in their cells and notice the results of copying the formula. The only references that change are those that refer to the hours in column A, which were relative. The references to rows 6 and 7, which were absolute, haven't changed when copied down the columns.
5. Press Ctrl+` to display values in their cells.
6. Save, print, and close the workbook.

2-9C Specifying Absolute Cell References

There is a concept referred to as the time value of money which describes how money increases when invested at compound interest (future value) and decreases due to inflation (present value). To calculate compound interest, you use the formula (1+r)N. To calculate the present value of an amount, the formula is

(1+r)-N. In both formulas, r is the rate of interest (or inflation) and N is the number of periods. Here you enter these formulas in a single cell and then use the fill command to copy them to other cells. The result is a table of values similar to those you find in the appendix of many accounting or finance books.

=(1+B$5)^$A6

	A	B	C	D	E	F	G	H	I	J	K
1	Type **Name: your name** into cell A1 and press **Enter**										
2	Filename: Time value of money										
3	30-Jan-96										
4											
5	Period	1%	2%	3%	4%	5%	6%	7%	8%	9%	10%
6	1	1.010	1.020	1.030	1.040	1.050	1.060	1.070	1.080	1.090	1.100
7	2	1.020	1.040	1.061	1.082	1.103	1.124	1.145	1.166	1.188	1.210
8	3	1.030	1.061	1.093	1.125	1.158	1.191	1.225	1.260	1.295	1.331
9	4	1.041	1.082	1.126	1.170	1.216	1.262	1.311	1.360	1.412	1.464
10	5	1.051	1.104	1.159	1.217	1.276	1.338	1.403	1.469	1.539	1.611
11	6	1.062	1.126	1.194	1.265	1.340	1.419	1.501	1.587	1.677	1.772
12	7	1.072	1.149	1.230	1.316	1.407	1.504	1.606	1.714	1.828	1.949
13	8	1.083	1.172	1.267	1.369	1.477	1.594	1.718	1.851	1.993	2.144
14	9	1.094	1.195	1.305	1.423	1.551	1.689	1.838	1.999	2.172	2.358
15	10	1.105	1.219	1.344	1.480	1.629	1.791	1.967	2.159	2.367	2.594
16	11	1.116	1.243	1.384	1.539	1.710	1.898	2.105	2.332	2.580	2.853
17	12	1.127	1.268	1.426	1.601	1.796	2.012	2.252	2.518	2.813	3.138
18	13	1.138	1.294	1.469	1.665	1.886	2.133	2.410	2.720	3.066	3.452
19	14	1.149	1.319	1.513	1.732	1.980	2.261	2.579	2.937	3.342	3.797
20	15	1.161	1.346	1.558	1.801	2.079	2.307	2.759	3.172	3.642	4.177
21	16	1.173	1.373	1.605	1.873	2.183	2.540	2.952	3.426	3.970	4.595
22	17	1.184	1.400	1.653	1.948	2.292	2.693	3.159	3.700	4.328	5.054
23	18	1.196	1.428	1.702	2.026	2.407	2.854	3.380	3.996	4.717	5.560
24	19	1.208	1.457	1.754	2.107	2.527	3.026	3.617	4.316	5.142	6.116
25	20	1.220	1.486	1.806	2.191	2.653	3.207	3.870	4.661	5.604	6.727
26	21	1.232	1.516	1.860	2.279	2.786	3.400	4.141	5.034	6.109	7.400
27	22	1.245	1.546	1.916	2.370	2.925	3.604	4.430	5.437	6.659	8.140
28	23	1.257	1.577	1.974	2.465	3.072	3.820	4.741	5.871	7.258	8.954

The Compound Sum of $1 Worksheet

1. Open the *Time value of money* workbook stored in the *Drill Workbooks* folder on the *Excel Student Resource Disk* and enter your name into cell A1.
2. On the *Compound Sum of $1* sheet, enter the formula **=(1+B$5)^$A6** into cell B6.
3. Select the cell with the formula and use the fill handle to fill the formula to all cells on the row out to cell K6.
4. Select cells B6 through K6 and use the fill handle to fill the formula to all rows down to row 30.
5. Print the worksheet.
6. Press Ctrl+` to display formulas in their cells and notice the results of copying the formula. The row or column references with dollar signs in front of them didn't change and those without them did. Check a few of the formulas to see exactly which rows and columns they refer to.
7. Press Ctrl+` to display values in their cells.
8. Click the tab at the bottom of the sheet labeled *Present Value of $1* to make it the active sheet.
9. Enter the formula **=1/(1+B$5)^$A6** into cell B6. Repeat Steps 3 and 4 to use the fill handle to fill the formula first into the cells to the right and then down.
10. Repeat Steps 6 through 7 for this table to see how the formula changes when copied.
11. Save the workbook and then close it.

7. Save the finished model and make a printout.
8. How much would you have to put in on the 31st day if you started with $1 instead of a penny? With $2? With fifty cents?
9. Close the workbook without saving your last what-if change.

2-3 Exploring Series of Numbers

In math, there are three common types of number series: arithmetic, geometric, and exponential. In this exercise, you enter a model that allows you to see the relationships among these three series.

1. Open the *Number series* workbook stored in the *Exercise Workbooks* folder on the *Excel Student Resource Disk* and enter your name into cell A1.
2. Use the **Format, Column, Width** command to set columns A, B, and C, to 15.
3. Enter the number **2** in cells A6, B6, and C6.
4. Enter and copy the formulas as described in the table "The Number Series Model's Formulas."
5. Save, print, and close the workbook.

The Number Series Model's Formulas

Cell	Formula
A7	*Arithmetic* is a reference to the number above it plus 1. Use the cell's fill handle to copy the formula down to cell A11.
B7	*Geometric* is a reference to the number above it times 2. Use the cell's fill handle to copy the formula down to cell B11.
C7	*Exponential* is a reference to the number above raised to the power of 2. Use the cell's fill handle to copy the formula down to cell C1.

2-4 Exploring Birthday Probabilities

Whenever there is a group of people together, the possibility that any two of them share the same birthday is surprisingly high. For example, if there is one other person in the room, the probability that they do not have the same birthday as you is 364/365, or 99.18%. The probability that the two of you do have the same birthday is therefore 100%–99.18%, or .82%. If there are two other people in the room, you can calculate the probability that they don't have the same birthday with the formula (364/365)*(363/365). If there were five people, you would use the formula (364/365)*(363/365)*(362/365)*(361/365)*(360/365). If there were 25 people, the formula would be five times as long. Let's see how easy it is to make this calculation by entering and copying a few simple formulas. When finished, your model should look like the figure "The Birthday Odds Model."

1. Open the *Birthday odds* workbook stored in the *Exercise Workbooks* folder on the *Excel Student Resource Disk* and enter your name into cell A1.
2. Enter and copy the formulas described in the table "The Birthday Odds Model's Formulas." You can see from the table that if there are 25 people in a room, the probability that two of them share a birthday is almost 60%.
3. Save, print, and close the workbook.

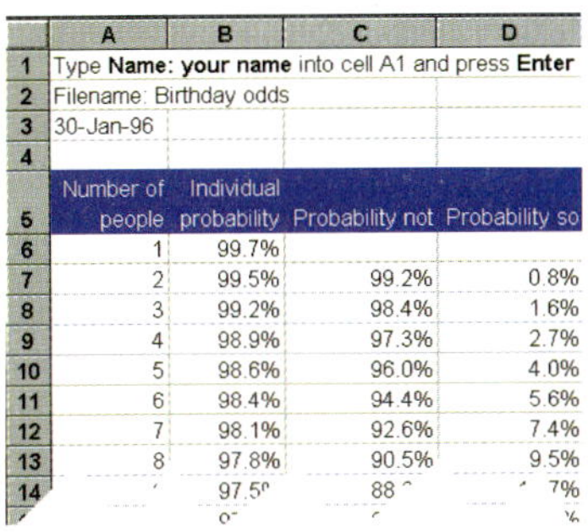

The Birthday Odds Model

The Birthday Odds Model's Formulas	
Cell	**Formula**
B6	Enter the formula **=(365-A6)/365** and use the cell's fill handle to copy the formula down to cell B30.
C7	Enter the formula **=B7*B6**.
C8	Enter the formula **=C7*B8** and use the cell's fill handle to copy the formula down to cell C30
D7	Enter the formula **=1-C7** and use the cell's fill handle to copy the formula down to cell D30.

2-5 Creating a Multiplication Table

Every math book you used in grade school probably had a multiplication table in the appendix. In this exercise, you create a multiplication table that allows you to display any range of numbers. When finished, your model should look like the figure "The Multiplication Table Model."

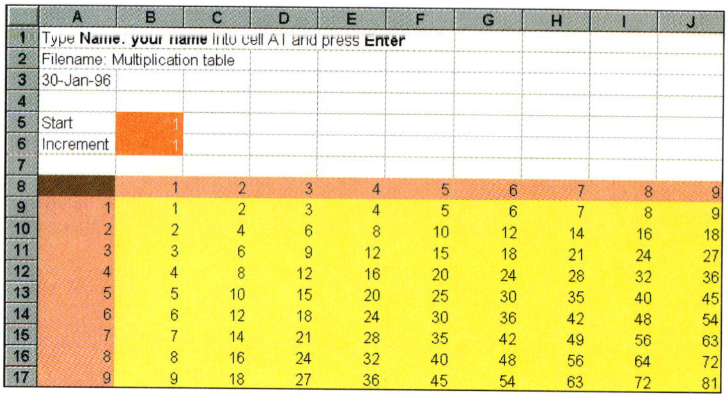

	A	B	C	D	E	F	G	H	I	J
1	Type **Name. your name** into cell A1 and press **Enter**									
2	Filename: Multiplication table									
3	30-Jan-96									
4										
5	Start	1								
6	Increment	1								
7										
8		1	2	3	4	5	6	7	8	9
9	1	1	2	3	4	5	6	7	8	9
10	2	2	4	6	8	10	12	14	16	18
11	3	3	6	9	12	15	18	21	24	27
12	4	4	8	12	16	20	24	28	32	36
13	5	5	10	15	20	25	30	35	40	45
14	6	6	12	18	24	30	36	42	48	54
15	7	7	14	21	28	35	42	49	56	63
16	8	8	16	24	32	40	48	56	64	72
17	9	9	18	27	36	45	54	63	72	81

The Multiplication Table Model

1. Open the *Multiplication table* workbook stored in the *Exercise Workbooks* folder on the *Excel Student Resource Disk* and enter your name into cell A1.
2. Enter the formulas described in the table "The Multiplication Table Model's Formulas," and copy the formulas to the indicated cells.
3. Save and print the worksheet.
4. Press Ctrl+` to display formulas in their cells and notice the results of copying the formula. Then press Ctrl+` to display values in their cells.
5. Change the start and increment numbers in cells B5 and B6, and watch the table change.
6. Close the workbook without saving your what-if changes.

The Multiplication Table Model's Formulas	
Cell	**Formula**
A9	Enter the formula **=B5**.
A10	Enter the formula **=A9+B$6** (so that the reference to cell B6 has the row reference absolute), and use the cell's fill handle to copy the formula down to A17.
B8	Enter the formula **=B5**.
C8	Enter the formula **=B8+$B6** (so that the reference to cell B6 has the column reference absolute), and use the cell's fill handle to copy the formula out to cell J8.
B9	Enter the formula **=$A9*B$8** (so that the reference to cell A9 has the column reference absolute and B8 has the row reference absolute), and use the cell's fill handle to copy the formula first to J9, then select B9:J9 and fill down to row 17.

2-6 Exploring Chain Letters

Have you ever received a chain letter asking you to send money to the sender? These letters always promise great rewards if you do so, and if you send copies of the letter to a number of other people who will then send you money. Because these letters are illegal, they are usually couched in some other terms; for example, you send $5 to the sender to buy mailing labels, which you in turn sell to others. Generally, these chain letters are a great investment—if you are the originator. The problem with them is that the number of people involved grows so fast that before too many mailings, the entire world population has to be involved. When finished, your model should look like the figure "The Chain Letter Analysis Model."

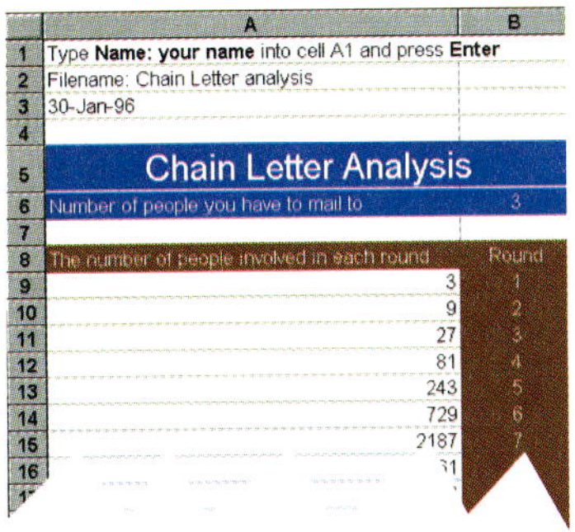

The Chain Letter Analysis

1. Open the *Chain letter analysis* workbook stored in the *Exercise Workbooks* folder on the *Excel Student Resource Disk* and enter your name into cell A1.
2. Use the **Format**, **Column**, **Width** command to set column A to 39.
3. Enter the formulas described in the table "The Chain Letter Analysis Model's Formulas," and copy the formulas to the indicated cells.
4. Save and print the worksheet.
5. Press Ctrl+` to display formulas in their cells, and notice the results of copying the formula. Then press Ctrl+` to display values in their cells.
6. The variable is the number of people that you have to mail to in cell B3. Change this to 4 and then to 5. How many people are involved on the tenth round? The thirtieth?
7. Close the workbook without saving your changes.

The Chain Letter Analysis Model's Formulas

Cell	Formula
A9	*The number of people involved in each round* is a reference to the number of people you have to mail to in cell B6.
A10	*The number of people involved in each round* is the value in cell A9 multiplied by the number of people you have to mail to in cell B6 (an absolute reference). Use the fill handle on cell A9 to copy the formula down to cell A38.

2-7 Calculating Currency Exchange Rates

With many transactions being international in nature, financial complications arise as currency exchange rates rise and fall. Profits made in one country have to be converted to the currency of the country in which a business is based. Prices and costs are frequently quoted in one currency but paid in another. To help people keep track, the daily exchange rates are always listed in the *Wall Street Journal*. In this exercise, you create a model that allows you to quickly convert from one currency to another based on that daily rate.

1. Open the *Exchange rates* workbook stored in the *Exercise Workbooks* folder on the *Excel Student Resource Disk* and enter your name into cell A1.
2. Enter and copy the formulas described in the table "The Exchange Rates Model's Formulas."
3. Save and print the workbook.
4. Explore what-ifs by changing the amount in cell D5.
5. Close the workbook without saving your what-if changes.

The Exchange Rates Model's Functions

Cell	Formula
C8	*Amount (in $)* is calculated by the formula **=B8*D$5**. Use the cell's fill handle to copy the formula down to cell C27.
D8	*Amount (in local)* is calculated by the formula **=D$5/B8**. Use the cell's fill handle to copy the formula down to cell D27.

TIP

Note On Projects

Each PicTorial in this text ends with a series of real-world projects that test and build on the skills you have developed as you learn how to use Excel. The projects are typical of the applications spreadsheets are used to analyze. To complete them, you must use the procedures already discussed in the text. However, they are designed to make you think about what you're doing as you use procedures to solve real-world problems. Don't be discouraged if they take some thought and effort to work through.

2-1 A Balance Sheet

The accounting balance sheet is appropriately named, for it must always balance. There are two sections of the balance sheet. The left side shows the firm's assets (what the firm owns). The right side shows the liabilities (what the firm owes) and the owner equity, which together represent the claims against the assets or how the firm paid for its assets. The balance sheet is a snapshot of a firm's condition at a given point in time, such as the end of the month, quarter, or year. In simple terms, a balance sheet is a record of what the company has done with its income and the money provided by creditors, lenders, and stockholders. Managers and owners use the balance sheet not only for evaluating financial conditions but also for setting management and company goals. The balance sheet is also a window through which others, such as bankers, creditors, and stockholders, can look at a company.

In this project, you create a balance sheet for a company that compares this year's results with last year's results. After completing this project, you will be able to enter and describe the elements that make up a balance sheet and explain how they relate to one another.

A typical balance sheet is shown in the figure "The Balance Sheet." Instead of being organized into left and right sides, liabilities are entered below assets to simplify its layout on the worksheet. This balance sheet, like most others that you will encounter, contains the formulas indicated on the illustration and described below. Using these descriptions, create a balance sheet just like the one illustrated. When finished, save it as *Balance sheet* in the *Project Workbooks* folder on the *Excel Student Resource Disk* and make a printout.

1. **Total current assets** is the sum of the firm's assets that are expected to be converted into cash in the course of the firm's operating year. Typical current assets include cash, marketable securities with maturities of less than a year (such as Treasury bills or money market securities), accounts receivable, notes receivable, inventory, and prepaid expenses such as insurance payments.

2. **Total fixed assets** is the sum of the assets acquired for the long-term use of the business. These assets are typically not for resale, and they are recorded on the balance sheet at their cost to the business less accumulated depreciation. Fixed assets include land, buildings, leasehold improvements, fixtures, furniture, machinery, tools, and equipment.

	A	B	C
1	Type **Name: your name** into cell A1 and press **Enter**		
2	Filename: Balance sheet		
3	30-Jan-96		
4			
5	BALANCE SHEET		
6	PACRIM Enterprises		
7	December 31, 199X		
8		This Year	Last Year
9	CURRENT ASSETS		
10	Cash	11,200	6,400
11	Accounts receivable	20,000	20,000
12	Inventory	70,000	70,000
13	Prepaid expense	3,400	3,400
14	Total current assets	104,600	99,800
15	FIXED ASSETS		
16	Buildings & equipment	30,000	30,000
17	Less accumulated depreciation	-10,000	-5,000
18	Land	20,000	5,000
19	Total fixed assets	40,000	30,000
20	OTHER ASSETS		
21	Patents	10,000	10,000
22	Total assets	154,600	139,800
23	CURRENT LIABILITIES		
24	Accounts payable	20,000	20,000
25	Accrued wages and taxes	10,000	10,000
26	Current portion of long term debt	5,000	5,000
27	Other current liabilities	5,000	5,000
28	Total current liabilities	40,000	40,000
29	LONG-TERM DEBT		
30	Bank loans	40,000	30,000
31	Other	10,000	20,000
32	Total liabilities	90,000	90,000
33	OWNER EQUITY		
34	Common stock	37,000	37,000
35	Retained earnings	27,600	12,800
36	Total owner equity	64,600	49,800
37	Total equity and liabilities	154,600	139,800

The Balance Sheet

3. **Total assets** is the sum of total current assets, total fixed assets, and all other assets such as goodwill, patents, trademarks, and organizational costs.
4. **Total current liabilities** is the sum of all claims of creditors against the assets of the business—in other words, debt owed by the business. Current liabilities are short-term obligations due on demand or within a year. Typical current liabilities include accounts payable for merchandise and services, loans payable within the year, taxes, and other accruals.
5. **Total liabilities** is the sum of the current liabilities and the itemized long-term debt items such as bank loans or bonds entered on the rows above.
6. **Total owner equity** (also called net worth) is the sum of the owners' investment and retained earnings entered on the rows above.
7. **Total equity and liabilities** is the sum of all liabilities and owner equity. This sum always equals total assets, and therefore, the balance sheet balances.

2-2 An Income Statement

Business owners and managers must have a way to measure the degree of success or failure of their business or department and to show the net results of subtracting expenses from sales or revenues. The income, or profit-and-loss, statement is the gauge most frequently used to determine profitability. The income statement shows the profit or loss over a period, usually a month, quarter, or year.

In this project, you create an income statement that shows the sales, expenses, and profits for a three-year period. After completing this project, you will be able to enter and describe the line items that make up an income statement and explain how they are related.

The income statement shown in the figure "The Income Statement" is typical of those used to show the performance of a business over a period of time. This income statement, like most others that you will encounter, contains the formulas indicated on the illustration and described below. Using these descriptions, create an income statement just like the one illustrated. When finished, save it as *Income statement* in the *Project Workbooks* folder on the *Excel Student Resource Disk* and make a printout. Then display formulas in their cells instead of the calculated values, narrow columns as much as possible, and make a printout so you have a record of the formulas in the model.

	A	B	C	D
1	your name			
2	Filename: Income statement			
3	30-Jan-96			
4				
5	PRO FORMA INCOME STATEMENT - FIRST THREE YEARS			
6	PACRIM Enterprises			
7	January 1, 199x -- December 31, 199x			
8		Year 1	Year 2	Year 3
9	SALES			
10	Gross sales	40,000	44,000	48,400
11	Discounts, returns, & allow.	2,000	2,200	2,420
12	Net sales	38,000	41,800	45,980
13				
14	COST OF GOODS SOLD			
15	Purchase price	22,800	25,080	27,588
16	Freight in	912	1,003	1,104
17	Total cost of goods sold	23,712	26,083	28,692
18	Gross profit	14,288	15,717	17,288
19				
20	OPERATING EXPENSES			
21	General and administrative	7,500	7,500	7,500
22	Selling expenses	3,750	3,750	3,750
23	Interest expenses	931	931	931
24	Depreciation	1,250	1,250	1,250
25	Total operating expenses	13,431	13,431	13,431
26				
27	Operating income/loss	857	2,286	3,857
28	Other income	10		15
29	Other expenses		12	
30	Income before taxes	867	2,274	3,872
31	Taxes	214	571	964
32	Net income/loss	653	1,702	2,908

The Income Statement

1. **Net sales** is gross sales minus discounts, returns, and allowances.
2. **Total cost of goods sold** is the sum of all costs of inventory or raw materials purchased by the firm, including the freight charges of having them delivered.
3. **Gross profit** is the money available to the firm after cost of goods sold is deducted from net sales.
4. **Total operating expenses** is the sum of all costs used to operate the business. Typical operating expenses include general and administrative costs, selling expenses, interest expenses, and depreciation.
5. **Operating income or loss** is calculated by subtracting total operating expenses from gross profit.
6. **Income before taxes** is calculated by adding other income to operating income or loss and then subtracting other expenses.
7. **Net income or loss**, frequently referred to as the bottom line, is income before taxes minus taxes.

What-Ifs

Using the finished *Income statement* model, explore the following what-ifs, and list the amounts for each item in the table "Exploring Sales What-Ifs." Compare the results of the changes with the original numbers. Which changes are for the better? For the worse?

A. What if sales in Year 1 are reduced to $37,000?

B. What if sales in Year 1 are increased to $43,000?

C. What if sales in Year 1 are $38,000 and the purchase price increases to $24,700?

Exploring Sales What-Ifs

What If	Original	A	B	C
Gross sales	______	______	______	______
Gross profit	______	______	______	______
Income before taxes	______	______	______	______

Assume that you are the manager of a small store and want to increase your profits. Using the income statement, make the following changes, and list the results from the "Year 1" column in the table "Exploring Other What-Ifs." Compare the results of the changes with the original numbers. Which changes are for the better? For the worse?

A. Assume that with better training, and no additional expenses, your sales help can increase gross sales to $50,000.

B. Return gross sales to the original $40,000, and then assume that you can strike a better deal with your supplier that will decrease purchase price to $20,900.

C. Return purchase price to the original $22,800, and then assume that by hiring a part-time salesperson sales can be increased. To do so, you must increase general and administrative expenses to $9,000 to increase gross sales to $45,000.

Exploring Other What-Ifs

What If	Original	A	B	C
Gross sales	______	______	______	______
Gross profit	______	______	______	______
Income before taxes	______	______	______	______
Net income/loss	______	______	______	______

2-3 Scaling Times

Have you ever wondered how people figure out those wonderful analogies about sizes and times—ones where the history of the earth is condensed into 24 hours? Well, here's an excerpt from a textbook on astronomy that does something similar.

"Some people have trouble comprehending millions and billions of years. These are big numbers, and after a while they lose their meaning. To better understand Earth's history, consider an analogy. Imagine the entire lifetime of Earth to be 50 years rather than 5 billion years. This time scale is then comparable to the human life span, making various highlights of Earth's history more understandable.

With this analogy in mind, we can say that there is no record whatever for the first 10 years of Earth's existence. Rocks hardened and life arose quickly thereafter. In particular, life originated about at least 35 years ago, when Earth was only 15 years old in our analogy. Our planet's middle age is largely a mystery, although we can be sure that life continued to evolve, and that mountain chains and oceanic trenches steadily built up and eroded down. Not until 5 years ago, in our 50-year analogy, did abundant life flourish throughout Earth's oceans. Life came ashore about 4 years ago, plants and animals mastered the land about 2 years ago, and dinosaurs reached their peak about 1 year ago, only to die suddenly about 8 months ago. Human-like apes changed into humans only last week, and the last major ice ages occurred only a few days ago. Homo Sapiens—our species—did not emerge in this 50-year analogy of Earth's history until about 4 hours ago. In fact, the invention of agriculture is only 1 hour old, and the Renaissance only 3 minutes old!"[1]

The model shown in the figure "The Scale Model" is one the author could have used to calculate these numbers. The formulas in it are numbered and described below. Using these descriptions, create a model just like the one illustrated. When finished, save it as *Scaling times* in the *Project Workbooks* folder on the *Excel Student Resource Disk* and make a printout.

	A	B	C	D	E	F
1	your name					
2	Filename: Scaling times					
3	30-Jan-96					
4						
5	Scaling Times					
6						
7	Age of Earth	1 5,000,000,000				
8	Scale to (in years)	50				
9	Scaling factor	0.00000001				
10						
11		Actual Age	Scaled Time 2	3 Scaled Time	Scaled Time 4	Scaled Time 5
12			(in years)	(In days)	(In hours)	(In minutes)
13	Earth	5,000,000,000	50	18250	438000	2628000
14	First life	3,500,000,000	35	12775	306600	1839600
15	Dinosaurs	500,000,000	5	1825	43800	262800
16	Man	1,500,000	0.015	5.475	131.4	788
17	First use of fire	500,000	0.005	1.825	43.8	262
18	Agriculture	10,000	0.0001	0.0365	0.876	52.5
19	Renaisance	500	0.000005	0.001825	0.0438	2.62

1. **Scaling factor** is calculated by dividing the *Scale to (in years)* value by the age of the earth.
2. **Scaled Time (in years)** is the actual age multiplied by the scaling factor.
3. **Scaled Time (in days)** is the scaled time in years multiplied by 365.
4. **Scaled Time (in hours)** is the scaled time in days multiplied by 24.
5. **Scaled Time (in minutes)** is the scaled time in hours multiplied by 60.

[1] Eric Chaisson, *Universe: An Evolutionary Approach to Astronomy* (Englewood Cliffs, NJ.: Prentice-Hall, 1988), p. 7.

PICTORIAL

THREE

FORMATTING AND REVISING MODELS

After completing this PicTorial, you will be able to:

- **Format text and numbers automatically and by using the toolbar and menus**
- **Copy formats to other cells**
- **Delete and clear the contents and formats from cells**
- **Change the page setup for printing**
- **Insert and delete rows and columns**
- **Move data from one location to another**

ONE of the best features of a spreadsheet is its revisability. You can start with small, simple models, and then add to their power and readability. For example, to change existing data or formulas in a model, you can edit them or erase them. To expand or condense your model, you can insert or delete rows and columns. When you want your models, whether on the screen or in printouts, to be attractive and easy to read, you use formats to align labels and format numbers or use patterns, borders, and fonts to highlight items.

3-1 AUTOFORMATTING

Excel's AutoFormat feature makes formatting fast and easy. All you have to do is select the area you want formatted and choose a professionally designed format from a list. The formats not only add borders and patterns; they also change column width and format numbers.

QUICKSTEPS

AutoFormatting

1. Select a single cell in the model you want formatted or select all of the cells you want formatted. (When you select more than one cell, only those cells are formatted. If you select just one cell, Excel analyzes the sheet and guesses at which cells should be formatted. Occasionally it will guess wrong.)
2. Pull down the **Format** menu and click the **AutoFormat** command to display the AutoFormat dialog box.
3. Select a format from the **Table Format** list, and it is illustrated in the Sample window.
4. Click the **Options** command button to display a list of formats you can turn on or off. Turn off any that you want to preserve in the table. For example, if you have already formatted numbers in the Currency format and don't want that format to change, click the **Number** check box to turn it off (☐).
5. Click the **OK** command button to apply the selected format to the table.

TUTORIAL

In this tutorial you are introduced to the command that automatically formats your model. The model you use is the one that calculates your budget.

Getting Ready

1. Open the *Budget* workbook stored in the *Tutorial Workbooks* folder on the *Excel Student Resource Disk*.

Formatting a Table

2. Select cells A6 through E21, pull down the **Format** menu, and click the **AutoFormat** command to display the AutoFormat dialog box.

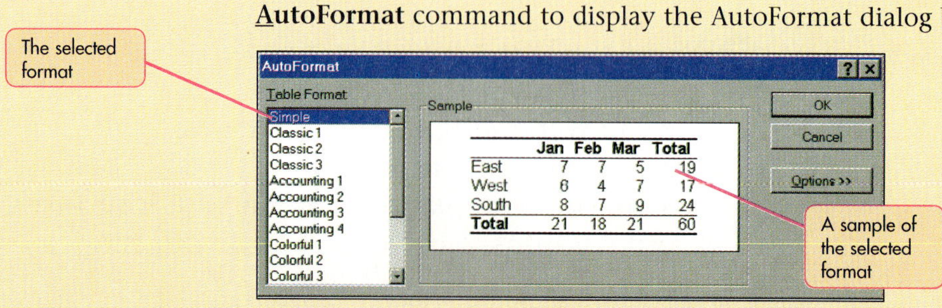

3. Select the *Accounting 2* format from the **Table Format** list, and it is illustrated in the *Sample* window.
4. Click the **OK** command button to apply the selected format to the table. Click anywhere outside of the table so you can see the formats without their being highlighted.

	A	B	C	D	E
1	Type **Name: your name** into cell A1 and press **Enter**				
2	Filename: Budget				
3	21-Mar-96				
4					
5	2-Year Budget				
6	**INCOME**	FALL	SPRING	FALL	SPRING
7	Bank balance	3,000	2,050	1,100	150
8	Income during semester	1,250	1,250	1,250	1,250
9	College loans	1,000	1,000	1,000	1,000
10	Total	5,250	4,300	3,350	2,400
11					
12	**EXPENSES**				
13	Tuition	1,000	1,000	1,000	1,000
14	Room & board	1,000	1,000	1,000	1,000
15	Books	200	200	200	200
16	Entertainment	300	300	300	300
17	Travel	500	500	500	500
18	Misc	200	200	200	200
19	Total	3,200	3,200	3,200	3,200
20					
21	**Balance**	2,050	1,100	150	-800
22					

The AutoFormat applied to selected cells

5. Click the **Save** button on the Standard toolbar to save your changes.
6. Click the **Print** button on the Standard toolbar to print the sheet.

PAUSING FOR PRACTICE

The AutoFormat command is such a useful feature that you should take the time to explore it. Pause here to repeat Steps 2 through 4 to select one or more additional formats.

Finishing Up

7. Close the workbook without saving your changes.

3-2 FORMATTING TEXT AND NUMBERS USING THE TOOLBAR

If you want to format cells individually instead of using AutoFormat, you can apply the most commonly used formats by clicking buttons on the Formatting toolbar.

Fonts and Sizes

Arial
Courier New
Times New Roman

Windows Font Faces

With Excel, you can select cells and then change the fonts used to format the cell contents. When you do so, you can select a new font design or a new size. The font design, called its *typeface*, determines the overall look of the type. Some fonts of a kind known as TrueType fonts are supplied with Windows. They include Arial, Courier New, and Times New Roman.

Many other fonts may be added to a system. The fonts available to you depend on what printer has been selected. If you change the printer selection, you may see a different list of fonts when you format characters.

Arial 8 point
Arial 10 point
Arial 12 point
Arial 14 point
Arial 18 point

Font Sizes

The font size determines the height and width of the characters and is specified in a unit of measurement called *points*. (Available font sizes vary depending on the capabilities of your printer.) A point is about 1/72 of an inch, so 72-point type is 1 inch high, 36-point type is fi inch high, and 18-point type is/inch high. Normally, body text in books, magazines, and newspapers will be 10 to 12 points in size.

QUICKSTEPS

Changing Fonts and Sizes

1. Select the cells to be formatted.
2. Click the drop-down arrow (▾) on the **Font** box or **Font Size** box on the Formatting toolbar to display a list of the fonts or font sizes available on your system.
3. Click the font or size you want to use.

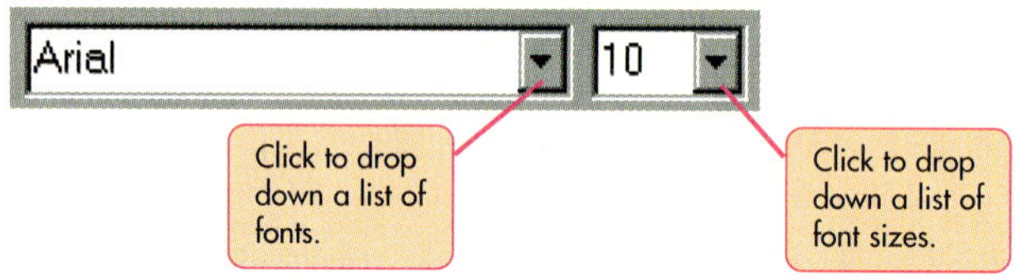

Font Style Buttons

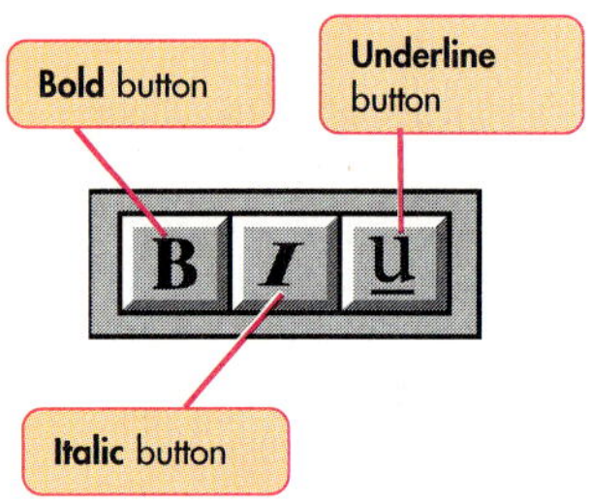

The **Bold**, **Italic**, and **Underline** buttons on the Formatting toolbar will **boldface**, *italicize*, or underline the contents of selected cells.

TIP

Repeating Commands

When using the same command a number of times, you need only do it once and then repeat it as needed. To repeat the previous command, select new cells (if appropriate), and either press F4, click the **Repeat** button on the Standard toolbar, or pull down the **Edit** menu and click the **Repeat** command (the most recent command is listed following the **Repeat** part).

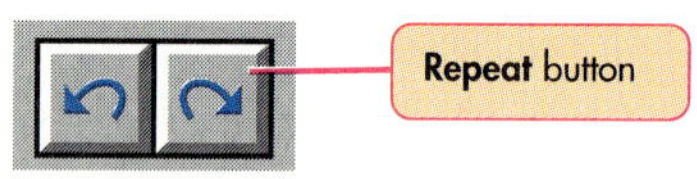

Alignment Buttons

The **Align Left**, **Center**, and **Align Right** buttons on the Formatting toolbar align data in selected cells with the left or right edge of the cells or center them between the edges.

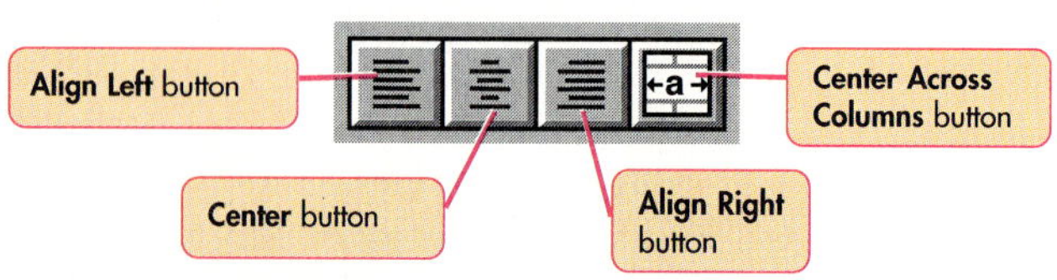

The **Center Across Columns** button is a little different. If you enter a heading or other text in the leftmost cell, select that cell and any number of cells to the right, clicking this button will center the text in the selected range. The text itself, however, remains in the leftmost cell in case you need to delete or edit it.

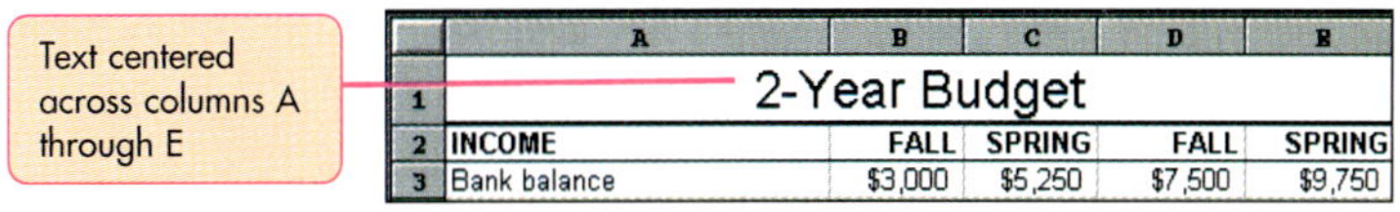

Number Format Buttons

The **Currency Style** ($100.00), **Percent Style** (10%), and **Comma Style** (1,000) buttons on the Formatting toolbar apply those styles to numbers in selected cells. You can also click the **Increase Decimal** or **Decrease Decimal** buttons to increase or decrease decimal places in selected numbers.

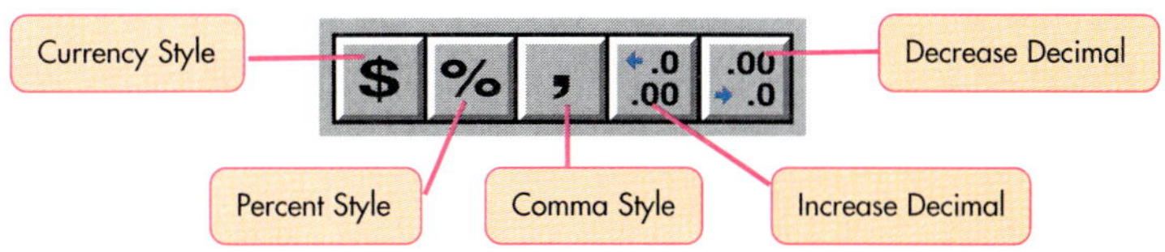

Border and Pattern Buttons

Many worksheets look much more attractive when borders are used to set off headings and sections. You can also apply colors to the borders, as background in cells, and to text and numbers. Although these colors will not print in color on most printers, they can still improve the worksheet's appearance on the screen. (Colors may print as various shades of gray on many printers, so you may have to run some tests to see if you like the results.)

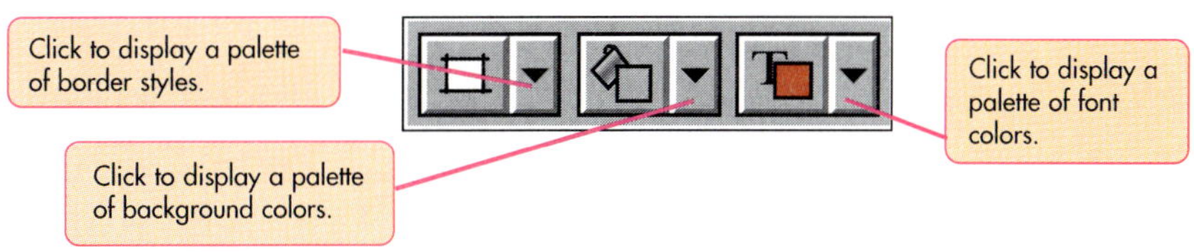

- Clicking the **Borders** drop-down arrow (▾) on the Formatting toolbar displays a palette of borders. Click the one you want to apply to the selected cells.

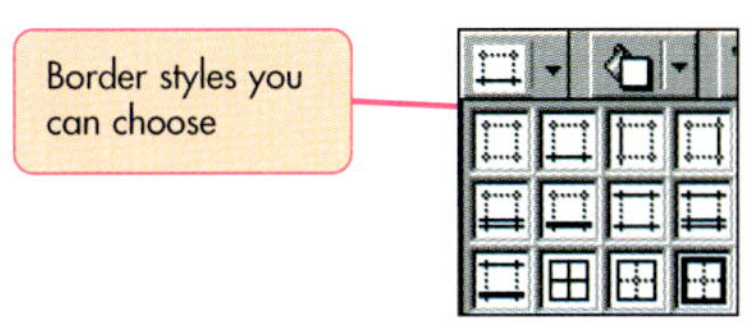

- Clicking the **Color** drop-down arrow (▾) on the Formatting toolbar displays a palette of colors. Click the one you want as a background in selected cells. The left part of the **Color** button shows the currently selected color. If you click that part of the button, it assigns the color to selected cells.

- Clicking the **Font Color** drop-down arrow (▾) on the Formatting toolbar displays a palette of colors. Click the one you want to apply to text and numbers in the selected cells. The left part of the **Font Color** button shows the currently selected color. If you click that part of the button, it assigns the color to selected text.

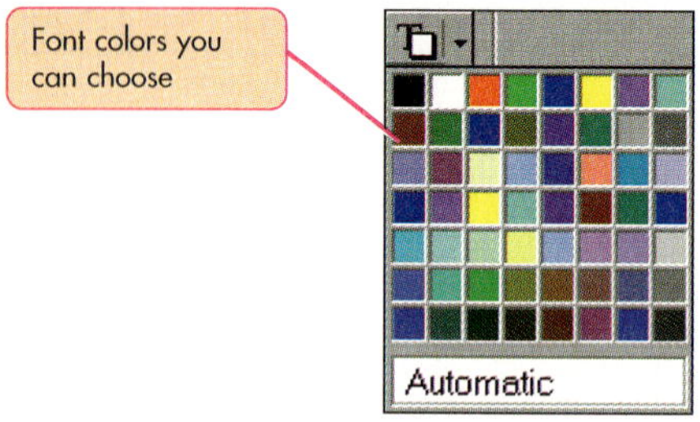

TUTORIAL

In this tutorial you format a table using the buttons on the Formatting toolbar. The model you format is the one that calculates a five-year plan.

Getting Ready

1. Open the *Five-year plan* workbook stored in the *Tutorial Workbooks* folder on the *Excel Student Resource Disk.*

Centering Text across Columns

2. Select cells A5 through F5 and click the **Center Across Columns** button on the Formatting toolbar to center the heading across the selected columns. Click the **Bold** button on the Formatting toolbar to boldface the heading.

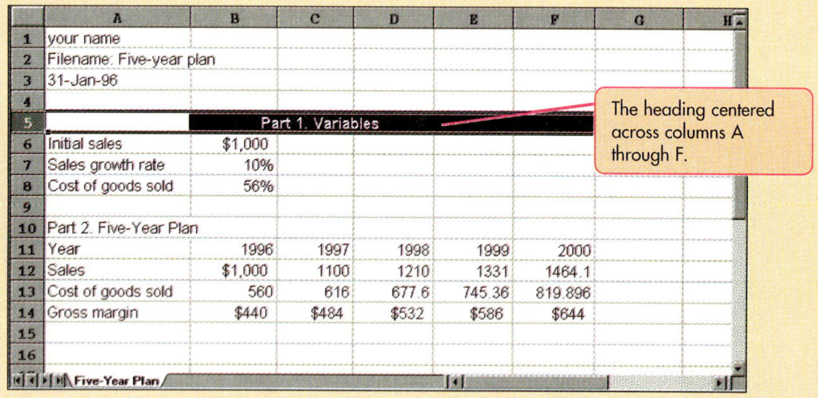

3. Select cells A10 through F10 and click the **Center Across Columns** button on the Formatting toolbar to center the heading across the selected columns. Click the **Bold** button on the Formatting toolbar to boldface the heading.

Formatting Numbers as Currency

4. Select cells B12 through F14 and click the **Currency Style** button on the Formatting toolbar to add dollar signs to the numbers.
5. With cells B12 through F14 still selected, click the **Decrease Decimal** button on the Formatting toolbar twice to remove decimal places from the numbers.

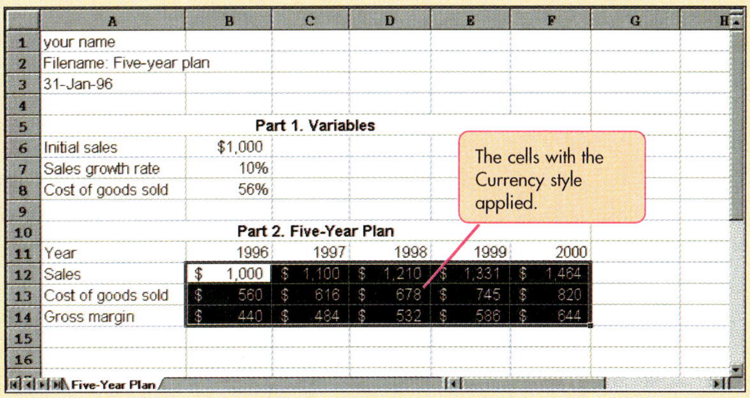

Formatting Numbers with Commas

6. Select cells B13 through F13 and click the **Comma Style** button on the Formatting toolbar to remove dollar signs from the numbers.
7. With cells B13 through F13 still selected, click the **Decrease Decimal** button on the Formatting toolbar twice to remove decimal places from the numbers but retain the commas that separate thousands.

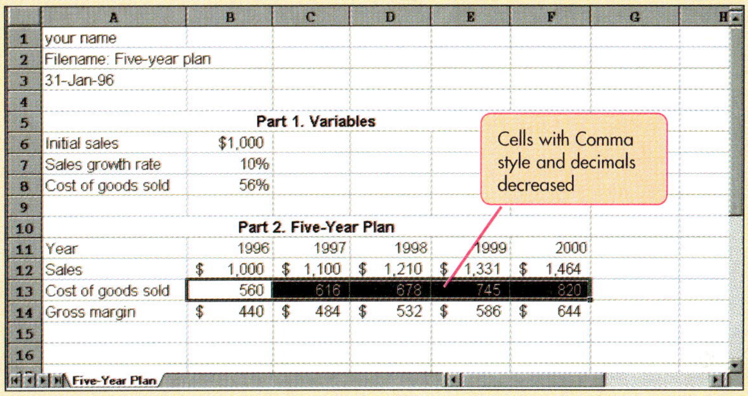

Using Colored Patterns

8. Select cells A5 through F5 and click the **Color** drop-down arrow (▾) on the Formatting toolbar to display a palette of colors.

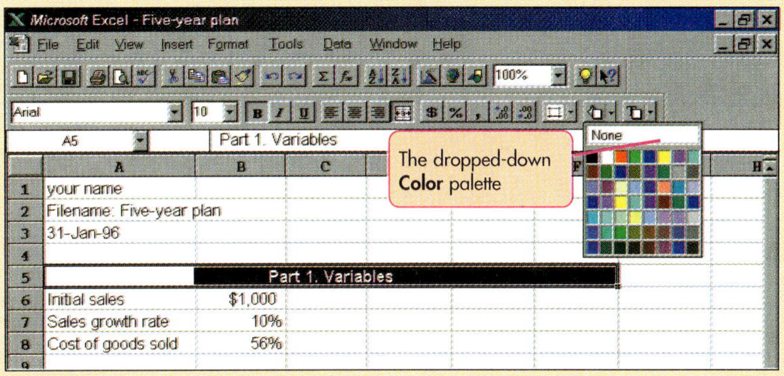

9. Click the leftmost color on the bottom row (a dark blue color) to format the selected cells. (In this and the following steps, you might want to click outside of the formatted area to see your results when they are not selected.)
10. Select cells A10 through F10 and press F4 to repeat the format command.

11. Select cells A6 through F8 and click the **Color** drop-down arrow (▾) on the Formatting toolbar to display a palette of colors.
12. Click the rightmost color on the top row (a light blue) to format the selected cells.
13. Select cells A11 through F14 and click the **Repeat** button on the Standard toolbar to repeat the format command.

Using Colored Text

14. Select cells A5 through F5 and click the **Font Color** drop-down arrow (▾) on the Formatting toolbar to display a palette of colors.

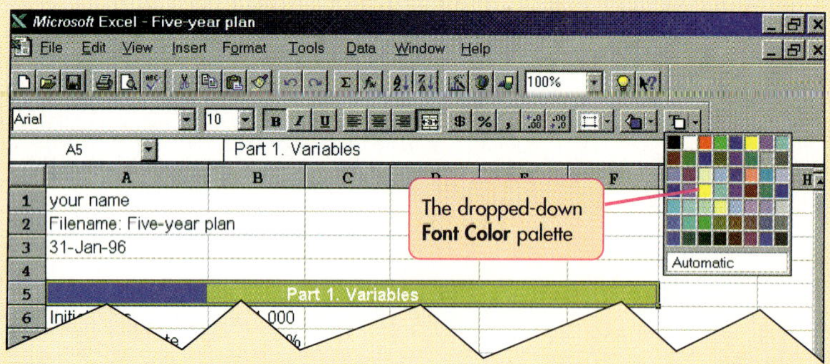

15. Click the second color from the left on the first row (white) to format the selected cells so they display white text against a deep red background.
16. Select cells A10 through F10 and click the **Repeat** button on the Standard toolbar to repeat the format command.

Finishing Up

17. Save, print, and close the workbook. Compare the printout to the screen display to see how various colors have printed.

3-3 FORMATTING TEXT AND NUMBERS USING THE MENU

When you want complete control over cell formats, you use the Format Cells dialog box.

QUICKSTEPS

Formatting Text and Numbers Using the Menu

1. Select the cells you want to format.
2. Pull down the **Format** menu and click the **Cells** command to display the Format Cells dialog box.
3. Choose any of the setting described in the box "Understanding the Format Cells Dialog Box."
4. Click the **OK** command button to apply the selected formats to the cells.

UNDERSTANDING
The Format Cells Dialog Box

When you pull down the **Format** menu and click the **Cells** command, the Format Cells dialog box appears. This dialog box contains six tabs with formats you can apply to the selected cells. To select a tab, click it, and it moves to the front of the pack. Change any settings you want to change, and then click the **OK** command button to apply them to the selected cells.

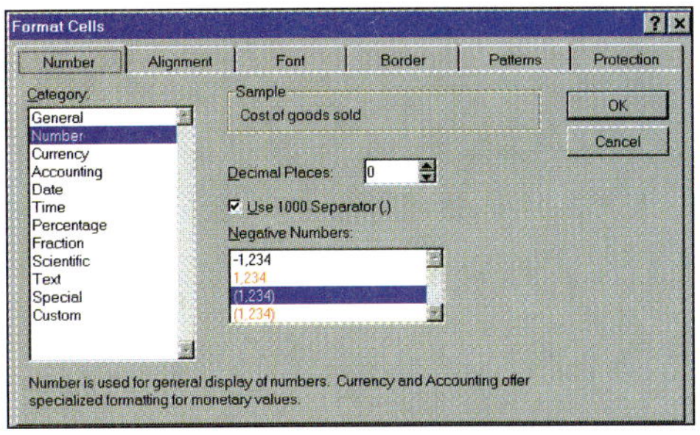

The *Number* tab lists formats you can apply to numbers. Click the desired category of formats in the **Category** list. Choices vary depending on the category you select. In some cases you can select a type with the category, specify decimal places, use a comma to separate thousands, or use dollar signs in front of numbers.

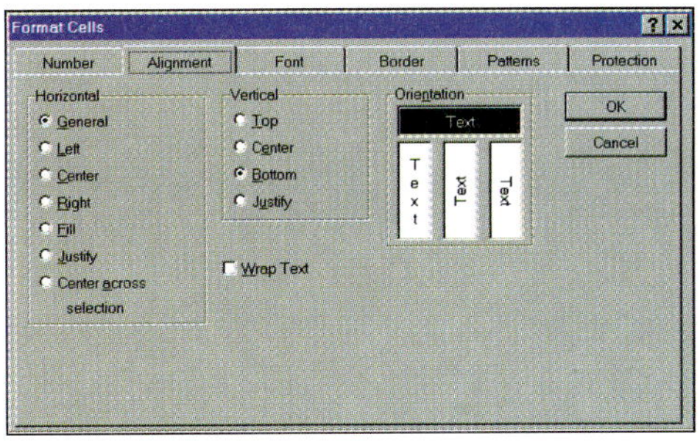

The *Alignment* tab lists horizontal and vertical alignments you can apply to text. Most of these are self-evident, but here are a few you may not already know:

Fill repeats the cell's entry so it fills the entire width of the cell. For example, if you enter / into a cell and apply this format, the cell will display //////.

Justify wraps text wider than the cell to more than one line and expands it so it has even left and right margins.

Wrap Text wraps the text to more than one line in the cell if it is too long to fit in the cell. The row height adjusts automatically to make room for the extra line(s).

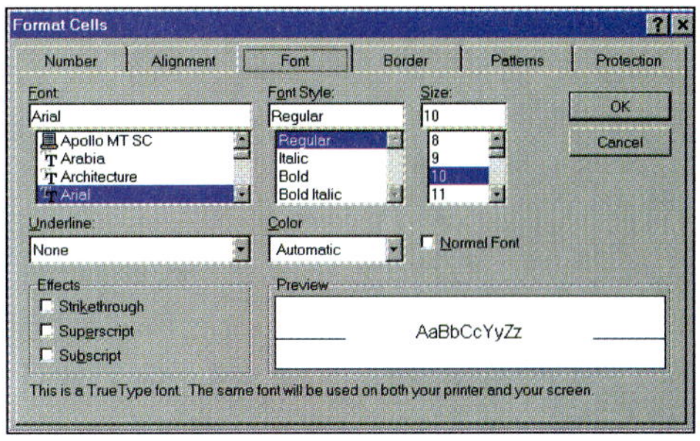

The *Font* tab lists fonts, styles, sizes, and colors that you can apply to text and numbers.

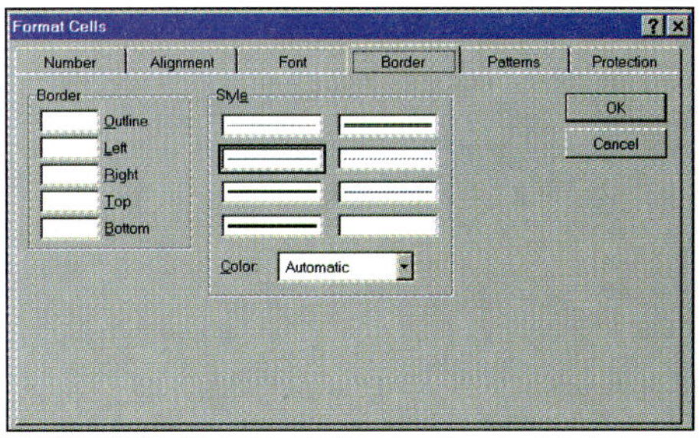

The *Border* tab lists border styles and border colors that you can apply.

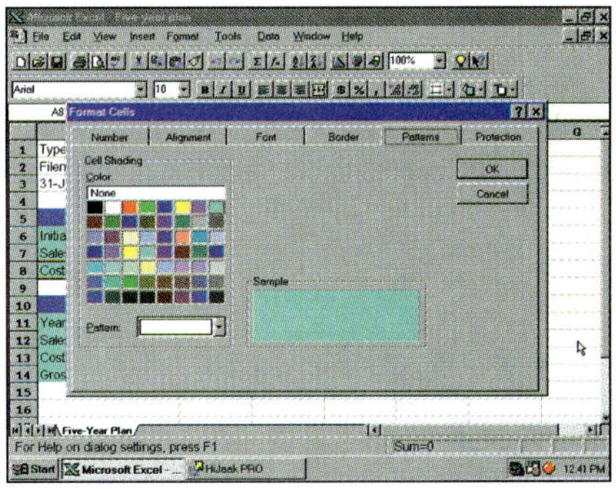

The *Patterns* tab lists background colors and patterns that you can apply.

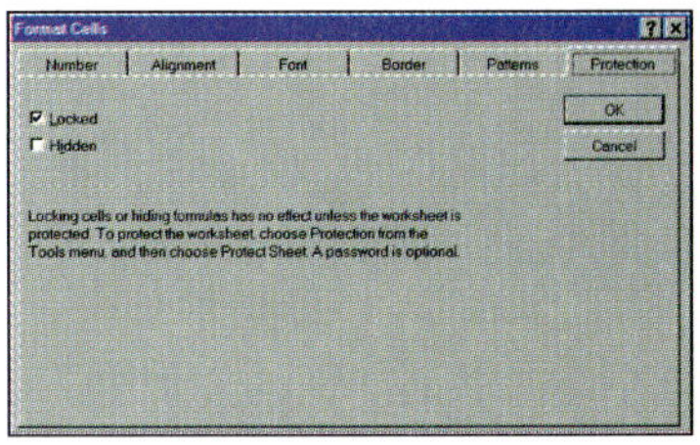

The *Protection* tab locks or unlocks selected cells. When locked, you cannot enter data into them when Protection is turned on. (To turn it on, pull down the **Tools** menu, click the **Protection** command to cascade the menu, and click **Protect Sheet** or **Protect Workbook**.)

TIP
Accounting Formats

Excel's Accounting format for numbers positions the dollar sign at the far left side of the cell, displays negative values in parentheses, and displays zero values as hyphens. This number format is used by the AutoFormat accounting formats and by the **Currency Style** button on the Formatting toolbar. You can also use it by pulling down the **Format** menu and clicking the **Cells** command to display the Format Cells dialog box. Then click the *Number* tab and select *Accounting* on the **Category** list.

TUTORIAL

In this tutorial you format a table using menu commands. The model you format is the one that calculates your budget.

Getting Ready

1. Open the *Budget* workbook stored in the *Tutorial* Workbooks folder on the *Excel Student Resource Disk.*

Formatting Numbers as Currency

2. Select cells B7 through E21, pull down the **Format** menu, and click the **Cells** command to display the Format Cells dialog box.
3. Click the *Number* tab to make it active.
4. Click *Accounting* under the **Category** list to select it. Click the **Decimal Places** spin button to set it to zero and click the **Use $** check box to turn it on.
5. Click the **OK** command button. Some of the numbers are now too large to be displayed in their cells so the cells display pound signs (######) instead.

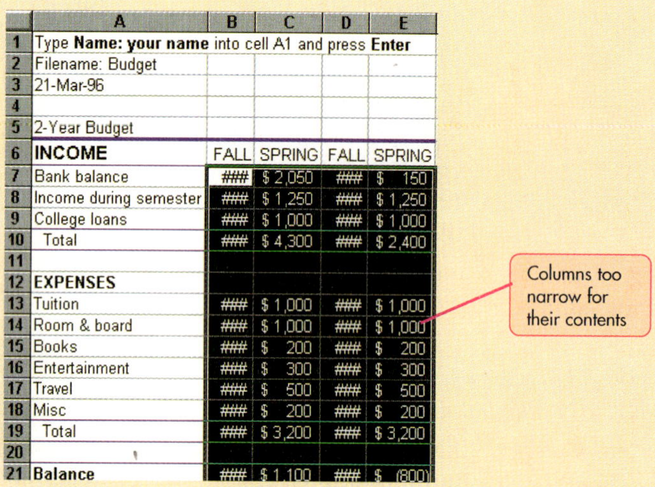

	A	B	C	D	E
1	Type **Name: your name** into cell A1 and press **Enter**				
2	Filename: Budget				
3	21-Mar-96				
4					
5	2-Year Budget				
6	**INCOME**	FALL	SPRING	FALL	SPRING
7	Bank balance	###	$ 2,050	###	$ 150
8	Income during semester	###	$ 1,250	###	$ 1,250
9	College loans	###	$ 1,000	###	$ 1,000
10	Total	###	$ 4,300	###	$ 2,400
11					
12	**EXPENSES**				
13	Tuition	###	$ 1,000	###	$ 1,000
14	Room & board	###	$ 1,000	###	$ 1,000
15	Books	###	$ 200	###	$ 200
16	Entertainment	###	$ 300	###	$ 300
17	Travel	###	$ 500	###	$ 500
18	Misc	###	$ 200	###	$ 200
19	Total	###	$ 3,200	###	$ 3,200
20					
21	**Balance**	###	$ 1,100	###	$ (800)

6. With the cells still selected, pull down the **Format** menu, point to the **Column** command to cascade the menu, then click the **AutoFit Selection** command to automatically adjust column widths.

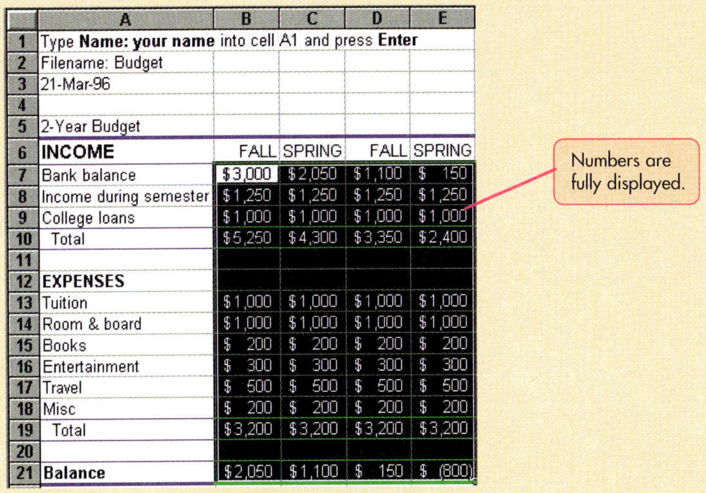

	A	B	C	D	E
1	Type **Name: your name** into cell A1 and press **Enter**				
2	Filename: Budget				
3	21-Mar-96				
4					
5	2-Year Budget				
6	**INCOME**	FALL	SPRING	FALL	SPRING
7	Bank balance	$3,000	$2,050	$1,100	$ 150
8	Income during semester	$1,250	$1,250	$1,250	$1,250
9	College loans	$1,000	$1,000	$1,000	$1,000
10	Total	$5,250	$4,300	$3,350	$2,400
11					
12	**EXPENSES**				
13	Tuition	$1,000	$1,000	$1,000	$1,000
14	Room & board	$1,000	$1,000	$1,000	$1,000
15	Books	$ 200	$ 200	$ 200	$ 200
16	Entertainment	$ 300	$ 300	$ 300	$ 300
17	Travel	$ 500	$ 500	$ 500	$ 500
18	Misc	$ 200	$ 200	$ 200	$ 200
19	Total	$3,200	$3,200	$3,200	$3,200
20					
21	**Balance**	$2,050	$1,100	$ 150	$ (800)

Formatting Numbers with Commas

7. Select cells B8 through E9, pull down the **Format** menu, and click the **Cells** command to display the Format Cells dialog box. The *Number* tab should still be displayed and the *Accounting* category still selected.
8. Click the **Use $** check box to turn it off, and then click the **OK** command button.
9. Select cells B14 through E18 and click the **Repeat** button on the Standard toolbar to repeat the command.

Aligning Text

10. Select cells B6 through E6, pull down the **Format** menu, and click the **Cells** command to display the Format Cells dialog box.
11. Click the *Alignment* tab to make it active.

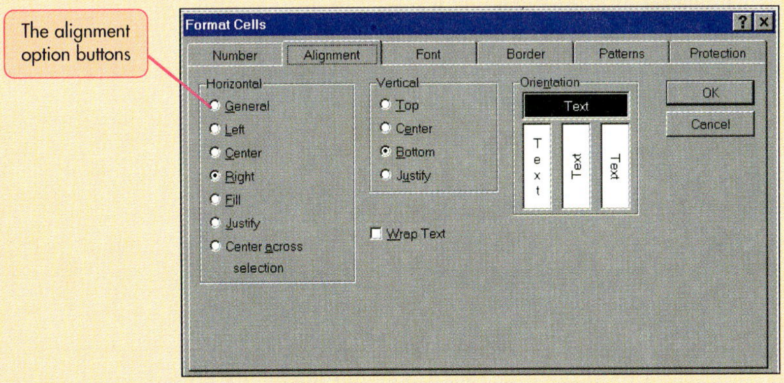

12. Click the **Center** option button under the *Horizontal* heading to turn it on (◉), then click the **OK** command button.

Finishing Up

13. Save, print, and close the workbook.

3-4 COPYING FORMATS

Excel's Format Painter allows you to quickly copy the format from one cell to any other cells.

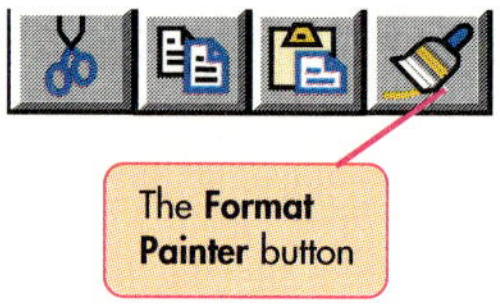

QUICKSTEPS

Copying Formats

Copying Formats to a Single Range

1. Select the cell that has the format you want to copy.
2. Click the **Format Painter** button on the Standard toolbar, and a paintbrush appears on the mouse pointer.
3. Select the range you want to apply the copied format to. When you release the mouse button, the paintbrush disappears from the mouse pointer.

Copying Formats to Multiple Ranges

1. Select the cell that has the format you want to copy.
2. Double-click the **Format Painter** button on the Standard toolbar, and a paintbrush appears on the mouse pointer.
3. Select the ranges you want to apply the copied format to. When you release the mouse button after painting each range, the paintbrush remains on the mouse pointer.
4. Click the **Format Painter** button on the Standard toolbar to turn it ff.

TUTORIAL

In this tutorial you copy formats from one range to another. The model you format is one designed to demonstrate the effects of these commands and others.

Getting Ready

1. Open the *Deleting and clearing* workbook stored in the *Tutorial Workbooks* folder on the *Excel Student Resource Disk* and enter your name into cell A1.

Copying Formats

2. Click cell A5 to select it, then click the **Format Painter** button on the Standard toolbar. The mouse pointer now has a paintbrush attached to it.

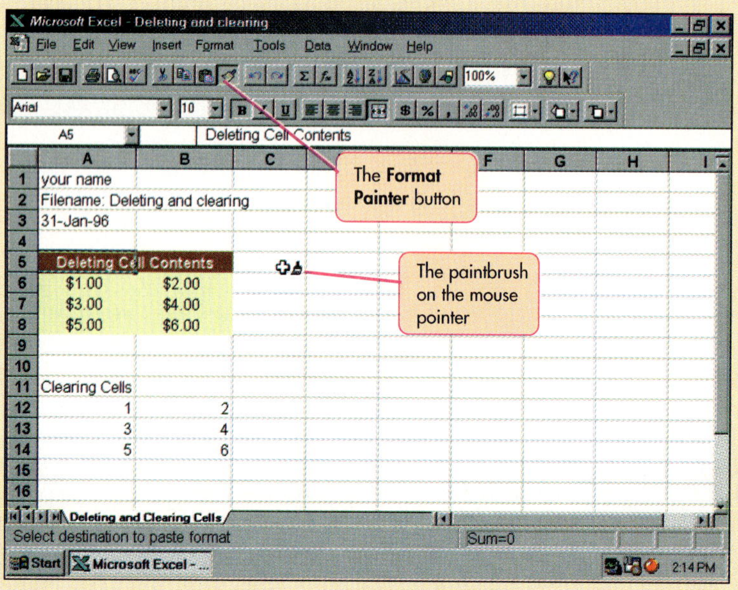

3. Select cells A11 through B11 and then release the mouse button to copy the format to those cells.

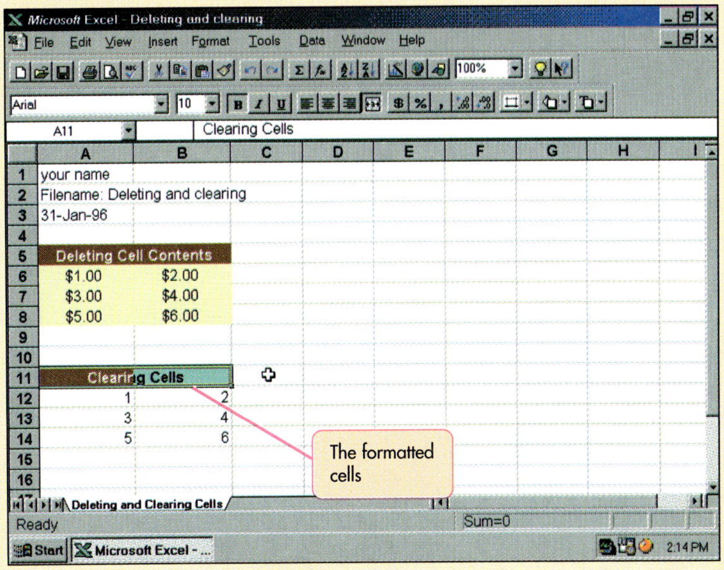

4. Click cell A6 to select it, then click the **Format Painter** button on the Standard toolbar. The mouse pointer again has a paintbrush attached to it.
5. Select cells A12 through B14 and then release the mouse button to copy the format to those cells.

Finishing Up

6. Save, print, and close the workbook.

3-5 DELETING AND CLEARING CELL CONTENTS

When revising a model, you can delete the contents of cells without deleting formats, or you can clear formats, contents, or both. (To delete the cells themselves, see Section 3-9 "Deleting Rows, Columns, and Cells").

QUICKSTEPS

Deleting and Clearing Cell Contents

- To delete the contents of cells (text, numbers, or formulas), select the cells and press Delete. This does not delete any formats applied to the cell.
- To clear the contents of cells (text, numbers, or formulas), select the cells, click the right mouse button in the highlighted area to display the shortcut menu, and then click the **Clear Contents** command. This does not delete any formats applied to the cell.
- To clear contents, formats, or notes from cells, select the cells, pull down the **Edit** menu and point to the **Clear** command to cascade the menu. Click one of the following:
  - **All** to clear all (formats, contents, and notes)
  - **Formats** to clear just formats
  - **Contents** to clear just contents
  - **Notes** to clear notes. (Notes are beyond the scope of this text.)

In this tutorial you explore the differences between deleting and clearing cells. The model you work on is one designed to demonstrate the effects of these commands and others.

Getting Ready

1. Open the *Deleting and clearing* workbook stored in the *Tutorial Workbooks* folder on the *Excel Student Resource Disk*.

Deleting the Contents of Cells

2. Select cells A6 through B8 and then press Delete to delete their contents.

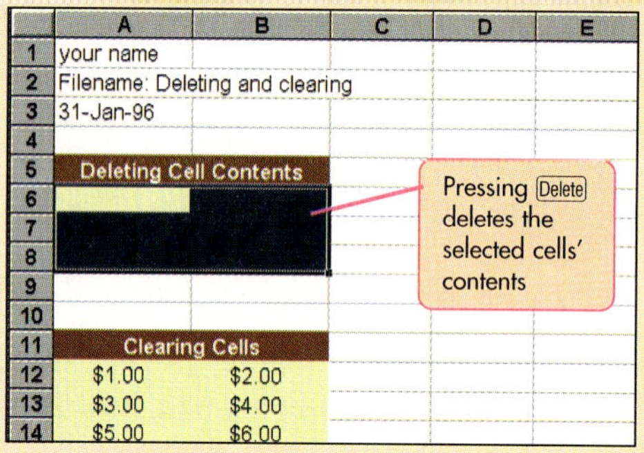

3. Type the numbers **1** through **6** back into the cells in any order and you'll see that the formats for the cell were not deleted along with their contents. All of the numbers are displayed as currency with two decimal places.

Clearing Cell Formats

4. Select cells A12 through B14, pull down the **Edit** menu and point to the **Clear** command to cascade the menu.
5. Click **Formats** to clear just the formats.

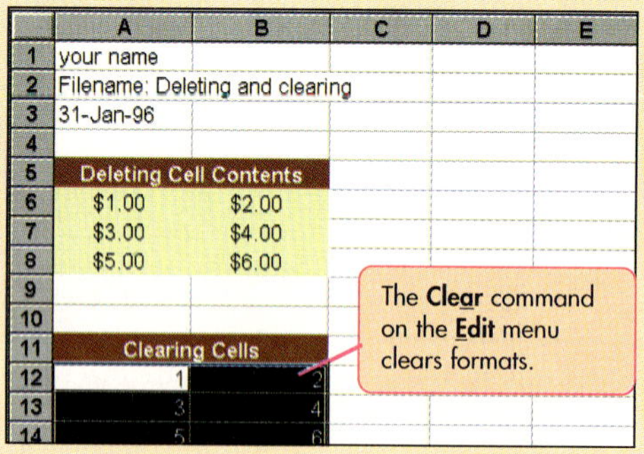

Finishing Up

6. Click the **Print** button on the Standard toolbar to print the sheet.
7. Close the workbook without saving your changes.

Up till now you have printed sheets by clicking the **Print** button on the Standard toolbar. Although fast and easy, this procedure doesn't give you much control over the results. To control your printouts, you need to be familiar with the Print dialog box and page setup commands. However, you can also save a lot of paper if you use the Print Preview command before you print the worksheet to see how the printout will look.

Using Print Preview

You can preview what a worksheet will look like when printed. The advantage of Print Preview is that it lets you catch layout mistakes before wasting time and paper printing the document. In this view, you can also adjust margins and column widths.

QUICKSTEPS

Previewing Printouts

1. Click the **Print Preview** button on the Standard toolbar, or pull down the **File** menu and click the **Print Preview** command.
2. Click any of the buttons described in the box "Understanding the Print Preview Toolbar."
3. Click the **Close** command to return to your previous view of the worksheet.

UNDERSTANDING

The Print Preview Toolbar

When you display the Print Preview toolbar, you have access to the following command buttons.

Next and **Previous** scroll you though the workbook's pages as they will appear when printed. If the worksheet will print on a single sheet, these buttons are dimmed.

Zoom zooms and unzooms the display. You can also do this by clicking the screen with the magnifying-glass-shaped mouse pointer.

Print prints the document.

Setup displays the Page Setup dialog box described below in "Changing Page Setup."

Margins displays handles on the page that you can drag to change margins and column widths.

Close returns you to your previous view of the worksheet.

Using the Print Dialog Box

To print an entire workbook, specific sheets, or a selected block of cells, you use the **Print** command on the **File** menu to display the Print dialog box.

QUICKSTEPS

Printing Workbooks

1. Pull down the **File** menu and click the **Print** command to display the Print dialog box.
2. Change any of the settings described in the box "Understanding the Print Dialog Box."
3. Click the **OK** command button to begin printing.

UNDERSTANDING

The Print Dialog Box

When you pull down the **File** menu and click the **Print** command, the Print dialog box appears. This box allows you to control all aspects of the printout.

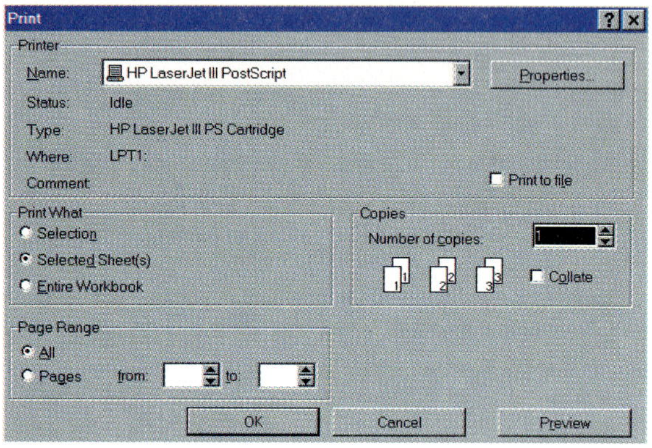

Printer Section

Name drop-down arrow displays a list of printers from which you can choose.

Properties button displays the properties of the printer so you can change its settings.

Print to file check box prints the document to a disk file instead of to the printer.

Print What Section

Normally, the active sheet is printed, but you can print just selected cells or all sheets in the workbook

Selection prints selected cells in selected sheets.

Selected Sheet(s) prints the entire print area in selected sheets.

Entire Workbook prints all sheets in the workbook.

Copies Section

Copies specifies the number of copies to be printed.

Collate check box arranges pages in order when on and multiple copies are printed.

Page Range Section

All prints all pages of the selected sheets.

Pages prints only the specified pages of the selected sheets. You enter the first page to print in the **From** text box and the last page in the **To** text box.

Command Buttons

Preview displays the document on the screen just the way it will look when printed. Use this command to check layout and click the **Next** or **Previous** command buttons to page through the worksheet. After you've done this, page breaks (the places where new pages begin) are shown on the sheet with dotted gridlines. These same gridlines appear after you have printed a document once.

OK prints the document with the current settings.

Managing Print Jobs

When you print a worksheet, you may want to check its status, pause it, or even cancel it. You can do so using the printer icon in the notification area on Windows' taskbar.

QUICKSTEPS

Managing Print Jobs

1. Do one of the following with the printer icon in the notification area on Windows' taskbar:
   - Double-click the printer icon.
   - Right-click the printer icon and then click the shortcut menu's **Open Active Printers** command.
2. Use any of the commands described in the box "Understanding the Printer's Dialog Box."

UNDERSTANDING

The Printer's Dialog Box

When you display the dialog box for the printer you are using, its name appears on the title bar. You can use any of the dialog box's commands to manage your print jobs.

Printer Menu

Pause Printing pauses all print jobs on the current printer. You have to click the command a second time to resume printing.

Purge Print Jobs cancels all jobs waiting to be printed.

Set as Default makes the current printer the default printer for your system.

Properties displays a dialog box where you can change the properties of your printer. For example, you can change the printing mode from portrait (normal) to landscape (text printed lengthwise on the page) or back again.

Close closes the dialog box.

Document Menu

Pause Printing pauses the printing of the document highlighted on the list. You have to click the command a second time to resume printing.

Cancel Printing cancels the printing of the document highlighted on the list.

View Menu

Status Bar turns the dialog box's status bar on or off.

Changing Page Setup

To change the orientation of the printed page, change margins, add headers and footers, or turn gridlines and row and column headings on or off, you have to change the page setup.

TIP

Landscape Orientation

With Excel it's easy to print a document on most laser printers across either the width or length of the page. The direction is called the orientation, and it can be either portrait or landscape. *Portrait orientation* is that of a normal printout—that is, text is printed across the width of the page. *Landscape orientation* rotates the printout 90 degrees so that it is printed along the length of the page. This orientation is useful when you are printing wide models.

QUICKSTEPS

Changing Page Setup

1. Pull down the **File** menu and click the **Page Setup** command.
2. Change any of the settings described in the box "Understanding Page Setup."
2. When finished, do one of the following:
   - Click the **OK** command button to return to the worksheet.
   - Click the **Print** button to display the Print dialog box so you can print the worksheet or preview the changes.
   - Click the **Cancel** button to cancel any changes you have made.

UNDERSTANDING
Page Setup

When you choose **Page Setup** from the **File** menu or click the Print dialog box's **Page Setup** command button, the Page Setup tabbed dialog box appears. To change aspects of page setup, click the appropriate tab.

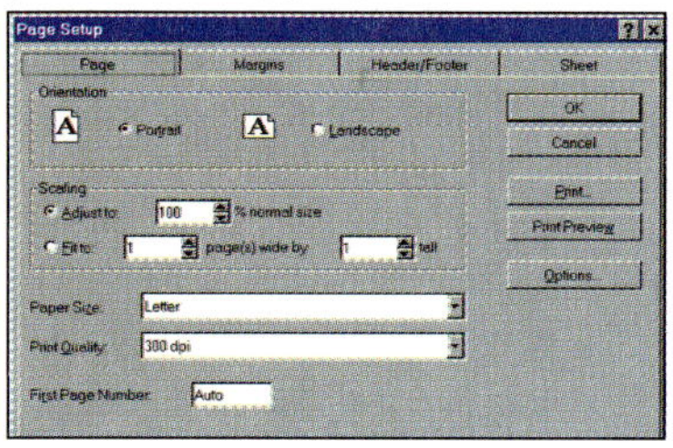

The *Page* tab lists options for paper orientation, scaling, and size. It also allows you to change the page number printed on the first and subsequent pages. One of the unique features on this tab is the **Fit to** spin buttons (⬍) that allow you to specify how many pages the document will be shrunk to. This is most useful when your model is just a little too wide or too long to print on a single sheet.

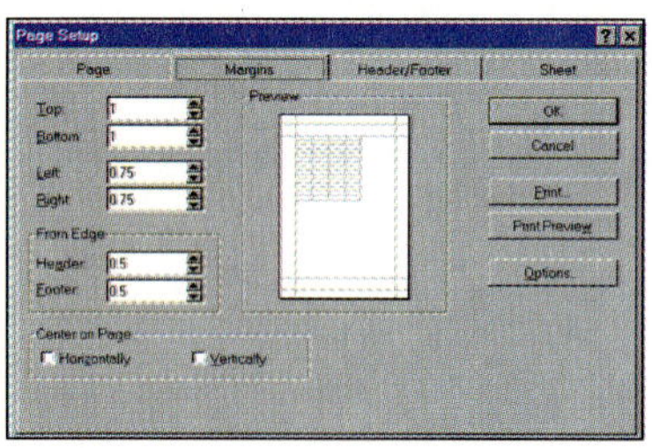

The *Margins* tab lists options for page margins and header and footer spacing. It also contains check boxes you can click to horizontally or vertically center the printout on the page. (You can also change margins by using the **Print Preview** command and then dragging handles on the margins.)

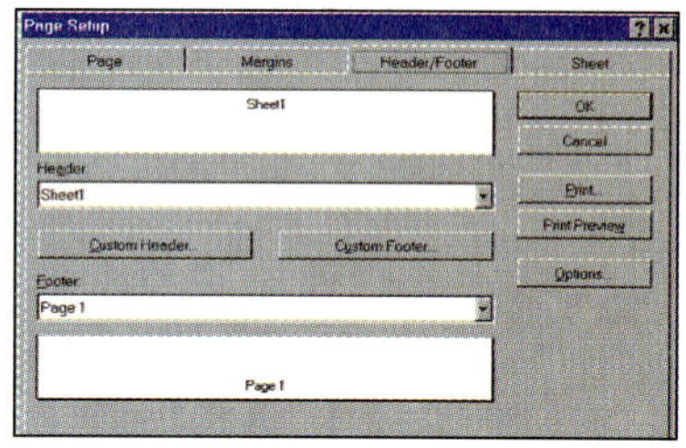

The *Header/Footer* tab has two drop-down arrows (▾) that display lists from which you can select headers and footers for the printout or create your own. Samples of each are shown above and below the drop-down lists.

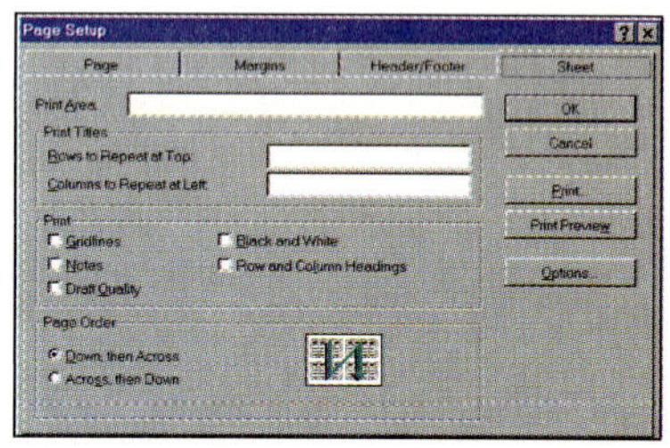

The *Sheet* tab allows you to print the same rows and columns on each page. It also allows you to choose whether gridlines and row and column headings are printed along with the model.

Print Titles are used when a model is too wide or long to print on a single sheet of paper. For example, if you use column A for row titles and print a wide model, column A appears only on the first page of the printout. This makes it hard to identify the contents of the rows on the second and subsequent pages. The same is true if you use row 1 for column titles and print a long model. The titles appear only at the top of the first page. In either case, if you specify that these columns or rows be treated as titles, they are printed on each page of the printout. To set print titles, click in the **Rows to Repeat at Top** or **Columns to Repeat at Left** text boxes and then select the rows or columns that you want to repeat.

TIP

Turning Gridlines and Row and Column Headings On and Off

When you are working on a model, it helps to print gridlines and row and column headings because they guide you in checking your results and troubleshooting any mistakes. However, you may not want to print them on the final printout. The best way to turn them off is to use the Page Setup dialog box's Sheet tab. However, you can also turn them off both on the screen and printout. To do so, pull down the **Tools** menu and click the **Options** command to display the Options dialog box. Click the *View* tab to select it, and then click the **Gridlines** or **Row and Column Headers** check boxes to turn them on (☑) or off (☐).

TUTORIAL

In this tutorial you use page setup commands to change a printout's orientation and gridlines. The model you print is the one you use to forecast a five-year business plan.

Getting Ready

1. Open the *Five-year plan* workbook stored in the *Tutorial Workbooks* folder on the *Excel Student Resource Disk*.

Changing Page Setup

2. Pull down the **File** menu and click the **Page Setup** command to display the Page Setup dialog box.
3. Click the *Margins* tab to select it, and then click the **Horizontally** and **Vertically** check boxes in the *Center on Page* section to turn them on (☑).

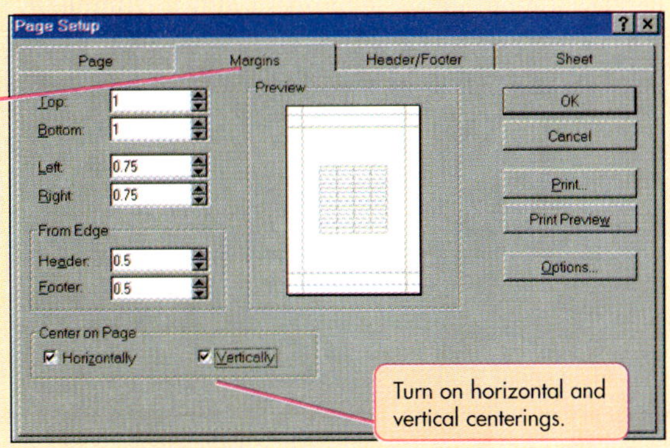

4. Click the *Sheet* tab to select it, and then turn off the **Gridlines** and **Row and Column Headings** check boxes in the Print section.

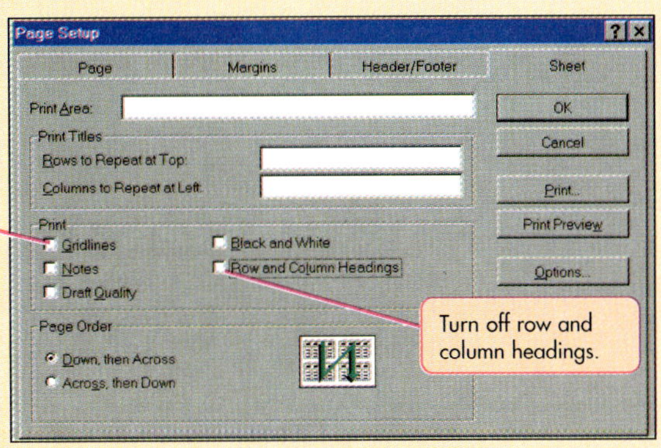

5. Click the *Header/Footer* tab to select it, and then click the **Header** box's drop-down arrow (▾) to display a list of possible headers.

6. Click the header that reads *Page 1 of ?* to select it (you may have to scroll to see it), and a sample is displayed in the box above.

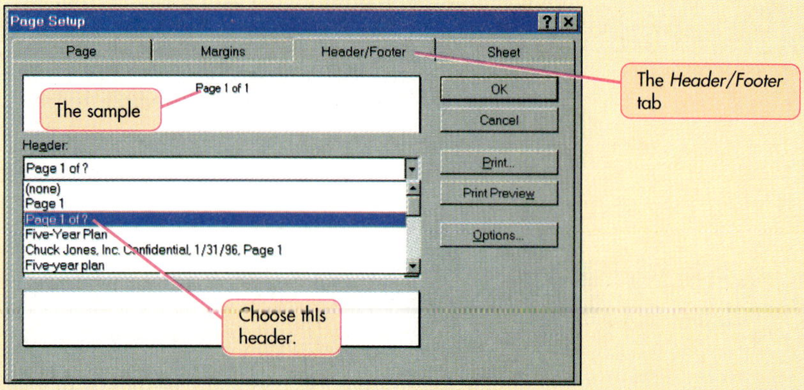

STOP
Does Your Printer Support Landscape Printing?

Step 7 should be completed only if your printer supports landscape printing. If you are not sure, ask. If it doesn't, skip this step and proceed directly to Step 8.

7. If your printer supports landscape printing, click the *Page* tab to select it, and then click the **Landscape** option button to turn it on (◉).

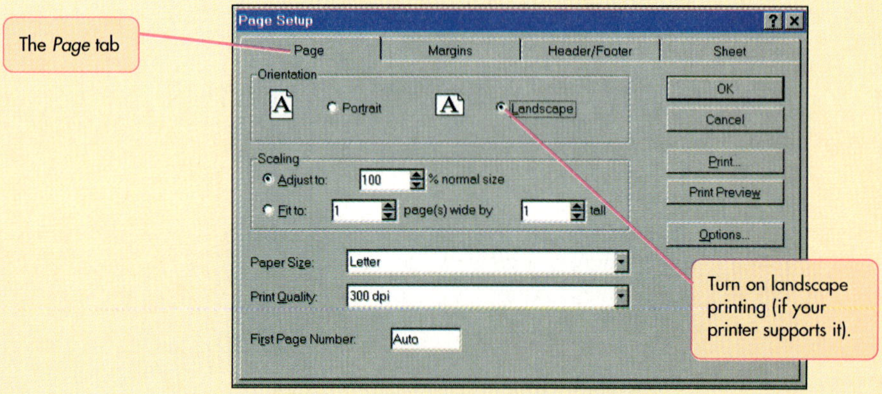

8. Click the **OK** command button to close the dialog box.

9. Click the **Print Preview** button on the Standard toolbar to preview the way the sheet will look when you print it. It's centered on the page which is turned sideways and has a header at the top.

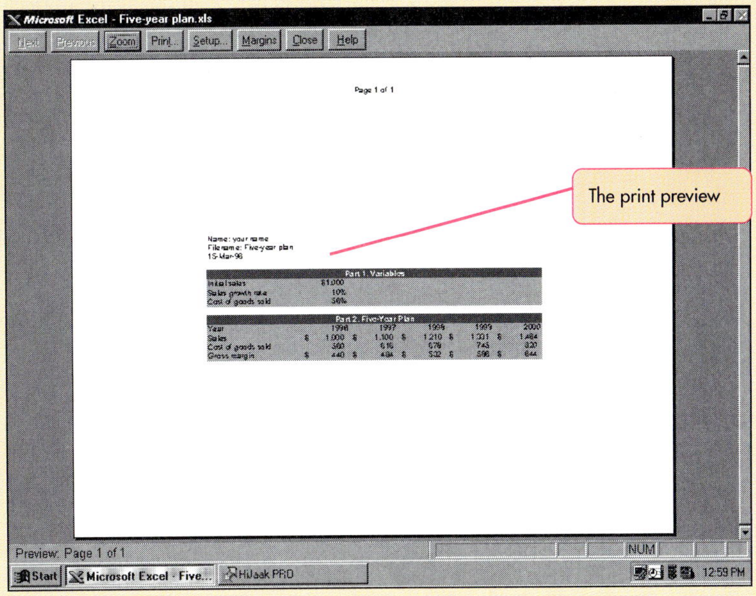

10. Click the **Print** command button on the Preview screen's button bar to display the Print dialog box, then click its **OK** button to print the worksheet.

Printing Row and Column Headers and Gridlines

11. Pull down the **File** menu and click the **Page Setup** command to display the Page Setup dialog box.

12. Click the *Sheet* tab to select it, then click both the **Gridlines** and **Row and Column Headings** check boxes under the Print heading so they have check marks in them (☑) to turn them on.

13. If you changed to landscape orientation in Step 7, click the *Page* tab to select it, then click the **Portrait** option button to turn it on (◉).

14. Click the **Print** command button to display the Print dialog box.

15. Click the **OK** command button to print the worksheet again. Compare this printout with the first one you made to see the effects of the changes you made.

Finishing Up

16. Click the **Save** button on the Standard toolbar to save your changes. Changes to Page Setup are saved along with the workbook.

17. Close the workbook.

3-7 SPELL-CHECKING A WORKSHEET

Excel contains a built-in spelling checker that compares words in your spreadsheet with those in its dictionary. When it finds a word in your spreadsheet that it can't find in its dictionary (the word isn't necessarily misspelled), it highlights the word and displays a list of words you can use to replace it.

QUICKSTEPS

Spell-Checking a Worksheet

1. Select the cells to be spell-checked, or select one cell to spell-check the entire sheet.
2. Click the **Spelling** button on the Standard toolbar, or click pull down the **Tools** menu and click the **Spelling** command to display the Spelling dialog box. If you select one cell, the sheet is checked from that cell down, and then a dialog box asks *Continue checking at beginning of sheet?* Click **Yes** to continue or **No** to close the Spelling dialog box.
3. When a word is found that isn't in the dictionary, it is listed following the *Not in Dictionary* heading. A list of possible replacement words is displayed in the **Suggestions** list, and the word Excel believes to be the most likely replacement is shown in the **Change To** box. To replace the word in the workbook with the word in the **Change To** box, click the **Change** command button. You can also use any of the commands described in the Box "Understanding the Spelling Dialog Box."
4. When a message box reads *Finished spell checking entire sheet,* click the **OK** button.

UNDERSTANDING

The Spellling Dialog Box

When you use Excel's built-in spelling checker, the following options are available in the Spelling dialog box:

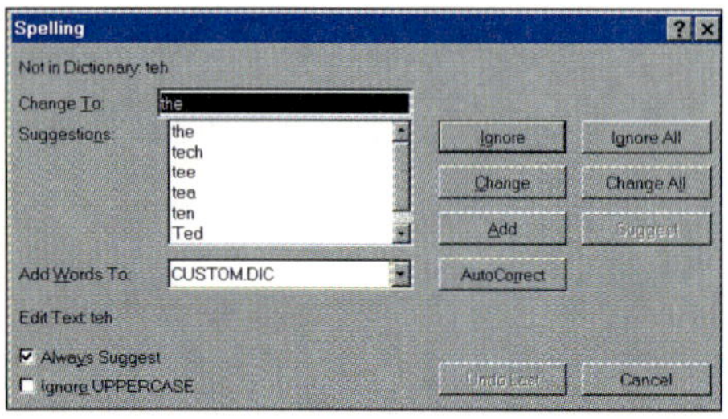

- **Change To** text box lists the word that Excel thinks you should use as the replacement. If you select another word from the **Suggestions** list, then that word is listed. To edit the entry displayed in this box, click the box to move the insertion point there, or press ← or → to remove the highlight from the current entry. Then edit the entry and click the **Change** command button to replace the word in the document with the edited word. If the edited word isn't in the dictionary, a dialog box tells you it isn't in the dictionary and asks *Change anyway?* Click **Yes** to change it.
- **Suggestions** list displays words that Excel thinks are possible replacements for the highlighted word.
- **Add Words To** drop-down list lets you select the dictionary that you add correctly spelled words to so they aren't flagged again.
- **Always suggest** check box, when on, has Excel always list words in the Suggestions lists.
- **Ignore UPPERCASE** check box, when on, tells Excel to skip words that contain only capital letters, such as RAM or ROM.
- **Ignore** leaves the currently highlighted term unchanged, and **Ignore All** does the same for the current and all subsequent occurrences.
- **Change** changes the term in the worksheet to the word currently in the **Change To** text box. **Change All** does the same and also changes any other occurrences in the worksheet.
- **Add** adds the highlighted word to the dictionary listed in the **Add Words To** box. When added, it won't be highlighted again in this or any other workbook.
- **Suggest** displays a list of suggested words when the **Always suggest** check box is off.
- **AutoCorrect** adds the word to the AutoCorrect list so Excel can correct it automatically as you type.

IN this tutorial you check and correct the spelling in a model. The model you spell-check is the one that calculates a grade point average.

Getting Ready

1. Open the *Grade point average* workbook stored in the *Tutorial Workbooks* folder on the *Excel Student Resource Disk.*

Spell-Checking the Worksheet

2. Select cell A1, then click the **Spelling** button on the Standard toolbar to begin spell-checking the document.

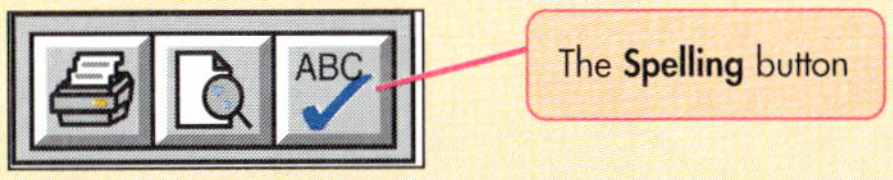

3. When Excel finds a word that is not in its dictionary (such as your name), it displays the Spelling dialog box. The "misspelled" word is displayed following the *Not in Dictionary* heading. A list of possible replacement words is displayed in the **Suggestions** window. The word that Excel thinks is the most likely choice is displayed in the **Change To** text box. (Remember you can grab the dialog box by the title bar and drag it out of the way if it hides the word it has highlighted.)
4. Click the **Change** command button to accept one of Excel's suggestions or click the **Ignore** command button to leave the word unchanged and continue spell-checking. (For help, see the table "Correcting Spelling.") A dialog box tells you spell-checking is finished.

Correcting Spelling

Highlighted Word	Action
your name	Ignore
Biologi	Change to *Biology*
Englsh	Change to *English*
Microcompoters	Change to *Microcomputers*
avarage	Change to *average*
GPA	Ignore

5. When a message box reads *Finished spell checking entire sheet,* click the **OK** command button. (Notice how the spelling checker did not find the word *Grad* in cell A11 that should read *Grade.* The word is spelled correctly; it's just the wrong word.)

Finishing Up

6. Save, print, and close the workbook.

3-8 INSERTING ROWS, COLUMNS, AND CELLS

Often you may find it necessary to insert rows or columns into the middle of an existing model. You can do this easily, and all formulas automatically adjust so that they continue to refer to the correct cells. If rows, columns, or cells are inserted within a range referred to by a formula, the range expands to include the new rows or columns. If rows or columns are inserted on the edge of the range, they are not included.

To insert rows, columns, or cells, you must select the adjoining area to tell Excel where the insertion should be made. The contents of the selected cells are not affected, but the cells move down or to the right to make room for the inserted cells.

QUICKSTEPS

Inserting Rows, Columns, and Cells

- To insert a single row or column, select the row above or the column to the right of where you want the insertion. Then pull down the **Insert** menu and click the **Rows** or **Columns** command.
- To insert multiple rows or columns, select the row above or the column to the right of where you want the insertion. Then extend the selection so you have selected as many rows or columns as you want inserted. Pull down the **Insert** menu and click **Rows** or **Columns** command.
- To insert cells, select a range the same size and in the same position as the one you want inserted. Then pull down the **Insert** menu and click the **Cells** command to display the Insert dialog box. Click one of the following option buttons to turn it on, (◉) and then click the **OK** command button to insert the cells:

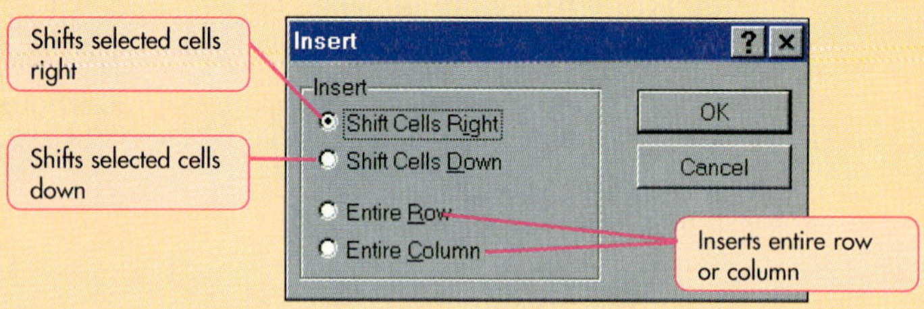

  - **Shift Cells Right** to insert the cells and have the currently selected cells move to the right to make room for the new cells.
  - **Shift Cells Down** to insert the cells and have the currently selected cells move down to make room for the new cells.
  - **Entire Row** to insert entire rows.
  - **Entire Column** to insert entire columns.

TIP
Using the Shortcut Menu

After selecting rows, columns, or cells, you can click with the right mouse button in the selected area to display a shortcut menu. You then click the menu's **Insert** command to insert rows, columns, or cells.

UNDERSTANDING
Inserting Cells

When you insert cells into a worksheet, Excel guesses whether you want the selected cells shifted down or to the right to make room for the inserted cells. You can accept the program's guess or click another choice.

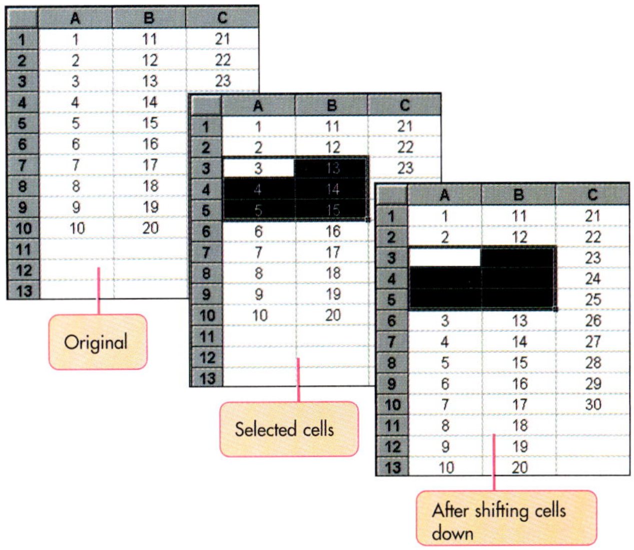

TUTORIAL

In this tutorial you insert rows to expand the model that calculates grade point averages. This allows you to add additional courses as you progress closer to a degree.

Getting Ready

1. Open the *Grade point average* workbook stored in the *Tutorial Workbooks* folder on the *Excel Student Resource Disk.*

Inserting Rows

2. Click the row heading for row 10 to select the entire row, pull down the **Insert** menu, and click the **Rows** command to insert one row.
3. Press Ctrl+` to display formulas in the cells instead of calculated results. Notice how the functions in cells B11 and E11 have not adjusted their ranges to include the new row. This is because the row you selected was at the bottom of the previous range.
4. Edit the function in cell B11 so it reads =SUM(B7:B10). Then edit the function in cell E11 to read =SUM(E7:E10).

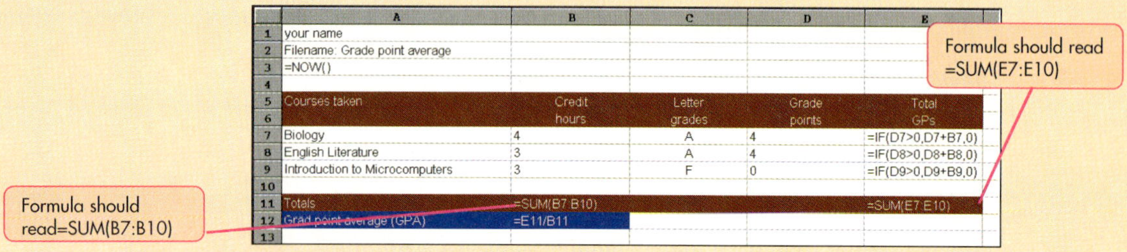

LOOKING AHEAD

SUM Function

Adding a row or column of numbers is easy when you use the SUM function. This function is entered using its name and the range of the cells to be added. For example, to add a column of cells entered between cells B7 and B10, you would enter the function **=SUM(B7:B10)**. The colon separates the first and last cell in the range of cells to be added.

5. Using the row headings, select the entire rows 10 through 15.
6. Right-click in the highlighted area to display a shortcut menu and click the Insert command to insert six rows. Notice how the functions have correctly adjusted their ranges to include the new rows. This is because the first row you selected was included in the previous range.

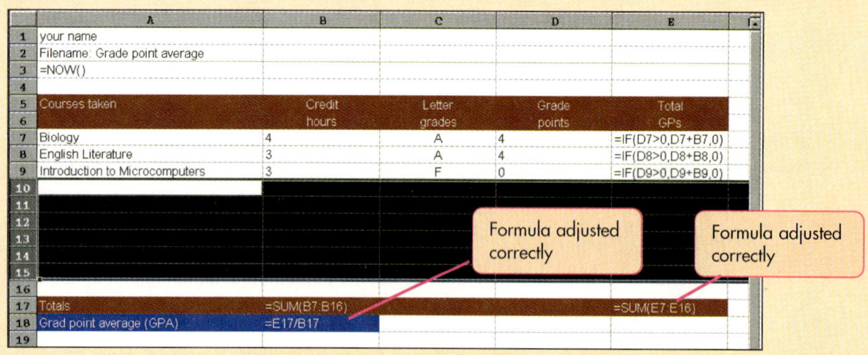

7. Press Ctrl+` to display calculated results in the cells instead of formulas.

Finishing Up

8. Save, print, and close the workbook.

3-9 DELETING ROWS, COLUMNS, AND CELLS

Deleting rows, columns, or cells has almost the same effect as inserting them. The worksheet closes up, and all formulas automatically adjust to refer to the correct cells.

There is one exception to the way formulas automatically adjust. If you delete any cells that remaining formulas refer to, those formulas display error values. For this reason, it is wise to save a workbook before making deletions. After making deletions, check to see if any error values (especially #REF!) appear in the cells. If you have any doubts, click the **Undo** button on the Standard toolbar or save the worksheet under a new filename so that you do not store it on top of, and erase, the original version.

If you do not delete the upper-left or lower-right corner of a range referred to by a formula, the range contracts or expands to accommodate the change. If these corners are deleted, the range is erased. If any formulas or functions refer to the range, they display a #REF! error value.

QUICKSTEPS

Deleting Rows, Columns, and Cells

- To delete rows or columns, first select the rows or columns to be deleted. Then pull down the **Edit** menu and click the **Delete** command. (Immediately click the **Undo** button on the button bar if you think you may have made a mistake.)
- To delete cells, first select the range to be deleted. Then pull down the **Edit** menu and click the **Delete** command. If you have selected a range of cells rather than a range of rows or columns, the Delete dialog box appears. Click one of the following option buttons and then click the **OK** command button:
  - **Shift Cells Left** to delete the cells and have those to the right move left to fill the deleted area.
  - **Shift Cells Up** to delete the cells and have those below move up to fill the deleted area.
  - **Entire Row** to delete the entire row.
  - **Entire Column** to delete the entire column.

COMMON WRONG TURNS

Whoops, Where Did My Budget Go?

When you delete a row or column, you delete it entirely, including any data that it contains. If some data aren't currently displayed on the screen, you may not even know you deleted them by mistake until later when you need them. A good way to check for unseen data in a row or column is to select a cell in the row of column to be deleted and press End and then one of the arrow keys. This shoots the selected cell along the row or column out to the boundary of the sheet unless it encounters data along the way.

Experienced model builders take this problem into consideration when they lay out a model. Sections are added stepwise rather than side by side or one above another. This way rows or columns can be deleted in one section without deleting them in another.

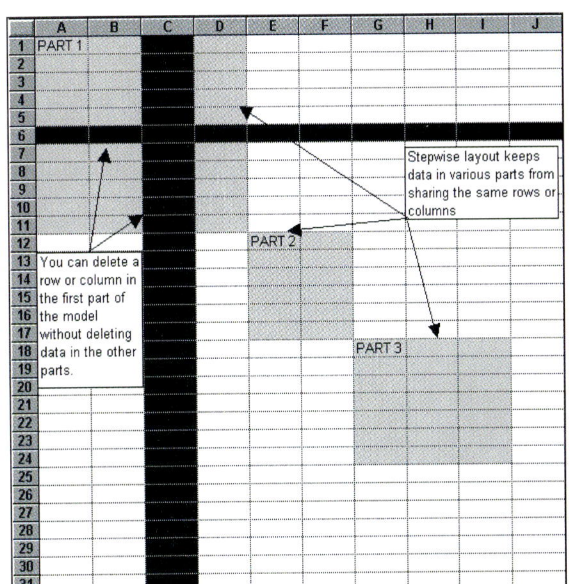

In this tutorial you delete rows in the model that calculates grade point averages. The purpose here is to just see how it's done. You then undo the changes and close the model without saving it.

Getting Ready

1. Open the *Grade point average* workbook stored in the *Tutorial Workbooks* folder on the *Excel Student Resource Disk.*

Deleting and Undeleting Rows

2. Press Ctrl+` to display formulas in the cells instead of calculated results.
3. Using the row headings, select the entire rows 10 through 16, pull down the **Edit** menu, and click the **Delete** command to delete the selected rows. Notice how the functions in cells B10 and E10 have adjusted their ranges.

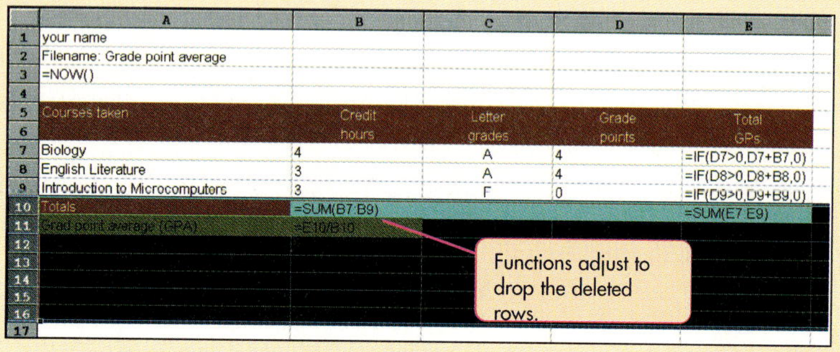

4. Click the **Undo** button on the Standard toolbar to undo the deletion.
5. Click the **Undo** button on the Standard toolbar again to redo the deletion.
6. Press Ctrl+` to display calculated results in the cells instead of formulas.

Finishing Up

7. Close the workbook without saving your changes.

3-10 MOVING DATA

You can move the contents of cells to other locations on the worksheet. Moving allows you to reorganize models as you create or revise them. To begin, you first select the cells you want to move. You then drag the selected cells' contents to a new location or cut them to Windows' Clipboard so you can paste them elsewhere in the workbook. Because they remain on the Clipboard until you cut (or copy) other cells or exit Windows, you can paste them in more than one place.

To insert moved cells among existing cells so the existing cells move aside to make room for them, right-drag them. When you release them, a shortcut menu appears that lets you choose which direction the existing cells shift. You can also hold down Shift while you drag and release them. When you point to the area where you want to insert the dragged cells, the mouse pointer turns into a horizontal or vertical I-beam shape (I). When vertical, the cells to the right move to the right to make room for the dragged cells. When horizontal, the cells below move down to make room.

When you move a range of cells, a duplicate of the cells' contents and formats is moved to the target range, and then the contents of the cells in the source range are automatically deleted.

- If the cells in the target range contain any data, a dialog box asks you if you want to replace the contents of the destination cells. If you choose to do so, the contents of the destination cells are overwritten, and the old data are lost.
- All formulas pasted into a new position will continue to refer to the same cells they referred to before they were cut.
- If any formulas refer to cells in the target range, they display the error value #REF!.

QUICKSTEPS

Moving by Dragging and Dropping

1. Select the cells to be moved.
2. Point to the border around them, and the mouse pointer will turn into an arrow.
3. Do one of the following:
   - Drag the outline of the cells to where you want it, and release the mouse button.
   - Right-drag the outline of the cells to where you want it, and release the mouse button to display a shortcut menu. Click one of the move commands.

QUICKSTEPS

Moving by Cutting and Pasting

1. Select the cells to be moved.
2. To move the data to the Clipboard, click the **Cut** button on the Standard toolbar or do any of the following:
   - Right-click the selected cells and click the shortcut menu's **Cut** command.
   - Pull down the **Edit** menu and click the **Cut** command.
   - Press Shift+Delete.

   The selected cells are highlighted by a moving border and the status line reads *Select destination and press ENTER or choose Paste.*
3. Select the cell that will be in the upper-left corner of the range of cells to be pasted in.
4. To paste in the data from the Clipboard, click the **Paste** button on the toolbar or do any of the following:
   - Right-click the cell that will be in the upper-left corner of the range of cells to be pasted in and click the shortcut menu's **Paste** command.
   - Pull down the **Edit** menu and click the **Paste** command.
   - Press Enter.
   - Press Shift+Insert.

   The cells highlighted by the moving border are moved to the new location.

In this tutorial you move data from one part of a model to another. The model you use is the one that calculates a five-year plan.

Getting Ready

1. Open the *Five-year plan* workbook stored in the *Tutorial Workbooks* folder on the *Excel Student Resource Disk*.

Moving a Range with Menu Commands

2. Select the range of cells from A5 to F14, pull down the **Edit** menu and click the **Cut** command. The selection is outlined with a moving border.

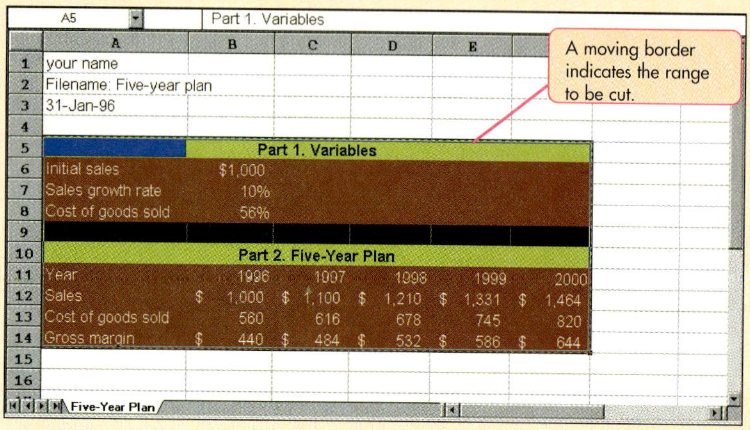

3. Select cell A6, pull down the **Edit** menu and click the **Paste** command. The entire selected area is moved down one row. Check the formulas in the moved cells, and you'll find that they have all automatically adjusted and still refer to the correct cells.

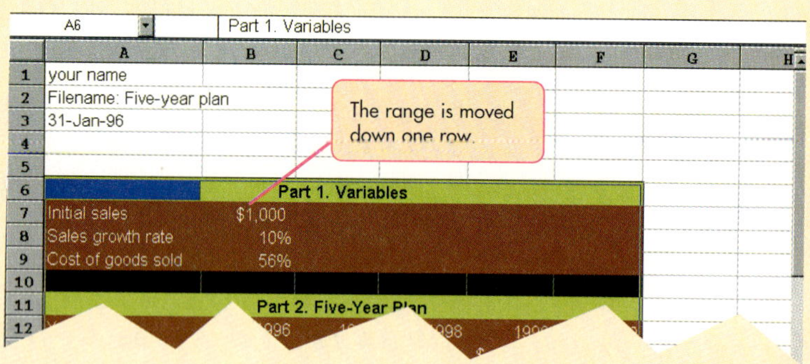

Moving a Range with Toolbar Buttons

4. Select the range of cells from A6 to F15 and click the **Cut** button on the Standard toolbar. The selection is outlined with a moving border.
5. Select cell A5 and click the **Paste** button on the Standard toolbar. The selection is moved back up one row.

Finishing Up

6. Close the workbook without saving your changes.

REVIEW QUESTIONS

TRUE-FALSE

T F **1.** Before using the AutoFormat feature, you must always select the area you want formatted.

T F **2.** The font size determines the height and width of characters.

T F **3.** To change the size of the font in selected cells, click the **Font** drop-down arrow on the Formatting toolbar.

T F **4.** You can add or subtract decimal places from selected numbers just by clicking buttons on the Formatting toolbar.

T F **5.** When formatting text using the **Center Across Columns** command, the text remains in the rightmost column.

T F **6.** To format numbers with menu commands, pull down the **Format** menu and click the **Cells** command.

T F **7.** To copy formats from one cell to another, you use the **Copy** and **Paste** buttons on the toolbar.

T F **8.** You can clear formats of cells without deleting the contents.

T F **9.** The best way to check the layout of your page is to print the document.

T F **10.** To cancel a print job before it is finished, you begin by double-clicking the printer icon on Windows' taskbar.

MULTIPLE CHOICE

1. ________ mode is the orientation of a normal printout.

a. Landscape b. Portrait
c. Snapshot d. Picture

2. ________ are used when a model is too wide or long to print on a single sheet of paper.

a. Print outlines b. Print profiles
c. Print titles d. Gridlines

3. If a column is not wide enough to display a value, ________ may appear in the column.

a. #### b. ****
c. !!!! d. """"

4. A font design is called its ________.

a. Font face b. Font style
c. Type style d. Typeface

5. A good way to check for unseen data in a row or column is to select a cell in the row or column to be deleted and press ________.

a. End and one of the arrow keys

b. Ctrl+End

c. Home and one of the arrow keys

d. Alt+End

6. Italic is an example of a ________.

a. Font style
b. Font face
c. Typeface
d. Type style

7. To insert a single column, select the column ________ where you want the insertion.

a. To the right of
b. To the left of
c. Above
d. Below

8. To repeat a cell's entry so it fills the entire width of a cell, use the **Format, Cells,** ________ command.

a. **Fill**
b. **Full**
c. **Fulfill**
d. **Repeat**

9. ________ mode rotates the printout 90 degrees so that it is printed along the length of the page.

a. Landscape
b. Portrait
c. Snapshot
d. Picture

10. To change the orientation of the printed page, you have to change the page's ________.

a. Size
b. Typeface
c. Column widths
d. Setup

FILL IN THE BLANK

1. The ________ determines the height and width of characters.

2. The ________ command is used to change printing modes, change margins, and add headers to a worksheet.

3. Font size is specified in a unit of measurement called ________.

4. To insert a single row, select the row ________ where you want the insertion.

5. To copy the same format to another range, use the ________.

6. To horizontally and vertically center a printout on the page, select the ________ tab in the **File**, **Page Setup** dialog box.

7. Instead of using AutoFormat to format cells individually, you can apply the most commonly used formats by clicking buttons on the ________.

8. The ________ button is used to repeat the previous command.

9. When you want complete control over cell formats, use the ________ Cells dialog box.

10. To have Excel's spelling checker skip over a word and all subsequent occurrences of the word, select the command ________ button.

LAB ACTIVITIES

DRILLS

3-1 AutoFormatting

When you use the **AutoFormat** command, you can choose from a list of predefined formats. In this drill you apply some of those to a model so you can see what they look like on the screen and printouts.

1. Open the *Using AutoFormat* workbook stored in the *Drill Workbooks* folder on the *Excel Student Resource Disk* and enter your name into cell A1.
2. Use the **AutoFormat** command on the **Format** menu to format each of the four models (including the *Profit & Loss* headings). Use a different Accounting format for each. As you do so, type the name and number of the format you used in column G next to the model so you can use the printout as a guide in your other work.
3. Save, print, and then close the workbook.

3-2 Formatting Text and Numbers Using the Toolbar

Formatting isn't always necessary when the model is for your personal use but it's important when you are sharing a model or printout with others. Good formatting makes a worksheet easier to read. Here you format an existing model and when finished, your results should match those shown in the figure " The Toolbar Formatting Model."

	A	B	C
1	Type **Name: your name** into cell		
2	Filename: Toolbar formatting		
3	31-Jan-96		
4			
5	**P&L Summary-Before**		
6	Sales	$11,000	100%
7	Expenses	7,000	64%
8	Profits	$ 4,000	36%
9			
10			
11	**P&L Summary-After**		
12	Sales	$11,000	100%
13	Expenses	7,000	64%
14	Profits	$ 4,000	36%

The Toolbar Formatting Model

1. Open the *Toolbar formatting* workbook stored in the *Drill Workbooks* folder on the *Excel Student Resource Disk* and enter your name into cell A1.
2. Select cell A5:C5 and use the **Bold**, **Center Across Columns**, **Color**, and **Font Color** buttons to format the range. (Choose any colors you like.)
3. Select cell A5 and use the **Font Size** drop-down arrow to change the heading's font size to 12.
4. Select cells B6 and then B8 one at a time and use the **Currency Style** and **Decrease Decimal** buttons to format them with dollar signs and no decimal places.
5. Select cell B7 and use the **Comma Style** and **Decrease Decimal** buttons to format it with a comma and no decimal places.
6. Select cell C6:C8 and use the **Percent Style** button to format the range as percentages.
7. Save, print, and then close the workbook.

3-3A Formatting Text and Numbers Using the Menu

When you pull down the **Format** menu and click the **Cells** command, the Format Cells dialog box is displayed. You can then click the *Number* tab to display a list of formats you can apply to values in selected cells. In this drill, you use many of these formats in a document that you can then use as a reference since it illustrates the results of each format. When finished, your results should match those shown in the figure "The Menu Formats Model."

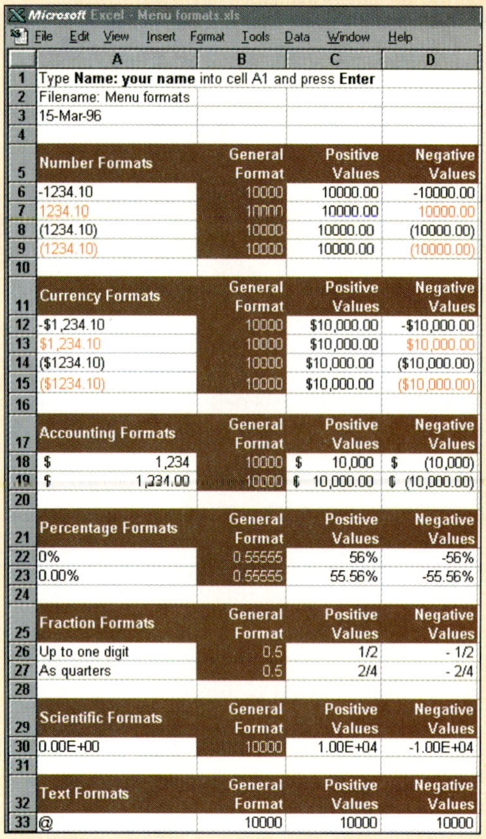

Microsoft Excel - Menu formats.xls

File Edit View Insert Format Tools Data Window Help

	A	B	C	D
1	Type **Name: your name** into cell A1 and press **Enter**			
2	Filename: Menu formats			
3	15-Mar-96			
4				
5	Number Formats	General Format	Positive Values	Negative Values
6	-1234.10	10000	10000.00	-10000.00
7	1234.10	10000	10000.00	10000.00
8	(1234.10)	10000	10000.00	(10000.00)
9	(1234.10)	10000	10000.00	(10000.00)
10				
11	Currency Formats	General Format	Positive Values	Negative Values
12	-$1,234.10	10000	$10,000.00	-$10,000.00
13	$1,234.10	10000	$10,000.00	$10,000.00
14	($1234.10)	10000	$10,000.00	($10,000.00)
15	($1234.10)	10000	$10,000.00	($10,000.00)
16				
17	Accounting Formats	General Format	Positive Values	Negative Values
18	$ 1,234	10000	$ 10,000	$ (10,000)
19	$ 1,234.00	10000	$ 10,000.00	$ (10,000.00)
20				
21	Percentage Formats	General Format	Positive Values	Negative Values
22	0%	0.55555	56%	-56%
23	0.00%	0.55555	55.56%	-55.56%
24				
25	Fraction Formats	General Format	Positive Values	Negative Values
26	Up to one digit	0.5	1/2	- 1/2
27	As quarters	0.5	2/4	- 2/4
28				
29	Scientific Formats	General Format	Positive Values	Negative Values
30	0.00E+00	10000	1.00E+04	-1.00E+04
31				
32	Text Formats	General Format	Positive Values	Negative Values
33	@	10000	10000	10000

The Menu Formats Model

1. Open the *Menu formats* workbook stored in the *Drill Workbooks* folder on the *Excel Student Resource Disk* and enter your name into cell A1.
2. Select each pair of numbers in columns C and D of the *Number Formats* section—for example, cells C6:D6. Then use the **Format**, **Cells** command to apply the format to them described or illustrated in column A on the same row. The formats needed for each section of the model are those listed when you display the Format Cells dialog box and then select **Number**, **Currency**, **Accounting**, **Percentage**, **Fraction**, **Scientific**, and **Text** from the **Category** list.
3. Save, print, and close the workbook.

3-3B Formatting Text and Numbers Using the Menu

Not all formatting commands are listed on the toolbar. In this drill you practice formatting using dialog boxes that are displayed when you choose menu commands.

1. Open the *Date & time formats* workbook stored in the *Drill Workbooks* folder on the *Excel Student Resource Disk* and enter your name into cell A1.
2. Use the **Format**, **Cells**, **Number**, **Date** (or **Time**) commands to format each of the dates and times in column B with the format described on the same row in column A. The numbers currently displayed in the cells have two parts. The first part, before the decimal, is the number of days between January 1, 1900 and today. The part after the decimal is a fraction representing the time from 0 (12:00:00 A.M.) to .99999999 (11:59:59 P.M.).
3. Save, print, and close the workbook.

3-4 Copying Formats

Once you have formatted one range, there is no need to repeat the same commands again elsewhere on the worksheet. Instead you can use Format Painter as you do in this drill.

1. Open the *Copying formats* workbook stored in the *Drill Workbooks* folder on the *Excel Student Resource Disk* and enter your name into cell A1.
2. Use the **Format Painter** button on the toolbar to copy formats from the formatted model to the other three unformatted models. If you make any mistakes, click the **Undo** button on the toolbar to undo them or just copy the formats again. When finished your three formatted models should look just like the top one.
3. Close the workbook without saving your changes.

3-5 Deleting and Clearing Cell Contents

Deleting removes cell contents; clearing removes that and more. In this drill you practice deleting and clearing to explore the differences between these two procedures. In the process, you also practice using the Undo command.

1. Open the *Whoops—undoing mistakes* workbook stored in the *Drill Workbooks* folder on the *Excel Student Resource Disk*.
2. Select any cells on rows 6 through 10 in the *Undoing* section that contain numbers and press [Delete] to delete them. Then immediately click the **Undo** button on the toolbar to undo the deletions. Repeat with other cells until you are comfortable with the procedure.
3. Select any cell on rows 6 through 10 that contain numbers, then pull down the **Edit** menu and click first **Clear** and then **All** to clear both the contents and formats from the cells. Immediately click the **Undo** button on the Standard toolbar to undo the changes. Repeat with other cells until you are comfortable with the procedure.
4. Close the workbook without saving your changes.

3-6 Printing and Page Setup

When working with application programs it's easy to go through lots of expensive paper as you make revisions. For this reason many programs have a print preview command that shows the worksheet on the screen just as it will look when printed. In this drill you use this feature to explore some of the setup options you can use on your printouts.

1. Open the *Exploring formulas* workbook stored in the *Drill Workbooks* folder on the *Excel Student Resource Disk* and enter your name into cell A1.
2. Using the **Page Setup** command on the **File** menu, make the following changes to the document.
   - On the **Page** tab change the orientation to **Landscape**.
   - On the **Margins** tab, change the left margin to 2, and center the page horizontally and vertically.
   - On the **Header/Footer** tab use the drop-down arrows ([▾]) to select the header *Understanding Formulas* and the footer *Page 1 of ?*.
   - On the **Sheet** tab, turn off both gridlines and row and column headings.
3. Use the **Print Preview** command button to see the results.
4. Close the document without saving any changes.

3-7 Spell-checking a Worksheet

As you have seen, checking the spelling in a document is very easy. In this drill you use Excel's spelling checker to check a document with built-in mistakes. You then use it to check the spelling in any workbooks you have entered text into.

1. Open the *Spelling checker practice* workbook stored in the *Drill Workbooks* folder on the *Excel Student Resource Disk* and enter your name into cell A1.
2. Click cell A1 to select it, then click the **Spelling** button on the Standard toolbar to correct any spelling mistakes in the worksheet.
3. Save and close the workbook.
4. For additional practice, repeat Steps 1 through 3 with any of your own workbooks.

3-8 Inserting Rows, Columns, and Cells

One of the best things about spreadsheets is how you can revise models on the fly. One of the main procedures you use to do so is inserting rows, columns, and cells. In this drill you practice those procedures. When finished your model should look like the figure "The Insert Model."

	A	B	C	D	E
1	Name: your name				
2	Filename: Inserting rows and columns				
3	15-Mar-96				
4					
5	Inventory				
6	**Item**	Stock #	*Quantity*	*Price*	***Total value***
7	Computer, desktop	1001	100	$ 1,300.00	$ 130,000
8	Computer, workstation	1002	20	1,500.00	30,000
9	Computer, notebook	1003	150	2,500.00	375,000
10	Printer, color laser	1004	5	2,000.00	10,000
11	Printer, laser	1005	75	1,200.00	90,000
12	Printer, inkjet	1006	25	500.00	12,500
13	Monitor, 17"	1007	125	350.00	43,750
14	Monitor, 21"	1008	25	1,800.00	45,000
15	Modem, 14.4 bps	1009	10	50.00	500
16	Modem, 28.8 bps	1010	100	175.00	17,500
17	CD-ROM drive	1011	200	300.00	60,000
18	*Total*		835		814,250

The Insert Model

1. Open the *Inserting rows & columns* workbook stored in the *Drill Workbooks* folder on the *Excel Student Resource Disk* and enter your name into cell A1.
2. Select all cells in column B between rows 5 and 14 inclusive and use the **Insert, Cells** command to insert cells. When prompted, have them shift to the right.
3. Use the row heading to select row 9 and use the **Insert, Rows** command to insert a row.
4. Use the row heading to select row 12 and use the **Insert, Rows** command to insert a row.
5. Use the row headings to select rows 15 and 16 and use the **Insert, Rows** command to insert two rows.
6. Select cell E8 and use the cell's fill handle to copy the formula down the column to cell E16.
7. Enter data in the inserted rows or columns to match the illustration. Center the data you enter into column B. When you enter data into columns C and D, the formula in column E fills in the values for you.
8. Check all of the formulas in the model, and you'll see that they have adjusted to refer to the correct cells.

9. Save and then close the workbook.

3-9 Deleting Rows, Columns, and Cells

Models, unlike our waistlines, don't always expand. Sometimes they shrink. The procedure you use to reduce them in size is the deletion or rows and columns. In this drill you practice those procedures.

1. Open the *Delete rows & columns* workbook stored in the *Drill Workbooks* folder on the *Excel Student Resource Disk* and enter your name into cell A1.
2. Use the row and column headings to select each of the rows and columns with the brownish-red (brick) background color one at a time and use the **Edit, Delete** command to delete them.
3. Check all of the formulas in the model, and you'll see that they have adjusted to refer to the correct cells.
4. Save and then close the workbook.

3-10 Moving Data

In addition to inserting and deleting rows and columns, one of the other major revision tools at your disposal is moving data. In this drill you practice moving data from one place to another on the worksheet.

1. Open the *Moving data practice* workbook stored in the *Drill Workbooks* folder on the *Excel Student Resource Disk* and enter your name into cell A1.
2. On the *Cutting & Pasting* sheet, use the **Cut** and **Paste** buttons on the Standard toolbar to cut each of the cell ranges with a yellow background and red border and paste them into the corresponding ranges with a red background and yellow border. When you do so, notice how none of the cell references change. They refer to the same cells in their new position as they did in their old.
3. On the *Dragging & Dropping* sheet, drag each of the four ranges of cells with a yellow background and red border from the *Drag From* section and drop them in the indicated spaces in the *Drag To* section.
4. Close the workbook without saving your changes.

EXERCISES

3-1 Formatting and Revising the Pricing Model

In this drill you revise and format the *calculating prices* model that you created in the exercises at the end of PicTorial 2. When finished, you model should look like the one shown in the figure "The Formatted Pricing Model."

	A	B
1	Filename: Calculating prices	
2	1-Feb-96	
3		
4	Part 1. Pricing Variables	
5	Manufacturer's suggested list price	$ 10.00
6	Your actual selling price	$ 11.00
7	Unit cost of freight-in	$ 0.20
8	Discount from manufacturer	40%
9		
10	Part 2. Pricing Analysis	
11	Unit cost from manufacturer	$ 6.00
12	Total unit cost of goods	$ 6.20
13	Gross profit per unit (in dollars)	$ 4.80
14	Percentage markup over unit cost of goods	77.42%
15	Gross margin per unit (%)	43.64%

The Formatted Calculating Prices Model

1. Open the *Calculating prices* workbook stored in the *Exercise Workbooks* folder on the *Excel Student Resource Disk.*
2. Change the width of column A to 45.
3. Select the cell range A5:B5 and format it as follows:
   - Center the heading using the **Center Across Columns** button on the Formatting toolbar.
   - Click the **Color** button on the Formatting toolbar and choose red on the first row of the palette.
   - Click the **Font Color** button on the Formatting toolbar and choose white on the first row of the palette.
   - Click the **Bold** button on the toolbar.
   - Click the **Font Size** drop-down arrow on the Formatting toolbar and choose 12.
4. Copy the formats from the cell range A5:B5 to the cell range A11:B11 using the **Format Painter** button on the Standard toolbar.
5. Formats cells B12:B14 as currency with two decimal places using the **Format**, **Cells**, **Currency**, **-$1,234.10** commands. Note that the format is different from the one in cells B6, B8, and B9. What caused the difference? Which format do you prefer? (The **Currency Style** button was used for the first entries; the **Format** menu for the later entries.)
6. Copy the format from cell B6 to the cell range B12:B14 using the **Format Painter** button on the Standard toolbar.
7. Select row 10 and use the **Insert**, **Rows** command to insert a blank row.
8. Use the **Cut** and **Paste** buttons on the Standard toolbar to move the cell range A7:B7 to the range A10:B10.
9. Delete the now blank row 7 using the **Edit**, **Delete** command.
10. Format the cell range B15:B16 as percentages with two decimal places using the **Percent Style** and **Increase Decimal** buttons on the Formatting toolbar.
11. Turn off gridlines and row and column headings using the **File**, **Page Setup** command.
12. Print the workbook, save it, and then close it.

3-2 Formatting and Revising the Model That Doubles a Penny Every Day

In this exercise you revise and format the *Doubling a penny daily* model that you created in the exercises at the end of PicTorial 2.

1. Open the *Doubling a penny daily* workbook stored in the *Exercise Workbooks* folder on the *Excel Student Resource Disk.*
2. Using the **Color** button on the Formatting toolbar, change the background colors of the following ranges:
   - cells A5 and B5 to dark blue (on the fourth row of the palette). Then use the **Bold** button on the Formatting toolbar to boldface the text in those cells.
   - cells A6:A36 to lime green color (fourth from the left on the top row of the palette)
   - cells B6:B36 to light yellow (third from left on the third row of the palette)
3. Using the **Font Color** button on the Formatting toolbar, change the colors of the contents in cells A5:B5 to bright red (on the first row of the palette).

4. Using the **Font Color** button on the Formatting toolbar, change the colors of the contents in cells A6:B36 to dark blue (on the first row of the palette).
5. Use the **Copy** and **Paste** buttons on the Standard toolbar to copy the entries in A5:B36 to cells D5:E36. This gives you a second copy of the model which you can use to practice clearing formats and data.
6. Select the new entries in columns D and E and use the **Edit**, **Clear** command to clear first the formats and then the contents.
7. Use the **File**, **Page Setup** command turn off the gridlines and row and column headings.
8. Save, print, and then close the workbook.

3-3 Formatting and Revising the Model That Explores Series of Numbers

In this exercise you revise and format the *Number* series model that you created in the exercises at the end of PicTorial 2.

1. Open the *Number series* workbook stored in the *Exercise Workbooks* folder on the *Excel Student Resource Disk*.
2. Change the font size of the entries in cells A5:C5 to 14 point bold using the **Font Size** drop-down arrow and **Bold** button on the Formatting toolbar.
3. Use the **Cut** and **Paste** commands to reverse the order of the data in columns A and C in three steps.
   - Move the data in column A (Arithmetic) to column D.
   - Move the data in column C (Exponential) to column A.
   - Move the data in column D (Arithmetic) to column C.
4. Use the **Bold** button on the Formatting toolbar to boldface all of the numbers in the cell range A6:C11.
5. Use the **Copy** and **Paste** buttons on the Standard toolbar to copy the cell range A11:C11 to rows 12 through 19. Notice how some of the numbers in column A are too large to be displayed.
6. Double-click the heading border between columns A and B to widen the column to fit the largest entry. The numbers in column A on rows 16 through 19 are too large to be calculated. On some systems you may not be able to see the entire column.
7. Select rows 14 through 19 and use the **Edit**, **Delete** command to delete them.
8. With cell A13 selected, use the **Format**, **Column**, **AutoFit Selection** command to narrow the column.
9. Select columns B and C and use the **Format**, **Column**, **AutoFit Selection** command to adjust the columns.
10. Use the **File**, **Page Setup** command turn off the gridlines and change to landscape orientation; then click the **Print Preview** button to preview your results.
11. Print the workbook.
12. Use the **File**, **Page Setup** command to return to portrait orientation.
13. Save and then close the workbook.

3-4 Formatting and Revising the Birthday Model

In this exercise you revise and format the *Birthday odds* model that you created in the exercises at the end of PicTorial 2. When finished, you model should look like the one shown in part in the figure "The Formatted Birthday Odds Model."

	A	B	C	D	E
1	Your Name				
2	Filename: Birthday odds				
3	1-Feb-96				
4					
5	Number of people (*n*th person)		Individual probability for *n*th person	Probability no two people have the same birthday	Probability two people do have same birthday
6	1		99.7%		
7	2		99.5%	99.2%	0.8%
8	3		99.2%	98.4%	1.6%
9	4		98.9%	97.3%	2.7%
10	5		98.6%	96.0%	4.0%
11	6		98.4%	94.4%	5.6%
12	7		98.1%	92.6%	7.4%
13	8		97.8%	90.5%	9.5%
14	9		97.5%	88.3%	11.7%
15	10		97.3%	85.9%	14.1%
16	11		97.0%	83.3%	16.7%
17	12		96	80.6	19
18				7	

The Formatted Birthday Odds Model

1. Open the *Birthday odds* workbook stored in the *Exercise Workbooks* folder on the *Excel Student Resource Disk.*
2. Select cells A5:D5 and use the **Font Size** drop-down arrow on the Formatting toolbar to change the font to 12 point.
3. Select the cells containing data on row 10 and use the **Format**, **Cells**, **Border** command to insert a bottom line border for the row of entries.
4. Use the **Repeat** button on the Standard toolbar to insert the bottom line border for entries in Row 15, 20, 25, and 30.
5. Use the **Center** button on the Formatting toolbar to center the entries in the range A5:A30.
6. Use the **Insert**, **Columns** command to insert a new column between columns A and B and change the width of the new column B to 2.
7. Use the **Color** button on the Formatting toolbar to change the background color to the same blue used for the headings for the empty cells in the range B6:B30. (It's the blue on the second row of the palette.)
8. Use the **File**, **Page Setup**, **Margins** command to vertically and horizontally center the page.
9. Save, print, and then close the workbook.

3-5 Formatting and Revising the Multiplication Table

In this exercise you revise and format the *Multiplication table* model that you created in the exercises at the end of PicTorial 2.

1. Open the *Multiplication table* workbook stored in the *Exercise Workbooks* folder on the *Excel Student Resource Disk.*
2. Select cells A5 and A6 and use the **Bold** button on the Formatting toolbar to boldface them.
3. Select all of the cells with numbers and use the **Center** button on the Formatting toolbar to center them.
4. Use the **File**, **Page Setup**, command to center the page horizontally and vertically on the page and to have row and column headings displayed but not gridlines.

5. Save, print, and then close the workbook.

3-6 Formatting On Your Own

In this exercise you put to work all that you have learned so far by formatting one or more models of your choice as you think best.

1. Open one of the workbooks *Chain letter analysis* or *Exchange rates.*
2. Format the model as you think best.
3. Save, print, and close the workbook.
4. Repeat Steps 1 through 3 for another model if you have time.

PROJECTS

3-1 A Balance Sheet

There are standard ways to format a balance sheet including the type of underlines used, number formats, spacing, and such. Here you use those rules to revise and format the *Balance sheet* workbook stored in the *Project Workbooks* folder on the *Excel Student Resource Disk* so it matches the one shown in the figure "The Formatted Balance Sheet." As you complete each sequence of corrections or formats, check them off on the "Balance Sheet Revision Checklist." When finished, save, print and close the workbook.

	A	B	C
1	Your Name		
2	Filename: Balance sheet		
3	1-Feb-96		
4			
5	BALANCE SHEET		
6	PACRIM Enterprises		
7	December 31, 199X		
8		**This Year**	**Last Year**
9			
10	**CURRENT ASSETS**		
11	Cash	$ 11,200	$ 6,400
12	Accounts receivable	20,000	20,000
13	Inventory	70,000	70,000
14	Prepaid expense	3,400	3,400
15	Total current assets	$104,600	$ 99,800
16			
17	**FIXED ASSETS**		
18	Buildings & equipment	$ 30,000	$ 30,000
19	Less accumulated depreciation	(10,000)	(5,000)
20	Land	20,000	5,000
27	**CURRENT LIABILITIES**		
28	Accounts payable	$ 20,000	$ 20,000
29	Accrued wages and taxes	10,000	10,000
30	Current portion of long-term debt	5,000	5,000
31	Other current liabilities	5,000	5,000
32	Total current liabilities	$ 40,000	$ 40,000
33			
34	**LONG-TERM DEBT**		
35	Bank loans	$ 40,000	$ 40,000
36	Other	10,000	10,000
37	Total liabilities	$ 90,000	$ 90,000

The Formatted Balance Sheet

Balance Sheet Revision Checklist

- ☐ Center the three-line heading on rows 5 through 7 across columns and format its color, size, and style.
- ☐ Boldface the all-capital headings and the two column headings.
- ☐ Insert blank rows between number sections (above all-capital headings).
- ☐ Format the indicated values as currency with 0 decimal places. Adjust column widths as necessary. Remove dollar signs where appropriate.
- ☐ Add single or double accounting underlines below number sections.

3-2 An Income Statement

There are standard ways to format income statements including the type of underlines used, formats, spacing, and such. Here you use those rules to revise and format the *Income statement* workbook stored in the *Project Workbooks* folder on the *Excel Student Resource Disk* so it matches the one shown in the figure "The Formatted Income Statement." As you complete each sequence of corrections or formats, check them off on the "Income Statement Revision Checklist." When finished, save, print and close the workbook.

Income Statement Revision Checklist

- ☐ Center the three-line heading on rows 5 through 7 head ing across columns and format its size and style.
- ☐ Insert a new row below the heading.
- ☐ Center the three annual column headings and change their color and style.
- ☐ Correct and revise all text.
- ☐ Boldface all-cap headings.
- ☐ Format the indicated values as currency.
- ☐ Move the three annual columns to reverse their order.
- ☐ Add single or double borders below number sections.

	A	B	C	D
1	Your Name			
2	Filename: Income statement			
3	16-Jan-96			
4				
5	**PRO FORMA INCOME STATEMENT--FIRST THREE YEARS**			
6	**PACRIM Enterprises**			
7	**January 1, 199X -- December 31, 199X**			
8				
9		Year 3	Year 2	Year 1
10	**SALES**			
11	Gross sales	$48,400	$44,000	$40,000
12	Discounts, returns, and allow.	2,420	2,200	2,000
13	Net sales	$45,980	$41,800	$38,000
14				
15	**COST OF GOODS SOLD**			
16	Purchase price	$27,588	$25,080	$22,800
17	Freight in	1,104	1,003	912
18	Total cost of goods sold	28,692	26,083	23,712
19	Gross profits	$17,288	$15,717	$14,288
20				
21	**OPERATING EXPENSES**			
22	General and administrative	$ 7,500	$ 7,500	$ 7,500
23	Selling expenses	3,750	3,750	3,750
24	Interest expenses	931	931	931
25	Depreciation	1,250	1,250	1,250
26	Total operating expenses	$13,431	$13,431	$13,431
27				
28	Operating income/loss	$ 3,857	$ 2,286	$ 857
29	Other income	$ 15		$ 10
30	Other expenses		12	
31	Income before taxes	$ 3,872	$ 2,274	$ 867
32	Taxes	964	571	214
33	Net income/loss	$ 2,908	$ 1,703	$ 653
34				

The Formatted Income Statement

PICTORIAL

FOUR

WORKING WITH FUNCTIONS

After completing this PicTorial, you will be able to:

- **Understand how functions work**
- **Use AutoSum and Function Wizard to enter functions**
- **Use names in functions and formulas**
- **Enter and calculate dates and times**
- **Use comparison operators and logical functions**
- **Use text in formulas and functions**

YOU have already been introduced to formulas. In this PicTorial you are introduced to a special type a formula called a function. A function will either perform a complex calculation or make a long formula simple to enter.

4-1 UNDERSTANDING FUNCTIONS

Excel contains many functions that have been built in to perform commonly used calculations. You enter them just like formulas, by typing them into cells.

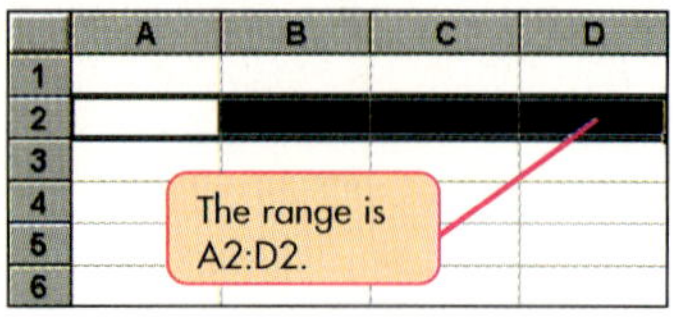

A row range

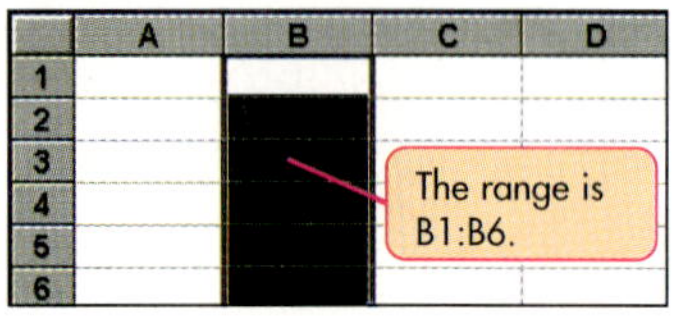

A column range

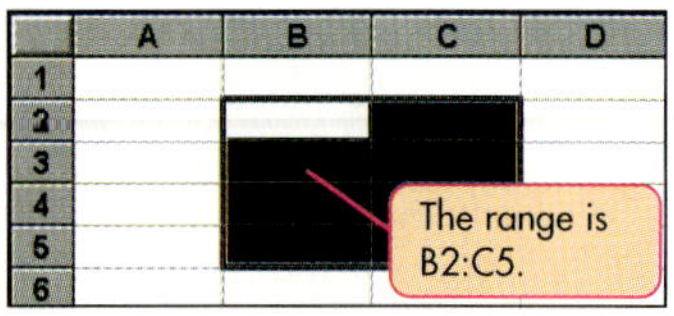

A rectangular range

Specifying Ranges

Functions frequently refer to a group, or *range* of cells. For example, a function can add all of the values entered into cells A1 through A5. This range of cells is specified in the function as A1:A5, where the colon means "through," as in cells A1 *through* A5.

To specify a range of cells falling on a row, you specify the leftmost and rightmost cells in the range, separated by a colon.

To specify a range of cells falling in a column, you specify the top and bottom cells in the range, separated by a colon.

To specify a range of cells falling in a rectangle, you specify the upper-left and lower-right cells in the range, separated by a colon.

TIP
Text and Blank Cells

- Cells containing text or blank cells have a numeric value of 0 when referred to in a function's range. For example, if a function reads =SUM(A1:A10) and cell A5 is blank or contains text, it is treated as a zero value.
- Statistical functions such as COUNT, AVERAGE, and MEDIAN treat blank cells and cells containing text differently from cells containing a zero. If you want a cell in the range ignored, leave it blank or containing text. If you want it to be treated as a zero value, enter a 0.

The Purpose of Functions

As mentioned earlier, functions will either make a complex formula simple to enter, or perform complex calculations. Let's look at some examples.

Functions often simplify the entry of long formulas. For example, to calculate the average of a list of 6 numbers in cells A1 through A6, you would have to enter the formula =(A1+A2+A3+A4+A5+A6)/6. The same calculation can be made with the function =AVERAGE(A1:A6). If the list of numbers were expanded to a hundred numbers, imagine how long the formula would be. The function, on the other hand, would be simply =AVERAGE(A1:A100).

In addition to simplifying formulas, functions can also perform complex calculations. We will see a few such functions in this PicTorial, but the most complex functions are beyond the scope of this text.

The Structure of Functions

Functions have a structure, or syntax, that you must follow when you enter them. The syntax includes an equal sign, a function name, and usually one or more values, called arguments, on which the function performs its calculations.

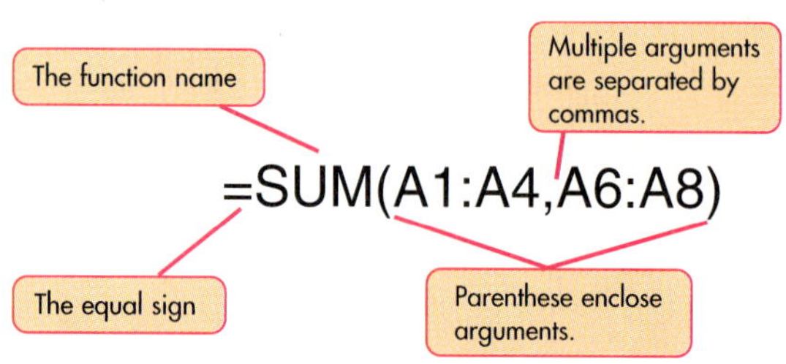

For example, the name of the function that sums the values in a range of cells is SUM, and the name of the function that averages the values in a range of cells is AVERAGE.

TIP

Function Names

When you enter a function name in lowercase letters, Excel will automatically convert it to uppercase when you press Enter↵ or click the Enter box. If it doesn't convert it to uppercase, and #NAME? is displayed in the cell, check for typos in the name.

Arguments follow the function's name. The most common kind of argument is the numbers that are to be calculated, or references to other cells containing the numbers.

- The arguments must be enclosed in parentheses that tell Excel where they begin and end.
- The arguments can be numbers, cell references, ranges, formulas, or other functions. For example, the function =SUM(10,20,30) sums the three numbers, and the function =SUM(A1:A5) sums the values in the range A1 through A5.
- If there is more than one argument, the arguments must be separated from each other by commas. (Do not use commas to separate thousands when you enter numbers into a function.) For example, the function =SUM(A1:A5,A7:A9) sums the values in the ranges A1:A5 and A7:A9.
- A few functions, such as PI or RAND, do not require arguments, but they must still have the parentheses for Excel to recognize them. For example, the function =PI() will calculate the value of pi for you, and =RAND() will generate a random number between 0 and 1.
- Some functions have optional arguments that you can enter but that are not required for the function to make a calculation.

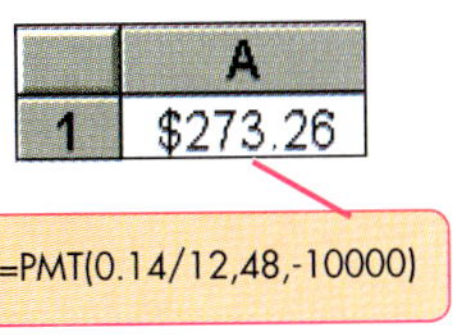

Let's look at an example of the function used to calculate monthly payments on a loan. The function's syntax is =PMT(*rate,nper,–pv*). The function's name is PMT (for **P**ay**M**en**T**). The arguments are rate (the interest rate), *nper* (number of payment periods), and *–pv* (present value of the loan—that is, the amount of the loan—expressed as a negative). The three arguments are separated from one another by commas and are enclosed in parentheses. You can substitute numbers in the function; for example, the function =PMT(.14/12,48,–10000) calculates and displays monthly payments of $273.26 on a $10,000 loan at 14% for 48 months (the 14% loan is divided by 12 in the function to convert it to a monthly rate that matches the term, which is expressed in months. You could also leave the .14 undivided by 12 and express the term in years (4) to calculate an annual payment.)

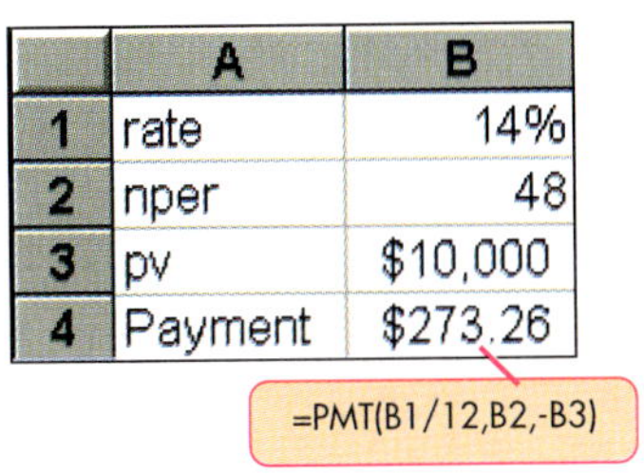

Instead of entering numbers as arguments in a function, you can enter them into other cells and then enter references to those cells as arguments in the function. The values in the referred-to cells are calculated just as if they were a part of the function. Entering the values into their own cells makes it easy to change them when updating a model or exploring what-ifs.

Functions can also be used in combinations. For example, the functions =ROUND(SUM(A1:A7),2) round the sum of the values in cells A1:A7 to two decimal places. When you include one function in another like this, the functions are *nested*.

TIP
Boldface Parentheses

As you enter a formula or function, when you type a right parenthesis, Excel will momentarily boldface the matching left parenthesis so you can be sure you have the correct number of opening and closing parentheses. When you are editing a formula, Excel momentarily boldfaces opening and closing parentheses whenever you move the insertion point past one or the other of them.

TUTORIAL

In this tutorial you look at a number of functions to see how they are structured. The functions you look at include those with no arguments, those with a range of cells as an argument, and those with multiple arguments.

Getting Ready

1. Open the *Forms of functions* workbook stored in the *Tutorial Workbooks* folder on the *Excel Student Resource Disk* and enter your name into cell A1.

Exploring Functions

2. Press Ctrl+` to display functions in the cells instead of their calculated values. Scroll the screen, if necessary, to see how the functions all work.

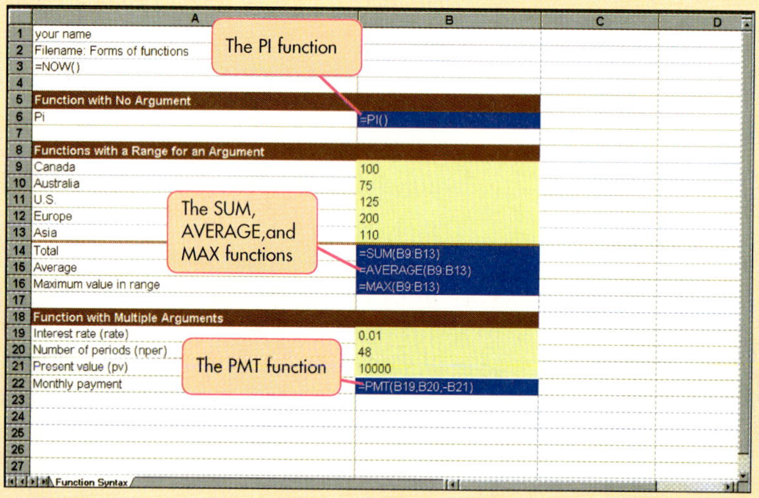

3. Notice how the function in cell B6 (which calculates the mathematical constant pi (π) to 15 digits) has no argument within its parentheses. A few functions don't require arguments—but they still require the parentheses.

TIP
Pi Are Round

Pi is the ratio of the circumference of a circle to its diameter. You may remember the formula for the area of a circle, πR^2 (pronounced "pi r squared"), from high school geometry. On the old George Burns and Gracie Allen radio program, Gracie played a dizzy wife to husband George's straight-man role. In one memorable scene, a suitor of a friend of theirs introduces himself as a teacher of geometry. Gracie demands "If you know so much about geometry, then say something in it." The befuddled suitor finally blurts out, "OK, pi r squared." Gracie shouts, "Ha—got you, everyone knows pies are round."

4. Cells B14, B15, and B16 each contain a function that refers to the same range of cells, B9:B13. The function in cell B14 sums the range, the one in cell B15 calculates the average value of the range, and the one in cell B16 calculates the maximum value in the range.
5. The function in cell B22 calculates the monthly payment on a loan. It has three arguments separated by commas. Its syntax is =PMT(*rate,nper,–pv*). Since it is referring to cells, it's calculating the numbers in those cells as =PMT(.01,48,–10000). The figure "The Function's Arguments" shows three ways to think of these arguments.

The Function's Arguments

18	Function with Multiple Arguments	
19	Interest rate (rate)	1%
20	Number of periods (nper)	48
21	Present value (pv)	$ 10,000.00
22	Monthly payment	$263.34

With descriptions =PMT(rate,nper,-pv)

With cell references =PMT(B2,B3,-B4)

With numbers =PMT(.01,48,-10000)

6. Press Ctrl+` again to return to displaying calculated values.

Finishing Up

7. Close the workbook without saving it.

4-2 USING AUTOSUM

The function that people use most frequently is the one that totals, or sums, columns or rows of numbers. This SUM function can be typed directly into a cell in the format =SUM(*range*). For example, to total all of the numbers in column B from rows 3 to 8 you would enter the function as =SUM(B3:B8).

	A	B	C	D	E
1	**Sales: First Quarter**				
2	**Item**	*Jan*	*Feb*	*Mar*	***Total***
3	Computer	$10,000	$11,000	$12,100	$33,100
4	Printer	300	330	363	$ 993
5	CD-ROM	400	440	484	$ 1,324
6	Monitor	250	275	303	$ 828
7	Mouse	50	55	61	$ 166
8	Software	350	385	424	$ 1,159
9	*Total*	$11,350	$12,485	$13,734	$37,569

=SUM(B3:B8)

The AutoSum button

However, you can also enter this function quickly and automatically using the **AutoSum** button on the Standard toolbar. When you do so, Excel analyzes the data and automatically enters an =SUM function and guesses at the range of cells to be added. If it guesses correctly, you just have to click the Enter box (☑) on the formula bar or press Enter ↵ to complete the entry.

QUICKSTEPS

Using AutoSum

1. Select the cells to be summed as described in the box "Understanding Selecting Cells to Be Summed."
2. Click the **AutoSum** button on the toolbar to enter the SUM function(s). If you selected a single cell, Excel enters the function for you and highlights the range of cells with a moving border.

- If the range is correct, press Enter ↵, click the Enter box (☑), or click the AutoSum button on the formula bar again.
- If the range isn't correct, edit the range highlighted in the active cell, and then press Enter ↵ or click the Enter box (☑). (You can also click the Cancel box (☒), select the range manually, and then repeat this step.)

UNDERSTANDING

Selecting Cells to Be Summed

When you click the **AutoSum** button on the Standard toolbar, your results depend on what cells you have selected.

- Select one blank cell below or to the right of the cells to be summed to sum the adjacent column or row.

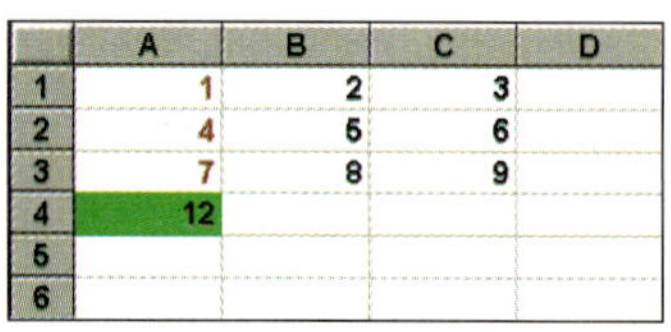

	A	B	C	D
1	1	2	3	
2	4	5	6	
3	7	8	9	
4	12			
5				
6				

- Select a range of blank cells below or to the right of the cells to be summed to sum the adjacent columns or rows.

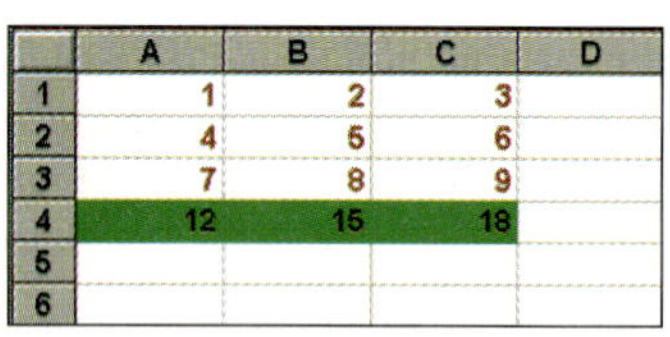

	A	B	C	D
1	1	2	3	
2	4	5	6	
3	7	8	9	
4	12	15	18	
5				
6				

- Select the cells to be summed to sum them on the row below the selected range.

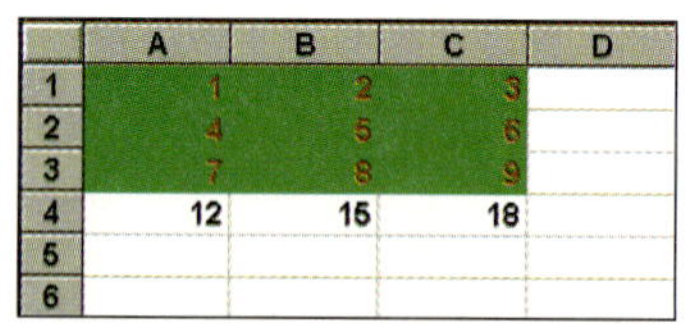

	A	B	C	D
1	1	2	3	
2	4	5	6	
3	7	8	9	
4	12	15	18	
5				
6				

- Select the cells to be summed and the row below and column to the right to sum both rows and columns.

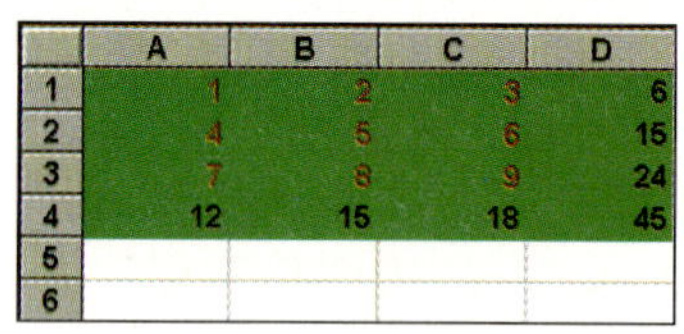

	A	B	C	D
1	1	2	3	6
2	4	5	6	15
3	7	8	9	24
4	12	15	18	45
5				
6				

TIP
Entering Grand Totals

If you use the SUM function to calculate subtotals, you can then select the range that includes those subtotals and click the **AutoSum** button to calculate grand totals. Excel ignores all numbers in the selected range and just sums those calculated by other SUM functions.

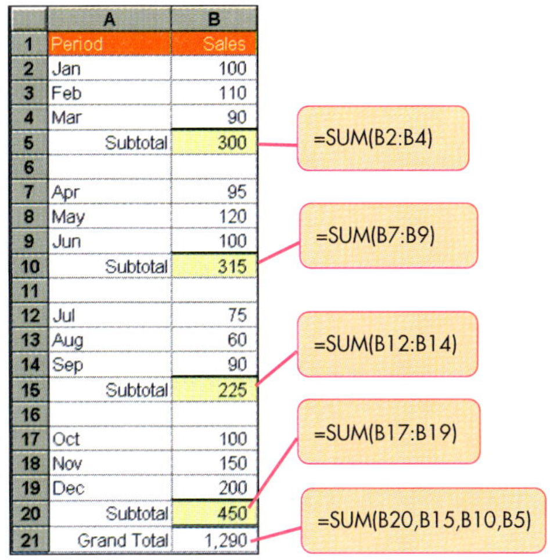

In this figure, cells B2 through B21 were selected, and then the **AutoSum** button was clicked. The function summed the number in cells B20, B15, B10, and B5—ignoring the other numbers in the column.

TUTORIAL

IN this tutorial you are introduced to the **AutoSum** command. You use it to quickly sum columns of income and expense numbers in the *Budget* model.

Getting Ready

1. Open the *Budget* workbook stored in the *Tutorial Workbooks* folder on the *Excel Student Resource Disk*.
2. Select any of the cells on the *Total* lines to see their formulas on the formula bar. You may remember all of the typing or pointing you had to do to enter these formulas that sum the cells above them. You are about to see how easily the same thing can be done.
3. Select cells B10 through E10 and then press Delete to delete their contents. (Don't worry that some of the cells fill with number signs.)
4. Select cells B19 through E19 and then press Delete to delete their contents.

Using AutoSum

5. Select cells B10 through E10 and click the **AutoSum** button on the Standard toolbar to sum the columns of data above. (Don't worry that one is too large to be displayed in its cell.) Click any cell on the row to see how SUM functions were automatically entered.

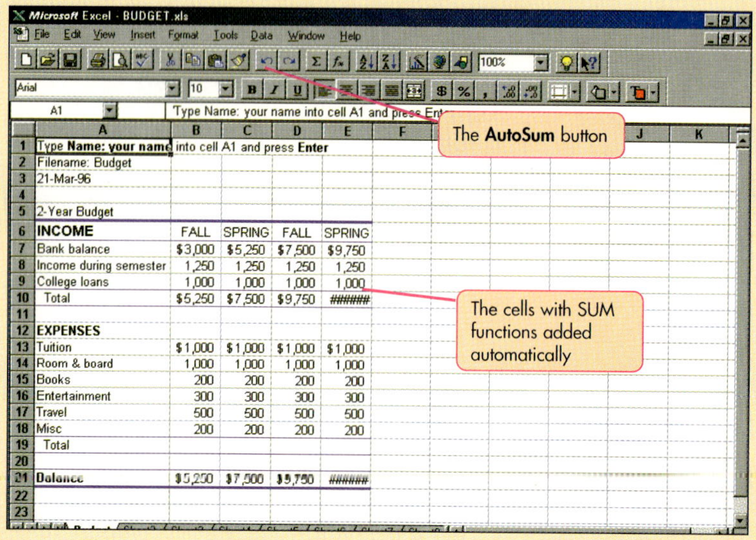

6. Select cells B19 through E19 and click the **AutoSum** button on the Standard toolbar to sum the columns of data above. Click any cell on the row to see how SUM functions were automatically entered

Finishing Up

7. Save, print, and close the workbook.

4-3 USING THE FUNCTION WIZARD

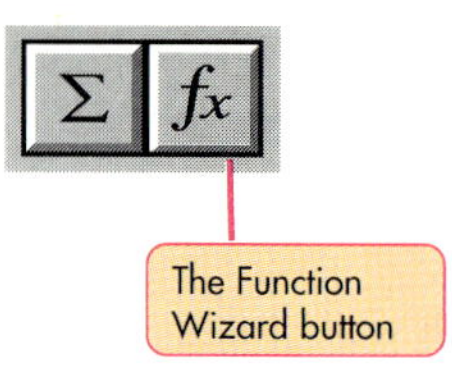

Although you can type a function directly into a cell, Excel's Function Wizard makes the process much easier. When you use the Function Wizard, a dialog box displays functions grouped by category. When you select the function you want to enter, you can then display a second dialog box that guides you through entering the arguments.

Excel has hundreds of functions from which you can choose. To help you locate them, related functions are grouped into the following families:

Database functions calculate averages and medians, count cells, and find maximum and maximum values, standard deviations, sums, and variances of databases and lists.

Date & Time functions calculate the current date and time or add or subtract dates and times.

Engineering functions perform calculations used by programmers, scientists, and engineers.

Financial functions calculate depreciation, present and future values, internal rates of return, periodic payments of an annuity, interest rates, and yields.

Information functions determine what type of data is in cells.

Logical functions perform conditional calculations (if x, then y), and connect arguments so one, both, or neither must be true for a conditional calculation to be performed in a given way.

Lookup & Reference functions look up values in a table and find locations of row and column references.

Math & Trig functions calculate absolute values, logarithms, pi, and random numbers.

Statistical functions calculate averages and medians, count cells, and find minimum and maximum values, standard deviations, sums, and variances.

Text functions convert text to numbers and vice versa, compare text entries, remove nonprintable text characters, join several text items into one item, compare two text values to see if they are identical, and change the case of characters.

Entering Functions with the Function Wizard

When you click the **Function Wizard** button on the Standard toolbar, the Function Wizard Step 1 of 2 dialog box is displayed. After selecting a function, you normally click the **Next** command button to display the Step 2 of 2 dialog box. (If you click the **Finish** command button, the selected function is entered into the active cell with the argument names inserted as placeholders. For example, if you insert the PMT function this way, the function =PMT(*rate,nper,pv,fv,type*) is entered in the cell and displayed on the formula bar so you can substitute values for the placeholders in the arguments.)

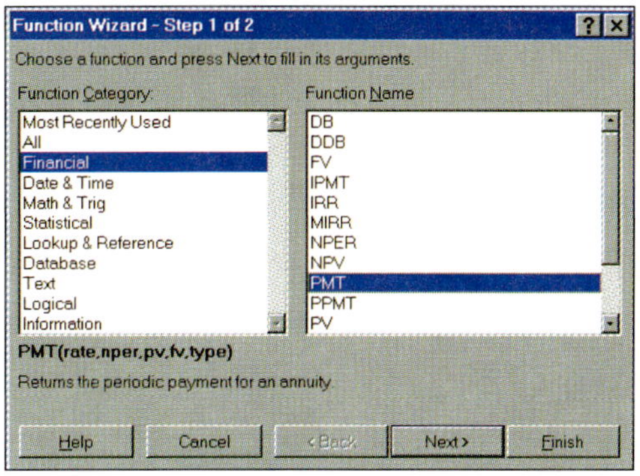

The Function Wizard Step 2 of 2 dialog box is where you enter a function's arguments (if any are required). The names of required arguments are boldfaced and the names of optional arguments are displayed in lighter type. When you enter a formula or cell reference in one of the argument edit boxes, the arguments are shown to the right of the edit box. The current calculated value of the function is displayed in the *Value* box in the upper-right corner of the dialog box.

You can click the **Function Wizard** button to the left of any argument in an edit box to open another instance of the Function Wizard dialog box. This lets you insert another function as an argument within the first one.

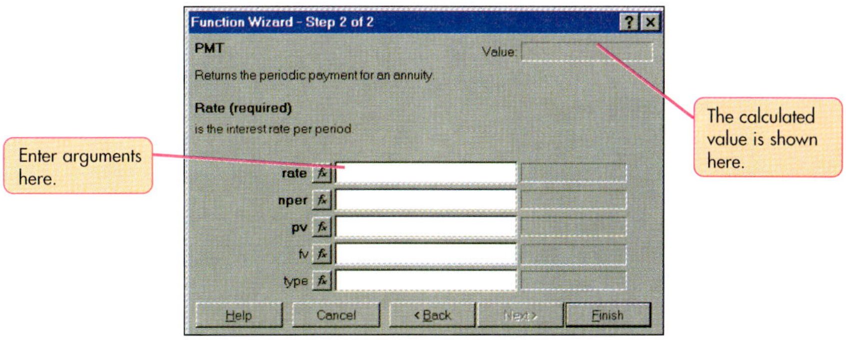

QUICKSTEPS

Entering Functions with the Function Wizard

1. Select the cell in which you want to enter the function, or begin entering a formula in which you want to enter a function.
2. Click the **Function Wizard** button on the Standard toolbar, or pull down the **Insert** menu and click the **Function** command to display the Function Wizard Step 1 of 2 dialog box.
3. Click the type of function you want to use in the **Function Category** list to select it and display that kind of function in the **Function Name** list.
4. Click the name of the desired function in the **Function Name** list to select it. A brief description of the function and its arguments is displayed below the lists.
5. Click the **Next** command button to display the Function Wizard Step 2 of 2 dialog box. (You can then click the **Back** command button at any point to return to Step 1 of 2.)
6. Enter the arguments for the function in the argument edit boxes, and then click the **Finish** command button to enter the function in the cell.

Editing Functions with the Function Wizard

When you select a cell that already contains a function and click the **Function Wizard** button on the Standard toolbar, the Editing Function 1 of 1 dialog box is displayed so you can edit the arguments. (The box is the same as the Step 2 of 2 box used to enter the function.) If the selected cell contains more than one function, the second number in the Editing Function box's title changes. If it reads 1 of 2, for instance, when you click the **Next** command button, the arguments are entered in the first function and the second function is displayed.

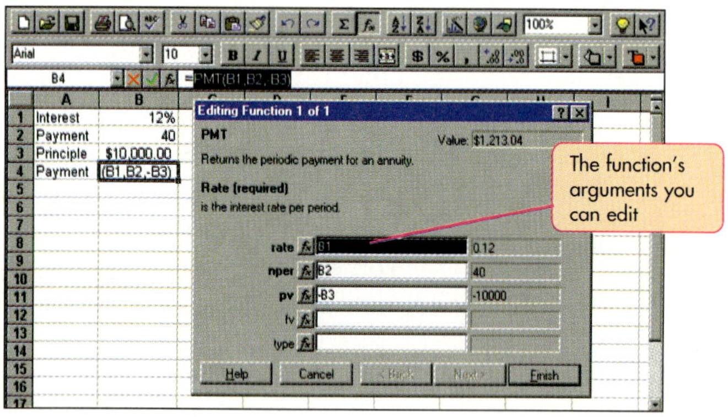

TUTORIAL

In this tutorial you use Excel's Function Wizard to enter a variety of commonly used functions. The model you use already has all of the arguments for each of the functions you enter. All you have to do is be sure you refer to the correct cells when entering the arguments asked for by the Function Wizard.

Getting Ready

1. Open the *Financial functions* workbook stored in the *Tutorial Workbooks* folder on the *Excel Student Resource Disk* and enter your name into cell A1.

Entering a Function with the Function Wizard

2. Select cell C11 and click the **Function Wizard** button on the Standard toolbar to display the Function Wizard's Step 1 of 2 dialog box.
3. Click *Financial* in the **Function Category** list to select it and display financial functions in the **Function Name** list.

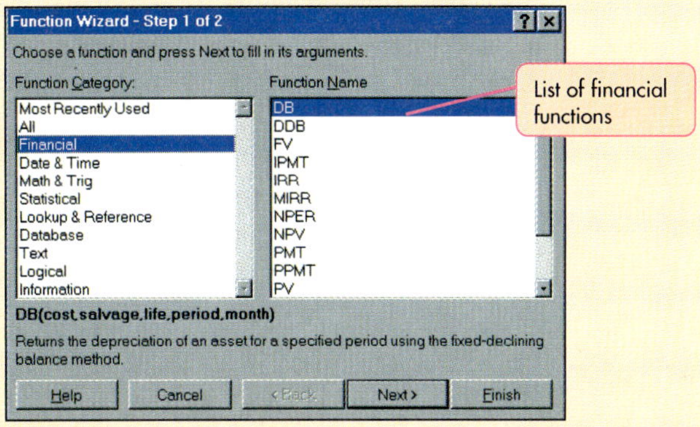

4. Click *DDB* in the **Function Name** list to select it, and notice how a description of the selected function, the double-declining balance method of depreciating assets, is displayed at the bottom of the dialog box.
5. Click the **Next** command button to display the Function Wizard Step 2 of 2 dialog box.
6. Enter the arguments shown here in the edit boxes (those that are boldfaced are required—the others are optional). The easiest way to enter an argument is to click in the argument's edit box to move the insertion point there, then click the appropriate cell in the model. If necessary, you can drag the dialog box out of the way.

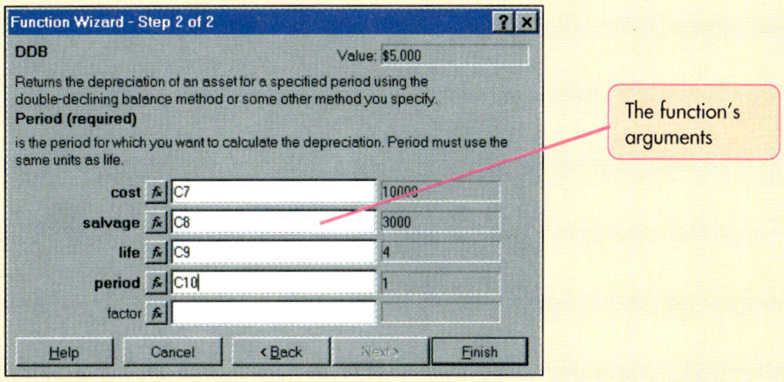

7. Click the **Finish** command button to enter the function in its cell. The result should be $5,000.

Entering Other Functions

8. Select cell C16 and use the Function Wizard to select the financial function *FV* (the future value of an investment) and specify the arguments as cells **C13** (*rate*), **C14** (*nper*), and **C15** (*pmt*). Then click the **Finish** command button. The result should be $98,347.

9. Select cell C23 and use the Function Wizard to select the financial function *IRR* (the internal rate of return) and specify the arguments as cells **B19:B23** (*values*) and **C19** (*guess*). Then click the **Finish** command button. The result should be 34.90%.
10. Select cell C28 and use the Function Wizard to select the financial function *PMT* (payment) and specify the arguments as cells **C25** (*rate*), **C26** (*nper*), and **C27** (*pv*). Then click the **Finish** command button. The result should be $1,338.79.
11. Select cell C33 and use the Function Wizard to select the financial function PV (the present value of an investment) and specify the arguments as cells **C30** (*rate*), **C31** (*nper*), and **C32** (*pmt*). Then click the **Finish** command button. The result should be $9,818.
12. Save and print the worksheet.

Exploring What-Ifs

13. Change any of the arguments for any of the functions, and watch the functions calculate new results.

Finishing Up

14. Close the workbook without saving your what-if changes.

4-4 USING NAMES

You can name ranges of cells and then refer to them by name rather than by their reference when entering formulas and functions, selecting cells, or completing dialog boxes. Names are useful because they are easy to remember. For example, a formula =A6–A7 has no meaning without referring to the referenced cell's descriptive labels. However, if you name cell A6 *Sales* and A7 *Expenses*, you could enter the formula as =*Sales–Expenses* and know immediately what it calculated. Also, you can use names instead of cell addresses or ranges in functions. For example, the function =SUM*(sales)* will total all of the numbers that fall in the range named *sales*.

When you first open a new workbook, there are no named ranges. However, you can name them using the Name box on the formula bar or by pulling down the **Insert** menu and clicking the **Name** command.

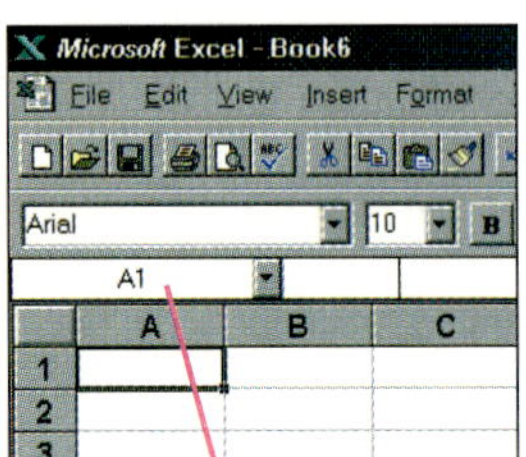

The Name box

Names and the Name Box

You can use the Name box on the formula bar to define names and then use those names to select cells or refer to them in formulas. To name a range of cells, select the range and then type a name into the Name box.

QUICKSTEPS

Naming Ranges Using the Name Box

1. Select the range of cells to be named.
2. Click the Name box on the formula bar, type a name, and then press Enter↵. The names you can use are described in the box "Understanding Names."

UNDERSTANDING Names

- The first character in the name must be a letter or underscore character. The characters that follow the first can also include numbers and periods.
- Spaces are not allowed in names. To separate words, enter underscore characters. For example, to name a range *Fall Sales*, enter the name as *Fall_Sales*.
- You can use upper- and lowercase letters, but Excel is not case-sensitive when you refer to names. For example, if you name a range *Sales*, the functions =SUM(sales), =SUM(Sales), and =SUM(SALES) all work identically.

Using Names in Formulas and Functions

Once you have named ranges, you can use the names by clicking the Name box's drop-down arrow (▾) to display them and then click one of the names to select it. What happens then depends on where you are in a procedure:

- If the formula bar is active (as it is after you press =), the selected name is inserted into the formula or function. The name in the formula or function acts just as the cell reference would and would be entered at the same point. For example, if the range A1:A5 has been named *sales*, the function =SUM(sales) is the same as the function =SUM(A1:A5). To enter this function, you type **=SUM(** and then click the Name box's drop-down arrow (▾) to select the name *sales*. At this point the function would read *=SUM(sales*. You would then type) to end the function and press Enter↵ to enter it in the cell.

- If the formula bar is not active, the range of cells to which the name has been assigned is selected. For example, if the range A1:A5 has been named *Sales*, that range is highlighted when you click *Sales* on the drop-down list. In other words, clicking the name is like using the **Go To** command on the **Edit** menu.

Names and the Insert Menu

You can define names using the **Name** command on the **Insert** menu, but it isn't as fast as using the Name box on the formula bar. The reason you use the **Name** command is that it allows you to delete names and apply names to cells based on the text in adjacent cells. For example, all cells in a column labeled *January* will be named *January*. All cells in a row labeled *Sales* will be named *Sales*.

	A	B	C	D	E
1		January	February	March	Apri
2	Sales	1000	1500	2000	250
3	Expenses	600	900	1200	150
4	Profit	400	600	800	100

Select the range that includes the names, and then pull down the **Insert** menu, click the **Name** command, and use the **Create** command to create names in the top row and left column.

	A	B	C	D	E
1		January	February	March	April
2	Sales	1000	1500	2000	2500
3	Expenses	600	900	1200	1500
4	Profit	400	600	800	1000

This row will be named *Sales*.

This column will be named *January*.

QUICKSTEPS

Naming Ranges with the Insert Menu

1. Select the range of cells that includes the cells containing the names and the cells to be named.
2. Pull down the **Insert** menu and point to the **Name** command to cascade the menu.
3. Make any of the choices described in the table "Understanding the Name Menu."

UNDERSTANDING

The Name Menu

When you pull down the **Insert** menu and click the **Name** command, the menu cascades to list the following commands:

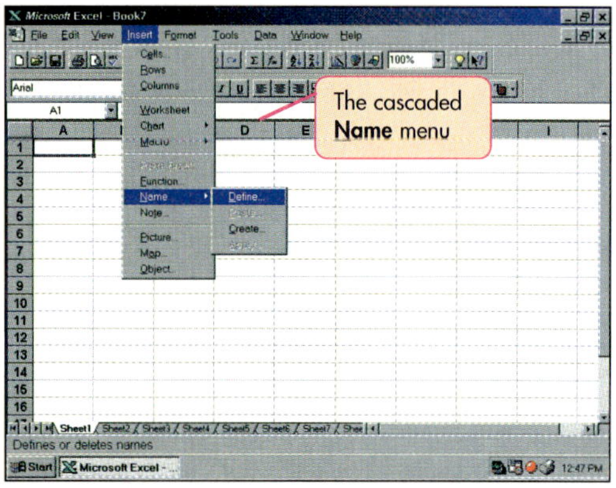

Define displays the Define Name dialog box. All defined names are displayed in the **Names in Workbook** window. You can enter a new name in the **Names in Workbook** text box and click the **Add** button to create a new name. You can also select any name on the list and click the **Delete** command button to delete it.

Paste inserts the selected name into the formula displayed on the formula bar.

Create displays the Create Names dialog box where you assign names to selected cells using the text in adjacent selected cells.

- **Top Row** uses the text in the top row to name the cells on the rows below. The name in the top cell of the selected range is applied to all of the selected cells below it in the column.
- **Left Column** uses the text in the left column to name the cells in the columns to the right. The name in the leftmost cell in the selected range is applied to all of the selected cells to the right of it on the row.
- **Bottom Row** uses the text in the bottom row to name the cells on the rows above.
- **Right Column** uses the text in the right column to name the cells in the columns to the left.

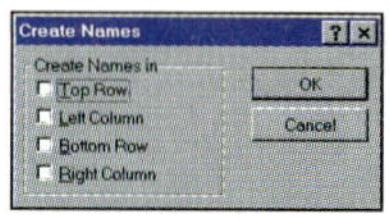

Apply replaces cell references in formulas with the selected name wherever the ranges match exactly. It does this for a selected range of cells, or for the entire worksheet when only a single cell is selected.

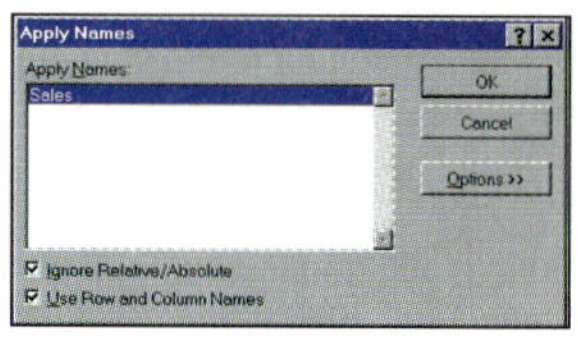

In this tutorial you define a name with the Name box on the formula bar. Then you use Excel's **Name** command to name cells by assigning them the row labels to their left and the column labels above them. You then enter formulas that use the assigned names rather than the cell addresses to which they refer.

Getting Ready

1. Open the *Names in calculations* workbook stored in the *Tutorial Workbooks* folder on the *Excel Student Resource Disk* and enter your name into cell A1.

Naming a Range

2. Select cells B6 through B9.
3. Click the Name box on the formula bar to select the cell's address, then type the name **sales** and press Enter↵.

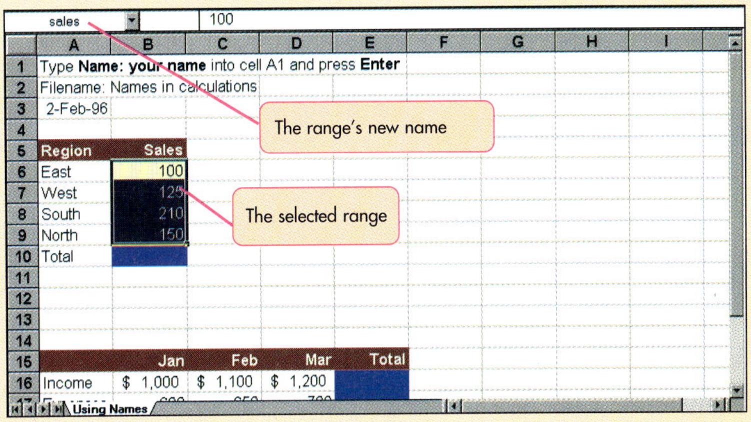

Selecting a Named Range

4. Click anywhere on the worksheet outside of the named range.
5. Click the Name box's drop-down arrow (▾) to display a list of names on the worksheet (*sales* is now the only one), and click the name *sales*. The range to which you assigned that name is immediately selected.

Referring to a Named Range in a Function

6. Select cell B10 and type the function **=SUM(sales)** and press Enter↵. The function sums the range just as if you had entered it as B6:B9.

Creating Names

7. Select the range of cells from A15 to D17.

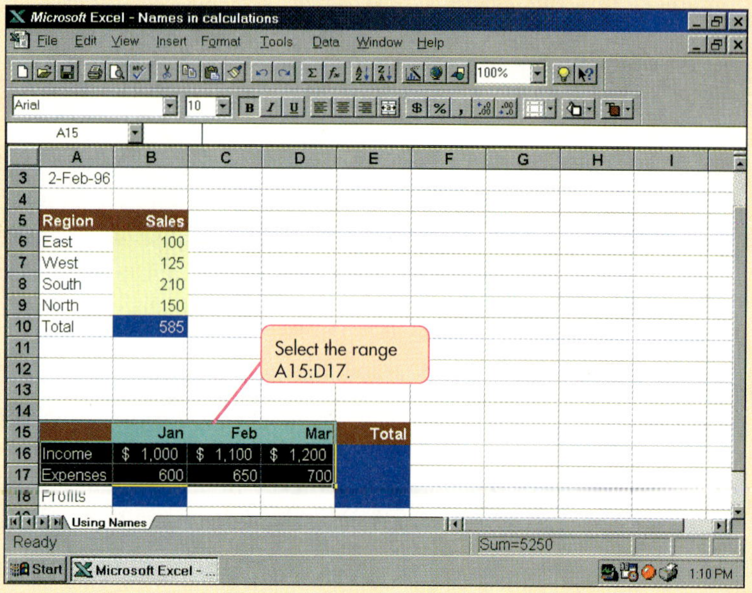

8. Pull down the **Insert** menu and point to the **Name** command to cascade the menu.
9. Click the **Create** command to display the Create Names dialog box. The check boxes for **Top Row** and **Left Column** should both be on (☑). If they are not, click them on.

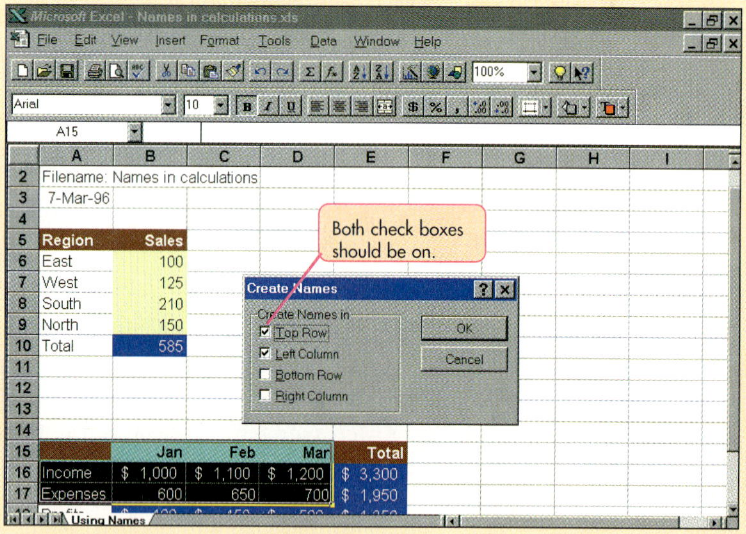

10. Click the **OK** command button to create the names.

Using Created Names in Formulas

11. Select cell B18, type the formula **=income–expenses** and press Enter.
12. Select cell B18 and point to the fill handle on the cell border so the mouse pointer turns into a small plus sign (+). Hold down the left mouse button, drag the fill handle to cell D18, and release the mouse button. The formula is copied to each of the cells you dragged the outline over.
13. Select cell E16, then type **=SUM(** and click the Name box's drop-down arrow (▾) to display a list of names on the worksheet.
14. Click *Income* to select it, then type) and press Enter.

15. Select cell E17, then type **=SUM(expenses)** and press Enter.

16. Select cell E18, then type **=SUM(income)–SUM(expenses)** and press Enter.

Displaying Formulas

17. Press Ctrl+` to display formulas in the cells instead of their calculated values. If necessary, scroll the screen to see how the formulas all work.

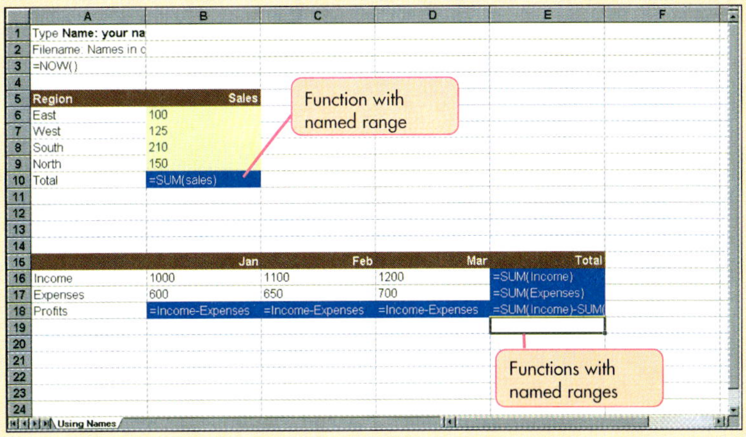

18. Press Ctrl+` again to return to displaying calculated values.

Finishing Up

19. Save, print, and close the workbook.

4-5 ENTERING DATES AND TIMES

To calculate with dates and times you must enter them in a specific way but you can then format them so they are displayed in a variety of formats.

Entering Dates and Times

When entering dates and times, if you enter them in a way that Excel recognizes, it will allow you to calculate with them and automatically format the cell to display them correctly. When they are entered correctly, Excel stores dates and times as values called *serial numbers* that it can add and subtract. For example, you can subtract two dates to see how many days fell between them. When they are entered in such a way that Excel does not recognize the format, they are stored as text. When entering dates or times, keep the following points in mind:

- To enter dates and times as text, precede them with an apostrophe.
- To enter today's date, press Ctrl+;
- To enter the current time, press Ctrl+: (you'll have to hold down Shift to type the :).
- To enter dates, separate days, months, and years with slashes (/) or hyphens (-). For example, enter January 30, 1996 as 1/30/96 or 1-30-96.
- To have Excel display a time in AM or PM format, type the time, then a space, then the AM or PM. If you leave out the space, Excel treats the entry as text. If

you do not type AM or PM, you must use 24-hour format to type a time. Thus, for 1:00 PM you would type 13:00.

- To enter a date and time in the same cell, separate them with a space.

TIP

Entering Dates and Times

When you enter dates and times in a form that Excel recognizes, the cell is automatically formatted. Here are some acceptable ways to enter dates and times so Excel recognizes them.

Date Formats	*Time Formats*
1/30/96	6:30 or 18:30
1-Jan-96	6:30 AM or 6:30 PM
1/30 or Jan-30	1/30/96 6:30
Jan-96	

Date Formats

Format	Examples
3/4	2/2
3/4/98	2/2/96
03/04/98	02/02/96
4-Mar	2-Feb
4-Mar-98	2-Feb-96
04-Mar-98	02-Feb-96
Mar-98	Feb-96
March-98	February-96
March 4, 1998	February 2, 1996
3/4/98 1:30 PM	2/2/96 1:32 PM
3/4/98 13:30	2/2/96 13:32

Time Formats

Format	Examples
13:30	13:32
1:30 PM	1:32 PM
13:30:55	13:32:15
1:30:55 PM	1:32:15 PM
30:55.7	32:14.8
26:30:55	842341:32:15
3/4/98 1:30 PM	2/2/96 1:32 PM
3/4/98 13:30	2/2/96 13:32

Using AutoFill to Enter a Series of Dates and Times

When you want to enter a series of dates quickly, you can use Excel's AutoFill feature. Select the cell containing a date and drag the fill handle to cells where you want the date added. As you do so, the date that will be entered into the current cell is displayed in the Name box on the formula bar. When you release the mouse button, the cells are filled with incremented dates. The same procedure will fill in a series of times incremented by one hour.

Formatting Dates and Times

When you enter a date or time, its format depends on the format you used to enter it. However, you can change the format at any time with the **Format**, **Cells**, **Number** dialog box. The formats you can use are shown in the tables at the left.

TUTORIAL

IN this tutorial you see how to enter dates and times in formats that Excel recognizes. You then see how they increment if you use the Fill command to copy them to adjacent cells.

Getting Ready

1. Open the *Dates and times workbook* stored in the *Tutorial Workbooks* folder on the *Excel Student Resource Disk* and enter your name in cell A1.

Entering Dates and Times

2. Column A shows some example forms in which you can enter dates and times so Excel recognizes them. Enter each date and time in column B as shown in the cell to its left. Not all entries will be displayed exactly as you type them. (The entries in column A are text because an apostrophe (') was typed before typing the date or time. Don't type this apostrophe in column B.)

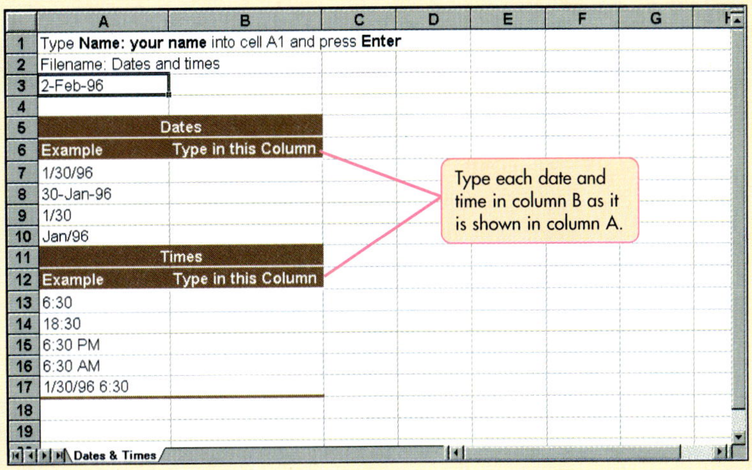

Filling Adjacent Cells

3. Click cell B7 to select it, then point to the fill handle on the lower-right corner of the cell until the mouse pointer turns into a small plus sign.
4. Drag the fill handle two cells to the right, and then release the mouse button to fill the cells with dates that increment by one day.

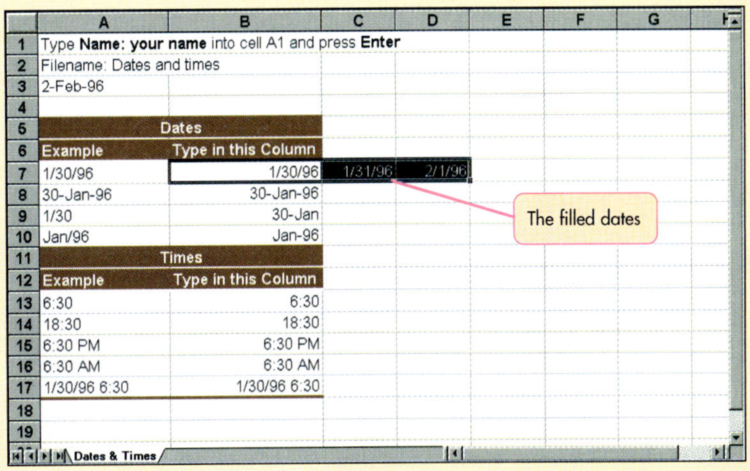

5. Click cell B16 to select it, then point to the fill handle on the lower-right corner of the cell until the mouse pointer turns into a small plus sign.
6. Drag the fill handle two cells to the right, and then release the mouse button to fill the cells with times that increment by one hour.

Finishing Up

7. Save, print, and close the workbook.

4-6 DATE AND TIME FUNCTIONS

Dates and times are important elements of many types of analysis. For example, a business's accounts payable and accounts receivable are due on certain dates. The time that a measurement is made in biology may have an influence on the results of an experiment. Since dates and times are so important, Excel provides functions that automatically calculate or operate on them for you.

Generating Date and Time Serial Numbers

To work with dates and times, you first have to enter them as described in Section 4-5 or generate them as serial numbers using one of the functions described in the table "Functions That Generate Date and Time Serial Numbers." These functions assign a numeric serial number to days and times.

- Date serial numbers are the number of days since January 1, 1900 inclusive. The serial number for that date is 1.
- Time serial numbers are fractional equivalents of the 24-hour period. For example, midnight is 0, noon is .5, and just before midnight is .999.

Functions That Generate Date and Time Serial Numbers

Function	Description
DATE	Calculates the serial number of the specified date
DATEVALUE	Calculates the serial number of the date entered as text
NOW	Calculates the serial number of the current date and time number based on your system's internal clock. When you use the =NOW() function, it updates whenever you open or recalculate the work sheet. You can use this to display the current date and time on the screen.
TIME	Calculates the serial number of the specified time
TIMEVALUE	Calculates the serial number of a time entered as text
TODAY	Calculates the serial number of today's date

Calculating with Dates and Times

Since dates and times are actually numbers, you can add and subtract them, for example, to find the number of days between two dates or the number of hours, minutes, and seconds between two times. To enter dates or times in formulas, enclose them in double quotation marks. For example, to subtract one date from another, enter the formula as **="1/30/96"-"1/30/95"**. You can also manipulate date and time serial numbers with the functions described in the table "Functions That Calculate with Date and Time Serial Numbers."

Functions That Calculate with Date and Time Serial Numbers

Function	Description
DAY	Converts a serial number to a day of the month
HOUR	Converts a serial number to an hour
MINUTE	Converts a serial number to a minute
MONTH	Converts a serial number to a month
SECOND	Converts a serial number to a second
WEEKDAY	Converts a serial number to a day of the week
YEAR	Converts a serial number to a year

TUTORIAL

IN this tutorial you use date functions to calculate the number of days, weeks, and years that you have been alive.

Getting Ready

1. Open the *Calculating with dates* workbook stored in the *Tutorial Workbooks* folder on the *Excel Student Resource Disk* and enter your name into cell A1.

Entering Dates

2. In cell B6, type **=DATE(70,1,1)** and press Enter↵ to display the number of days from January 1, 1900 to January 1, 1970 inclusive.
3. In cell B7, type **=NOW()** and press Enter↵ to calculate the number of days from January 1, 1900 to today. (Some numbers will be different from those in the illustration because today's date depends on which day you do this tutorial.)

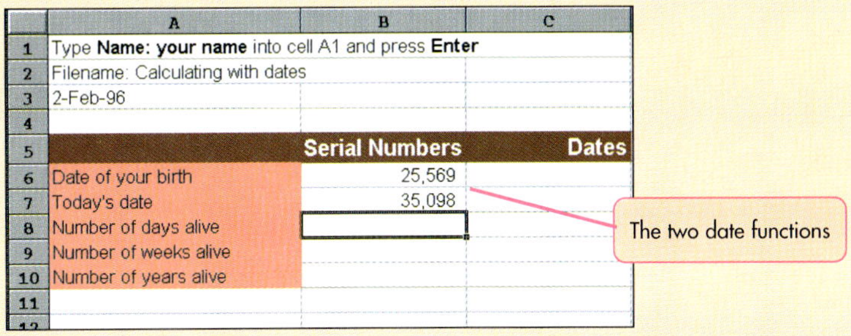

Calculating Dates

4. In cell B8, enter the formula **=B7–B6** to calculate the number of days you have been alive as of today if you had been born on January 1, 1970.
5. In cell B9, enter the formula **=B8/7** to calculate the number of weeks you have been alive as of today.
6. In cell B10, enter the formula **=B8/365** to calculate the number of years you have been alive as of today.

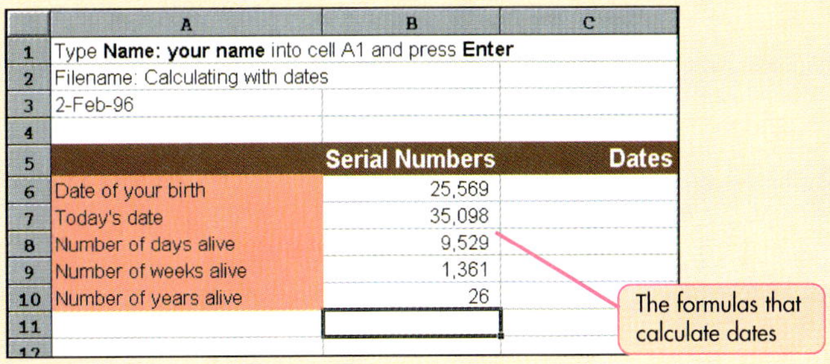

Formatting the Dates

7. Select cells B6 through B10 and drag the fill handle one column to the right to copy the dates and formulas into column C.
8. Select cells C6 and C7, point to the selected cells and click the **RIGHT** mouse button to display a shortcut menu.
9. Click the **Format Cells** command to display the Format Cells dialog box.
10. Click the *Number* tab to display that dialog box, and click *Date* in the **Category** list to display date formats.
11. Click the *4-Mar-95* format in the **Type** list, and then click the **OK** command button to apply the selected format to the cells.

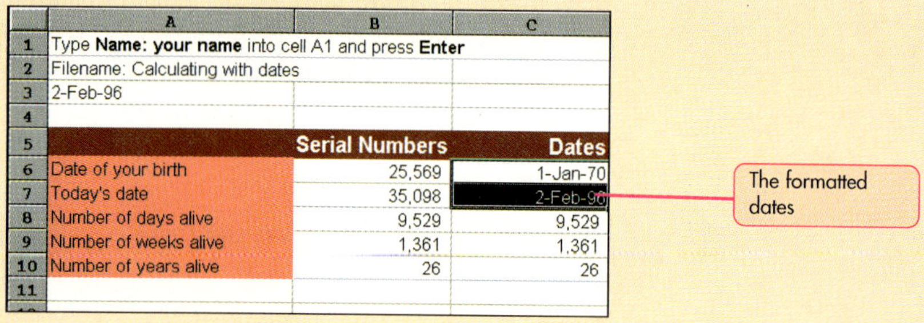

Finishing Up

12. Save and print the workbook.
13. Edit the date function in cell C6 so that it is your birth date (or a friend's). Replace the 70 with the year you were born, the first 1 with the month (1-12), and the second 1 with the day of the month (1-31). The numbers in cells C8 through C10 now are accurate for you or your friend.
14. Close the workbook without saving your changes.

4-7 COMPARISON OPERATORS AND LOGICAL FUNCTIONS

When entering functions and formulas, some of the most powerful tools that you have are comparison operators and logical functions. These operators determine the truth or falsity of statements. For example, they can determine if Sally's sales are higher or lower than John's. When used with IF functions, these operators can cause a calculation to branch to two or more possible outcomes. For example, the function can calculate that if Sally's sales are higher, she gets a bonus; if John's are higher, he gets it.

Comparison Operators

Operator	Description
=	Equal to
>	Greater than
<	Less than
>=	Greater than or equal to
<=	Less than or equal to
<>	Not equal to

Comparison Operators

You use comparison operators to evaluate the relationship between two values. Excel then checks to see if the comparison is true or false. Using these operators, you can determine if one number is equal to, less than, or greater than another number. For example, the comparison operator > (greater than) in the formula =A1>1000 calculates TRUE if the value in cell A1 is larger than 1000 and FALSE if it is less than or equal to 1000. (TRUE has the numeric value of 1 and FALSE has the numeric value of 0.)

Logical Functions

The logical functions AND, OR, and NOT are used to test one or more statements. For example, the statement =OR(A1>1000,A2>1000) calculates 1 (TRUE) if the value in either cell A1 or A2 is larger than 1000 and 0 (FALSE) if both are less than or equal to 1000.

Logical Operators

Operator	Description
AND	All following conditions must be met
OR	At least one following condition must be met
NOT	Following condition(s) must not be met

One way to look at logical operators is the way an engineer would when designing a simple electrical circuit, such as those used in your home to turn lights on and off. For current to flow to the light, the appropriate switches must be closed.

With the AND operator, both switches A and B must be closed for the circuit to be completed and the light to turn on.

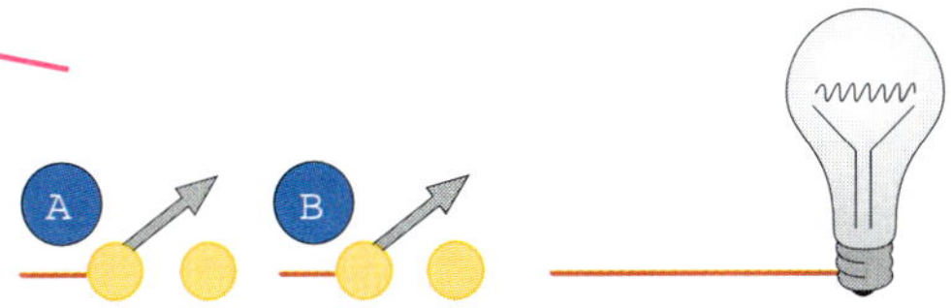

With the OR operator, if either switch A or B is closed, the circuit will be completed and the light will turn on.

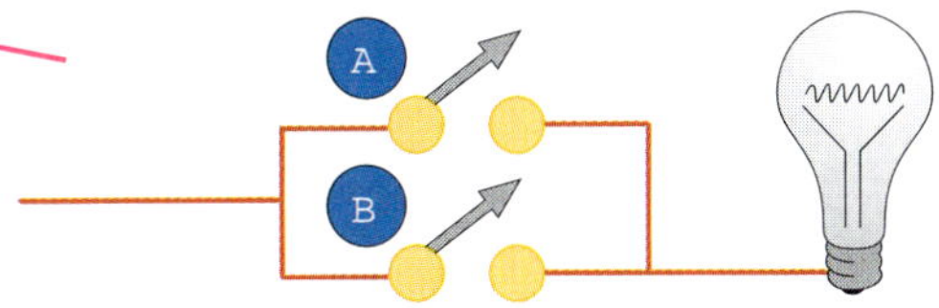

With the NOT operator, one of the switches, A or B, must NOT be open for the circuit to be completed and the light to turn on.

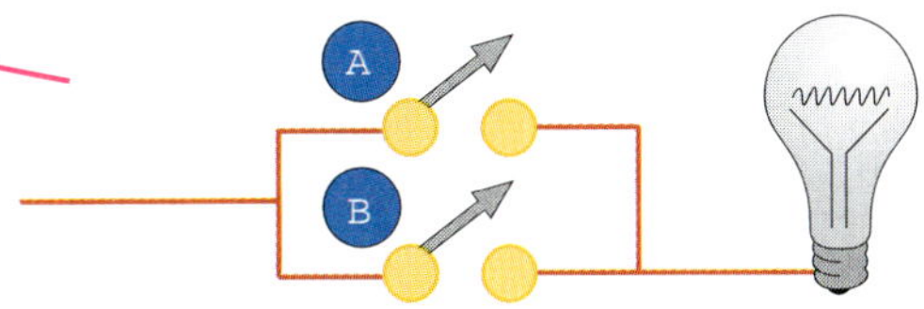

IF Functions

You use Excel's IF function to branch calculations. You do so by establishing a logical test that must be met. If the criterion is true, one calculation is made. If the criterion is false, another calculation is made. For example, let's say your business gave a 20% discount for all orders over $100. You could use the IF function =IF(order_amount>100,order_amount*discount,0) to calculate "IF the order amount is greater than $100, then multiply the order amount by 20% to calculate the discount; otherwise the discount is zero."

Since the functions normally refer to cells where the arguments are entered, the IF function we're describing might actually look like the one shown in the figure "The Discount Model—Original." It would actually read =IF(B1>100,B2*B1,0) where B1 is the order amount and B2 is the discount. Let's look closely at this function. The logical test B1>100 branches the calculation to one of two following possibilities depending on whether it is true or not. If the order is over $100, the B2*B1 part of the function calculates a discount. If the order is less than $100, the 0 part of the function is calculated.

You can expand on the model by using an AND function so the discount only applies to orders that are both over $100 and also $500 or less. The function would state "IF the order is greater than $100 and $500 or less, then multiply the order by 20% to calculate the discount, otherwise the discount is zero." The statement as shown in the figure "The Discount Model—Revised" would actually read =IF(AND(B1>100,B1<=500),B2*B1,0).

IF statements are also used to prevent #DIV/0! error messages from being displayed in cells. These error messages are displayed whenever you use the division operator (/) in a formula and the cell containing the denominator is blank. For example, if you enter the formula =B1/B2, it displays #DIV/0! when cell B2 is blank or contains a zero. To prevent this error message, you embed the formula in an IF function. For example, IF(B2>0,B1/B2,"N/A"). This formula now reads, "If the value in cell B2 is greater than 0, then divide the value in cell B1 by the value in cell B2; otherwise, display N/A."

=IF(B1>100,B2*B1,0)

=B1-B3

	A	B
1	Order amount	$ 110
2	Discount for orders over 100	20%
3	Discount for this order	$ 22
4	Amount due	$ 88

The Discount Model—Original

=IF(AND(B1>100,B1<=500),B2*B1,0)

=B1-B3

	A	B
1	Order amount	$ 501
2	Discount for orders over 100	20%
3	Discount for this order	$ -
4	Amount due	$ 501

The Discount Model—Revised

=B1/B3

	A	B
1	Total	1
2	Number	0
3	Average	#DIV/0!

=IF(B2>0,B1/B2,"N/A")

	A	B
1	Total	1
2	Number	0
3	Average	N/A

TUTORIAL

If you are running a successful business, you might be confronted with the need to expand spend money to increase sales beyond present production capacity. In this tutorial you enter an IF function in a model that calculates how your breakeven point changes when you have to invest in expansion. Since the goal of most businesses is to keep breakeven as low as possible, a higher breakeven point may be a source of concern. When finished with the model, it will look like the one shown in the figure "The Breakeven Model."

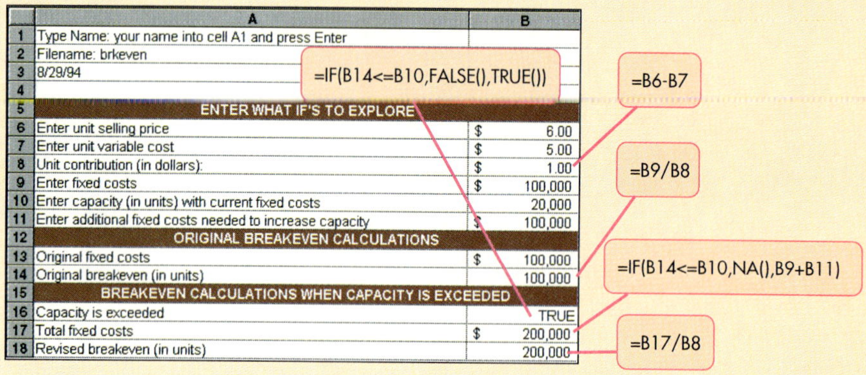

The Breakeven Model

Getting Ready

1. Open the *Breakeven analysis* workbook stored in the *Tutorial Workbooks* folder on the *Excel Student Resource Disk* and enter your name into cell A1.

Entering Formulas and Functions

2. Enter the formulas and the function shown in the figure "The Breakeven Model:"
   - The first function, in cell B16, reads in English "If the original breakeven is less than or equal to the capacity with current fixed costs, then display TRUE in the cell; otherwise display FALSE."
   - The second function, in cell B17, reads in English "If the original breakeven is less than or equal to the capacity with current fixed costs, then display #NA in the cell; otherwise add additional fixed costs to increase capacity to fixed costs."

Finishing Up

3. Save, print, and close the workbook.

4-8 WORKING WITH TEXT

Excel lets you use text in IF functions to display messages that make your models easier for others to use. When you do so, you enclose the text in quotation marks.

IN this tutorial you explore using text instead of numbers in functions. The model you create displays the terms *Fire* or *Promote* depending on how a salesperson performs.

Getting Ready

1. Open the *Fire or promote* workbook stored in the *Tutorial Workbooks* folder on the *Excel Student Resource Disk* and enter your name into cell A1.

Entering and Copying a Function

2. In cell C6, type **=IF(B6<10000,"Fire","Promote")** and press Enter. The function reads in English "IF the sales in cell B6 are less than $10,000, display the word *Fire*, otherwise display the Word *Promote*." In this case, the function displays the character string *Promote* because sales in cell B6 are not less than 10000.
3. Use the cell's fill handle to copy the function in cell C6 to cells C7 through C11. If sales in a cell in column B are less than 10000, the function in the adjoining cell displays *Fire*. If any value in a cell in column B is 10000 or more, the function displays *Promote*.

	A	B	C	D
1	Type **Name: your name** into cell A1 and press Enter			
2	Filename: iffire			
3	02-Feb-96			
4				
5	Name	Sales	Action	
6	Smith	10,000	*Promote*	
7	Jones	9,000	*Fire*	
8	Lewis	12,000	*Promote*	
9	Washington	15,000	*Promote*	
10	Lee	23,000	*Promote*	
11	Gonzalez	11,000	*Promote*	

Revising the Function

4. Revise the function in cell C6 to add the part shown in boldface here: **=IF(B6=10000,"Retain"**,IF(B6<10000,"Fire","Promote")). Be sure to add the closing parenthesis at the end of the function.
5. Use the cell's fill handle to copy the function in cell C6 to cells C7 through C11. The functions now work just as they did before; however, they now display *Retain* in any cell where sales are equal to 10000.

	A	B	C	D
1	Type **Name: your name** into cell A1 and press Enter			
2	Filename: iffire			
3	02-Feb-96			
4				
5	Name	Sales	Action	
6	Smith	10,000	*Retain*	
7	Jones	9,000	*Fire*	
8	Lewis	12,000	*Promote*	
9	Washington	15,000	*Promote*	
10	Lee	23,000	*Promote*	
11	Gonzalez	11,000	*Promote*	

6. Change some of the numbers in column B to numbers more than, less than, or equal to, 10,000 and watch the function change the displayed string.

Finishing Up

7. Save, print, and close the workbook.

REVIEW QUESTIONS

TRUE-FALSE

T F 1. Spaces are allowed in range names.

T F 2. The formula **=A1>1000** calculates **TRUE** if the value in cell A1 is greater than or equal to 1000.

T F 3. When referred to in a function's range, cells containing text or blank cells have a numeric value of 1.

T F 4. There can be more than one argument in a function.

T F 5. When you enter a function name in lowercase letters, Excel will automatically convert it to uppercase letters when you press Enter↵.

T F 6. Numbers cannot be used in range names.

T F 7. Time serial numbers are fractional equivalents of the 24-hour period.

T F 8. You can add and subtract dates.

T F 9. The statement **=OR(A1>1000,A2>1000)** calculates 1 if the value in either cell is larger than 1000.

T F 10. IF functions are used to branch calculations.

MULTIPLE CHOICE

1. All functions begin with a(n) ________.

a. = b. +
c. @ d. "

2. Arguments in functions must be enclosed in ________.

a. Quotation marks b. Colons
c. Parentheses d. Asterisks

3. The symbol used to separate the beginning and ending of a range is a(n) ________.

a. Quotation mark b. Colon
c. Parentheses d. Apostrophe

4. Which of the following is not an example of a logical function:

a. AND b. NOW
c. OR d. NOT

5. To enter dates and times as text, type a(n) ________ before typing the date or time.

a. Quotation mark b. Equal symbol
c. Plus symbol d. Apostrophe

6. To enter today's date, type ________ and press Enter.

a. =NOW
b. Ctrl+;
c. Ctrl+Shift+;
d. =TODAY

7. Date serial numbers are the number of days since ________.

a. January 1, 1900
b. January 1, 1950
c. January 1, 0001
d. None of the above

8. Which of the following is not an example of a comparison operator:

a. +
b. =
c. >
d. <

9. The first character in a range name must be a(n) ________.

a. Letter or an underscore
b. Quotation mark
c. Equal symbol
d. Plus symbol

10. When entering text directly into formulas or functions, enclose the strings in ________.

a. Quotation marks
b. Double quotation marks
c. Parentheses
d. Apostrophes

FILL IN THE BLANK

1. You can use ________ operators to determine if one number is equal to another number.
2. In functions, ________ must be enclosed in parentheses.
3. ________ functions are used to convert text to numbers and vice versa.
4. The ________ displays functions grouped by category.
5. To enter a date and time in the same cell, separate them with a(n) ________.
6. The ________ function calculates the serial number of today's date.
7. Arguments in functions can be ________, ________, ________, ________, or ________.
8. To specify a range of cells falling in a rectangle, you specify the ________-left and ________ right cells in the range, separated by a colon.
9. AND is an example of a ________ function.
10. When using comparison operators, TRUE has a numeric value of ________ and FALSE has a numeric value of ________.

LAB ACTIVITIES

DRILLS

4-1 Understanding Functions

In this drill you enter a PMT function in a model that calculates the monthly payment on a loan at any given interest rate, term, and loan amount.

1. Open the *Loan payments* workbook stored in the *Drill Workbooks* folder on the *Excel Student Resource Disk* and enter your name into cell A1.
2. Type the function **=PMT(B6/12,B7,-B8)** into cell B9 and press Enter. With cell B9 selected, look at the function displayed on the formula bar and notice the order in which the cells are listed.
3. Change the interest rate to 8% and look at the new monthly payment.
4. Save, print, and close the workbook.

4-2 Using AutoSum

The function that people use most often is SUM. Because it is used so extensively, Excel has an AutoSum feature that automatically sums numbers. In this drill you practice using that feature.

1. Open the *Using AutoSum* workbook stored in the *Drill Workbooks* folder on the *Excel Student Resource Disk* and enter your name into cell A1.
2. Select the cells with the red borders in each group but the last and then click the **AutoSum** button on the Standard toolbar to automatically enter the function in the selected cell(s). When you select only one cell, you have to click the Enter box (☑) on the formula bar to complete the entry.
3. In the last group ("Summing Totals and Grand Totals") select each cell individually and in sequence from top to bottom. For each, click the **AutoSum** button on the Standard toolbar, and then click the Enter box (☑) on the formula bar to complete the entry. You'll see that the last cell automatically totals the sums above it.
4. Save, print, and close the workbook.

4-3 Using the Function Wizard

Excel's Function Wizard makes it easy to enter functions step by step. In this drill you use Function Wizard to enter a series of statistical functions that all calculate the same list of numbers. When finished, your model should look like the one in the figure "The Statistical Functions Model."

	A	B
1	Your Name	
2	Filename: Statistical functions	
3	2-Feb-96	
4		
5	Region	Sales
6	Central	678
7	East	1,018
8	Northeast	1,515
9	Northwest	1,956
10	Southeast	965
11	Southwest	965
12	West	1,789
13		
14	Average (AVERAGE)	1269.428571
15	Count (COUNT)	0
16	Max (MAX)	1956
17	Min (MIN)	678
18	Standard deviation (STDEVP)	447.2132304
19	Sum (SUM)	8886
20	Variance (VARP)	199999.6735

The Statistical Functions Model

1. Open the *Statistical functions* workbook stored in the *Drill Workbooks* folder on the *Excel Student Resource Disk* and enter your name into cell A1.
2. Select the cells in the range B6:B12 and type the name **Sales** into the name box to name the range.
3. Use the Function Wizard to enter the functions listed on rows 14 through 20 in column B on the same row as its name.
   - The name of each function is listed in column A, for example, AVERAGE, COUNT, and MAX.
   - The functions are all under the *Statistical* **Function Category** in Function Wizard's first dialog box except SUM, which is *Math & Trig*.
   - The functions all have the same argument, the range of cells B6:B12 which you can type in as the only required argument in each of the functions.
4. Save the model and make a printout.
5. Change any of the sales for one or more regions and watch the statistical functions calculate new results.
6. Close the screen without saving your what-if changes.

4-4 Using Names

When you name cells or ranges of cells, you can then use those names in formulas and functions instead of cell references. In this drill you open an existing model and enter new functions that refer to a named range. When finished, your model should look like the one in the figure "The Statistical Functions Model with Names."

	A	B	C
1	Your Name		
2	Filename: Statistical functions		
3	=NOW()		
4			
5	Region	Sales	
6	Central	678	
7	East	1018	
8	Northeast	1515	
9	Northwest	1956	
10	Southeast	965	
11	Southwest	965	
12	West	1789	
13			
14	Average (AVERAGE)	=AVERAGE(B6:B12)	=AVERAGE(Sales)
15	Count (COUNT)	=COUNTA(B6:B12)	=COUNT(Sales)
16	Max (MAX)	=MAX(B6:B12)	=MAX(Sales)
17	Min (MIN)	=MIN(B6:B12)	=MIN(Sales)
18	Standard deviation (STDEVP)	=STDEVP(B6:B12)	=STDEVP(Sales)
19	Sum (SUM)	=SUM(B6:B12)	=SUM(Sales)
20	Variance (VARP)	=VARP(B6:B12)	=VARP(Sales)
21			

The Statistical Functions Model with Names

1. Open the *Statistical functions* workbook stored in the *Drill Workbooks* folder on the *Excel Student Resource Disk.*
2. Select the range of cells B6:B12, click in the Name box on the formula bar, and enter the name *Sales.*
3. In cells C14 through C20 enter the same functions entered into column B on the same rows, but this time specify the range as *Sales*. For example, in cell C14, enter the function **=AVERAGE(sales)** not **=AVERAGE(B6:B12)**.
4. Save the workbook.
5. Press Ctrl+` to display the formulas and functions in their cells, narrow column A, and make a printout.
6. Close the workbook without saving your changes.

4-5 Entering Dates and Times

The form in which you enter dates affects their format and the way they are displayed. In this drill you practice entering dates in a variety of formats.

1. Open the *Dates 2* workbook stored in the *Drill Workbooks* folder on the *Excel Student Resource Disk* and enter your name into cell A1.
2. Enter dates shown in column A on the same row in column B. The last two entries enter dates and times when you press Ctrl+; and Ctrl+Shift+; (expressed on the model as Ctrl+:). After pressing the correct keys, you must press Enter to complete the entry.
3. Save, print, and close the workbook.

4-6 Date and Time Functions

After you have entered dates or times, you can change their format. In this drill you enter date and time functions and format them using the available formats. When finished, your model should look like the one in the figure "The Date & Time Functions & Formats Model."

	A	B
2	Filename: Date & time functions & formats	
3	2/2/96	
4		
5	Exploring Date Functions & Formats	
6	Date function	=DATE(96,1,11)
7	Serial number	35075
8	3/4	1/11
9	3/4/95	1/11/96
10	3/4/95	01/11/96
11	4-Mar	11-Jan
12	4-Mar-95	11-Jan-96
13	4-Mar-95	11-Jan-96
14	Mar-95	Jan-96
15	Mar-95	January-96
16	4-Mar-95	January 11, 1996
17	3/4/95 13:30	1/11/96 12:00 AM
18	3/4/95 13:30	1/11/96 0:00
19		
20	Exploring Time Functions & Formats	
21	Time function	=TIME(12,1,45)
22	Serial number	0.501215278
23	13:30	12:01
24	1:30 PM	12:01 PM
25	13:30:55	12:01:45
26	1:30:55 PM	12:01:45 PM
27	30:55.7	01:45.0
28	26:30:55	12:01:45
29	3/4/98 1:30 PM	1/0/00 12:01 PM
30	3/4/98 13:30	1/0/00 12:01

The Date & Time Functions & Formats Model

1. Open the *Date & time functions & formats* workbook stored in the *Drill Workbooks* folder on the *Excel Student Resource Disk* and enter your name into cell A1.
2. Enter the function **=DATE(96,1,11)** in cell B6, and use the cell's fill handle to copy the function to cells B7 through B18. Use the **Format Painter** button on the Standard toolbar to copy the red line in cell B30 back into cell B18 where it was erased by the fill command.
3. Enter the time function **=TIME(12,1,45)** in cell B21, and use the cell's fill handle to copy the function to cells B22 through B30. Use the **Format Painter** button on the Standard toolbar to copy the line in cell B18 back into cell B30.
4. Format the cells as follows:
    - Edit the contents of cells B6 and B21 to enter an apostrophe in front of the equal sign. This will display the function in the cell as text. Right-align the functions in their cells.
    - Format cells B7 and B22 using the **Format**, **Cells**, **Number**, **General** commands.
    - Format each of the other functions using the date or time formats listed on the same row in column A. To do so, use the **Format**, **Cells**, **Number**, **Date** or **Time** commands.
5. Save, print, and close the workbook.

4-7 Comparison Operators and Logical Functions

You can create a truth table for comparison operators. By changing the numbers in cells B5 and B6, you can establish if the relationships are true or false. When finished, your model should look like the one in the figure "The Comparison Operators Model."

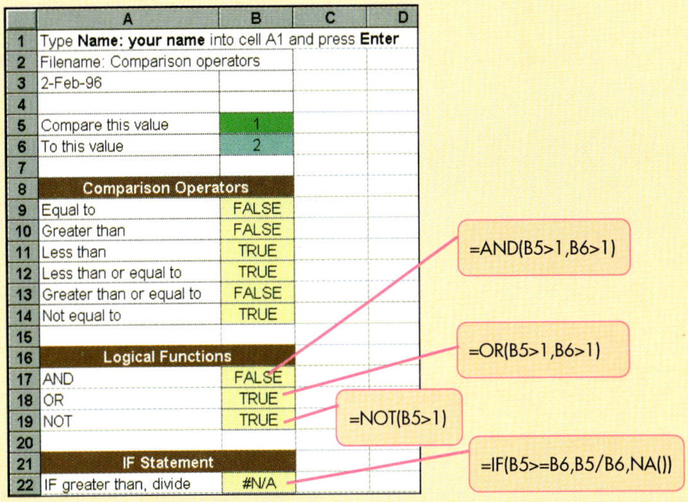

The Comparison Operators Model

1. Open the *Comparison operators* workbook stored in the *Drill Workbooks* folder on the *Excel Student Resource Disk* and enter your name into cell A1.
2. In the sections "Comparison Operators" enter formulas that compare the value in cell B5 with the value in B6. For example, in cell B9 the formula is =B5=B6 and in B10 it is =B5>B6. Only the comparison operator changes in each formulas.
3. In the section "Logical Functions" enter the functions shown in the figure "The Comparison Operators Model."

4. In cell B22, enter the function **=IF(B5>=B6,B5/B6,NA())** and press Enter.
5. Save and print the workbook.
6. Change the values in cells B5 and B6 to combinations such as 1 and 1, 1 and 2, and 2 and 1 to see how the formulas and functions calculate. Try to figure out why each one calculates what it does when you change the numbers.
   - What combination of the numbers 1 and 2 make cell B22 display a value? Why?
   - What combination of the numbers 1 and 2 make NOT false? Why?
7. Close the workbook without saving your changes.

4-8 Working with Text

If you owned a store, you might want to separate daily cash transactions from charge account transactions. In this drill you create a model that does so with two IF functions that evaluate text entered into the model. The first function, in cell D6, checks to see if you have entered Y into cell C6. If the cell does contain a Y, the function carries the amount the customer spent to the *Cash Amount* column. The other function checks to see if cell C6 contains an N. If it does, the function carries the amount the customer spent to the *Charge Amount* column. When finished, your model should look like the one in the figure "The Text in Calculations Model."

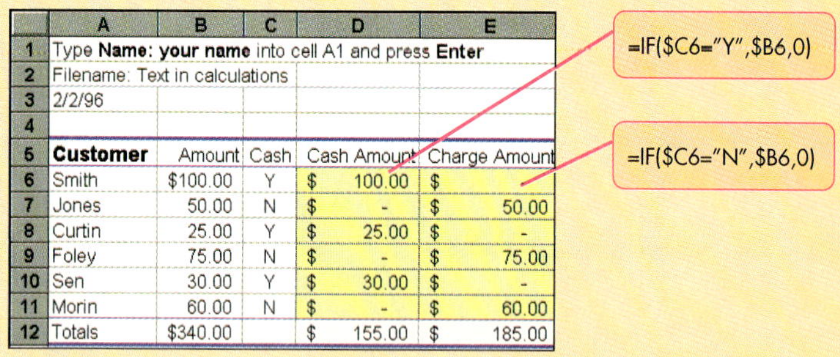

	A	B	C	D	E
1	Type **Name: your name** into cell A1 and press **Enter**				
2	Filename: Text in calculations				
3	2/2/96				
4					
5	**Customer**	Amount	Cash	Cash Amount	Charge Amount
6	Smith	$100.00	Y	$ 100.00	$
7	Jones	50.00	N	$ -	$ 50.00
8	Curtin	25.00	Y	$ 25.00	$ -
9	Foley	75.00	N	$ -	$ 75.00
10	Sen	30.00	Y	$ 30.00	$ -
11	Morin	60.00	N	$ -	$ 60.00
12	Totals	$340.00		$ 155.00	$ 185.00

The Text in Calculations Model

1. Open the *Text in calculations* workbook stored in the *Drill Workbooks* folder on the *Excel Student Resource Disk* and enter your name into cell A1.
2. In cells D6 and E6, enter the two functions shown in the figure "The Text in Calculations Model."
3. Select cells D6:E6 and use the fill handle to copy the formulas down to row 11.
4. Save and print the workbook.
5. Change any Y to N or N to Y in column C and watch the values move between the *Cash Amount* and *Charge Amount* columns.
6. Close the workbook without saving your changes.

EXERCISES

4-1 Balancing a Checkbook

One of the chores that each of us has to perform is balancing our checkbook. If we don't do it, or don't do it correctly, checks begin to bounce. In this exercise, you create a model that makes the checkbook-balancing calculations for you. To keep a checkbook in balance, you start with a known balance and subtract withdrawals and deposits. In the *Checkbook register* workbook, you could do this with a simple formula. In cell F8 you could enter =F7-D8+E8 and copy the formula all the way down column F. However, you can make the model a little more sophisticated by using a function to enter *NA* in the balance column for rows past the final record. When finished, your model should look like the figure "The Checkbook Register Model."

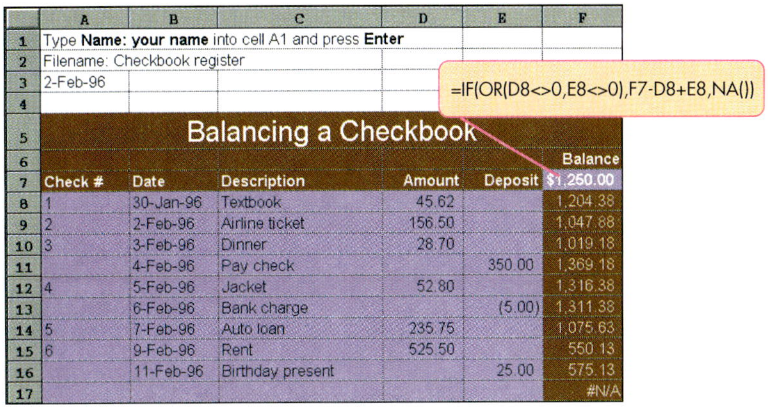

The Checkbook Register Model

1. Open the *Checkbook register* workbook stored in the *Exercise Workbooks* folder on the *Excel Student Resource Disk* and enter your name into cell A1.
2. Enter the dates in column B shown in the figure "The Checkbook Model."
3. In cell F8, enter the function **=IF(OR(D8<>0,E8<>0),F7-D8+E8,NA())**. The formula reads (in English) "If either cell D8 or cell E8 has any value other than zero, subtract any value in cell D8 from F7 and add cell E8; otherwise, display #N/A in cell F8."
4. Select cell F8 and use its fill handle to copy the formula from cell F8 to cells F9 through F17.
5. Save and print the workbook.
6. Explore what-ifs by changing the opening balance in cell F7, or any of the numbers in the *Amount* or *Deposit* column.
7. Close the workbook without saving your changes.

4-2 Calculating an Auto Loan

The *Auto loan analyzer* model is designed to make it easy to determine the monthly payments on a variety of auto loans. When finished, your model should look like the figure "The Auto Loan Analyzer Model."

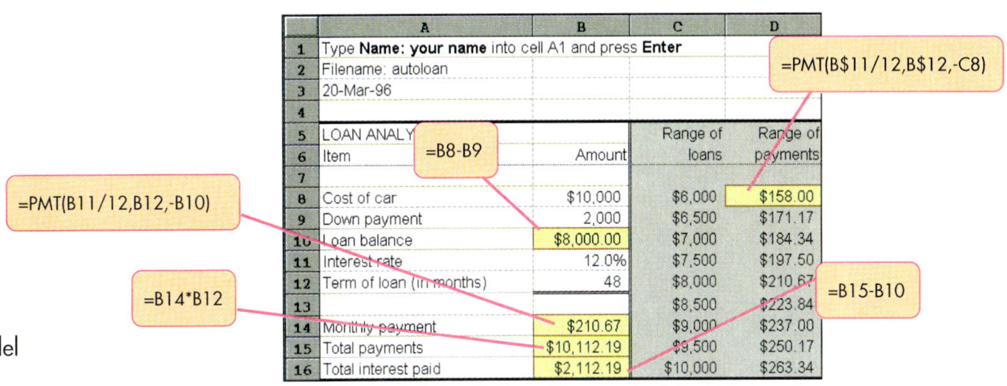

The Auto Loan Analyzer Model

1. Open the *Auto loan analyzer* workbook stored in the *Exercise Workbooks* folder on the *Excel Student Resource Disk* and enter your name into cell A1.

2. Enter the formulas and functions shown on the figure "The Auto Loan Analyzer Model." After entering the function into cell D8, select it and use its fill handle to copy the function to the cells below. Note that the two PMT functions divide the interest rate by 12 to convert it to a monthly interest rate.
3. Use the **Format**, **Cells**, **Border** commands to restore the border under cell D16.
4. Format all of the cells where you entered formulas using an accounting format with two decimal places.
5. Save and print the workbook.
6. Explore what-ifs by changing the *Cost of car, Down payment, Interest rate,* or *Term of loan.* Then close the workbook without saving your what-if changes.

4-3 Calculating Travel Expenses

When traveling on business, you are normally reimbursed for your expenses if you work for a large company, or you can deduct your expenses from your gross income for tax purposes when working on your own. In this application, you build a model that allows you to keep track of your expenses.

The expenses that are reimbursed vary from company to company. Normally, they cover only those expenses directly related to the business trip. Side trips or entertainment while traveling are not usually covered. Obviously, you do not create a good impression by billing for things that are not covered by the company. Where possible, attach receipts for each item you are billing to support the claim. When finished, your model should look like the figure "The Travel & Entertainment Model."

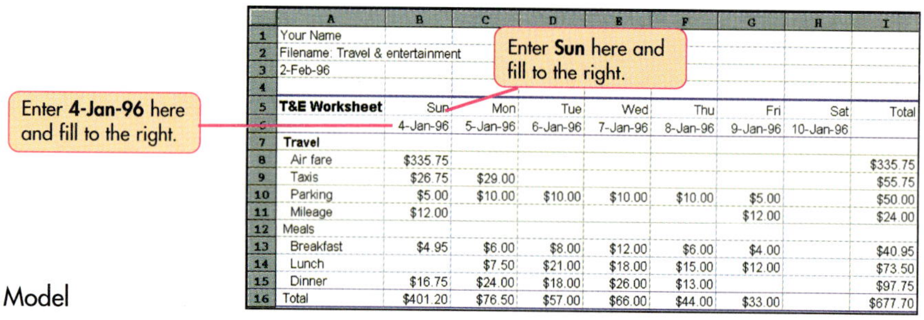

	A	B	C	D	E	F	G	H	I
1	Your Name								
2	Filename: Travel & entertainment								
3	2-Feb-96								
4									
5	**T&E Worksheet**	Sun	Mon	Tue	Wed	Thu	Fri	Sat	Total
6		4-Jan-96	5-Jan-96	6-Jan-96	7-Jan-96	8-Jan-96	9-Jan-96	10-Jan-96	
7	**Travel**								
8	Air fare	$335.75							$335.75
9	Taxis	$26.75	$29.00						$55.75
10	Parking	$5.00	$10.00	$10.00	$10.00	$10.00	$5.00		$50.00
11	Mileage	$12.00					$12.00		$24.00
12	Meals								
13	Breakfast	$4.95	$6.00	$8.00	$12.00	$6.00	$4.00		$40.95
14	Lunch		$7.50	$21.00	$18.00	$15.00	$12.00		$73.50
15	Dinner	$16.75	$24.00	$18.00	$26.00	$13.00			$97.75
16	Total	$401.20	$76.50	$57.00	$66.00	$44.00	$33.00		$677.70

The Travel & Entertainment Model

1. Open the *Travel & entertainment* workbook stored in the *Exercise Workbooks* folder on the *Excel Student Resource Disk* and enter your name into cell A1.
2. Select the cell range B8:I16 and use the **AutoSum** button on the Standard toolbar to enter sum functions in the *Total* column and row.
3. Enter the text **Sun** into cell B5 and use the cell's fill handle to copy it to other cells on the row through cell H5. It automatically changes to Mon, Tue, and so on.
4. Enter the date 4-Jan-96 into cell B6 and use the fill handle to copy it to other cells on the row through cell H6. It automatically changes to 5-Jan-96, 6-Jan-96, and so on.
5. Use the **Format**, **Cells** commands to format your model to match the figure "The Travel & Expense Model."
6. Select columns B through I and use the **Format**, **Column** commands to autofit their width to their contents.
7. Display the model in Print Preview, then click the **Setup** button to display Page Setup dialog box.

8. On the **Page** tab, turn on the **Fit to** option button to print the model on one sheet.
9. On the **Sheet** tab to turn off gridlines and row and column headings and then make a printout.
10. Save and close the workbook.

4-4 Calculating Lottery Payments

Almost all state lotteries offer huge prizes, but they spread their payment over a number of years. This stretched-out payment schedule saves the states a lot of money compared to what it would cost to pay winners a lump sum. In fact, you can say that these lotteries are guilty of false advertising. The tool you use to analyze the true value of payments over time is called present value analysis.

In this exercise, you enter a model that allows you to determine how much a lottery prize, or any other payment stretched over a period of years, is worth if you were to receive all of it today. The model shows how much a series of payments is worth in today's dollars, after accounting for interest you would have earned had you invested annual payments at a given interest rate.

1. Open the *Lottery payoffs* workbook stored in the *Exercise Workbooks* folder on the *Excel Student Resource Disk* and enter your name into cell A1.
2. In cell B7, enter the formula =B5/B6 to calculate the yearly payment.
3. In cell B9, enter the function =PV(B8,B6,-B7). l. As you can then see, $1 million spread in equal payments over 20 years is worth only $490,907 in today's dollars. If you had $490,907 and invested it for 20 years at 8%, you would have $1 million.
4. Save the finished model and make a printout without gridlines.
5. Change the size of the prize or the interest rate, and see how the present value changes. For example, what is the present value of a $10,000 prize spread over five years with interest rates at 12%?
6. Close the workbook without saving your what-if changes.

4-5 Calculating Running Totals and Running Averages

One useful application of absolute and relative references is to anchor one end of a range while letting the other end remain relative. This way, you can enter a function that includes the first number in a range, but when you copy it, additional numbers are included. In this exercise, you use this technique to calculate running totals and averages.

1. Open the *Running totals & averages* workbook stored in the *Exercise Workbooks* folder on the *Excel Student Resource Disk* and enter your name into cell A1.
2. In cell C6, enter the function **=SUM(B$6:B6)** being sure to use the correct relative and absolute addresses.
3. In cell D6, enter the function =**AVERAGE(B$6:B6)** being sure to use the correct relative and absolute addresses.
4. Select cells C6 and D6 and use the fill handle to copy the formulas down to row 17. Each cell in column C displays the cumulative total of numbers in column B and each cell in column D displays the cumulative average of numbers in that column.
5. Press Ctrl+` to display formulas in their cells and notice the results of copying the formula. Then press Ctrl+` to display values in their cells.
6. Save, print, and close the workbook.

4-1 Buying a House: The Cash Needed

When you buy a home, you need money for the down payment and other costs called closing costs. In this project you create a model that calculates closing costs when you purchase a new home. To begin, open the *Purchasing a house* model stored in the *Project Workbooks* folder on the *Excel Student Resource Disk*. This model contains all of the text you'll need but none of the numbers, formulas, or formats. The finished model is shown in the figure "The Purchasing a House Model," and its formulas are indicated on the illustration and described below. Using these descriptions and formatting commands, make your model look just like the one illustrated. When finished, change the size of the loan to $125,000, save the workbook, and make a printout.

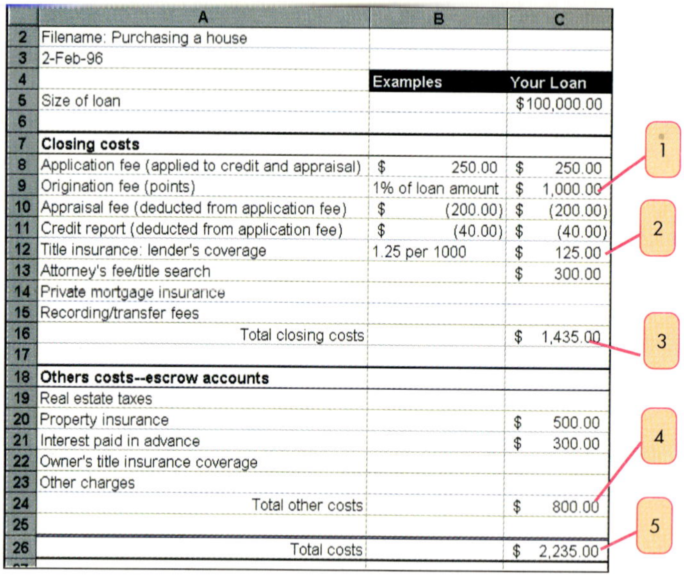

	A	B	C
2	Filename: Purchasing a house		
3	2-Feb-96		
4		Examples	Your Loan
5	Size of loan		$100,000.00
6			
7	**Closing costs**		
8	Application fee (applied to credit and appraisal)	$ 250.00	$ 250.00
9	Origination fee (points)	1% of loan amount	$ 1,000.00
10	Appraisal fee (deducted from application fee)	$ (200.00)	$ (200.00)
11	Credit report (deducted from application fee)	$ (40.00)	$ (40.00)
12	Title insurance: lender's coverage	1.25 per 1000	$ 125.00
13	Attorney's fee/title search		$ 300.00
14	Private mortgage insurance		
15	Recording/transfer fees		
16	Total closing costs		$ 1,435.00
17			
18	**Others costs--escrow accounts**		
19	Real estate taxes		
20	Property insurance		$ 500.00
21	Interest paid in advance		$ 300.00
22	Owner's title insurance coverage		
23	Other charges		
24	Total other costs		$ 800.00
25			
26	Total costs		$ 2,235.00

The Purchasing a House Model

1. **Origination fee**, known as points, is a one-time charge used to adjust the yield on the loan to what market conditions demand. Each point is equal to 1% of the loan amount.
2. **Title insurance** protects you and the lender from other people making claims on the property. It is usually bought at a given amount per $1,000 of mortgage.
3. **Total closing costs** is the sum of all closing costs broken down above.
4. **Total other costs** is the sum of all other costs broken down above. These include such items as money required for tax prepayments or escrow accounts.
5. **Total costs** is the sum of total closing costs and total other costs.

4-2 Buying a Home: The Mortgage

Shopping for the best mortgage credit available can save you money. Real estate mortgage loans differ in rate of interest, length of repayment period, and size. Some have penalties for prepayment. Because these factors can make a big difference in the ultimate cost of your real estate, it is worthwhile to shop for the type of loan and the terms that best suit your needs.

For each individual, there is a particular set of arrangements for down payment and length of time to repay the loan that will prove best. A desirable contract provides for payments as large as you can afford at the present time, with the right to repay the loan at a faster rate than originally agreed on if you later find that you want to.

In this project, you create a model that calculates the payments due on a home loan of any amount, for any period, at any interest rate. The emphasis is on mortgages, but the principles and calculations apply to almost any type of loan. After completing this project, you will be able to enter and describe how loan payments are calculated and how the terms affect the payments due.

The finished model is shown in the figure " The Mortgages Model," and its formulas are indicated on the illustration and described below. When finished, save the model as *Mortgages* in the *Project Workbooks* folder of the *Excel Student Resource Disk*.

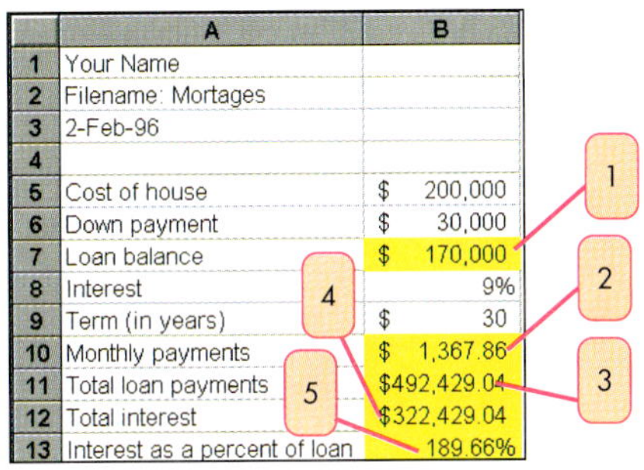

The Mortgages Model

1. **The loan balance** is the amount of the loan minus the down payment that you pay yourself without a bank's help. Your ability to make a large down payment can save you money on the cost of a mortgage. A large down payment usually has these advantages:
   - You may find it easier to obtain a loan.
   - You may be able to get a loan at a more reasonable rate of interest.
   - Your total interest expense will be lower.
   - Your equity in your home will be greater.

   On a 25-year, 12-percent loan, every $1,000 of down payment decreases the amount of total interest paid by about $2,160. For example, if you make a down payment of $10,000, the cost of interest over the 25-year period amounts to about $129,580. If you make a down payment of $20,000, the total cost of interest is about $107,990.
2. **The monthly payment** is calculated by a function that refers to cells B8, B9, and B7 in that order. The interest is divided by 12 and the number of periods is multiplied by 12 so both are expressed in months instead of years. The amount of the loan is entered as a negative value.
   - The interest rate you agree to pay affects the total cost of your loan. Because the amount borrowed is large and repayment extends over many years, a variation of one-half of 1 percent can make a big difference. For example, on a 30-year, $50,000 mortgage, you would pay about $6,960 more in interest on a 12fi-percent loan than on a 12-percent loan.
   - The term is the length of time you take to repay a loan, and it has a bearing on the amount of interest you pay. The shorter the time taken to repay the loan, the lower the total cost of interest to you; the longer the time to repay, the higher the total cost. The advantage of spreading payments over

a long period is the smaller monthly payment, which may make financing easier for you because it leaves more for current living. The disadvantage is the larger amount paid out in interest for the loan. When the annual rate is 12 percent, the total interest paid on a loan repaid in 20 years is about one-half more than the amount of the original loan, and in 25 years, it will almost double the original loan. If you take as long as 30 years to repay, the amount you pay in interest is almost triple the amount of the original loan.

3. **The total loan payment** is the monthly payment times the number of months that you must pay it.
4. **Total interest** is the *Total loan payment* minus the *Loan balance.*
5. **Interest as a percent of loan** is calculated the way you calculate any percentage.

4-3 The Computer System Pricing Model

Over the past few years, the power of desktop computers has increased dramatically. At the same time, the power required by newer programs such as Microsoft Windows has increased just as dramatically. Many new programs require a great deal of memory and hard disk storage, as well as a fast processor to operate well. In addition, a number of useful peripheral devices, such as scanners and CD-ROM disks, have dropped in price to where they are now affordable for many business and personal applications.

Before you purchase a system, you should carefully analyze your needs over the next three years and buy a system you won't outgrow. Because new programs require more sophisticated systems, older computers can be purchased for less than $1,000. If you don't anticipate needing newer programs, one of these systems can be a great buy. However, if you plan to use the latest software, or to use your computer for applications such as graphics or desktop publishing, a more powerful and more expensive system may be cheaper in the long run.

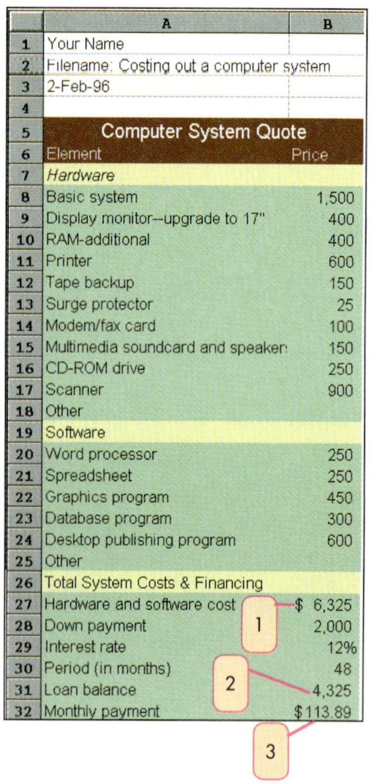

	A	B
1	Your Name	
2	Filename: Costing out a computer system	
3	2-Feb-96	
4		
5	Computer System Quote	
6	Element	Price
7	*Hardware*	
8	Basic system	1,500
9	Display monitor--upgrade to 17"	400
10	RAM-additional	400
11	Printer	600
12	Tape backup	150
13	Surge protector	25
14	Modem/fax card	100
15	Multimedia soundcard and speaker	150
16	CD-ROM drive	250
17	Scanner	900
18	Other	
19	Software	
20	Word processor	250
21	Spreadsheet	250
22	Graphics program	450
23	Database program	300
24	Desktop publishing program	600
25	Other	
26	Total System Costs & Financing	
27	Hardware and software cost	$ 6,325
28	Down payment	2,000
29	Interest rate	12%
30	Period (in months)	48
31	Loan balance	4,325
32	Monthly payment	$ 113.89

The Computer System Model

Open the *Costing out a computer system* workbook stored in the *Project Workbooks* folder of the *Excel Student Resource Disk.* This model contains all of the text and numbers you'll need but none of the formulas or formats. The finished model is shown in the figure "The Computer System Model," and its formulas are indicated on the illustration and described below. Using these descriptions and formatting commands, make your model look just like the one illustrated. When finished, change the price of the basic system to $1,250, save the workbook, and make a printout.

1. **Hardware and software cost** is the sum of all of the individual costs.
2. **Loan balance** is the total hardware and software cost minus the down payment.
3. **The monthly payment** is calculated by the PMT function based on the given *Interest rate* (divided by 12), *Period* (in months), and *Loan balance* (expressed as a negative value).

PicTorial

FIVE

EXPLORING WORKBOOKS, CHARTS, AND MACROS

After completing this PicTorial, you will be able to:

- **Manage the sheets in a workbook**
- **Create and modify embedded charts**
- **Create and modify chart sheets**
- **Use different types of charts to best represent your data**
- **Record and play back macros**

ENTERING data on a single sheet gives you a powerful analytical tool. However, Excel allows you to store a number of related sheets together in the same workbook and to chart that data on those worksheets. Finally, you can record keystrokes and play them back to automate repetitive tasks. These features greatly expand on the power and ease of use of the program.

5-1 MANAGING A WORKBOOK

When building models, it's important for you to know how to manage workbooks. You can rename sheets, add and delete them, or copy and move them. Normally, only one sheet is selected. This is called the active sheet. Any data that you type is entered into the *active sheet*. You can select another sheet by clicking its tab with the mouse.

QUICKSTEPS

Managing a Workbook

Opening New Workbooks

- To open a new workbook, pull down the **File** menu and click the **New** command.

Renaming Sheets

- To rename a sheet, double-click its tab (or right-click its tab and click the shortcut menu's **Rename** command) to display the Rename Sheet dialog box. Type the new name into the **Name** text box and click the **OK** command button.

Moving Around a Workbook with the Keyboard

- Press Ctrl+PageDown to move to the next sheet.
- Press Ctrl+Page Up to move to the previous sheet.

Scrolling Tabs into View with the Tab Scrolling Buttons

- Click the two end buttons to display the first or last tab.
- Click the two middle buttons to display the previous or next tab.

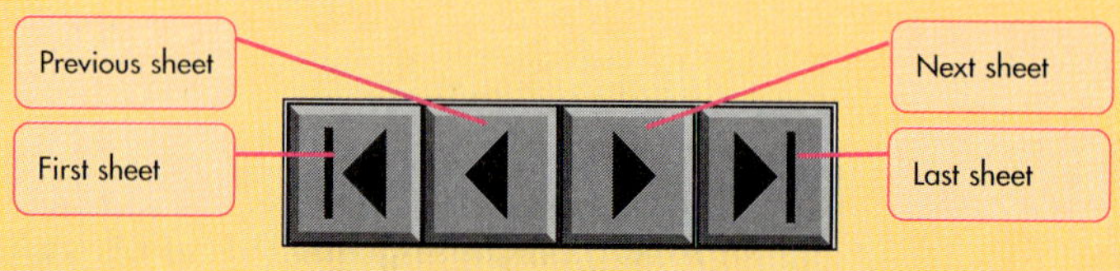

Selecting Sheets

- Click a sheet's tab to select it.
- To select a series of adjacent sheets, click the first and then hold down Shift while you click the last.
- To select a series of nonadjacent sheets, click the first and then hold down Ctrl while you click others.
- To select all sheets, right-click any tab and click the shortcut menu's **Select All Sheets** command.

Unselecting Sheets

- When you have more than one sheet selected, the word [Group] is displayed on the title bar, and the tabs of the selected sheets are white. To unselect the sheets, right-click any selected sheet tab and click the shortcut menu's **Ungroup Sheets** command.

(Continued on next page)

QUICKSTEPS

Managing a Workbook (*cont.*)

Inserting Sheets

1. To insert a sheet, do one of the following:
   - Click the tab on the sheet to the right of where you wanted it inserted, pull down the **Insert** menu and click the **Worksheet** command.
   - Right-click click the tab on the sheet to the right of where you wanted it inserted, click the shortcut menu's **Insert** command, then click the dialog box's **OK** button.

Deleting Sheets

1. To delete a sheet, do one of the following:
   - Click the sheet's tab to make it the active sheet, then pull down the **Edit** menu and click the **Delete Sheet** command.
   - Right-click the sheet's tab, then click the shortcut menu's **Delete** command,

   A dialog box warns you that the sheet will be permanently deleted.
2. Click the **OK** button to delete the sheet.

Moving Sheets

- Point to the tab of the sheet you want to move, drag the page icon to the tab you want it to be moved in front of, and drop it.
- Right-click click the tab on the sheet you want to move, and click the shortcut menu's **Move or Copy** command. Click the name of the sheet you want to move it in front of, and click the **OK** button.

Copying Sheets

- Point to the tab of the sheet you want to copy, hold down Ctrl and drag the page icon to the tab you want it to be copied in front of.
- Right-click click the tab on the sheet you want to copy, and click the shortcut menu's **Move or Copy** command. Click the name of the sheet you want to copy it in front of, click to turn on the **Create a Copy** check box, and click the **OK** button.

TUTORIAL

In this tutorial you are introduced to managing a workbook and tasks such as renaming moving, copying, and deleting sheets. The model you use is a master budget where one sheet summarizes a number of regional budgets.

Getting Ready

1. Open the *Master budget* workbook stored in the *Tutorial Workbooks* folder on the *Excel Student Resource Disk* and enter your name into cell A1.

Changing the Active Sheet

2. Click each of the first five sheet tabs (*Sheet1* through *Sheet5*) one after the other to make each sheet active so you can see what's on it. Then click the *Sheet1* tab to again make that the active sheet. (You may have to click a tab scroll button (◀) to see it.)

Renaming Sheets

3. Double-click the tab for *Sheet1* to display the Rename Sheet dialog box, type **Master Budget** into the **Name** text box, and then click the **OK** command button. The name appears on the sheet tab.

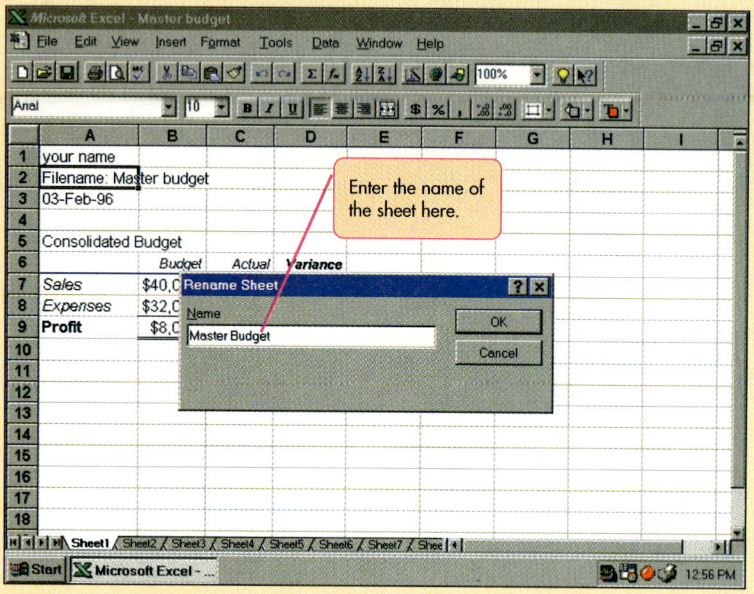

4. Double-click the tab for *Sheet2* to display the Rename Sheet dialog box, type **East** into the **Name** text box, and then click the **OK** command button.
5. Right-click the tab for *Sheet3* and click the shortcut menu's **Rename** command to display the Rename Sheet dialog box. Type **West** into the **Name** text box, and then click the **OK** command button.
6. Right-click the tab for *Sheet4* and click the shortcut menu's **Rename** command to display the Rename Sheet dialog box. Type **Southeast** into the **Name** text box, and then click the **OK** command button.
7. Right-click the tab for *Sheet5* and click the shortcut menu's **Rename** command to display the Rename Sheet dialog box. Type **Southwest** into the **Name** text box, and then click the **OK** command button.

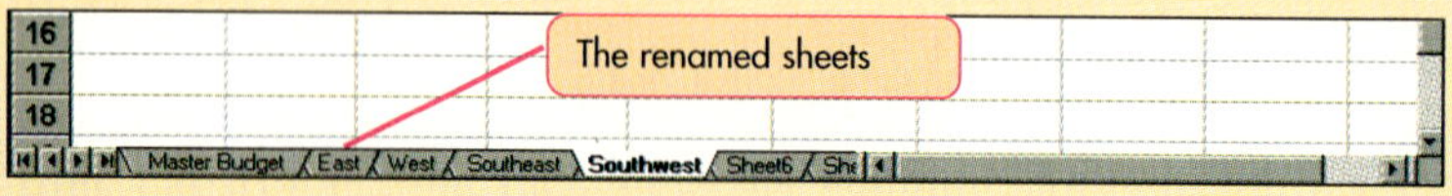

Moving Sheets

8. Point to the *East* tab and hold down the left mouse button. A downward-pointing arrowhead appears on the tab, and a sheet of paper appears on the mouse pointer.

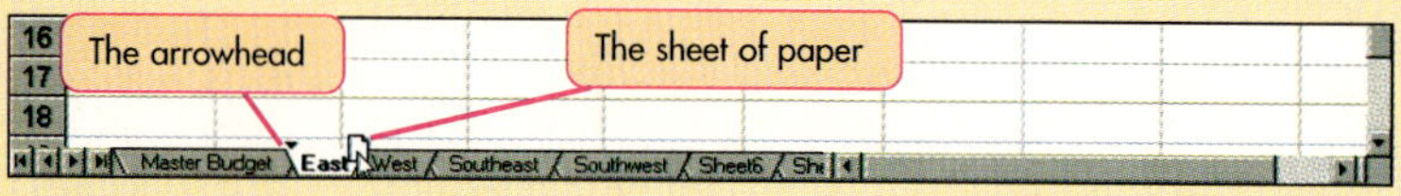

9. Drag the mouse pointer to the left side of the *Southwest* tab (the downward-pointing arrowhead shows where the sheet will move to—between the *Southeast* and *Southwest* sheets) and release the mouse button.

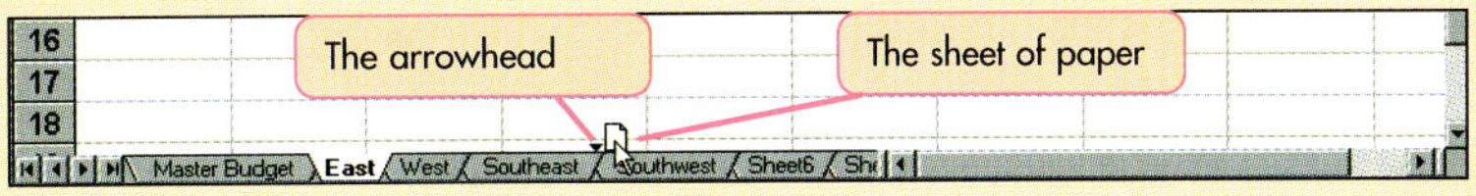

Copying Sheets

10. Point to the *East* tab again, hold down Ctrl and the left mouse button (the sheet of paper attached to the mouse pointer displays a plus sign to indicate you are copying). Drag a copy of it back to its original position—release the mouse button and Ctrl with the downward-pointing arrowhead positioned between the *Master Budget* and *West* tabs. The copy is named *East (2)*.

Using Tab Scrolling Buttons

11. Explore moving through the 16 sheets using the tab-scrolling buttons. Click the two end buttons to move to the first and last sheets and the two middle buttons to move forward or back one sheet.

Deleting a Sheet

12. Click the *East (2)* tab, pull down the **Edit** menu, and click the **Delete Sheet** command. A dialog box asks you to confirm the deletion.

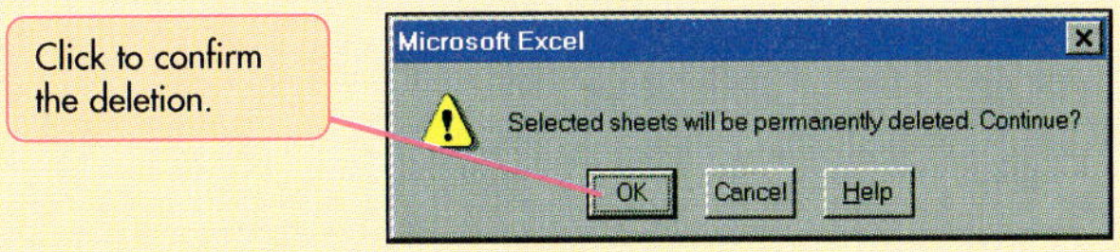

13. Click the **OK** command button to delete the sheet.

Selecting and Deleting Multiple Sheets

14. Click the *Sheet6* tab to select it.
15. Click the right end tab-scrolling button to move to the last sheet, hold down Shift, and click the *Sheet16* tab. Sheets 6 through 16 are now selected.

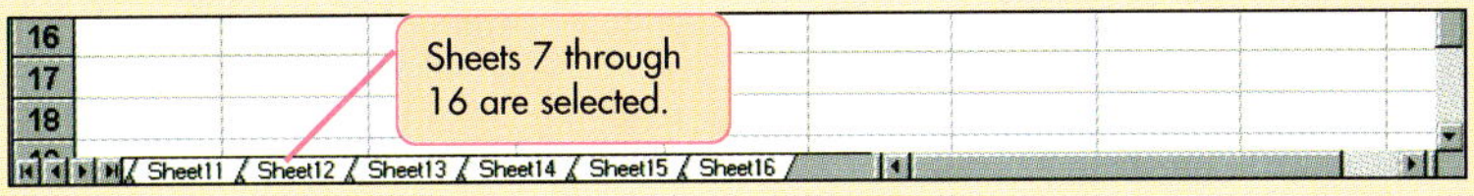

16. Pull down the **Edit** menu and click the **Delete Sheet** command. A dialog box asks you to confirm the deletion.
17. Click the **OK** command button to delete the selected sheets. Now only the five worksheets that you renamed are in the workbook.

Finishing Up

18. Save the workbook to save the names you assigned to sheets, and then close it.

5-2 CREATING EMBEDDED CHARTS

Excel can create charts of the data on your worksheets. The power of a chart is that it plots the values stored in a range of cells and remains linked to those cells. This way, when any of the values in those cells are changed, the chart immediately and automatically reflects those changes. This makes charts powerful analytical tools since you can explore changes in your model graphically instead of trying to interpret columns or rows of numbers.

When you create a chart, you can embed it on the same sheet as the data that it's based on or put it on a sheet by itself. The first type of chart is called an *embedded chart* and the second a *chart sheet*. In this section, we introduce the embedded chart. To create an embedded chart, you use Excel's ChartWizard. After you select the data you want to plot, the ChartWizard guides you through the process of creating the chart.

Selecting Chart Ranges

Since the only step where the ChartWizard doesn't guide you is in selecting the data, let's look at this procedure. Data that you chart on most charts has two axes—a value axis against which numbers are plotted, and a category axis that contains the labels for the data being plotted. For many charts the value axis is what is called the Y or vertical axis, and the category axis is called the X or horizontal axis.

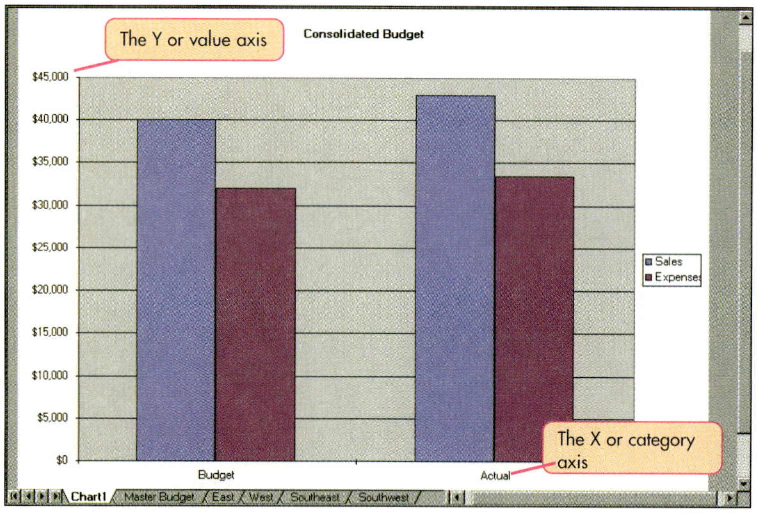

The data that is plotted is taken from cells on rows or in columns. The data in each row or column forms a data series, and all of the points in a data series are shown on the chart in the same color or pattern. Different data series are shown in different colors or patterns so they can be distinguished from one another. A data series can be best seen in a line chart since a line connects each of the points that represents one of the values in the series.

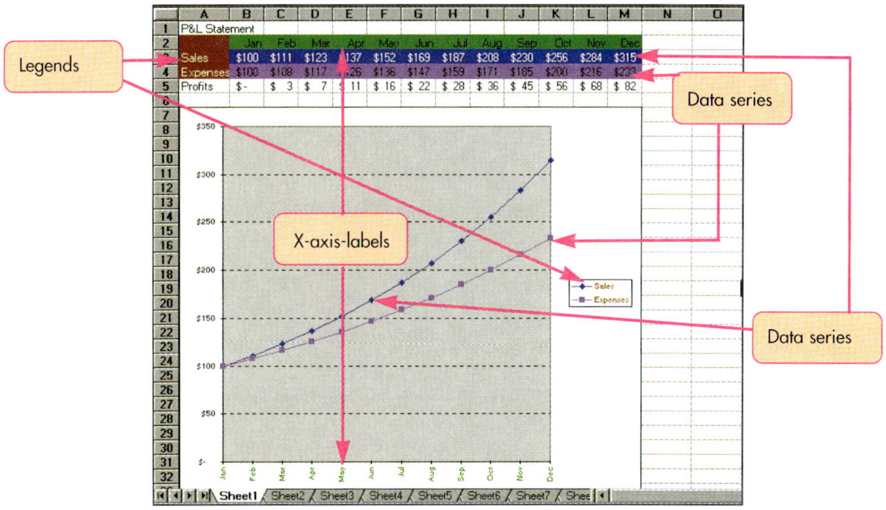

When you create a model to be used for a chart, the data normally takes the form of a table. When you chart this data, you can select which way the data series are oriented—whether they are in columns or rows. When you are creating the chart, Excel will guess at which way the data series run, but you can change its guess.

If you tell Excel the data series are in columns, it uses the top cell in each column as a legend and the text or values in the leftmost column as category axis labels.

When you specify that data is in columns, the first column is used to label the category axis (the countries), and the data from each of the three data columns is plotted against those labels. The first cell in each column is used as a label in the legends box to identify the data series.

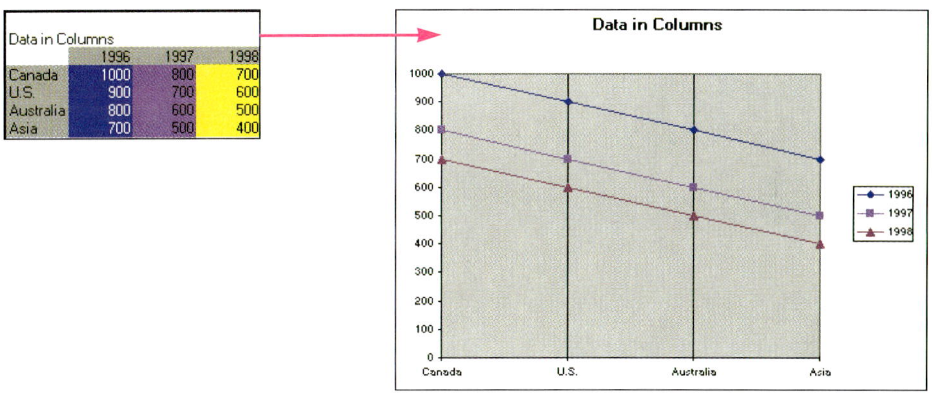

If you tell Excel the data series are in rows, it uses the left cell on each row as a legend and the text or values in the top row as category axis labels.

When you specify that data is in rows, the first row is used to label the category axis (the years) and data from each of the four data rows is plotted against those labels. The first cell in each row is used as a label in the legends box to identify the data series.

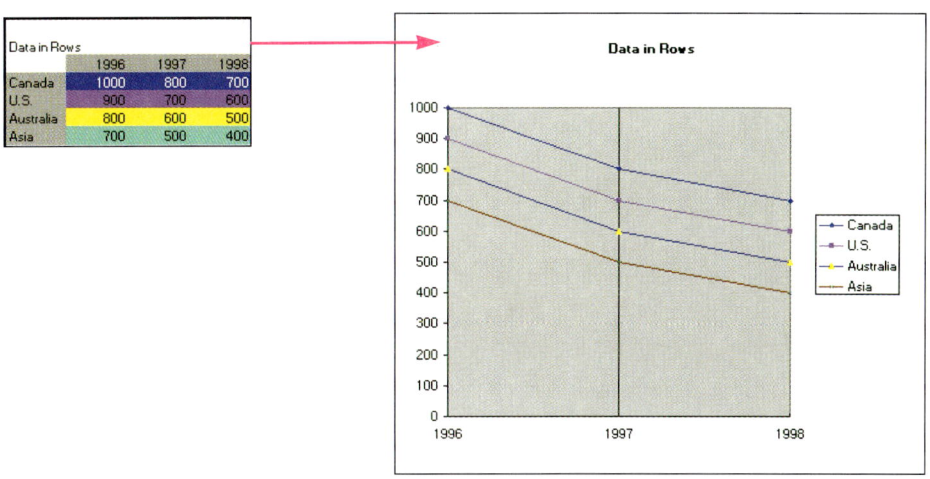

TIP
Selecting Chart Ranges

- Include row and column headings in the selection if you want category axis labels and legends.
- Select nonadjacent rows or columns by selecting the first, then holding down Ctrl while you select each of the others. Each row or column to be plotted must have the same number of cells.
- If there are rows or columns that you do not want included in a chart, you can set their height or width to zero to hide them. (See Section 2-10, "Adjusting Column Widths and Row Heights.")

Using the ChartWizard

After selecting the ranges to be plotted, you can use the ChartWizard to lead you step by step through a series of dialog boxes. In each of these boxes, you can check, and if you want to, change any of Excel's guesses about how your chart should be presented. In addition, you can add optional items such as legends and titles to make your chart more understandable to yourself and others. As you create the chart, a sample of it is shown in the dialog box so you have a preview of the finished chart.

The **ChartWizard** button

QUICKSTEPS
Creating Embedded Charts

1. Select the ranges for the chart as described in the section "Selecting Chart Ranges."
2. Click the **ChartWizard** button on the Standard toolbar, or pull down the **Insert** menu, point to the **Chart** command to cascade the menu, and then click **On This Sheet** to display the mouse pointer as a cross hair with a chart attached.
3. Point to the upper-left corner of where you want the chart to appear. Hold down the left mouse button, and drag the box to the size and shape that you want the chart to be. Release the mouse button to display the first ChartWizard dialog box.
4. Follow the instructions as you proceed through the ChartWizard dialog boxes described in the box "Understanding the ChartWizard."
5. When the chart is finished, click anywhere outside of the chart to unselect it and return the menu bar commands to normal (they change to chart-specific commands when a chart is activated).

UNDERSTANDING
The ChartWizard

Excel's ChartWizard makes creating charts a simple-to-follow step-by-step process. When the ChartWizard dialog boxes are displayed, click the <**Back** or **Next**> command buttons to move through the series of dialog boxes and make choices as you go. When the chart is the way you like it, click the **Finish** button. If you want to quit at any point, click **Cancel** or click the **Help** button for help.

Step 1 of 5 is where you confirm that you selected the correct range.

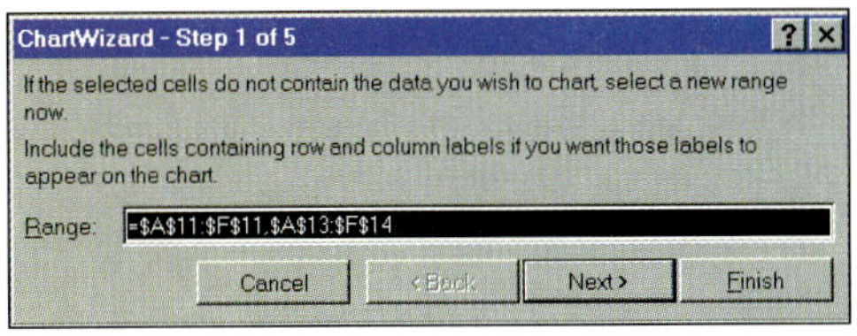

Step 2 of 5 is where you select a chart type by clicking a graphic image of it. The default chart type is a column chart.

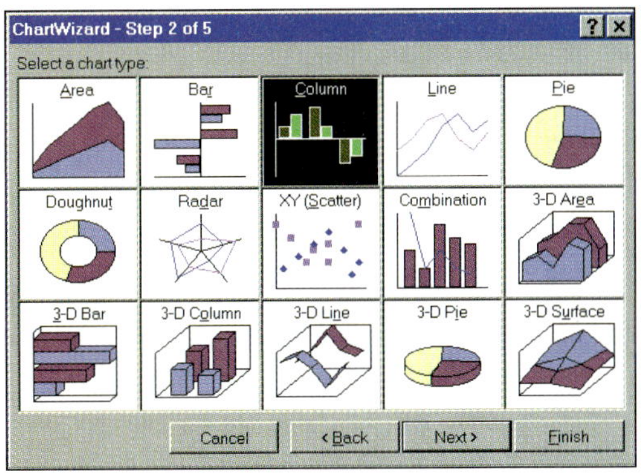

Step 3 of 5 is where you select a format by clicking a graphic image of it. The choices on this dialog box vary depending on the type of chart you selected in Step 2. The default format has gridlines.

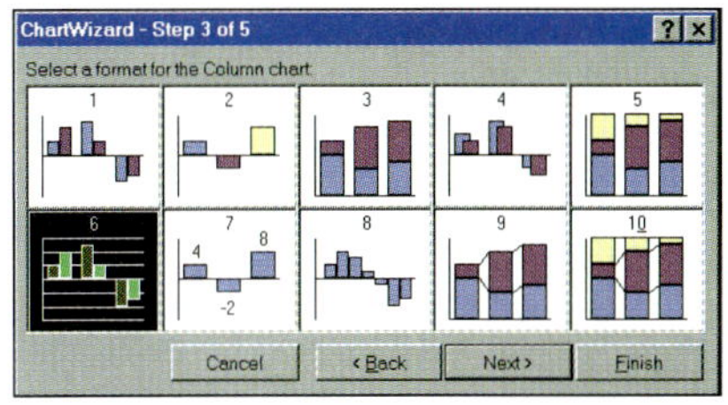

Step 4 of 5 is where you confirm or change Excel's guess about your data.

- **Data series in** specifies if the data series run along Rows or down Columns.
- **Use First Row(s)** and **Use First Column(s)** specifies what rows or columns are to be used for such chart elements as titles, legends, and category axis labels. The choices vary with the chart type.

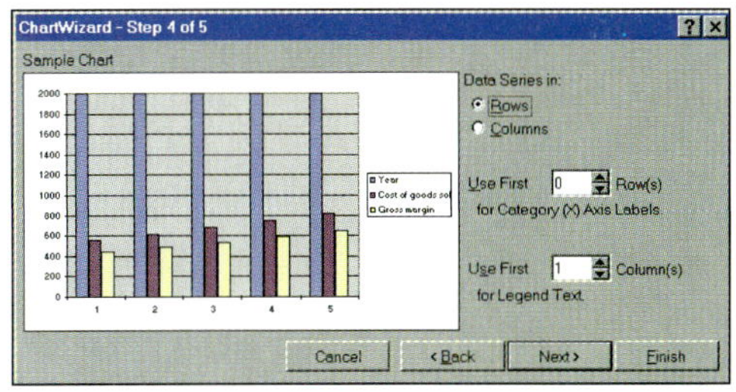

Step 5 of 5 is where you specify if the chart is to have a legend and where you type in titles for the chart and the category and value axes. The default chart has legends added.

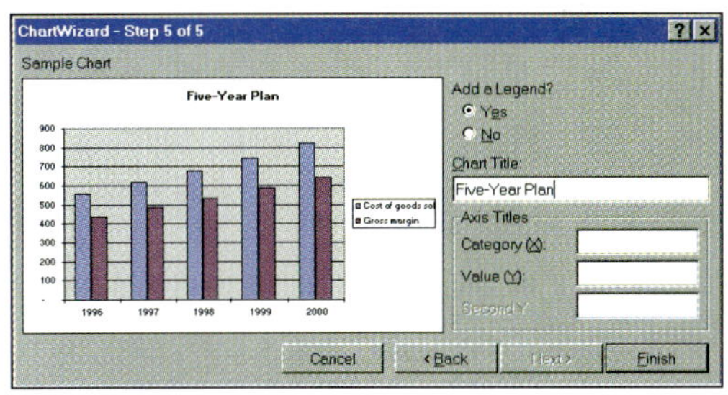

TUTORIAL

In this tutorial you use the ChartWizard to create an embedded chart of the five-year plan model. The chart will show the relationship between cost of goods and gross margin.

Getting Ready

1. Open the *Five-year plan* workbook stored in the *Tutorial Workbooks* folder on the *Excel Student Resource Disk.*

2. If necessary, change the numbers in the variables section to read $1,000 as the initial sales (cell B6), 10% as the sales growth rate (cell B7), and 56% as cost of goods sold (cell B8).

Creating the Chart

3. Select cells A11 to F11, then hold down Ctrl and select cells A13 to F14. Release Ctrl and the mouse button, and the selected cells remain highlighted.

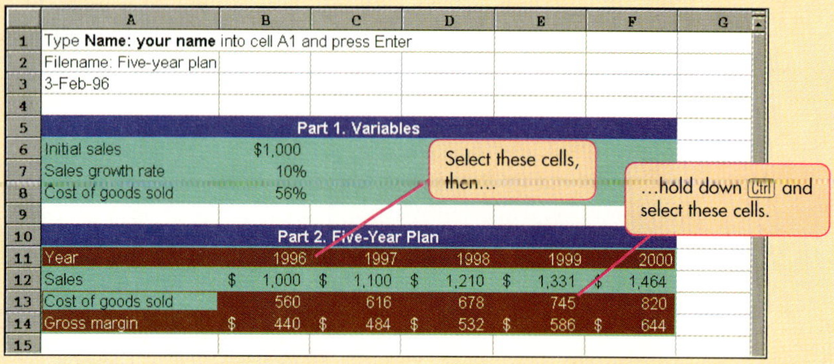

4. Click the **ChartWizard** button on the Standard toolbar. The selected cells are highlighted by moving borders, and the mouse pointer turns into a cross hair with a chart symbol.

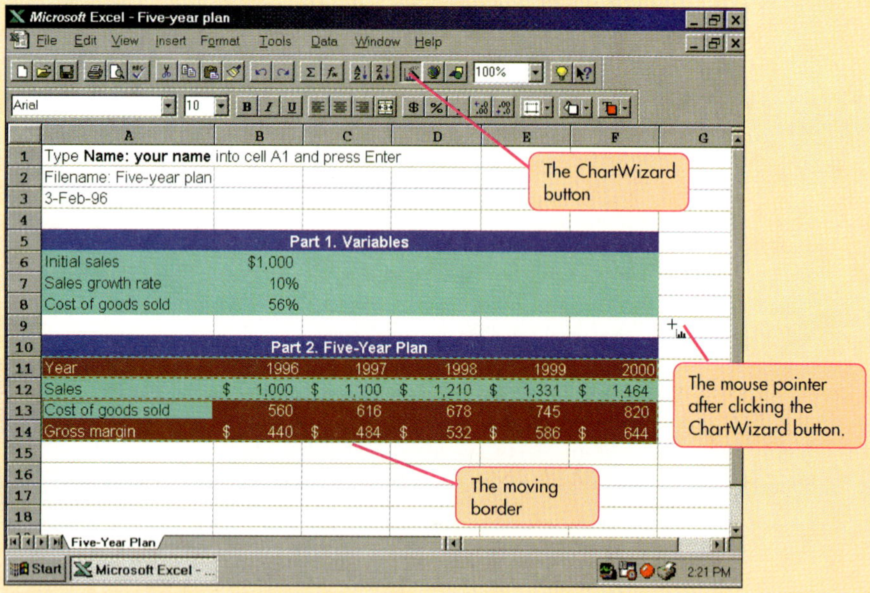

5. Point to the upper-left corner of cell A16 and hold down the left mouse button. Drag the mouse pointer to the lower right corner of cell D30 to draw a box where you want the chart to appear. (The screen will scroll for you when you drag against the lower window border.)

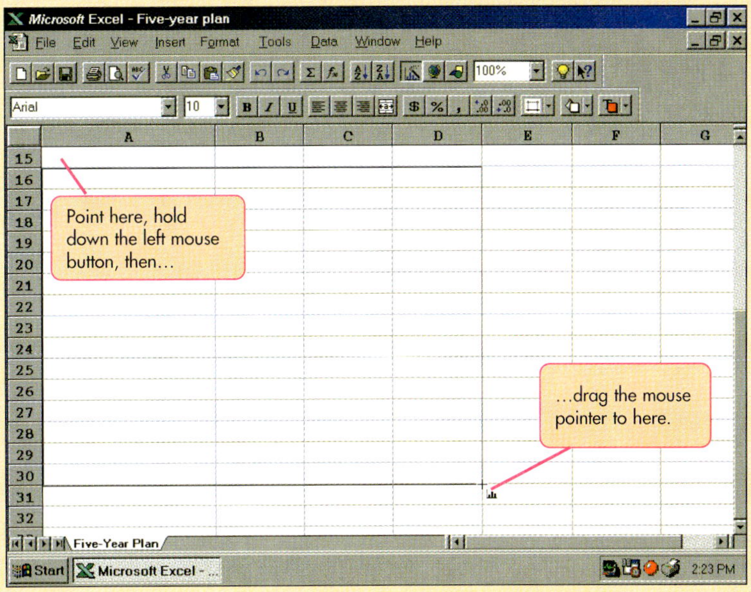

6. Release the mouse button to display the ChartWizard *Step 1 of 5* dialog box. The **Range** text box lists the two ranges that you selected for the chart.

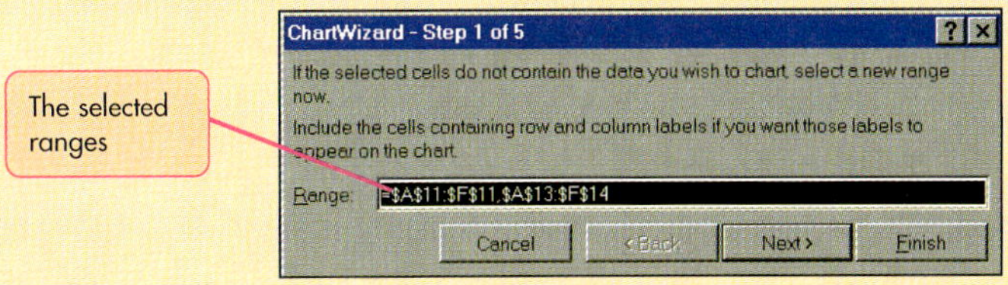

7. Click the **Next>** command button to display the *Step 2 of 5* dialog box illustrating chart types you can use; the **Column** type should be selected.

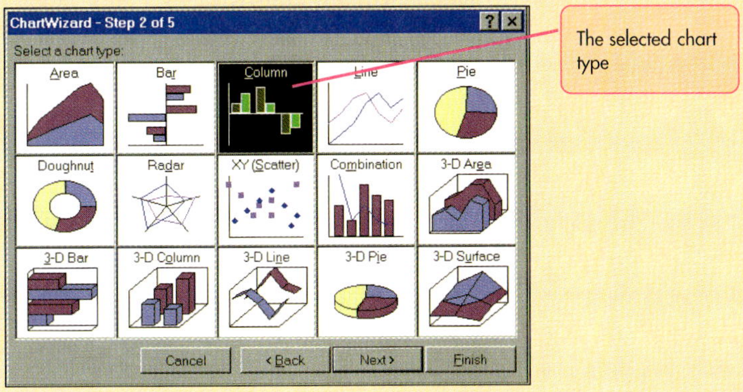

8. Click the **Next>** command button to display the *Step 3 of 5* dialog box illustrating formats you can use; number 6 should be selected.

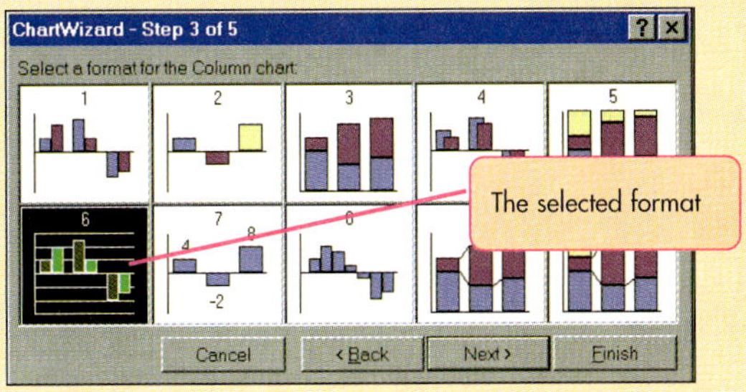

9. Click the **Next>** command button to display the *Step 4 of 5* dialog box illustrating a sample chart. It shows three data series when you only selected two. Read the legend in the sample chart in the ChartWizard and you'll see that Excel has treated the year as if it were a data series, when you want it to be used as a label instead.

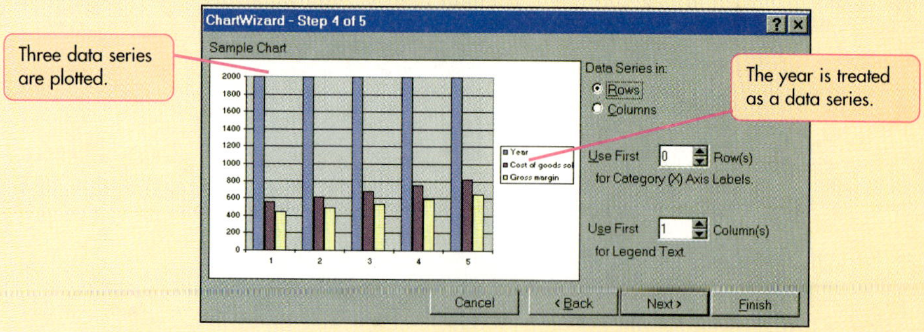

10. Click the up spin arrow (⬍) on the box for **Use First 0 Row(s) for Category [X] Axis Labels** to change it to 1. Immediately, the Y-axis changes and only two bars are plotted for each period.

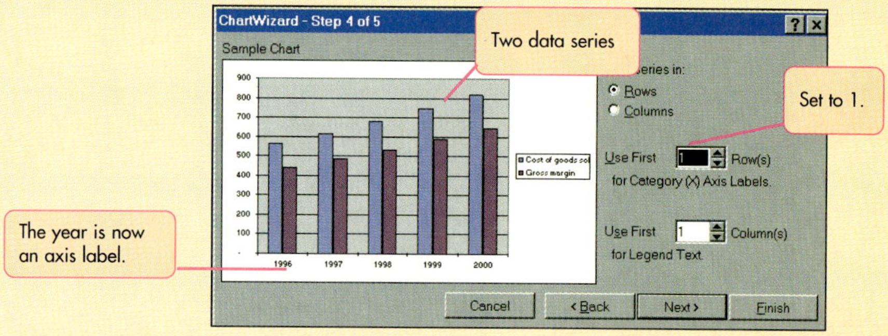

11. Click the **Next>** command button to display the *Step 5 of 5* dialog box. Click in the **Chart Title** text box to move the insertion point there, and type **Five-Year Plan**.

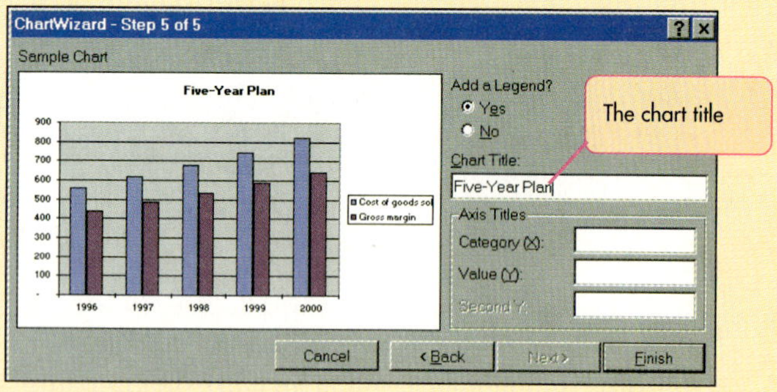

12. Click the **Finish** command button to display the chart on the worksheet.

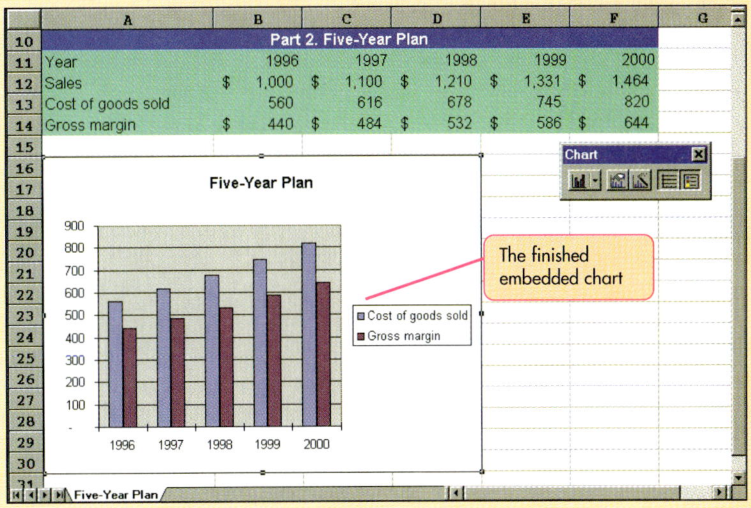

Finishing Up

13. Click the **Save** button on the Standard toolbar to save your changes.

14. Click the **Print Preview** button on the Standard toolbar to see how the table and chart will appear when printed. (Displaying this preview may take a few moments.) Click the chart to enlarge it on your screen.

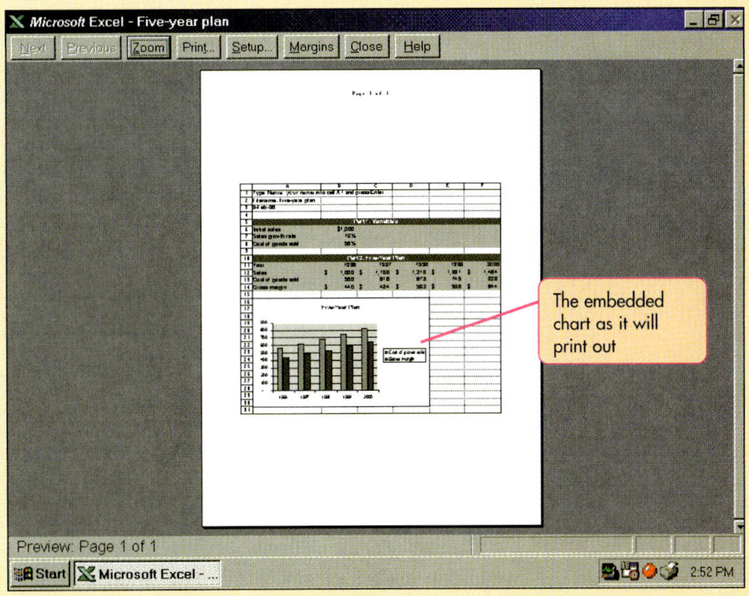

15. If you have time to print the sheet (this can take a long time on some systems), click the **Print** button on the preview screen; or click the **Close** command button to return to the document.

16. Close the workbook.

5-3 MOVING, SIZING, AND DELETING EMBEDDED CHARTS

After embedding a chart on a worksheet, you may find that it isn't the right size or in the right place. To refine its layout, you can drag it to a new position or drag one of its corners or sides to shrink or enlarge it. To move, size, or even delete a chart, you must first click it to select it.

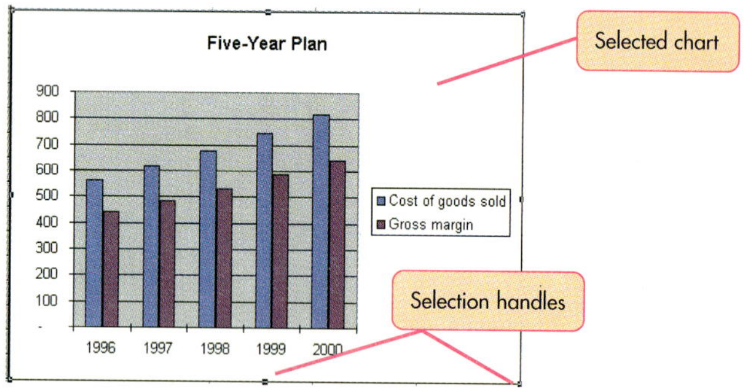

QUICKSTEPS

Moving, Sizing, and Deleting Embedded Charts

- To select a chart, click it anywhere. When you do so, *selection squares* appear on the top and bottom, sides, and corners of a frame around the chart.
- To move a selected chart, point anywhere in the chart, hold down the left button and drag the chart to where you want it. As you drag it, a dotted border indicates its new position. To drop the box into position, release the mouse button.
- To size a selected chart, point to any selection square until the mouse pointer turns into a diagonal two-headed arrow. Then drag the selection square. When the chart is the shape you want it, release the mouse button. To retain its proportions, hold down Shift when you drag one of the corners in and up or out and down.
- To delete a selected chart, press Delete. (If you find you have made a mistake, immediately click the **Undo** button on the Standard toolbar.)

COMMON WRONG TURNS

Activating a Chart by Mistake

If you double-click an embedded chart, you activate it rather than selecting it. When it is activated, the commands on the menu bar change, and you can only move it by dragging it by its border. To deactivate it, click anywhere outside of the chart.

TUTORIAL

In this tutorial you size and move the embedded chart that you created on the five-year plan in the previous section.

Getting Ready

1. Open the *Five-year plan* workbook stored in the *Tutorial Workbooks* folder on the *Excel Student Resource Disk.*

Sizing the Chart

2. Click anywhere in the chart to select it. When you do so, sizing handles appear on the four sides and corners.

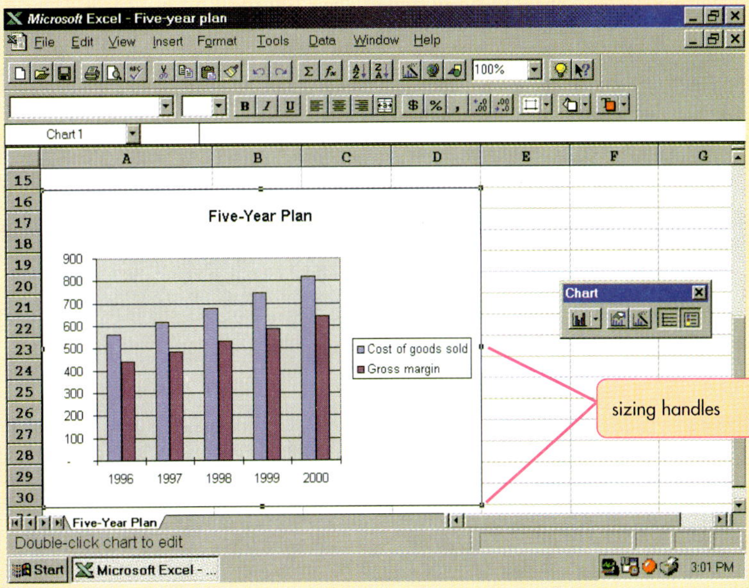

3. To change the size and proportions of the chart, point to the lower-right corner of the chart until the mouse pointer turns into a diagonal two-headed arrow. Then hold down the mouse button, and drag the corner in and up or out and down to shrink or expand the size of the chart. When it's a size you like, and can see on your screen, release the mouse button. Then click the **Undo** button on the Standard toolbar to undo the change.
4. To change the size but retain the proportions of the chart, point to the lower-right corner of the chart until the mouse pointer turns into a diagonal two-headed arrow. Then hold down [Shift] and the mouse button, and drag the corner in and up or out and down to shrink or expand the size of the chart while retaining its proportions. When it's a size about four columns wide, release the mouse button.

Moving the Chart

5. Point anywhere in the chart, hold down the left mouse button, and drag the outline of the chart so it's centered under the model.

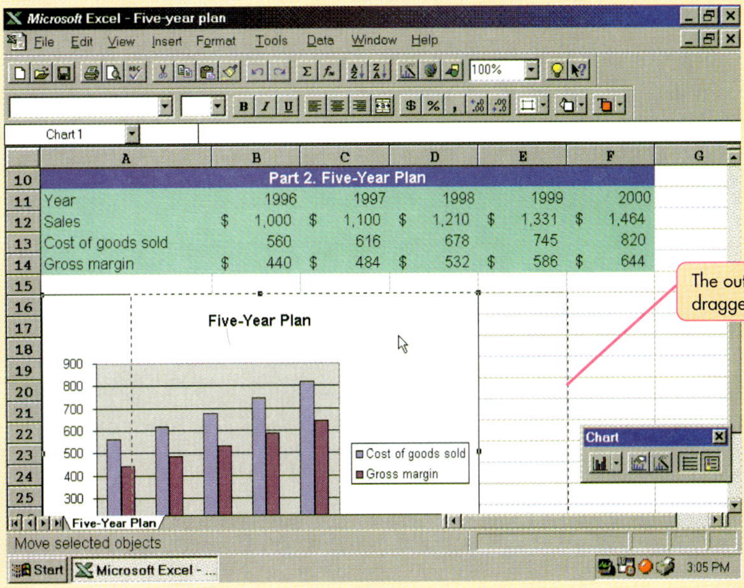

6. Release the mouse button to drop the chart into position.

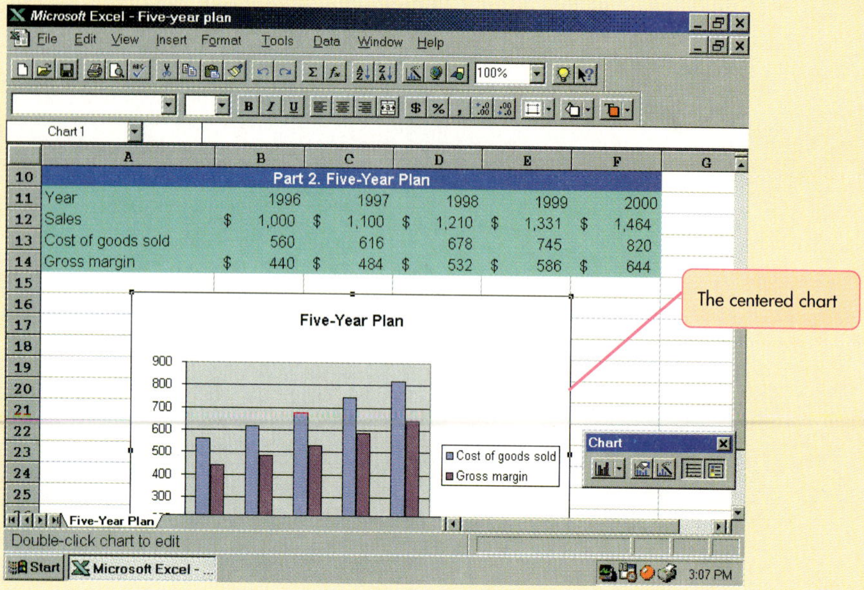

Finishing Up

7. Click the **Save** button on the Standard toolbar to save your changes.
8. Click the **Print Preview** button on the Standard toolbar to see how the resized and moved chart will appear when printed. (Displaying this preview may take a few moments.)
9. If you have time to print the sheet (this can take a long time on some systems), click the **Print** button on the preview screen; or click the **Close** command button to return to the document without printing the chart.
10. Close the workbook.

5-4 CREATING CHART SHEETS

When you don't want a chart embedded on the same worksheet as the data it is based on, you can create it on its own sheet in the workbook. You create a chart sheet the same way you create an embedded chart, with one exception: you must use the **Chart** command on the **Insert** menu and specify that the chart be on a new sheet.

QUICKSTEPS

Creating Chart Sheets

1. Select the ranges for the chart as described in the section "Selecting Chart Ranges" in Section 5-2, "Creating Embedded Charts."
2. Pull down the **Insert** menu, point to **Chart** to cascade the menu, and then click **As New Sheet** to display the first ChartWizard dialog box.
3. Follow the instructions as you proceed through the ChartWizard dialog boxes described in the box "Understanding the ChartWizard" in Section 5-2, "Creating Embedded Charts."

LOOKING BACK

Renaming a Sheet

Chart sheets are initially named *Chart1*, *Chart2*, and so on, but you can change the name. To do so, double-click the sheet's tab to display the Rename Sheet dialog box. Type the new name into the **Name** text box and click the **OK** command button.

QUICKSTEPS

Deleting a Chart Sheet

1. Click the sheet's tab to make it active.
2. Do one of the following:
   - Pull down the **Edit** menu and click the **Delete Sheet** command.
   - Right-click the sheet's tab and click the shortcut menu's **Delete** command.
3. Click the **OK** command button when a dialog box asks you to confirm the deletion.

TUTORIAL

In this tutorial you create a chart of the master budget on its own sheet. The chart will show the relationship between budgeted and actual sales and expenses so you can easily compare them.

Getting Ready

1. Open the *Master budget* workbook stored in the *Tutorial Workbooks* folder on the *Excel Student Resource Disk*.

Creating the Chart

2. With the *Master Budget* sheet active (click its sheet tab if necessary), select cells A6 through C8, then pull down the **Insert** menu, and point to the **Chart** command to cascade the menu.

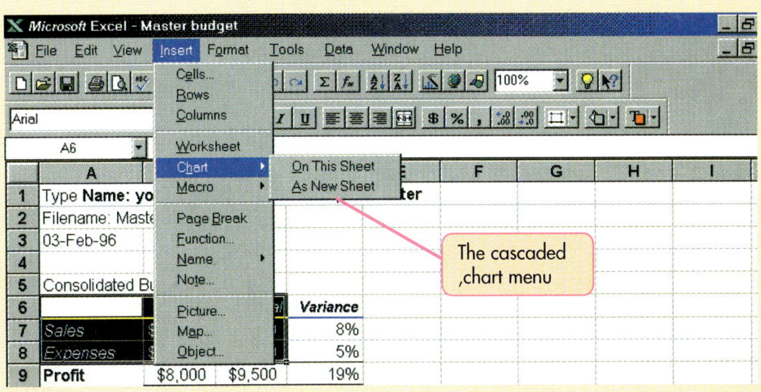

3. Click the **As New Sheet** command to display the ChartWizard *Step 1 of 5* dialog box. The **Range** text box lists the range that you selected for the chart.

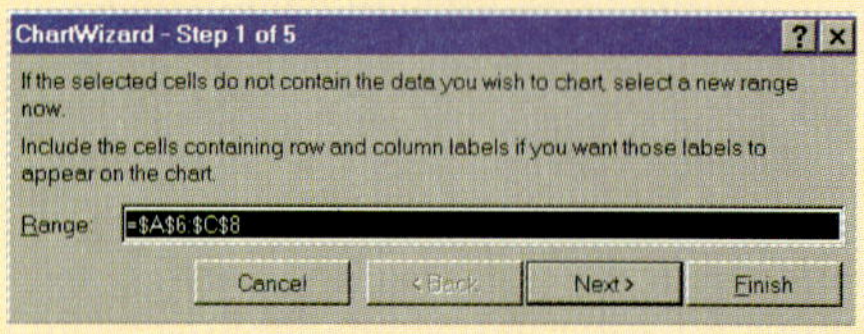

4. Click the **Next>** command button to display the *Step 2 of 5* dialog box illustrating chart types you can use; the **Column** type should be selected.

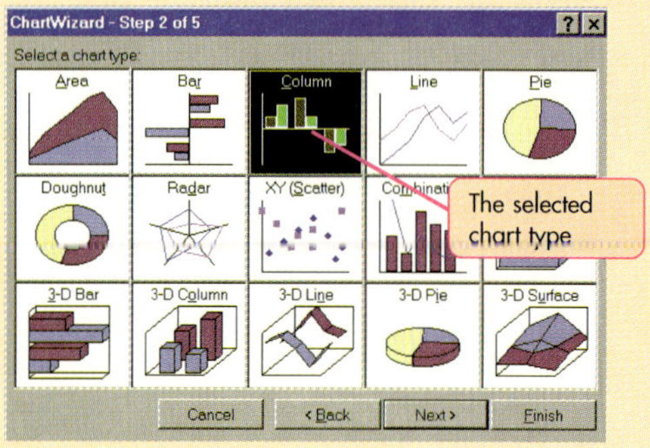

5. Click the **Next>** command button to display the *Step 3 of 5* dialog box illustrating formats you can use; number 6 should be selected.
6 Click the **Next>** command button to display the *Step 4 of 5* dialog box showing a sample chart.
7. Click the **Next>** command button to display the *Step 5 of 5* dialog box showing a sample chart again. Click in the **Chart Title** text box to move the insertion point there, and type **Consolidated Budget**.

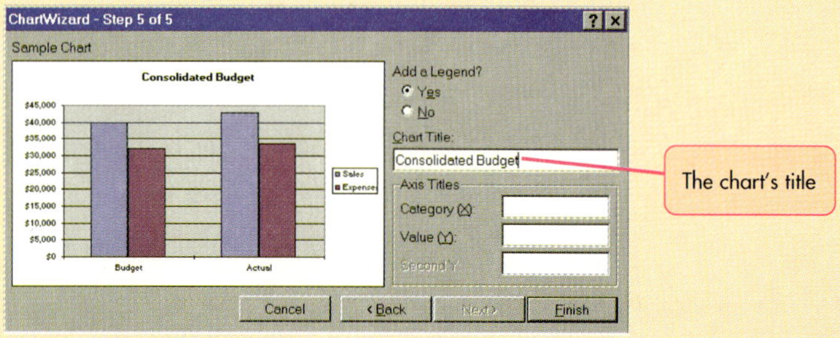

8. Click the **Finish** command button to display the chart on the worksheet.

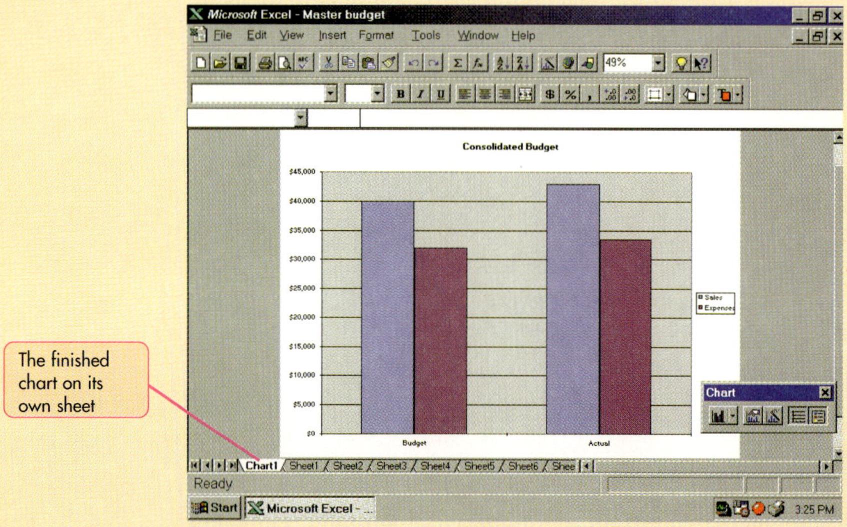

Finishing Up

9. Click the **Save** button on the Standard toolbar to save your changes.
10. Click the **Print Preview** button on the Standard toolbar to see how the chart will appear when printed. (Displaying this preview may take a few moments.) Notice how the chart has automatically incorporated the text you selected in the model along with the numbers.
11. If you have time to print the sheet (this can take a long time on some systems), click the **Print** button on the preview screen; or click the **Close** command button to return to the document.
12. Close the workbook.

5-5 EDITING AND REVISING CHARTS

Excel offers you a lot of control over the way your data is presented on a chart. You can add new elements, revise existing ones, or add formats such as font changes, boxes, and borders.

Activating a Chart

To make any changes to a chart you have created, you must first activate it. This allows you to select elements within the chart, and it also changes the menus to list chart commands. When a chart is active, the menu bar and menu commands change to those you use to work with charts.

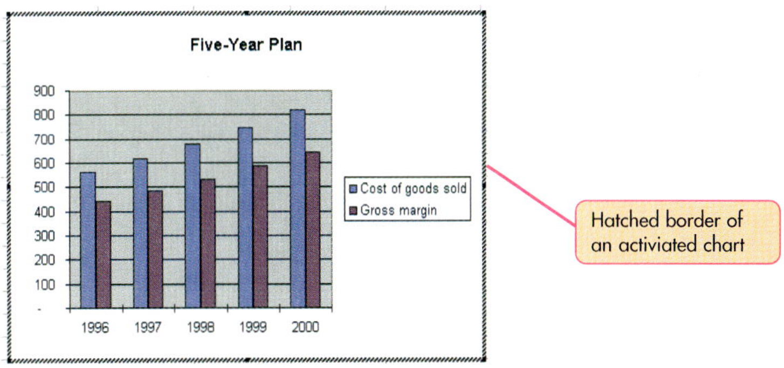

QUICKSTEPS

Activating and Deactivating Charts

- To activate an embedded chart, double-click it. When it is activated, its border changes from a thin line to a hatched border.
- To activate a chart page, click its tab. It's activated when it's displayed and its tab is white.
- To deactivate a chart and return the menu bar to normal, click anywhere outside of an embedded chart or click any other tab in the workbook.

Adding Elements to an Activated Chart

Once you have activated a chart, you can add elements to it that may be missing. These include titles, data labels, legends, axes, and gridlines.

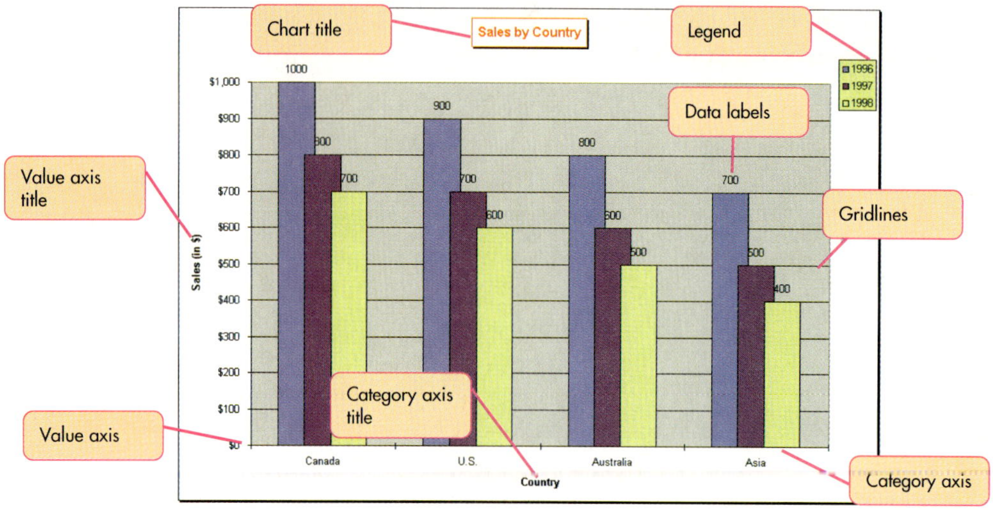

QUICKSTEPS

Adding Elements to an Activated Chart

1. Activate the chart and then pull down the **Insert** menu.
2. Select any of the commands described in the box "Understanding the Insert Menu."

UNDERSTANDING

The Insert Menu

To add elements to an activated chart, pull down the **Insert** menu and then click any of the following commands:

Titles displays the Titles dialog box. When you turn the check boxes on (☑) and then click the **OK** command button, the placeholder terms *Title*, *X*, and *Y* appear on the chart. Click one to select it, and then click again to delete it and enter your own title.

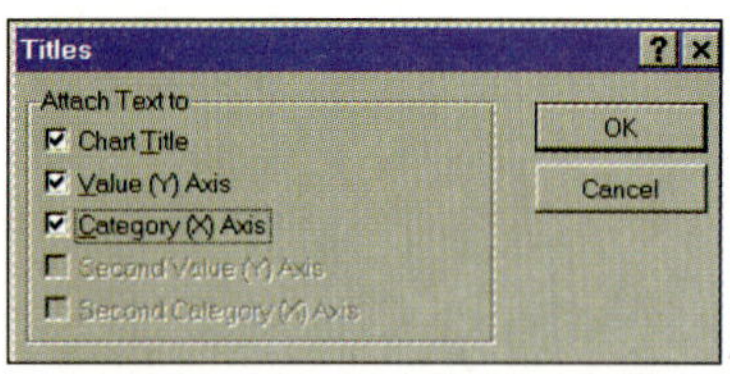

Data Labels displays the Data Labels dialog box. Click any of the available option buttons (◉) and then click the **OK** command button. The selected data labels will appear above the data points they refer to.

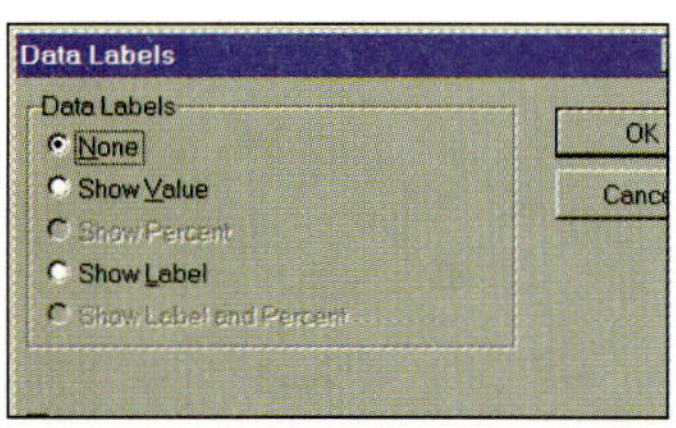

Legend inserts the legend to the right of the chart area.

Axes displays the Axes dialog box. Check either or both Axes check boxes to turn them on (☑) or off (☐) and then click the **OK** command button. When they are off, tick marks and labels are not displayed.

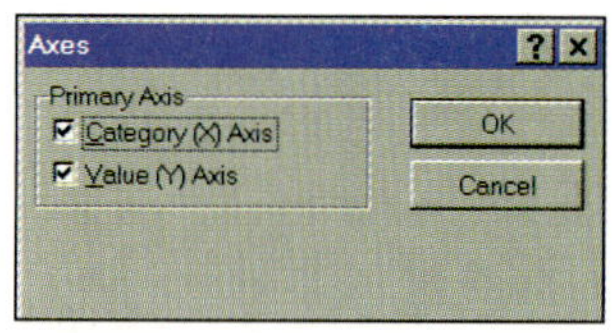

Gridlines displays the Gridlines dialog box. Click any check boxes to display major or minor gridlines extending from the category or value axis, and then click the **OK** command button.

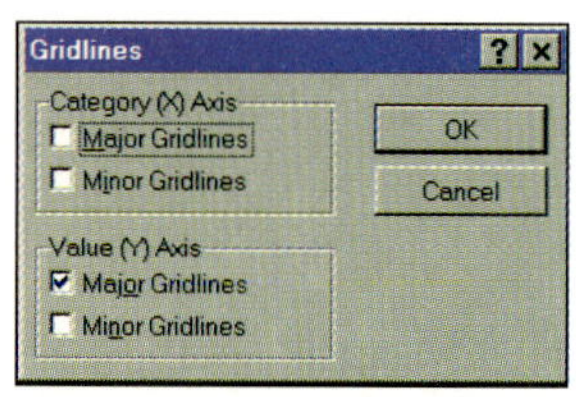

TIP
Transferring Worksheet Titles to a Chart with Cell References

You can use text that you enter into worksheet cells as titles for your chart or as legends. This makes it easy to revise the chart because changing the text in the worksheet cells changes the chart automatically. To refer to cells, select the text box on the chart, type [=], then click the tab of the sheet you want to refer to, click the cell and press [Enter↵]. Once you establish such a link, you can only edit the text in the cell it's linked to—not on the chart itself.

Editing Elements of an Activated Chart

Once you have activated a chart, you can select any of the text elements on the chart to edit them.

QUICKSTEPS
Editing Chart Elements

1. Activate the chart and then click the text element to select it.
2. Click the element again to move the insertion point into it.
3. Edit the text just as you would any other text.
4. Click anywhere outside of the element.

Formatting Elements of an Activated Chart

Once you have activated a chart, you can format any of its elements. The name of the selected element is displayed in the Name box on the formula bar. Selection handles will also appear on the element within the chart. You can move it by dragging it by its border or change its size by dragging one of the selection squares.

Once you have selected one element, you can press the arrow keys to move the selection from item to item on the chart. Press [↑] and [↓] to move from item to item. Press [←] and [→] to move between items within a group.

The elements that you can select for formatting include the following:

- *Chart Area* can have a border or pattern added, or you can change its fonts. (To select the entire chart, click the chart when not pointing to a specific item.)
- *Plot Area* can have a border or pattern added. (To select the plot area, click anywhere in it except on a data marker.)
- *Data Series* allows you to change patterns and add or remove data labels. You can also change the ranges plotted on the chart. Changes you then make affect the entire series. To select a single data marker in a series, select the series, and then click the data marker. Changes you then make affect only the selected marker.
- *Text* can have its pattern, font, or alignment changed.
- *Value axis* or *Category axis* can have their pattern, font, number format, alignment, or scale changed.
- *Gridlines* can have their pattern or scale changed.
- *Legend* can have its pattern, font, or placement changed. (To select a specific legend, select the legend box and then click the legend.)

- *Data labels* can have their pattern, font, number format, or alignment changed.

QUICKSTEPS

Formatting Chart Elements

1. Activate the chart and then do one of the following to format the chart parts described in the text.
   - Double-click the element to display a relevant dialog box.
   - Click the element to select it, and then pull down the **Format** menu. On this menu, click the topmost command that begins **Selected** followed by the name of the item you have selected. This displays a tabbed dialog box containing the formatting commands you can use (the commands vary depending on what you have selected).
2. Click anywhere outside of the element.

Adding Data Series and Data Points

To add data series or data points to a chart, select the cells on the worksheet, drag them onto the chart, and release them.

TUTORIAL

In this tutorial you edit and revise the chart you created for the five-year plan. In doing so, you will revise the chart title and format the Y-axis values to display them as currency.

Getting Ready

1. Open the *Five-year plan* workbook stored in the *Tutorial Workbooks* folder on the *Excel Student Resource Disk*.

Revising the Chart Title

2. Double-click the embedded chart to activate it. When activated, it has a hatched border around it.

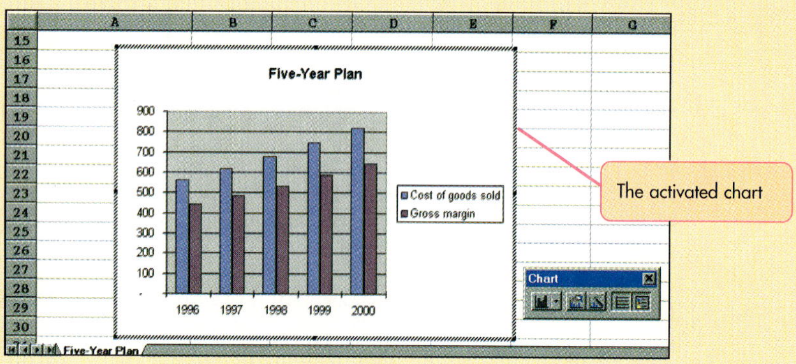

3. Click the chart title (*Five-Year Plan*) to select it and then click it again to move the insertion point into it. *Title* is displayed in the Name box on the formula bar indicating that is the chart element you have selected.
4. Press End to move the insertion point to the end of the title, press Spacebar, and type **(1996-2000)**.

Formatting the Y-Axis Values

5. Click the Y-axis (the vertical axis) to select it, and selection squares appear at the top and bottom of the axis. *Axis 1* is displayed in the Name box on the formula bar.

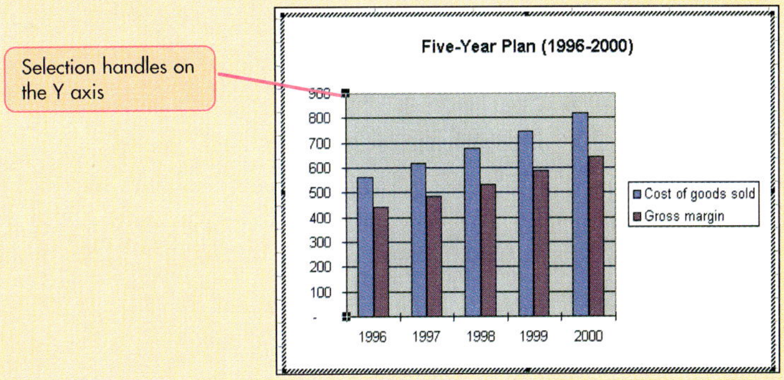

6. Press [↑] to scroll the selection handles through all of the selectable items in the chart. As you do so, watch the name of the selected items change in the Name box on the formula bar. When finished, press [↑] or [↓] to again display *Axis 1* appears in the Name box.
7. Pull down the **Format** menu and click the **Selected Axis** command to display the Format Axis dialog box.
8. Click the *Number* tab to display that dialog box, and Change the following settings:
   - Click *Currency* in the **Category** list.
   - Click the red (1,234.10) to select it on the list.
   - Set **Decimal Places** to 0.
   - Turn on the **Use $** check box.

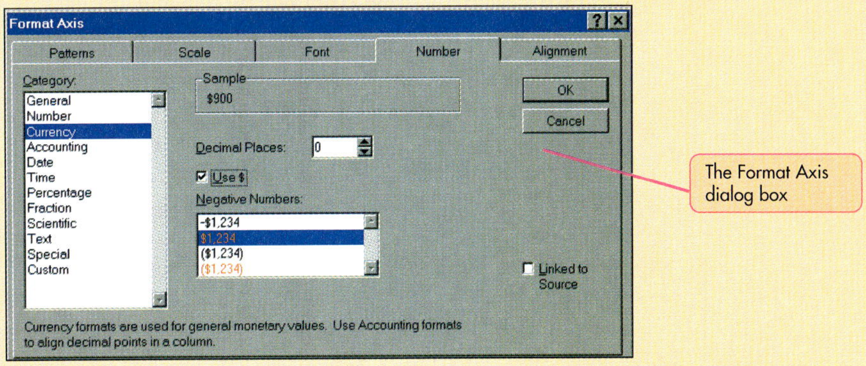

9. Click the **OK** command button to format the axis with dollar signs.
10. Click the **Save** button on the Standard toolbar to save your changes.
11. Click the **Print Preview** button on the Standard toolbar to see how the revised chart will appear when printed.
12. If you have time to print the sheet (this can take a long time on some systems), click the **Print** button on the preview screen; or click the **Close** command button to return to the document.

PAUSING FOR PRACTICE

Continue selecting other elements on the chart, then pull down the **Format** menu and click the **Selected** command to change formats for the element. Don't worry about making mistakes since you'll close the workbook without saving it. Explore how the various formats affect the look of the chart.

Finishing Up

13. Close the workbook without saving your changes.

5-6 EXPLORING CHART TYPES AND AUTOFORMATS

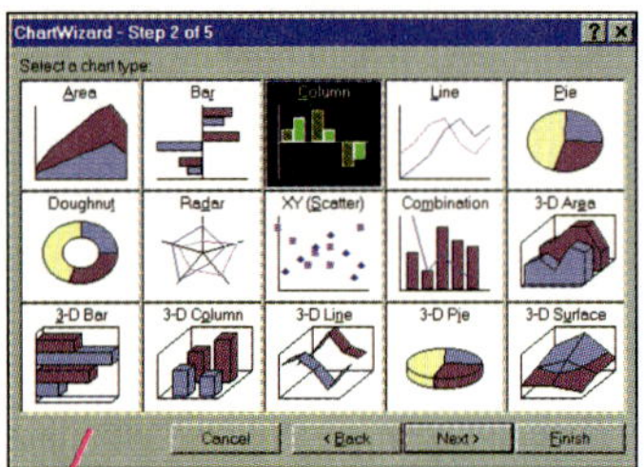

Excel offers these chart types.

One of the most important decisions you make when creating charts is what chart type to use. Excel has fifteen basic chart types and many subtypes. Choosing the right type determines how well your data is conveyed.

Normally you will be charting one of two types of data: discrete or continuous data. The chart type you choose should depend on the kind of data you are plotting.

Discrete data consist of values measured at a series of selected points. When plotted on a chart, all data between those points are meaningless. Charts of this kind are frequently called time-series charts and are used in business to plot sales, profits, inventory, and other important financial values. The best chart types to use for this kind of data include bar and column charts.

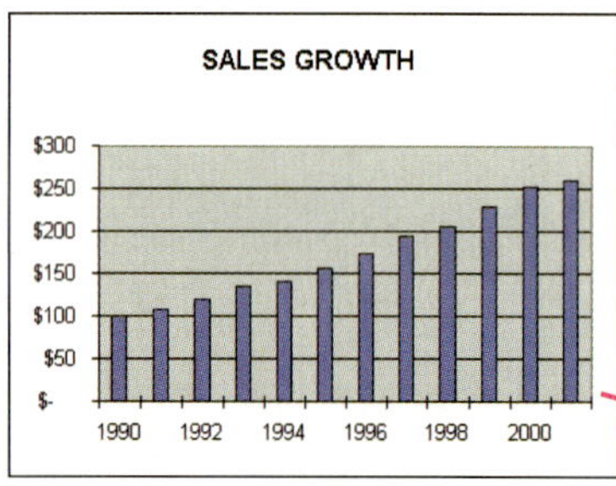

Discrete data are values representing specific periods of time or other units.

Continuous data occur when measurements have been sampled to determine a trend. Although each data point is a discrete value, the points are sampled so that when plotted, values between the measured data points can be estimated from the chart. This estimation of values falling between the points that were actually measured and plotted is called interpolation. When charting continuous data, a general rule is that the more data points you measure and plot, the more accurate the chart is. The best chart types to use for this kind of data include line and area charts.

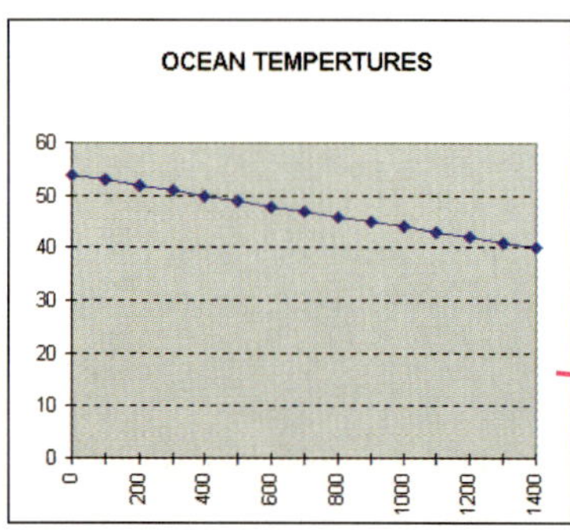

Continous data represent an unbroken range of values.

Percentages of a whole data are those where you have a data series that contains parts equaling a significant whole such as sales of various products in a product line and market shares. When you have only one data series, the best chart for this kind of data is a pie chart where the pie represents "the whole" or 100 percent, and the individual slices represent parts of the whole. The relative sizes of the parts are indicated by the sizes of the pie slices.

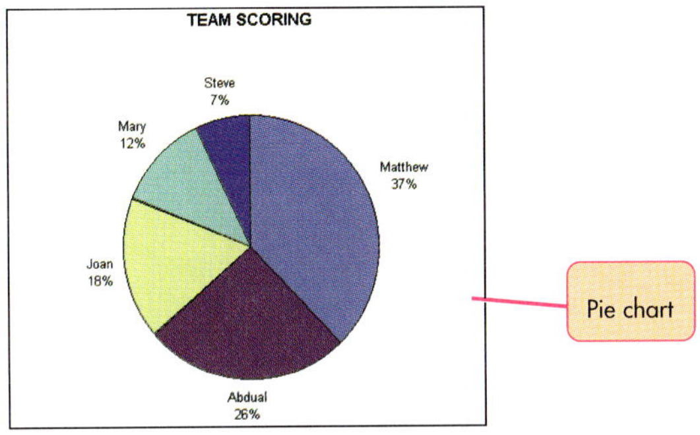

When you have more than one data series, you can create a pie chart for each series or plot them on a 100% bar or column chart where Excel will convert each data point to a percentage of the whole. You can also use a doughnut chart which plots data series in concentric circles.

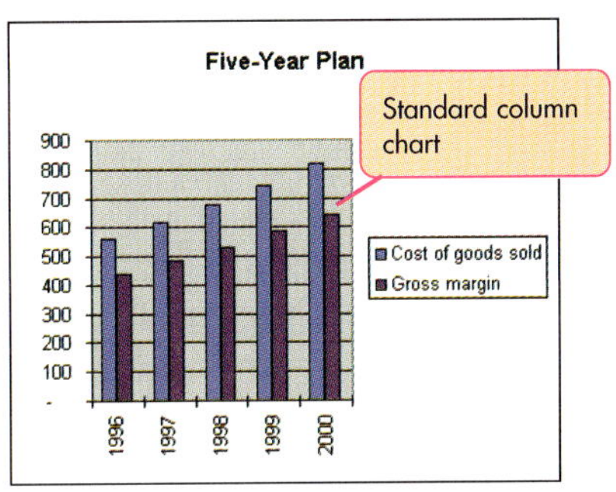

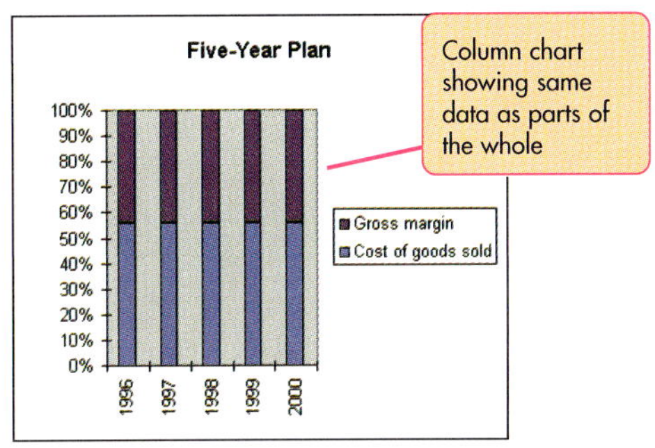

Many chart types include normal 2-D versions and more graphic 3-D versions that use depth to add emphasis.

Data in Columns

	1996	1997	1998
Canada	1000	800	700
U.S.	900	700	600
Australia	800	600	500
Asia	700	500	400

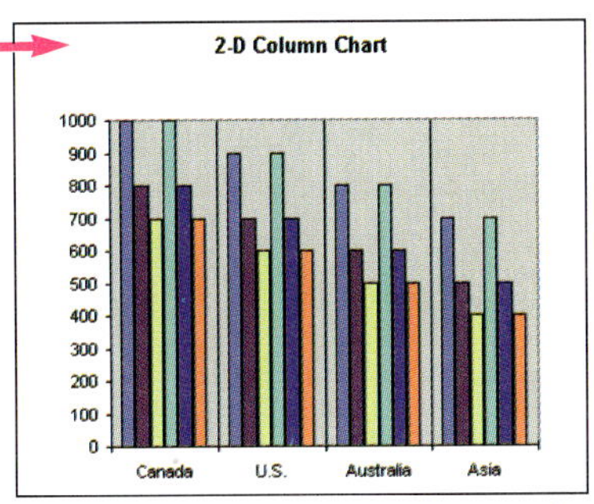

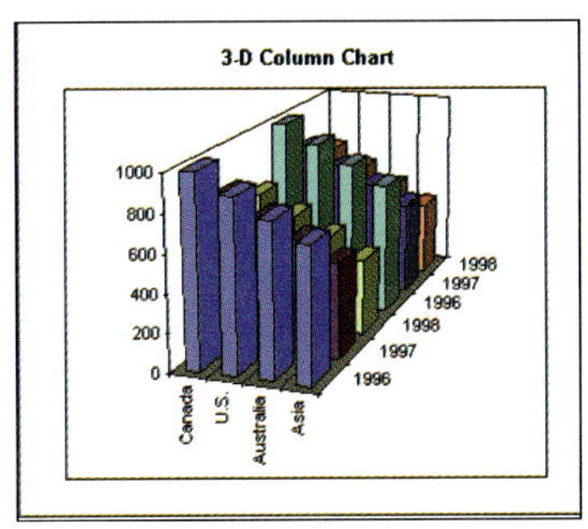

Changing Chart Types

One way to revise a chart is to change its type. For example, you can change a line chart to a bar or column chart for more impact. You can also change the type of individual data series. For example, you can have sales appear as a line and costs appear as bars. If you select one or more data series in the chart before using the **Chart Type** command, the **Selected Series** option button will be turned on (◉) in the dialog box and the chart type you select will be applied only to the selection.

QUICKSTEPS

Changing Chart Types with the Format Menu

1. Double-click an embedded chart to activate it or click the tab of a chart sheet to make it active.
2. Pull down the **Format** menu and click the **Chart Type** command to display the Chart Type dialog box.

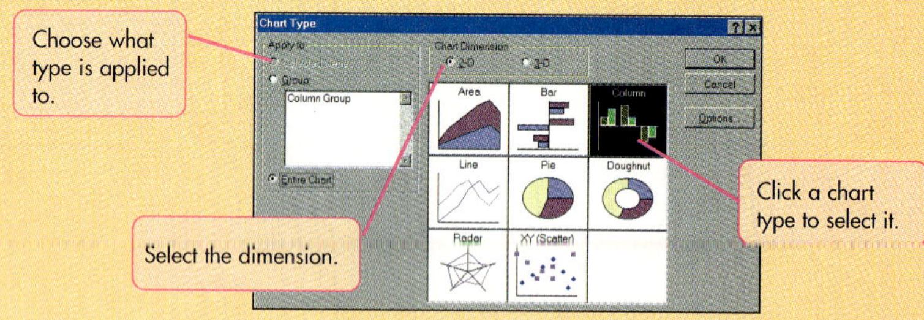

3. Click a type to select it, and then click the **OK** command button.

AutoFormatting Charts

Excel's AutoFormat command recognizes various parts of a chart and applies stored formats to them automatically.

QUICKSTEPS

Changing Formats and Chart Types with the AutoFormat Command

1. Double-click an embedded chart to activate it or click the tab of a chart sheet to make it active.
2. Pull down the **Format** menu and click the **AutoFormat** command to display the AutoFormat dialog box.

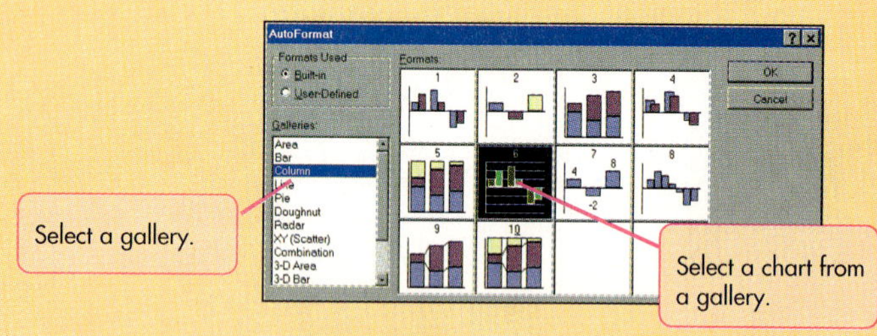

3. Click any chart type on the **Galleries** list to display the **Formats** palette of subtypes. Click the format you want to use, and then click the **OK** command button to apply it to the activated chart. The format you apply with this command does not affect the data in the chart, but it changes the look of the chart and overrides any chart formatting you may have already applied.

TIP
Logarithmic Scales

Logarithm scales on charts allow you to plot very large and very small values on the same chart. To create a log scale, double-click the value axis to display the Format Axis dialog box. Click the *Scale* tab, click the **Logarithmic Scale** check box to turn it on (☑), and then click the **OK** command button.

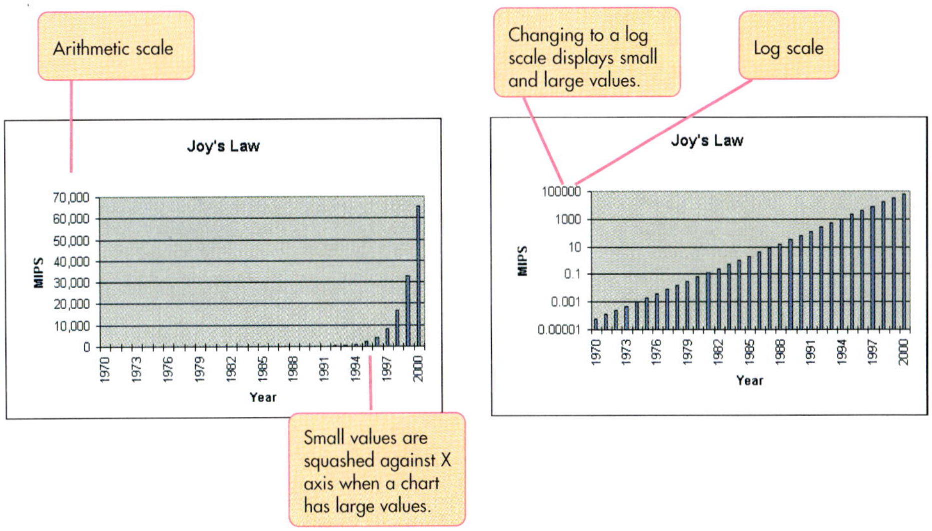

TUTORIAL

In this tutorial you explore how to change chart types and how to automatically format charts. Both of these procedures make it possible to refine your presentation so your data is best illustrated.

Getting Ready

1. Open the *Five-year plan* workbook stored in the *Tutorial Workbooks* folder on the *Excel Student Resource Disk.*

Changing the Chart Type

2. Double-click the embedded chart to activate it, and its border changes to a hatched pattern.
3. Pull down the **Format** menu and click the **Chart Type** command to display the Chart Type dialog box. The *Column* chart type should be selected.

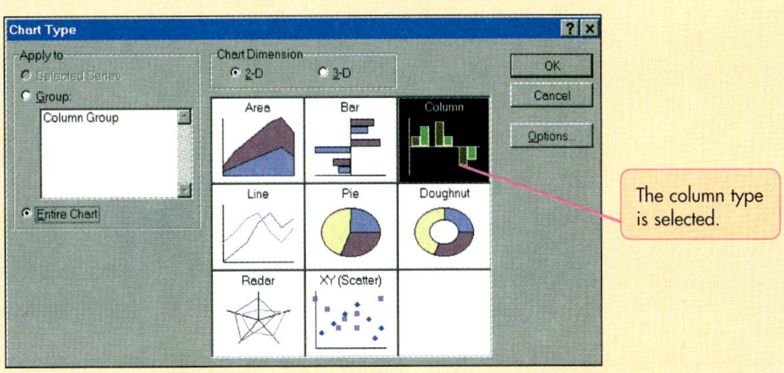

4. Click the **Options** command button to display the Format Column Group dialog box. With the *Subtype* tab selected, click the second type from the left (stacked columns) in the **Subtype** window.

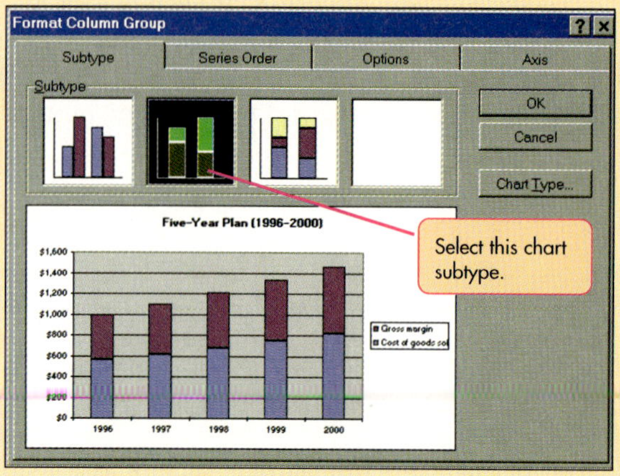

5. Click the **OK** command button to close the dialog box and display the chart in the new format.

Exploring AutoFormats

6. With the chart still activated, pull down the **Format** menu and click the **AutoFormat** command to display the AutoFormat dialog box.
7. Click the *Bar* choice in the **Galleries** list to display a variety of bar chart types in the **Formats** section.

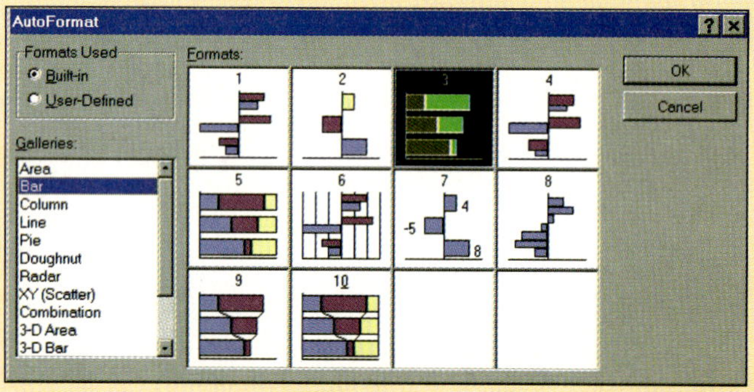

8. Click number *4* in the **Formats** window to select it and then click the **OK** command button to change the chart.
9. Repeat Steps 6 through 8 but select these chart types:

Galleries	Formats
Bar	9
Area	4
3-D Bar	4
3-D Column	4

Finishing Up

10. Save, print, and close the workbook. If your printer takes a long time to print charts, you may want to use Print Preview to see your chart instead of printing it.

5-7 RECORDING AND PLAYING BACK MACROS

Macros are a way to store commands so that they can be played back later. They can save you from having to rekey repetitive data or commands. It is like making a piano into a player piano; the only difference is the computer's keys do not move up and down and the mouse doesn't move about—it is all done electronically. You use macros to quickly execute any sequence of commands that you find yourself doing over and over again. These might include such procedures as:

- Entering a heading (for example, entering your name in cell A1 on each new model that you retrieve).
- Formatting a range of cells as currency with zero decimal places
- Querying a list (lists are the subject of PicTorial 6)
- Adding borders and patterns to headings or changing their font
- Widening columns

To use a macro, you must first record it. You can then play it back by selecting its name from a menu or by clicking a button. To record a macro, you use Excel's Macro Recorder to create Visual Basic code. This code, like that used to create any program, contains commands that Excel can interpret and execute. You'll see an example of this in this section's tutorial.

Recording Macros

To record a macro, you turn recording on, enter the keystrokes or commands you want recorded, and then turn recording off.

The **Stop** button

QUICKSTEPS

Recording Macros

1. Pull down the **Tools** menu and point to the **Record Macro** command to cascade the menu.
2. Click the **Record New Macro** command to display the Record New Macro dialog box and begin recording.
3. Enter any of the commands described in the box "Understanding the Record New Macro Dialog Box."
4. Click the **OK** command button to begin recording the macro. The status bar reads *Ready Recording*, and the **Stop** button from the Visual Basic toolbox is displayed on the screen.
5. Execute the commands you want recorded.
6. Click the **Stop** button from the Visual Basic toolbox, or, pull down the **Tools** menu, point to the **Record Macro** command to cascade the menu, and then click the **Stop Recording** command to end macro recording.

UNDERSTANDING
The Record New Macro Dialog Box

When you use the command to record a macro, the Record New Macro dialog box appears. All of the settings in this box are optional, but it is recommended that you assign a name to the macro so you'll be able to recognize it later.

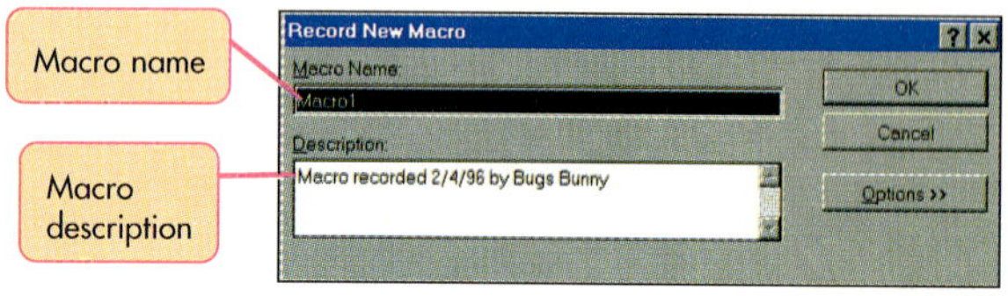

Macro Name text box is where you enter the name that will be listed when you use the command that runs macros. If you don't enter a name here, Excel will give the macro a sequential name such as Macro1, Macro2, Macro3, and so on.

Description text box is where you enter a description of the macro so you'll know what it does when you look it up later. If you don't enter a description, Excel gives just the date and the name of the person who recorded it.

Command Buttons

Options button expands the dialog box to offer these choices.

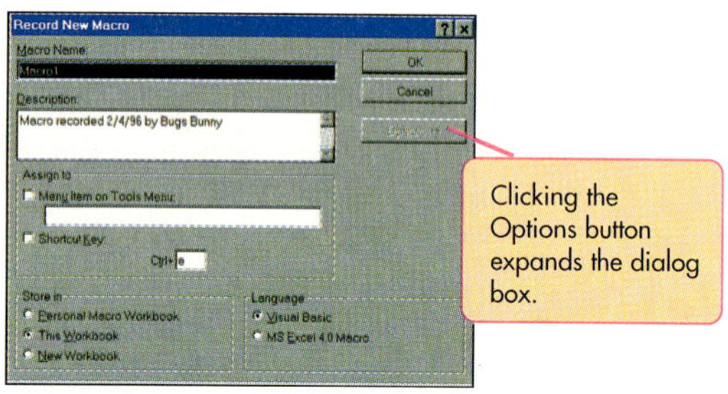

Assign To Section

Menu Item on Tools Menu check box is where you click to add the macro to the **Tools** menu. (You can also do this later.) After clicking the check box, type the name of the macro as you want it to appear on the menu.

Shortcut Key check box is where you click if you want to be able to execute the macro by holding down Ctrl while pressing one of the letter keys on the keyboard. After turning the check box on (☑), enter the letter you want to assign the macro to in the **Ctrl+** text box.

Store in Section

Personal Macro Notebook option button, when on (◉), stores macros all on the same sheet in a hidden workbook. To see it, pull down the **Window** menu and click the **Unhide** command to display a list of hidden workbooks.

This Workbook option button, when on (◉), stores the macro's code on a sheet in the same workbook named Module1, Module2, and so on.

New Workbook option button, when on (◉), stores the macro's code in a separate workbook. To see it, pull down the **Window** menu and click its name at the bottom of the menu.

Language Section

Visual Basic option button, when on (◉), generates the macro using Visual Basic code and stores it on a sheet named *Module1, Module2,* and so on.

MS Excel 4.0 Macro option button, when on (◉), generates the macro in Excel's own specific language and stores it on a sheet named *Macro1, Macro2,* and so on.

Playing Back Macros

Once a macro has been recorded, you can play it back by selecting its name from a menu or by holding down Ctrl and pressing the letter you assigned it to if you specified a shortcut key in the **Ctrl+** text box when recording the macro.

QUICKSTEPS

Playing Back Macros

1. Pull down the **Tools** menu and click the **Macro** command to display the Macro dialog box.
2. Click the name of the macro you want to run in the **Macro Name/Reference** list to select it.
3. Click the **Run** command button.

TIP

Interrupting a Running Macro

If you find you are running the wrong macro, or want to stop it for some other reason, you can do so by pressing Esc. This will display the Macro Error dialog box. To close the dialog box, press Esc again or click the **End** command button.

TUTORIAL

In this tutorial you record and play back a macro that enters the three-line heading found at the top of all workbooks included with this text. You see how to run the macro using menu commands and also how to assign it to a keyboard key so you can execute it by holding down Ctrl while pressing that key.

Getting Ready

1. Click the **New Workbook** button on the Standard toolbar to open a new document.

Recording a Macro

2. Pull down the **Tools** menu and point to the **Record Macro** command to cascade the menu.
3. Click the **Record New Macro** command to display the Record New Macro dialog box.

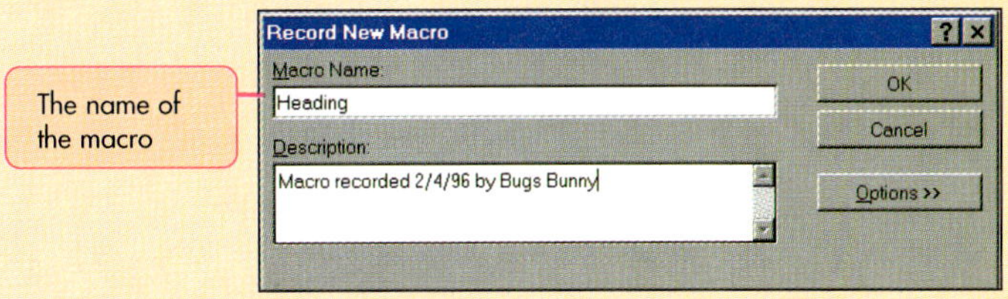

4. Type **Heading** in the **Macro Name** text box and then click the **OK** command button to begin recording the macro. The status bar reads *Ready Recording* and the **Stop** button from the Visual Basic toolbox is displayed on the screen.
5. Execute the following commands so they are recorded.
   - Press Ctrl+Home to select cell A1 (even if it is already selected).

- Type **Name:** press [Spacebar] and type your name.
- Press [Enter ↵] to select cell A2, and type **Filename: Macro workbook**
- Press [Enter ↵] to select cell A3 and type **=NOW()** and press [Enter ↵].
- With cell A3 selected, pull down the **Format** menu and click the **Cells** command to display the Format Cells dialog box.
- Click the *Number* tab to display that dialog box, then click *Date* in the **Category** list.
- Click *3/4/95* in the **Type** list, and then click the **OK** command button.

6. Click the **Stop** button from the Visual Basic toolbox to end macro recording.

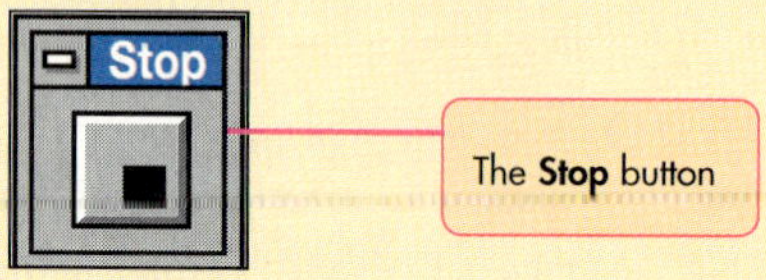

Displaying the Macro

7. Scroll the sheet tabs till you see Sheet16, and the one following it is named *Module1*. Click that tab to display the macro you just recorded.

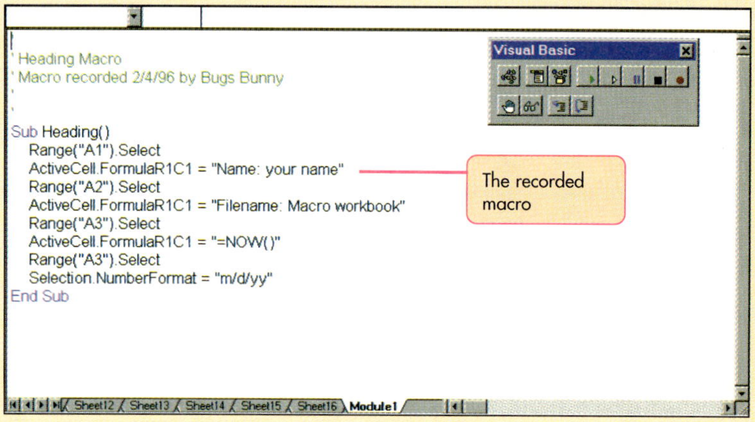

Playing Back a Macro from the Menu

8. Scroll the sheet tabs till you see *Sheet2*, and click that tab to display a blank sheet.
9. Pull down the **Tools** menu and click the **Macro** command to display the Macro dialog box.

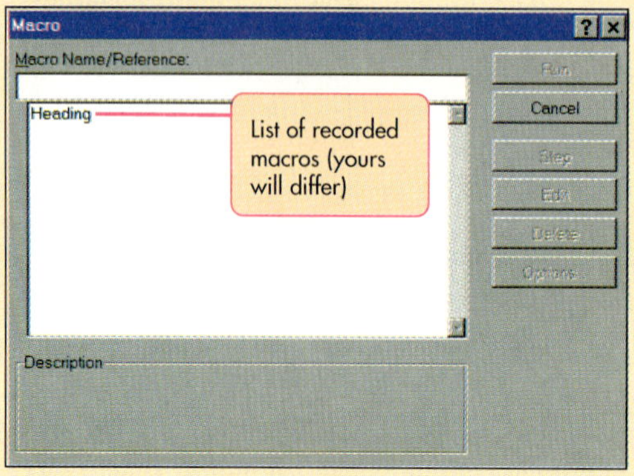

10. Click the macro named *Heading* to select it in the **Macro Name/Reference** list, and then click the **Run** command button. The macro automatically enters the three-line heading at the top of the sheet.

Assigning a Macro to Shortcut Keys

11. Pull down the **Tools** menu and click the **Macro** command to display the Macro dialog box.

12. Click the *Heading* macro on the **Macro Name/Reference** list and then click the **Options** command button to display the Macro Options dialog box.

13. Click the **Shortcut Key** check box to turn it on (☑), then type **h** in the **Ctrl+** text box.

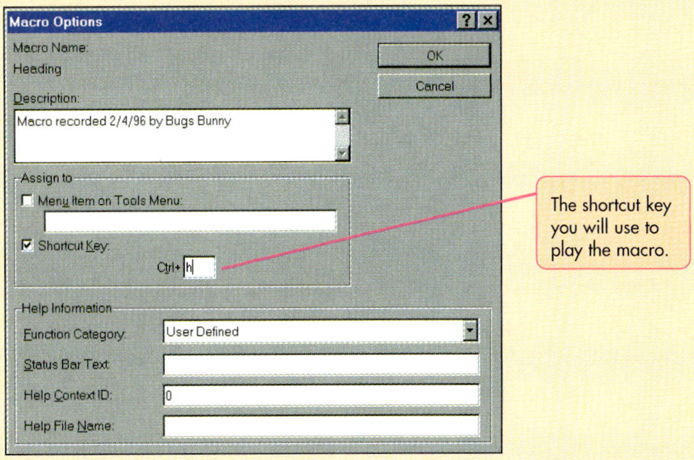

14. Click the **OK** command button to close the Macro Options dialog box.

15. Click the **Close** command button to close the Macro dialog box.

Playing Back a Macro from the Shortcut Keys

16. Click the sheet tab for *Sheet3* to display a blank sheet.

17. Press Ctrl+H to play back the macro and enter the heading.

Finishing Up

18. Click the **Save** button on the Standard toolbar, and save your workbook as *Macro workbook* in the *Tutorial Workbooks* folder on the *Excel Student Resource Disk*.

19. Click the *Module1* sheet to make it active, and then click the **Print** button on the Standard toolbar to print the sheet.

20. Close the workbook.

REVIEW QUESTIONS

TRUE-FALSE

T F **1.** If you double-click an embedded chart, you select it.

T F **2.** Text in worksheet cells can be used as titles for a chart.

T F **3.** To create a macro, you must understand how to program in Visual Basic.

T F **4.** A chart is linked to data in a worksheet.

T F **5.** When creating a chart, select the data before activating the ChartWizard.

T F **6.** If after creating an embedded chart, you change the data in the worksheet, the graph must be recreated.

T F **7.** All charts must have a data range.

T F **8.** An embedded chart is displayed and printed on the same sheet as the data on which it is based.

T F **9.** If you tell Excel the data series are in rows, it uses the text or values in the topmost row as category axis labels.

T F **10.** To select nonadjacent sheets, click the first sheet tab and then hold down [Shift] and click another sheet.

MULTIPLE CHOICE

1. Bar and column charts are best suited for ________ data.

a. Continuous
b. Percentages of whole
c. Discrete
d. Placid

2. On a chart, the ________ axis contains the labels for the data being plotted.

a. Value
b. Topic
c. Category
d. Topical

3. When you have only one data series, the best chart to use is a ________ chart.

a. Pie
b. Bar
c. Line
d. Area

4. To stop a macro while it is running, press ________.

a. [Esc]
b. **Pause**
c. [Ctrl]+[Break]
d. [End]

5. The number of items in a legend on a chart is based upon the number of ________.

a. Titles b. Data series

c. Labels d. Bars

6. ________ identify the symbols or patterns used to plot charts so that data series can be distinguished from one another.

a. Titles b. Legends

c. Scales d. Axes

7. Area and line charts are best suited for ________ data.

a. Continuous b. Percentages of whole

c. Discrete d. Placid

8. On a chart, the axis against which numbers are plotted is called the ________ axis.

a. Value b. Topic

c. Category d. Topical

9. To copy a sheet, point to its tab, hold down ________ and the left mouse button and drag the page icon to the tab you want it to be copied in front of.

a. Ctrl b. Alt

c. Ctrl+Shift d. Shift

10. To select adjacent sheets, click the first sheet tab and then hold down ________ and click the next one.

a. Ctrl b. Alt

c. Ctrl+Shift d. Shift

FILL IN THE BLANK

1. If you want category axis labels and legends on a chart, include ________ in the data selection range.
2. When you select a chart, ________ appear on the top and bottom, sides, and corners of a frame around the chart.
3. ________ data occurs when measurements have been sampled to determine a trend.
4. For many charts the value axis is what is called the Y or ________ axis.
5. When creating a pie chart, you can have ________ data series(s).
6. ________ scales on charts allow you to plot very large and very small values on the same chart.
7. To create a chart, you must have at least ________ data series.
8. ________ data are those where you have a data series that contains parts equaling a significant whole.
9. If you tell Excel the data series are in rows, it uses the leftmost cell on each row as a ________.
10. ________ data consists of values measured at a series of selected points.

LAB ACTIVITIES

DRILLS

5-1 Managing a Workbook

The advantage of workbooks is that they contain many sheets, each of which you can use for a related model. In this drill, you practice naming, deleting, copying, and moving sheets.

1. Open a new workbook.
2. Double-click the first three sheet tabs and change their names as follows.
   - Rename *Sheet 1* to **Master Budget**
   - Rename *Sheet 2* to **Income Budget**
   - Rename *Sheet 3* to **Expense Budget**
3. Select sheets 4 through 16, then delete them with the **Edit**, **Delete Sheet** commands.
4. Drag the *Expense Budget* sheet in front of the *Income Budget* sheet.
5. Use Ctrl to drag a copy of the *Expense Budget* sheet so it is the last sheet.
6. Delete the duplicate *Income Budget* sheet using the **Edit**, **Delete Sheet** command.
7. Close the workbook without saving your changes.

5-2 Creating Embedded Charts

Charts allow you to view data in a new way, making some things stand out better for analysis. In this drill, you create a chart that illustrates the sales for all of the regions to see how they compare. When finished, your chart should look like the one shown in the figure "Sales by Region."

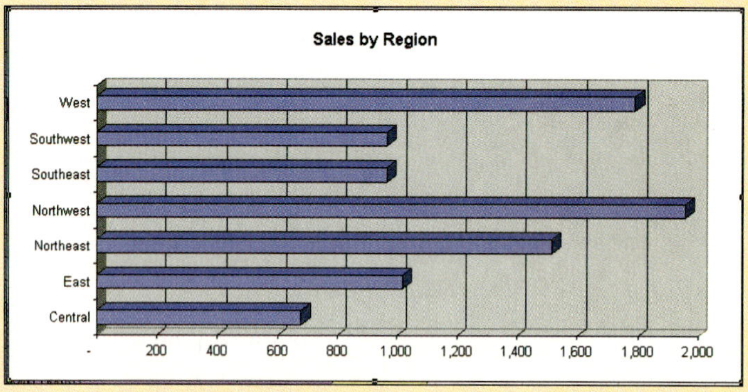

Sales by Region

1. Open the *Statistical functions* workbook stored in the *Drill Workbooks* folder on the *Excel Student Resource Disk*.
2. Select the cell range A5:B12 and click the **ChartWizard** button. Draw an outline showing where you want the chart, starting in the upper-left corner of cell A1 and ending in the lower-right corner of cell C16.

3. Click the **Next>** command button to display the ChartWizard *Step 2 of 5* dialog box, and click the **3-D Bar** chart type to select it.
4. Click the **Next>** command button three times to display the *Step 5 of 5* dialog box, then:
   - Click the **No** option button (◉) under the heading *Add A Legend?* to turn it off.
   - Enter the title **Sales by Region** in the **Chart Title** text box.
5. Click the **Finish** command button to display the chart. Don't worry that the chart covers the model; you'll fix that in the next drill.
6. Save, print, and close the workbook.

5-3 Moving, Sizing, and Deleting Embedded Charts

Once you have created an embedded chart, you can easily move, size, or delete it. In this drill you practice those procedures. When finished, your chart should be the size and in the position shown in the figure "The Sized Chart."

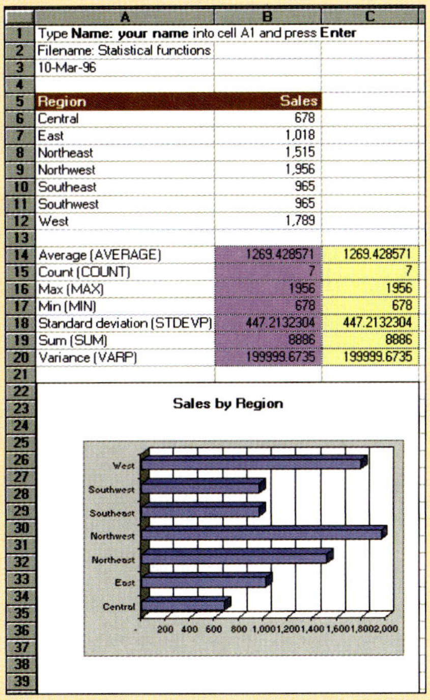

The Sized Chart

1. Open the *Statistical functions* workbook stored in the *Drill Workbooks* folder on the *Excel Student Resource Disk*.
2. Drag the chart below the model, then scroll the screen so you can see the entire chart or at least the lower right corner of it.
3. Use the lower-right selection square to make the chart as wide as the model above it. Be sure to hold down [⇧ Shift] so it is sized proportionally. When you release the mouse button, not all seven Y-axis labels may be displayed now. Also, the X-axis labels may not displayed correctly. We'll fix the Y-axis labels now and then fix the X-axis labels in a later drill.
4. If all seven Y-axis labels are not displayed, use the selection square on the bottom of the chart to drag it down until all seven Y-Axis labels are displayed. (It may take a few tries.)
5. Save, print, and close the worksheet.

5-4 Creating Chart Sheets

Unlike embedded charts, chart sheets are on their own sheet in the workbook. In this drill you create a chart sheet that illustrates the sales for all of the regions using the same model on which you created an embedded chart. When finished, your chart should look like the figure "The Statistical Functions Chart Sheet."

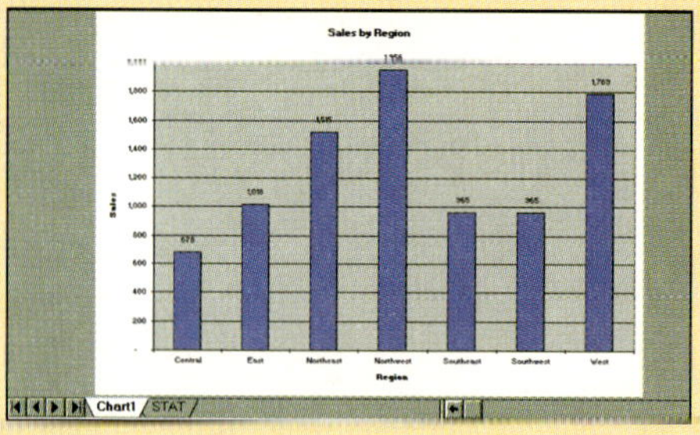

The Statistical Functions Chart Shoot

1. Open the *Statistical functions* workbook stored in the *Drill Workbooks* folder on the *Excel Student Resource Disk*.
2. Select the cell range A5:B12, then use the **Insert**, **Chart**, **As New Sheet** commands to display the ChartWizard *Step 1 of 5* dialog box.
3. Click the **Next>** command button four times to display the ChartWizard *Step 5 of 5* dialog box:
   - Click to turn on the **No** option button (◉) under the heading *Add A Legend?* to turn it off.
   - Enter the three titles **Sales by Region**, **Region**, and **Sales** in the appropriate text boxes.
4. Click the **Finish** command button to display the chart on its own sheet.
5. Insert data labels on the chart by selecting the **Insert**, **Data Labels** command. When the Insert Data Labels dialog box appears, click on the **Show Value** option button (◉), then click the **OK** command button.
6. Save the workbook, print the chart sheet, and then close the workbook.

5-5 Editing and Revising Charts

In this drill you revise the embedded chart you created in Drill 5-2 by changing its title and removing gridlines. When finished, your chart should look like the one shown in the figure "The Revised Sales Chart."

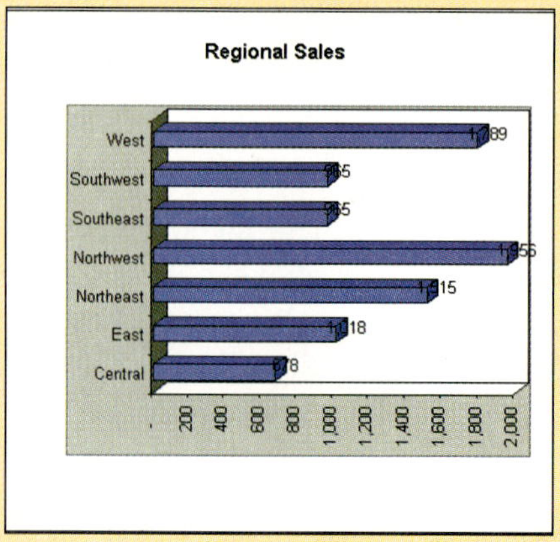

The Revised Sales Chart

1. Open the *Statistical functions* workbook stored in the *Drill Workbooks* folder on the *Excel Student Resource Disk* and click the sheet tab labeled *STAT*.

2. Double-click the embedded chart to activate it (it's the one on the same sheet as the model).
3. Click the chart title to select it, then click it again and change the title to *Regional Sales*. Click anywhere outside of the title area so it isn't selected.
4. Remove the gridlines with the **Insert**, **Gridlines** command and click off the **Major Gridlines** check box under the heading *Value (Z) Axis*. Click the **OK** command button to close the dialog box.
5. Double-click the X axis (the horizontal axis) to display the Format Axis dialog box. (If the wrong dialog box appears, click its **Cancel** command button and try again.). On the **Alignment** tab select the middle vertical choice under the **Orientation** heading and click the **OK** command button. Notice how the X-axis labels now run vertically so there is room for all of them to be displayed.
6. Click outside the chart so it is no longer activated.
7. Save the workbook, print the worksheet, and then close the workbook.

5-6 Exploring Chart Types and AutoFormats

The type of chart you choose determines how easy it is to interpret your data. One nice thing about spreadsheet graphics is that you can display the same data in a variety of ways to see which chart type best represents the data you are presenting. When finished, your chart should look like the figure "The Pie Chart."

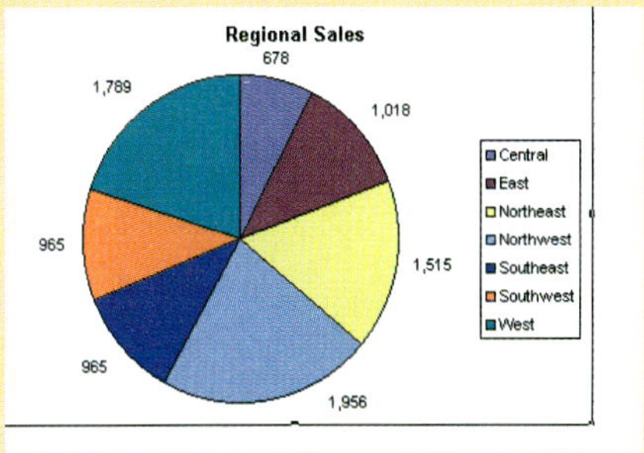

The Pie Chart

1. Open the *Statistical functions* workbook stored in the *Drill Workbooks* folder on the *Excel Student Resource Disk*.
2. On the sheet named *STAT*, double-click the embedded chart to activate it. Then use the **Format**, **Chart Type**, **2-D**, **Pie** commands to change it to a pie chart.
3. Insert legends on the chart using the **Insert**, **Legend** command.
4. Save the workbook, print the worksheet, and then close the workbook.

5-7 Recording and Playing Back Macros

When creating models, you often want to print them out with row and column headings and cell gridlines so you can troubleshoot them or have a record of their final form. Here you record a macro that includes directions for turning off row and column headings and turning off gridlines. You then record another that turns them on.

1. Open the *Loan payments* workbook stored in the *Drill Workbooks* folder on the *Excel Student Resource Disk*.
2. Turn on macro recording by selecting **Tools**, **Record Macro**, **Record New Macro**. In the Record New Macro dialog box, enter the macro name **heads_grids_off**.

3. To turn off row and column headings on your printouts, use the **File**, **Page Setup**, **Sheet** commands. Click off the **Gridlines** and **Row & Column Headings** check boxes if they are on. Close the dialog box.
4. Turn off macro recording by clicking the **Stop** button displayed in the screen area.
5. Repeat steps 2 through 4 but name the macro **heads_grids_on** and click on both **Gridlines** and **Row & Column** Headings settings.
6. Save the worksheet.
7. Execute each macro using the **Tools**, **Macro** commands. Select the name of the macro, and click the **Run** command button.
8. Make printouts after executing each macro.
9. Close the workbook.

EXERCISES

5-1 The Pennies Model

The rate of growth of doubling a penny every day is amazing. In this exercise you create an embedded area chart that plots this growth. When finished, your chart should look like the one shown in the figure "The Doubling a Penny Daily Chart."

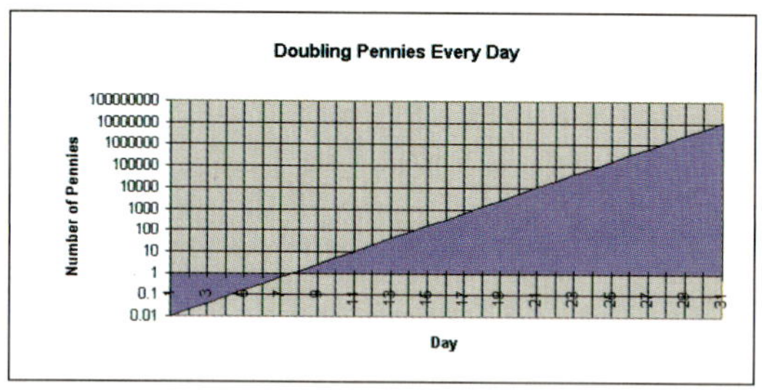

The Doubling a Penny Daily Chart

1. Open the *Doubling a penny daily* workbook stored in the *Exercise Workbooks* folder on the *Excel Student Resource Disk*.
2. Use the **ChartWizard** button on the Standard toolbar to create an embedded chart of the data in the range A5:B36. Embed the chart in the range C1:F14.
3. Use the Chart Wizard dialog boxes to specify the following:
   - On the *Step 2 of 5* dialog box select the Area chart.
   - On the *Step 4 of 5* dialog box, set **Use First X Column(s) for Category** (X) **Axis Labels** to *1*.
   - On the *Step 5 of 5* dialog box turn off the legend and enter the three titles **Doubling Pennies Every Day**, **Day**, and **Number of Pennies**.
4. Click the **Finish** command button to display the finished embedded chart. Notice how the chart of the first days is squashed against the category axis.
5. Activate the chart, then double-click the value axis to display the Format Axis dialog box.
6. On the **Scale** tab, turn on the **Logarithmic Scale** check box, and then return to the worksheet. The chart is now displayed using a logarithmic scale. Size the chart so you can see all of the Value axis labels.

7. Save, print, and close the workbook.

5-2 Birthday Probabilities

In this exercise, you create an embedded 3-D Column chart of the probabilities that two people might share the same birth date. When finished, your chart should look like the one shown in the figure "The Birthday Odds Chart."

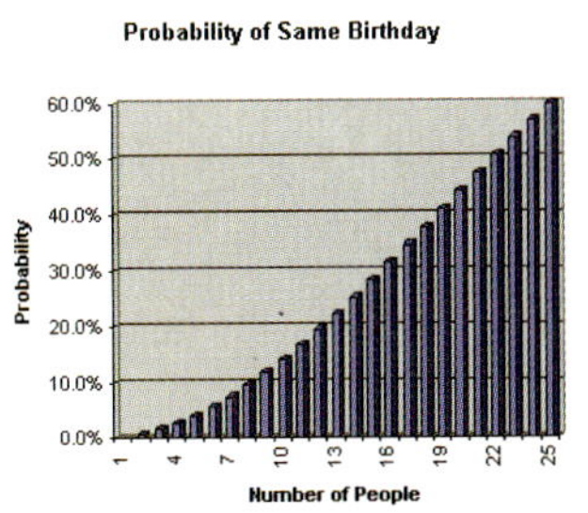

The Birthday Odds Chart

1. Open the *Birthday odds* workbook stored in the *Exercise Workbooks* folder on the *Excel Student Resource Disk*.
2. Use the **ChartWizard** button on the Standard toolbar to create an embedded chart of the data in the ranges A5:A30 and E5:E30 (use Ctrl to select the ranges). Embed the chart in the range A32:E50.
3. Use the Chart Wizard dialog boxes to specify the following:
   - On the *Step 2 of 5* dialog box, select **3-D Column** chart.
   - On the *Step 4 of 5* dialog box set **Use First X Column(s) for Category (X) Axis Labels** to *1*.
   - On the *Step 5 of 5* dialog box, turn off legends and enter the three titles **Probability of Same Birthday**, **Number of People**, and **Probability**.
4. Click the **Finish** command button to display the finished embedded chart.
5. Save, print, and close the workbook.

5-3 Loan Payments

In this exercise you create a 2-D Column chart that shows how payments change depending on the amount of a loan. When finished, your chart should look like the one shown in the figure "The Loan Payments Chart."

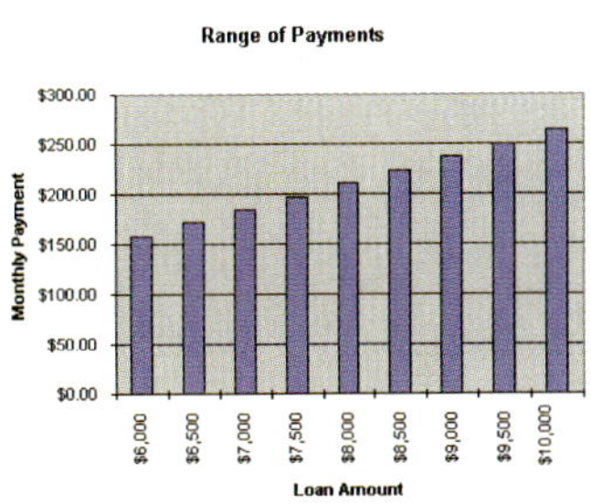

The Loan Payments Chart

1. Open the *Auto loan analyzer* workbook stored in the *Exercise Workbooks* folder on the *Excel Student Resource Disk*.
2. Use the **ChartWizard** button on the Standard toolbar to create an embedded chart of the data in the range C5:D16. Embed the chart in the range A20:D40.
3. Use the Chart Wizard dialog boxes to specify the following:
   - On the *Step 4 of 5* dialog box notice how there are two data series plotted. Set **Use First X Columns(s) for Legend Text** to *1*. Now there is just one bar.
   - On the *Step 4 of 5* dialog box notice how there is no bar for the first amount in the sample graph. Set **Use First X Row(s) for Legend Text** to *3*. Now there is a bar for the first amount.
   - On the *Step 5 of 5* dialog box, turn off legends and enter the three titles **Range of Payments**, **Loan Amount**, and **Monthly Payment**.
4. Click the **Finish** command button to display the finished embedded chart.
5. Save, print, and close the workbook.

5-4 Charting the Series Model

One thing you should avoid doing is plotting very large and very small data ranges on the same chart. In this exercise, you chart the *Number series* model to demonstrate the problems this can cause. You then use a log axis to correct the problem. When finished, your line chart should look like the one shown in the figure "The Number Series Chart."

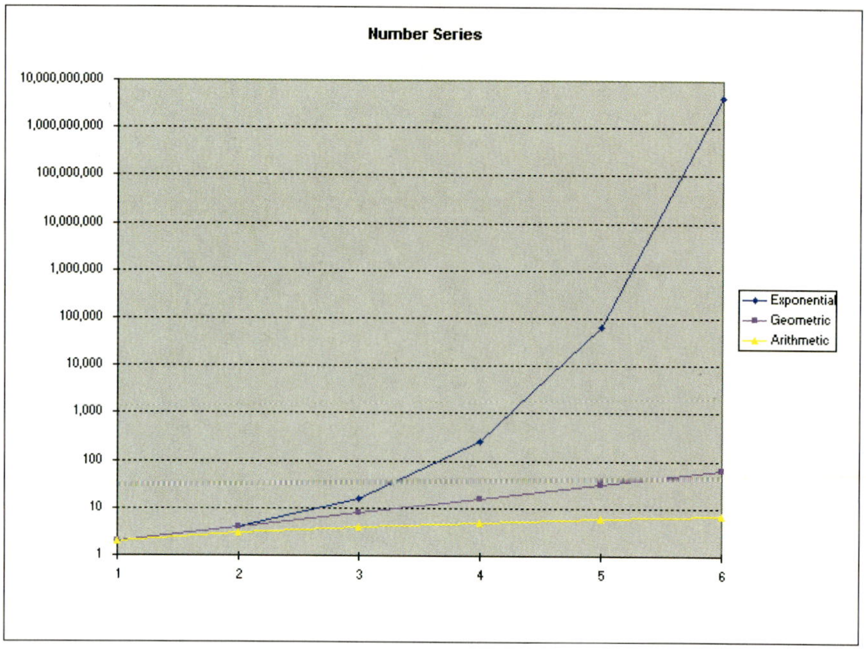

The Number Series Chart

1. Open the *Number series* workbook stored in the *Exercise Workbooks* folder on the *Excel Student Resource Disk.*
2. Select the range A5:C11 to be charted(don't select the last two rows—they are too large) and use the **Insert**, **Chart** commands to specify a new chart sheet for the graph and display the ChartWizard dialog box.
3. Use the Chart Wizard dialog boxes to specify the following:
   - On the *Step 2 of 5* dialog box, select **Line** as the chart type.
   - On the *Step 5 of 5* dialog box, enter the chart title **Number Series.**
4. Click the **Finish** command button to display the embedded chart. Notice how the lines for two of the series are pressed against the category axis because the values on the other series are so large.
5. Double-click the Y-axis scale to select it and display the Format Axis dialog box. On the **Scale** tab turn on the **Logarithmic Scale** check box. The chart is now displayed using a logarithmic scale and all three lines are clearly visible.
6. Save, print, and close the workbook.

PROJECTS

5-1 A Balance Sheet

Using the *Balance sheet* workbook you created earlier, create the chart shown in the figure "The Balance Sheet Chart," and add titles and legends to match the illustration. The chart plots total assets, total liabilities, and total owner equity for this year and last year. The category axis is the range that includes the column headings on row 8. When you are finished, save the workbook, and make a printout of the chart.

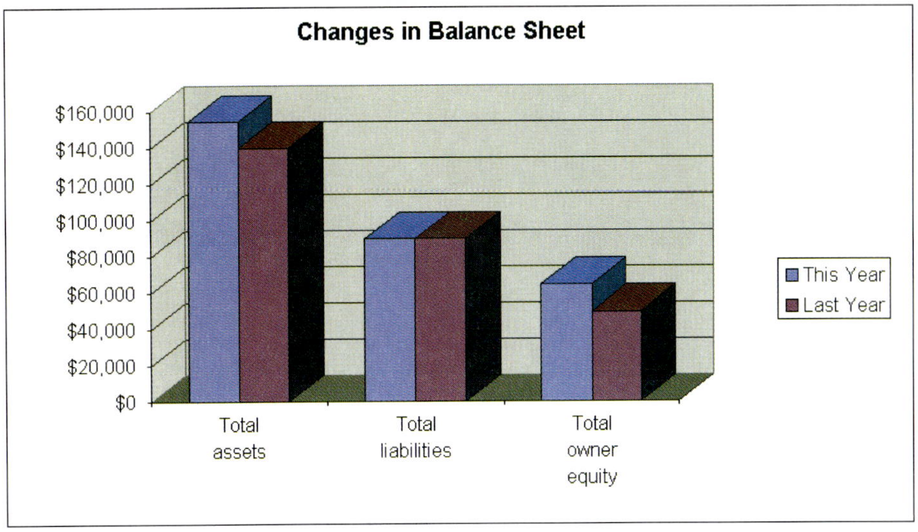

The Balance Sheet Chart

5-2 An Income Statement

Using the *Income statement* workbook you created earlier, create the chart shown in the figure "The Income Statement Chart," and add titles and legends to match the illustration. The chart plots total cost of goods and gross profits over the three-year period covered by the statement. The category axis includes the labels that head the yearly columns. When you are finished, save the workbook, and make a printout of the chart.

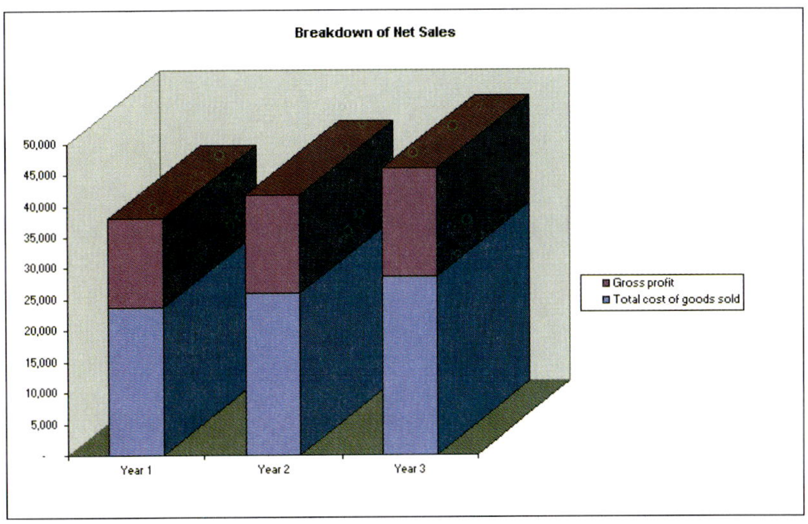

The Income Statement Chart

5-3 The Cost of Smoking

Everyone but the tobacco company managements knows that smoking is not good for you. No one knows this better than insurance companies that vary their rates for smokers and nonsmokers. Here is a worksheet that shows the rates from one company. Open the *Smoking costs* workbook stored in the *Project Workbooks* folder of the *Excel Student Resource Disk* and create the chart shown in the figure "One Cost of Smoking." The chart makes it easier to see the difference between males and females and smokers and nonsmokers.

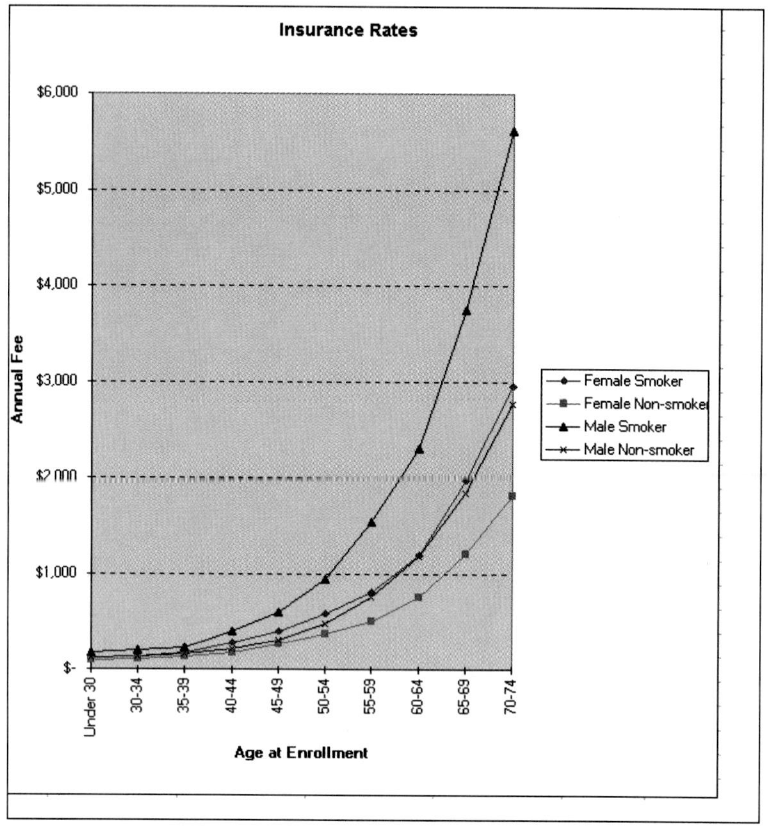

One Cost of Smoking

PicTorial

SIX

MANAGING LISTS

After completing this PicTorial, you will be able to:

- **Define the terms *field, record, list,* and *database***
- **Create lists of data so they can be used as a database of information**
- **Sort the data in a list into ascending or descending order**
- **Use criteria to find specific records in the list**
- **Filter a list to hide all records that don't match the specified criteria**
- **Use database functions to summarize data**
- **Automatically subtotal related groups of records**

MUCH information can be arranged in the form of a table called a *list* or *database*. Once a list has been set up correctly, Excel can quickly find information in the list, sort it into any desired order, and subtotal groups of related records. These capabilities are ideal for analyzing lists containing sales figures, inventory, mailing or distribution lists, customer accounts, check registers, or any other data that needs to be collected, sorted, and analyzed. Lists are created with most of the same commands used to create a model. In fact, a *list* is just a model organized into fields and records.

6-1 THE ANATOMY OF A LIST

When creating or working with a list, you need to understand the three parts of which it is constructed:

- *Column labels* (also called *field names*) are entered on the first row of the list and identify the contents of the columns where data are entered. These cells must be formatted differently from the records below them so Excel can recognize them as headings.
- *Records* are entered on the second and subsequent rows of the list. Each record is a set of related data, much like a Rolodex card that contains a person's name, address, and phone number.
- *Fields* are the columns of information that make up a record. Each column forms a separate field like an individual item on a Rolodex™ card—the person's name, street address, city, state, ZIP code, or phone number.

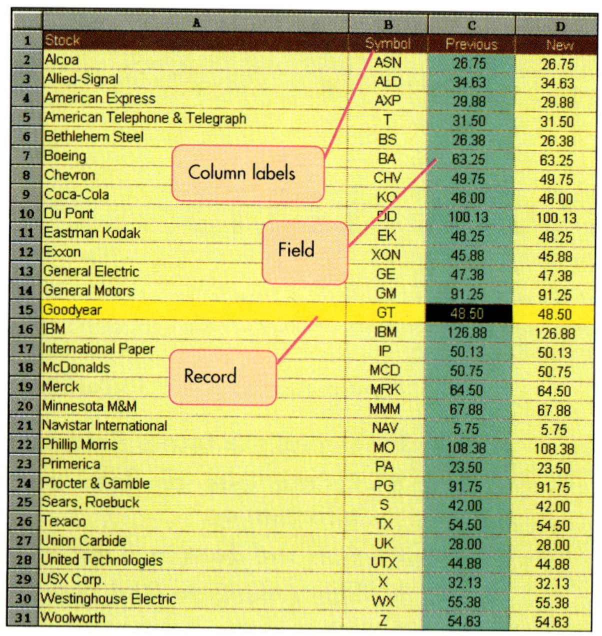

	A	B	C	D
1	Stock	Symbol	Previous	New
2	Alcoa	ASN	26.75	26.75
3	Allied-Signal	ALD	34.63	34.63
4	American Express	AXP	29.88	29.88
5	American Telephone & Telegraph	T	31.50	31.50
6	Bethlehem Steel	BS	26.38	26.38
7	Boeing	BA	63.25	63.25
8	Chevron	CHV	49.75	49.75
9	Coca-Cola	KO	46.00	46.00
10	Du Pont	DD	100.13	100.13
11	Eastman Kodak	EK	48.25	48.25
12	Exxon	XON	45.88	45.88
13	General Electric	GE	47.38	47.38
14	General Motors	GM	91.25	91.25
15	Goodyear	GT	48.50	48.50
16	IBM	IBM	126.88	126.88
17	International Paper	IP	50.13	50.13
18	McDonalds	MCD	50.75	50.75
19	Merck	MRK	64.50	64.50
20	Minnesota M&M	MMM	67.88	67.88
21	Navistar International	NAV	5.75	5.75
22	Phillip Morris	MO	108.38	108.38
23	Primerica	PA	23.50	23.50
24	Procter & Gamble	PG	91.75	91.75
25	Sears, Roebuck	S	42.00	42.00
26	Texaco	TX	54.50	54.50
27	Union Carbide	UK	28.00	28.00
28	United Technologies	UTX	44.88	44.88
29	USX Corp.	X	32.13	32.13
30	Westinghouse Electric	WX	55.38	55.38
31	Woolworth	Z	54.63	54.63

You must enter a list in such a way that Excel can recognize it as a list. This allows many of Excel's list management procedures to work automatically.

There are some easy-to-remember rules for labels, layout, and data entry that you should follow.

General Guidelines

- Have only one list on a worksheet, since some list management procedures can only work with a single list.
- Leave at least one blank row or column between a list and any other data on the worksheet so Excel can automatically identify the list when you select just a single cell within it. (If Excel can't recognize the list, you must select the entire list with the mouse before using list management procedures.)

- Avoid entering important data on the same rows on the sheet as the list. Some rows may be hidden during some list management operations, and this data would be hidden from view.

Column Label Guidelines

- The column labels (field names) must be entered as the first row of the list.
- When Excel sorts or otherwise manipulates the data in a list for you, it needs to be able to tell the difference between the column labels (which shouldn't be sorted) and the records in the list. To allow it to identify these separate parts of the list, format the column labels differently than the records below them. To do so, use a different font, data type, alignment, format, pattern, border, or capitalization style.

Row and Column Layout Guidelines

- Don't leave blank rows between column labels and records.
- Apply the same formats to all cells in a column (except the column label).

Data Entry Guidelines

- A list must have the same type of data in each field (column). For example, do not enter text in a field in some records and numbers, formulas, or dates in the same field of other records.
- All text or numbers in a column should have the same format.
- When entering numbers as text (as in phone numbers or ZIP codes) or combinations of numbers and text (as in 1, 2, 2a, 2b, 3, 3b, and so on), make sure they are all in a text format (type an apostrophe (') as the first character).
- Don't insert a space as the first character since it will be treated as a character and will affect sorting and searching.
- Be consistent with case since Excel can differentiate between lowercase and uppercase characters if you ask it to when sorting. (Normally Excel will ignore the case of characters. For example, it will treat *Product, product,* and *PRODUCT* the same during sorting.)

TIP

Wrapping Column Labels to Narrow Columns

To fully display long column labels, you may widen a column. However, there is no need to have a column wider than the data that it contains. To narrow a column that is too wide just because of the column label, wrap the long heading into two or more lines in the same cell. To do so, select the cell, pull down the **Format** menu and click the **Cells** command to display the Format Cells dialog box. Click the *Alignment* tab, click the **Wrap Text** check box to turn it on (☑), and then click the **OK** command button.

QUICKSTEPS

Creating Database Lists

1. Enter column labels for the list following the guidelines in the text.
2. Type data into the rows below the column labels following the guidelines discussed in the text.

TUTORIAL

In this tutorial you create a list and format the column labels so Excel recognizes them as list headings.

Getting Ready

1. Open the *Sales list 1* workbook stored in the *Tutorial Workbooks* folder on the *Excel Student Resource Disk* and enter your name in cell A1.

Entering Column Labels

2. Enter the column labels and records shown here just as you would type them into a regular model.

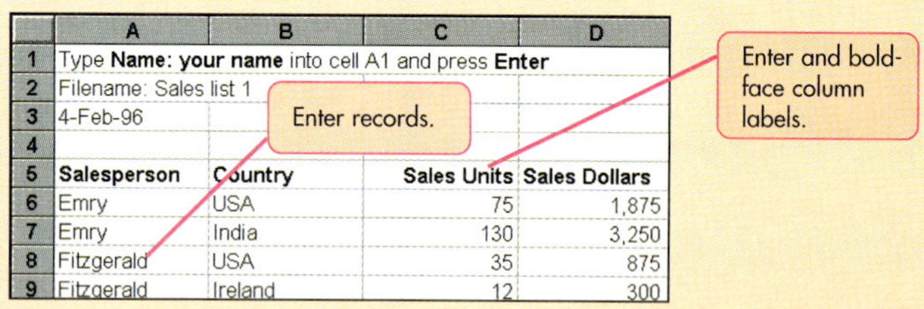

	A	B	C	D
1	Type **Name: your name** into cell A1 and press **Enter**			
2	Filename: Sales list 1			
3	4-Feb-96			
4				
5	**Salesperson**	**Country**	**Sales Units**	**Sales Dollars**
6	Emry	USA	75	1,875
7	Emry	India	130	3,250
8	Fitzgerald	USA	35	875
9	Fitzgerald	Ireland	12	300

3. Select the column headings on row 5 and click the **Bold** button on the Formatting toolbar to boldface them. Then use the **Align Right** button on the same toolbar to align the text in cells C5 and D5.

Finishing Up

4. Save, print, and close the workbook.

6-2 ENTERING AND EDITING DATA USING A DATA FORM

When you work with a list, you can display it using a special dialog box called the *data form* that displays all of the fields for a single record. The parts of a data form are described in the box "Understanding the Data Form."

To enter or edit data in a data form, you use the form's edit boxes. Each of the edit boxes is labeled with a field name automatically taken from the list's column labels. Data you enter into an edit box is inserted into the list in the column of the same name.

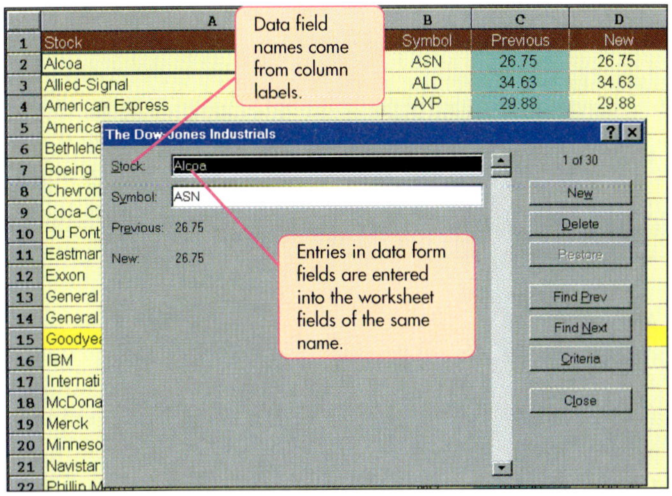

If you make mistakes when entering data, or if you want to modify a previously entered record, you can display it in the form and then edit it. You edit the contents of edit boxes the same way you edit the contents of text boxes in dialog boxes. For example, click to move the insertion point where you want it in an edit box, and then insert or delete characters. Double-click the edit box to select the entire entry, and then type a new entry or press Delete to delete the existing one.

QUICKSTEPS

Entering and Editing Data Using a Data Form

1. Select any cell in the list, pull down the **Data** menu, and click the **Form** command to display the data form. Data from the first record in the list (if any exists) will be displayed in the form.
2. Enter or edit data using these commands and others described in the box "Understanding the Data Form." (If a dialog box reads "No headers detected," refer to the box "Excel Cannot Identify the Column Labels.")
   - To enter a new record, click the **New** command button to display a blank form.
   - To display an existing record for editing, click the **Find Prev** or **Find Next** command buttons or use the scroll bar to display it. (See the Tip box "Using the Data Form's Scroll Bar.")
   - To enter or edit data, just type it into the edit boxes. You can press Tab or click the mouse to move between edit boxes. When finished entering or editing a record, press Enter or click the **New** command button to enter it into the list and display a new blank form.
3. When finished entering or editing data, click the **Close** command button to close the data form dialog box.

UNDERSTANDING
The Data Form

When you pull down the **Data** menu and click the **Form** command, the data form is displayed.

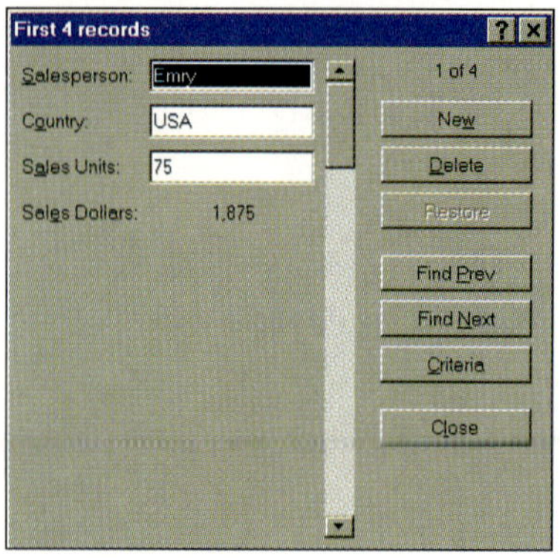

The *title bar* at the top of the dialog box displays the name of the worksheet.

Data form fields display the contents of the fields from a single record (up to 32). Those you can edit are displayed in edit boxes. Those you can't edit (computed fields containing formulas) are displayed without an edit box. The width of the widest column in the list determines the length of edit boxes.

Field names taken from the list's column labels identify the contents of each data form field. (To change these names, you must change the list's column labels.)

A scroll bar allows you to quickly scroll through records in the list. (See the Tip box "Using the Data Form's Scroll Bar.")

The *record number indicator* lists the number of the displayed record and the total number of records in the list.

Command buttons execute the following commands:

New enters any data currently display in the data form into the list on the worksheet and displays a new blank form.

Delete deletes the record displayed in the form and also deletes it from the list on the worksheet. When you click this command, a dialog box asks you to confirm the deletion. When you use this command to delete a record from the worksheet, all records below it move up to fill the gap left in the list.

Restore cancels any changes you have made to the record that is currently displayed. (This button is dimmed until you enter or change data in an edit box.)

Find Prev displays the previous record, if any.

Find Next displays the next record, if any.

Criteria searches for any records on the list that match the criteria you specify. (See Section 6-5, "Filtering Records.")

Close closes the data form dialog box.

TIP
Using the Data Form's Scroll Bar

You can use the scroll bar to scroll through the records in the list.

- To move to the same field in the previous or next record, click the up or down scroll arrows.
- To move to the same field in a record 10 before or 10 after the current record, click above or below the scroll box.
- To move to the first or last record, drag the scroll box to the top or bottom of the scroll bar and release it.

COMMON WRONG TURNS
Excel Cannot Identify the Column Labels

When you pull down the **Data** menu and click the **Form** command, a dialog box may appear that reads *No headers detected. Assume top row is header row?* Click the **OK** command button if it is a header row. Otherwise, click the **Cancel** command button, select the list manually (including the headings), and repeat the command. To permanently fix the problem, format the headings differently in some respect from the records that follow them and be sure they are not separated from the records by one or more blank rows.

IN this tutorial you open an existing list and then use a data form to add records to it. The records are added to the end of the list.

Getting Ready

1. Open the *Sales list 1* workbook stored in the *Tutorial Workbooks* folder on the *Excel Student Resource Disk.*

Entering Data

2. Select any cell in the list on rows 5 through 9, pull down the **Data** menu, and click the **Form** command to display a data form. The first record in the list is displayed in the form's edit boxes.

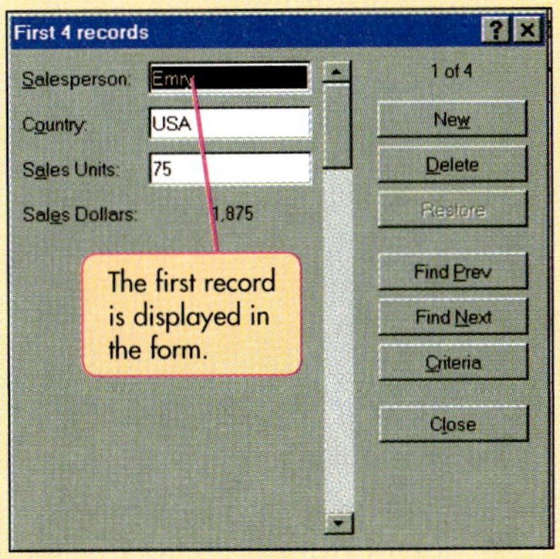

3. Click the **New** command button to display a blank form for a new record.
4. Enter the records shown in rows 10-15 as follows (as you enter each, it is added to the end of the list):
   - To fill in a record, type data into each edit box, pressing Tab to move the insertion point to the next edit box.
   - When finished with a record, click the **New** command button to enter the data into the list as a new record and display a blank form for another record. (You can also press Enter with the insertion point in the last field.)

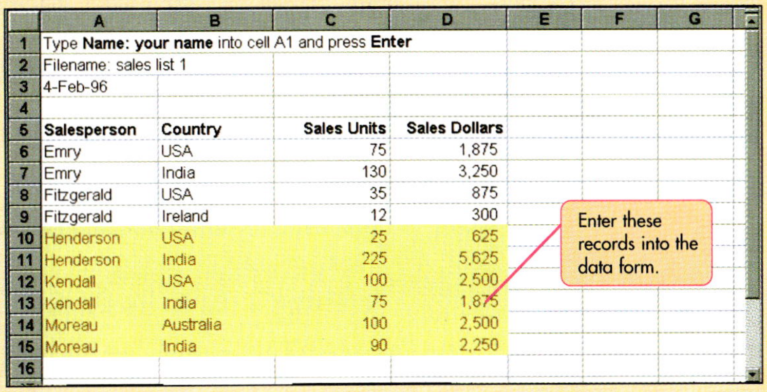

Finishing Up

5. After entering the last record, click the **Close** command button to close the data form dialog box.

6. Save, print, and close the workbook.

6-3 PERFORMING SIMPLE SORTS

	A	B	C
1	Random	Ascending sort	Descending sort
2	3	-2	Liz
3	1	-1	Dennis
4		10%	Cathy
5		20%	Bob
6	2	30%	Alice
7	5	1	1/30/97
8	4	2	1/30/96
9	-1	3	1/30/95
10	-2	4	1/30/94
11	20%	5	5
12	10%	1/30/94	4
13	30%	1/30/95	3
14	Alice	1/30/96	2
15	Bob	1/30/97	1
16	Cathy	Alice	30%
17	Liz	Bob	20%
18	Dennis	Cathy	10%
19	1/30/96	Dennis	-1
20	1/30/95	Liz	-2
21	1/30/97		
22	1/30/94		

Sort Orders

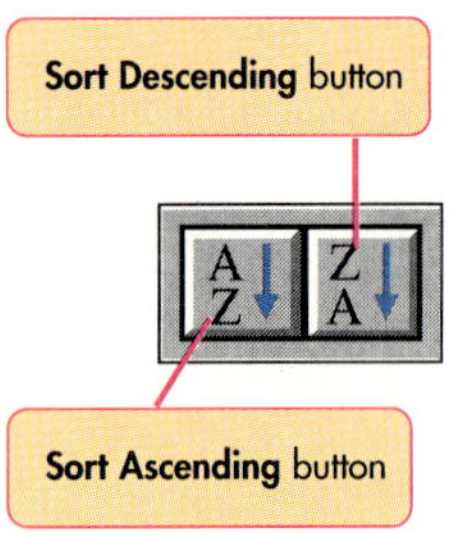

Sorting arranges entire rows in a list based on the contents of a single column—called the *Sort By* column. Sorting arranges the contents of the Sort By column in alphabetic or numeric order. (Column labels are not sorted.)

Sort Orders

Lists can be sorted into ascending or descending order. In an ascending sort, Excel puts numbers before dates before text before blank cells. It puts numbers in the order of smallest to largest, dates in the order of earliest to latest, and text in alphabetical order. In the default sort, Excel doesn't distinguish uppercase from lowercase letters. But if you check the Case Sensitive box in the Sort Options dialog box, it will sort in this order: *SORT, Sort, sort.* In a descending sort, all of this is reversed except that blank cells are still put last. The figure "Sort Orders" illustrates how various types of data are arranged when sorted.

Sorting by Single Columns

When you need to sort a list based on the contents of a single column, you can do so with just a couple of mouse clicks. For example, to sort a list so it's arranged by people's last names, click anywhere in the column where last names are listed and then click one of the Sort buttons on the Standard toolbar.

In some cases, you may want to sort based on more than one column. To do so, sort the least important column first and the most important column last. For example, if you sort a list just by last names, the people with the same last name will be listed in the order in which their first names were entered. To have both first and last names listed alphabetically, first sort by the first name column and then sort by the last name column.

QUICKSTEPS

Sorting by Single Columns

1. Select any cell in the column you want to sort by.
2. Click the **Sort Ascending** or **Sort Descending** button on the Standard toolbar.

TIP

Returning a List to Its Original Order

You can always sort a list back into its original order if you plan ahead. Before sorting the list, label one column *Original Order.* Then enter the number 1 in that field of the first record, hold down Ctrl and drag the fill handle down the column to the last record and release it. The column will be filled with a series of sequential numbers you can use to sort the list back into its original order at any time.

Sorting by Multiple Columns

With Excel's **Data**, **Sort** command, you can sort a list by more than one field at a time whenever you want related items to be subsorted. For example, if you were sorting a database by name, you would want to sort first by the *Last Name* field and then by the *First Name* field. This way, the name Jones, Smith would follow the name Jones, Ozzie. To subsort like this, specify the *Last Name* field as the field to **Sort By** and the *First Name* field as the **Then By** field to sort. If you wanted to subsort the second field, perhaps by department, you would specify that field as the second **Then By** field to sort.

	A	B
1	Original Order	
2		
3		
4	**Last Name**	**First Name**
5	Henderson	Carolyn
6	Fitzgerald	Liz
7	Emry	Barbara
8	Fitzgerald	Dennis
9	Emry	Alonzo
10	Emry	Judy
11	Henderson	Richard
12	Henderson	Ann
13	Fitzgerald	Frank
14	Fitzgerald	Jackie
15	Emry	Matthew

The original order of first and last names is random.

	A	B
1	Sorted Just by Last Name	
2		
3		
4	**Last Name**	**First Name**
5	Emry	Barbara
6	Emry	Alonzo
7	Emry	Judy
8	Emry	Matthew
9	Fitzgerald	Liz
10	Fitzgerald	Dennis
11	Fitzgerald	Frank
12	Fitzgerald	Jackie
13	Henderson	Carolyn
14	Henderson	Richard
15	Henderson	Ann

When sorted just by last name, first names are out of order.

When sorted by last name and then by first name, first names are in order.

	A	B
1	Sorted by Last Name,	
2	then by First Name	
3		
4	**Last Name**	**First Name**
5	Emry	Alonzo
6	Emry	Barbara
7	Emry	Judy
8	Emry	Matthew
9	Fitzgerald	Dennis
10	Fitzgerald	Frank
11	Fitzgerald	Jackie
12	Fitzgerald	Liz
13	Henderson	Ann
14	Henderson	Carolyn
15	Henderson	Richard

QUICKSTEPS

Sorting by Multiple Columns

1. Select any cell in the list, pull down the **Data** menu, and click the **Sort** command to display the Sort dialog box and automatically select the list. (If the list isn't selected correctly, click the **Cancel** command button, select the list manually, and then repeat this step.)
2. Use any of the commands described in the box "Understanding the Sort Dialog Box."
3. Click the **OK** command button to sort the list based on the settings you have made in the Sort dialog box.

TIP

Sorting Part of a List

To sort only part of a list, select the cells to be sorted before choosing the **Sort** command. Excel will ask you to confirm the sort since this will rearrange parts of records and could substantially affect their content. If you proceed with the sort and don't like the results, immediately click the **Undo** button on the Standard toolbar.

UNDERSTANDING
The Sort Dialog Box

When you pull down the **Data** menu and click the **Sort** command, the Sort dialog box is displayed. You use this dialog box to specify the Sort By columns and other options.

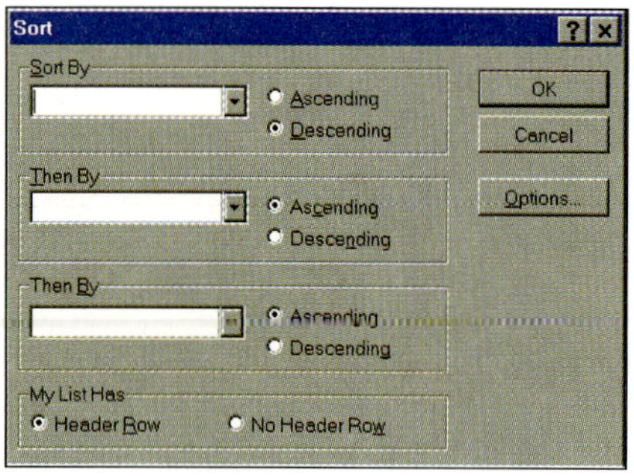

Sort By Section

The **Sort By** section specifies the column that will determine the main sort order.

Sort By drop-down arrow (▾) displays the column labels from the list so you can select one by clicking it.

Ascending or **Descending** option buttons (◉) specify the sort order.

Then By Sections

There are two **Then By** sections that you can use to break ties. The first breaks ties in the **Sort By** sort order. The second breaks ties in the first **Then By** sort. Each section has drop-down arrows (▾) and option buttons like those of the Sort By section.

My List Has Section

Header Row or **No Header Row** option buttons (◉) specify if the list you are sorting has a row of column labels. (Excel will guess the correct setting most of the time if the labels are formatted differently from the rest of the data in the list.)

Options Command Button

Options command button displays the Sort Options dialog box offering the following options:

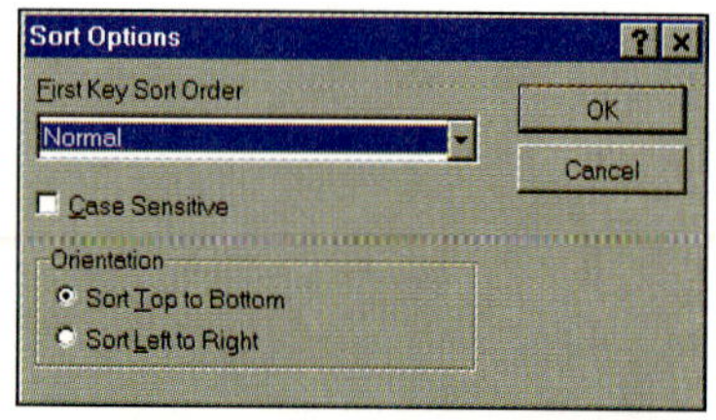

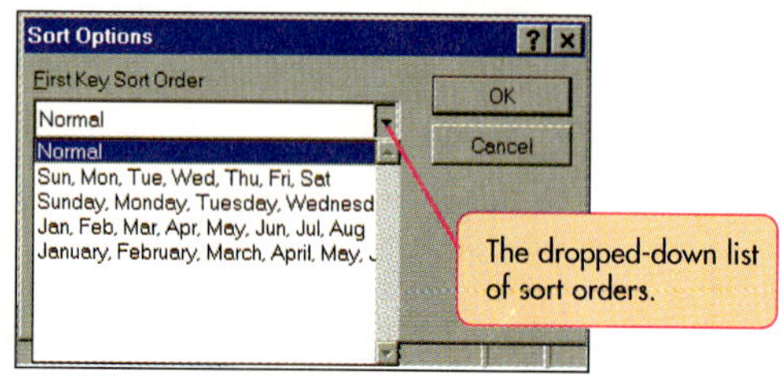

First Key Sort Order drop-down arrow (▾) displays a list of custom sort orders. Using these, you can sort by day of the week or month instead of alphabetically. (You can't use this option in the **Then By** boxes.

Case Sensitive check box specifies if Excel should ignore the case of text characters when off (☐) or use it as the basis for the sort when on (☑).

Sort Top to Bottom or **Sort Left to Right** option buttons (◉) specify if the list is to be sorted by rows (the default setting) or by columns.

TUTORIAL

In this tutorial you sort a list by one or more columns and undo the sort.

Getting Ready

1. Open the *Sales list 2* workbook stored in the *Tutorial Workbooks* folder on the *Excel Student Resource Disk* and enter your name in cell A1. This is an expanded version of the list you have been entering. Notice how the list is sorted randomly.

Sorting the Database Using a Single Column

2. Select any cell in the *Salesperson* column (column A) of the list and first click the **Sort Descending** button on the Standard toolbar and then click the **Sort Ascending** button.

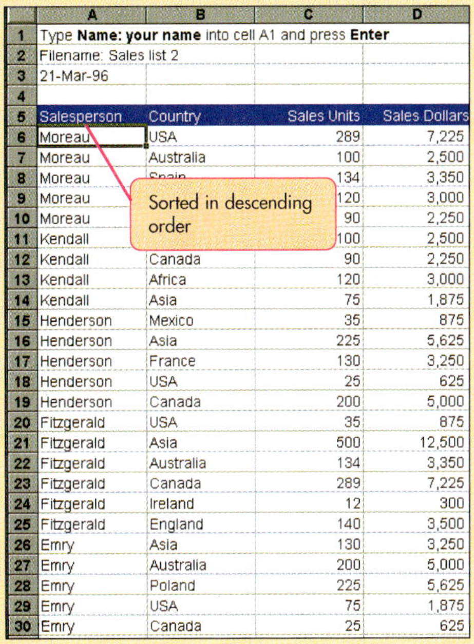

	A	B	C	D
1	Type **Name: your name** into cell A1 and press **Enter**			
2	Filename: Sales list 2			
3	21-Mar-96			
4				
5	Salesperson	Country	Sales Units	Sales Dollars
6	Moreau	USA	289	7,225
7	Moreau	Australia	100	2,500
8	Moreau	Spain	134	3,350
9	Moreau	[illegible]	120	3,000
10	Moreau	[illegible]	90	2,250
11	Kendall	[illegible]	100	2,500
12	Kendall	Canada	90	2,250
13	Kendall	Africa	120	3,000
14	Kendall	Asia	75	1,875
15	Henderson	Mexico	35	875
16	Henderson	Asia	225	5,625
17	Henderson	France	130	3,250
18	Henderson	USA	25	625
19	Henderson	Canada	200	5,000
20	Fitzgerald	USA	35	875
21	Fitzgerald	Asia	500	12,500
22	Fitzgerald	Australia	134	3,350
23	Fitzgerald	Canada	289	7,225
24	Fitzgerald	Ireland	12	300
25	Fitzgerald	England	140	3,500
26	Emry	Asia	130	3,250
27	Emry	Australia	200	5,000
28	Emry	Poland	225	5,625
29	Emry	USA	75	1,875
30	Emry	Canada	25	625

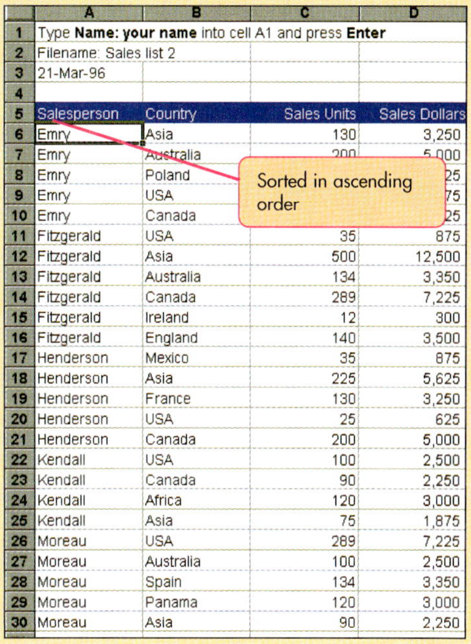

	A	B	C	D
1	Type **Name: your name** into cell A1 and press **Enter**			
2	Filename: Sales list 2			
3	21-Mar-96			
4				
5	Salesperson	Country	Sales Units	Sales Dollars
6	Emry	Asia	130	3,250
7	Emry	Australia	200	5,000
8	Emry	Poland	[illegible]	[illegible]25
9	Emry	USA	[illegible]	[illegible]75
10	Emry	Canada	[illegible]	[illegible]25
11	Fitzgerald	USA	35	875
12	Fitzgerald	Asia	500	12,500
13	Fitzgerald	Australia	134	3,350
14	Fitzgerald	Canada	289	7,225
15	Fitzgerald	Ireland	12	300
16	Fitzgerald	England	140	3,500
17	Henderson	Mexico	35	875
18	Henderson	Asia	225	5,625
19	Henderson	France	130	3,250
20	Henderson	USA	25	625
21	Henderson	Canada	200	5,000
22	Kendall	USA	100	2,500
23	Kendall	Canada	90	2,250
24	Kendall	Africa	120	3,000
25	Kendall	Asia	75	1,875
26	Moreau	USA	289	7,225
27	Moreau	Australia	100	2,500
28	Moreau	Spain	134	3,350
29	Moreau	Panama	120	3,000
30	Moreau	Asia	90	2,250

3. Select any cell in the *Country* column (column B) of the list and first click the **Sort Descending** button on the Standard toolbar and then click the **Sort Ascending** button.

4. Select any cell in the *Sales Units* column (column C) of the list and first click the **Sort Descending** button on the Standard toolbar and then click the **Sort Ascending** button.

Sorting the Database In Descending Order Using Multiple Columns

5. Select any cell in the list, pull down the **Data** menu, and click the **Sort** command to display the Sort dialog box and highlight the entire list.

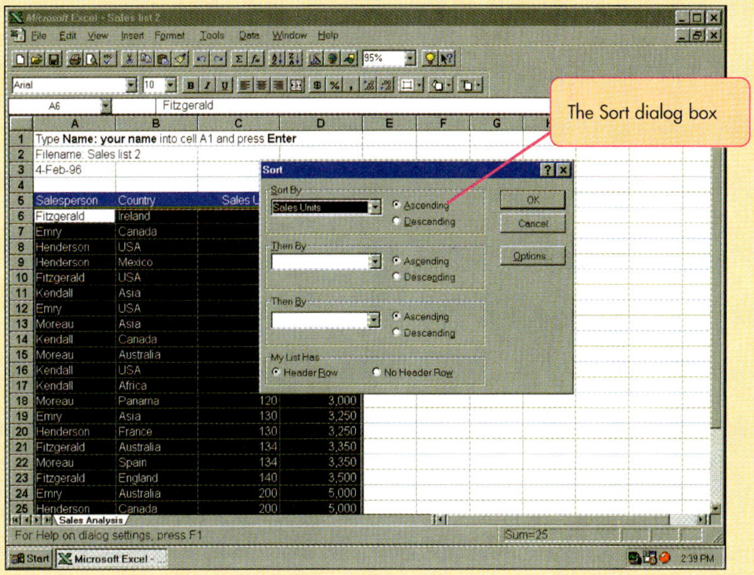

6. Click the **Sort By** drop-down arrow (▾), select the *Salesperson* field, and check that the **Ascending** option button is on (◉).

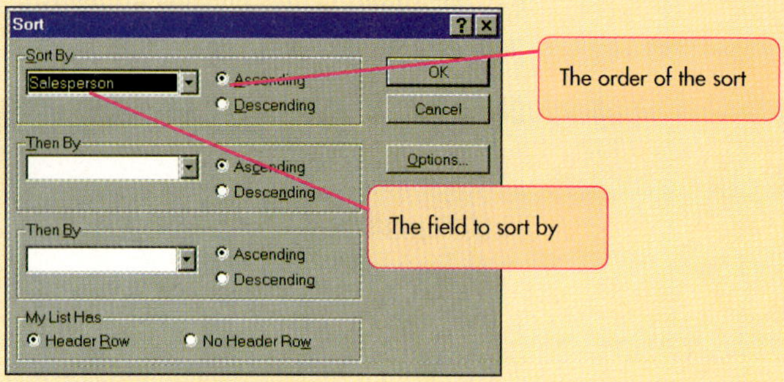

7. Click the **Then By** drop-down arrow (▾), select the *Sales Units* field, and click the **Descending** option button to turn it on (◉).

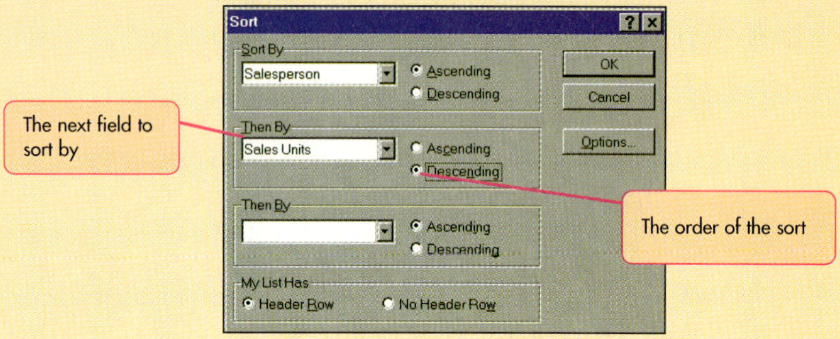

8. Click the **OK** command button to sort the list first by name of salesperson in ascending order and then by each salesperson's sales units in descending order.

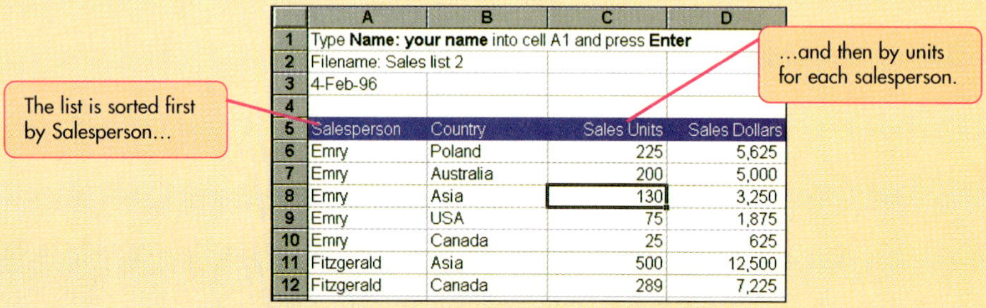

	A	B	C	D
1	Type **Name: your name** into cell A1 and press **Enter**			
2	Filename: Sales list 2			
3	4-Feb-96			
4				
5	Salesperson	Country	Sales Units	Sales Dollars
6	Emry	Poland	225	5,625
7	Emry	Australia	200	5,000
8	Emry	Asia	130	3,250
9	Emry	USA	75	1,875
10	Emry	Canada	25	625
11	Fitzgerald	Asia	500	12,500
12	Fitzgerald	Canada	289	7,225

Undoing a Sort

9. Select any cell in the *Salesperson* column (column A) of the list and click the **Sort Descending** button on the Standard toolbar.
10. Click the **Undo** button on the Standard toolbar to return the list to its previous order.
11. Click the **Print** button on the Standard toolbar to print the sheet.

PAUSING FOR PRACTICE

Continue sorting the list until you have mastered the concepts involved and can predict the outcome of any sort before you perform it.

Finishing Up

12. Close the workbook without saving your changes.

6-4 FINDING RECORDS USING THE DATA FORM

With short lists you can quickly find a record by looking at the list on the worksheet, or you can scroll through records on the data form by clicking the **Find Prev** or **Find Next** command or using the scroll bar. However, with longer lists, the fastest way to locate records is by using comparison criteria. Comparison criteria can be either text or a number. For example, you can enter a comparison criterion such as *Computer* or *100* to locate records that have those entries in the specified field. You can also use comparison operators such as > (greater than) or < (less than) to find records whose value in the field is greater than or less than the one you specify in the comparison criteria. For example, the comparison criterion *>100* will locate records that have numbers greater than 100 in the specified field. The comparison criterion *>F* will locate entries that begin with any letter from G to Z.

QUICKSTEPS

Finding Records Using a Data Form

1. Select any cell in the list, pull down the **Data** menu, and click the **Form** command to display the data form.
2. Click the **Criteria** command button to display the Criteria dialog box. (The dialog box changes slightly from the data form so you can enter comparison criteria that Excel will use to search the list and identify records. The changes are minor—*Criteria* is displayed instead of the record number indicator, and the **Delete** and **Criteria** command buttons change to **Clear** and **Form**.)
3. Enter your comparison criteria in one or more of the edit boxes, and then click the **Form** command button to return to the data form.
4. Click the **Find Next** or **Find Prev** buttons to locate records that match the criteria. Only those that do will be listed in the form where you can edit or delete them.
5. To change or remove the criteria, click the **Criteria** button again. Then enter a new criterion, or, to gain access to all records, click the **Clear** command button.
6. When finished, click the **Close** command button to close the data form.

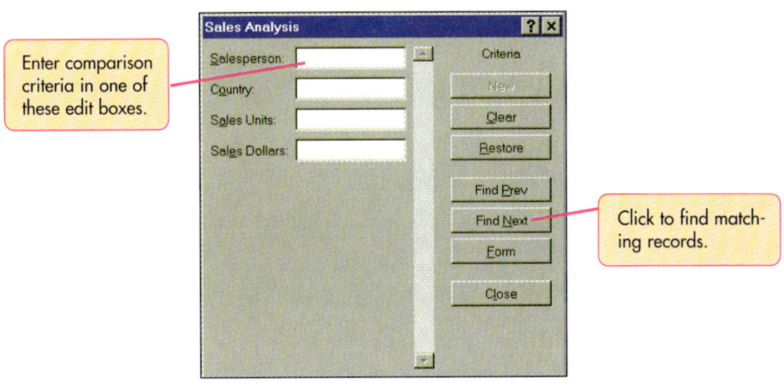

Finding Exact Matches

To find records that contain a specific value in a field, pull down the **Data** menu and click the **Form** command to display the data form. Click the **Criteria** command button to display the Criteria dialog box, and type the text or number you want to match in the field's edit box. For example, to find any records with the number 1000 in the *Quantity* field, enter **1000** in the *Quantity* edit box on the form. To find records with **CA** in the *State* field, enter CA in the State edit box. After entering your criteria, click the **Find Next** command button. What happens next depends on whether or not a match is found. If a match is found, the dialog box switches back to the data form and the first record on the list that matches your criteria is displayed in the form. You can click the **Find Prev** or **Find Next** command buttons to display others. (They only move between records that match the criteria.)

TIP

Using Text as a Criterion

When you enter text as a criterion, Excel will find all records with text in the field that begins with the characters you enter. For example, searching for *Head* will find both *Head* and *Headache*. Normally this saves you a great deal of time since you only have to type enough characters to uniquely identify what you are searching for. However, you can also find exact matches. To do so, enter the criterion in the form =*text* where *text* stands for the text you want to match exactly. For example, to find just *Head* and not *Headache*, enter the criterion as =*Head*.

UNDERSTANDING

Comparison Operators

You use comparison operators in criteria to look for ranges of records. For example, you could specify one of the following numeric criteria to search the *Quantity* field or the text criteria to search the *Company* field. If you enter the criteria shown in the *Criteria* column, you'll display records show in the *Result* column:

Number Criteria	Result
=1000	numbers equal to 1000 (this is the same as entering the number by itself)
>1000	numbers greater than 1000
<1000	numbers less than 1000
>=1000	numbers greater than or equal to 1000
<=1000	numbers less than or equal to 1000
<>1000	numbers not equal to 1000

Text Criteria	Result
Gen	text that begins with the letters *Gen*
>*Gen*	text that begins with letters alphabetically later than *Gen*, for example, *Geo*
<*Gen*	text that begins with letters alphabetically earlier than *Gen*, for example, *Gem*
>=*Gen*	text that begins with letters alphabetically later than *Gen* or beginning with *Gen*
<=*Gen*	text that begins with letters alphabetically earlier than *Gen* or beginning with *Gen*
<>*Gen*	text that does not begin with the letters *Gen*
=*Gen*	*Gen* only, and not *General*, *Generic*, *Genetic*, and so on

Finding Ranges of Matches

There are many times when you are not looking for an exact match, but rather for records that are above or below a certain value. For example, you may want to find all salespeople whose sales were below $10,000 or those above $50,000 for the month. Or you may want to find all products that have prices above $100 or below $200. To make searches of this kind, you use *comparison operators* that compare data in the specified field against a text or number value that you specify.

Using Wildcards

You can use the wildcard symbols when entering text criteria.

- The * (asterisk) substitutes for any characters from the position of the asterisk to the end of the text. For example, the criterion **J* Watson** would find any records for Watson with a first name that began with the letter J.
- The ? (question mark) stands for any single character in the same position as the question mark. For example, **h?t** would find *hut, hat, hitman, Hitachi, hot,* and *hit.*

To use the asterisk or question mark in your text criteria without having them act as wildcards, precede them with a tilde character (~). For example, to find *True?*, enter the criterion as **True~?**.

TUTORIAL

In this tutorial you display a list using a data form and then find data in the list. You find exact matches and use comparison operators to find ranges of matches.

Getting Ready

1. Open the *Sales list 2* workbook stored in the *Tutorial Workbooks* folder on the *Excel Student Resource Disk.*

Finding Exact Matches

2. Select any cell in the list, then pull down the **Data** menu and click the **Form** command to display the data form.
3. Click the **Criteria** command button to display the Criteria dialog box.

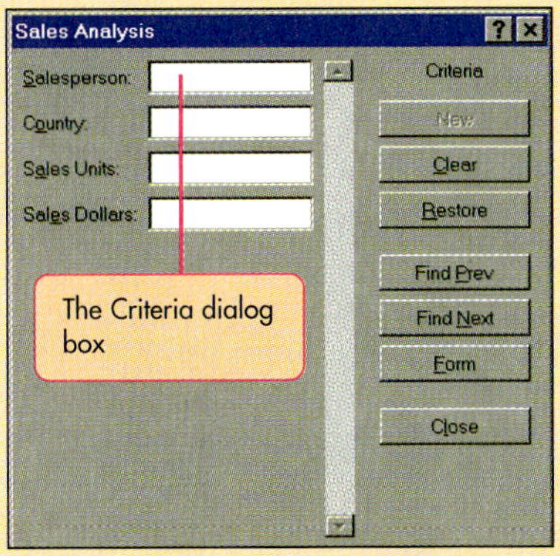

4. Type **Fitzgerald** in the **Salesperson** edit box and click the **Find Next** command button several times to scroll through Fitzgerald's records. Clicking the button when there are no more records rings a bell.

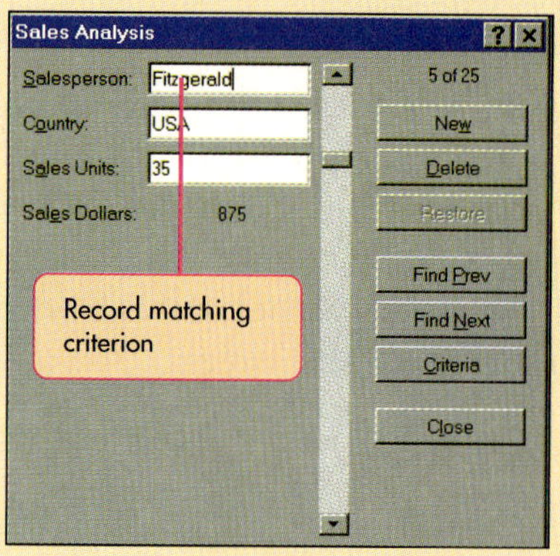

Using Comparison Operators

5. Click the **Criteria** command button to display the Criteria dialog box.
6. Click the **Clear** command button to clear the current criterion.
7. Type **<150** in the **Sales Units** edit box and click the **Find Next** or **Find Prev** buttons to scroll through the records with unit sales of less than 150.

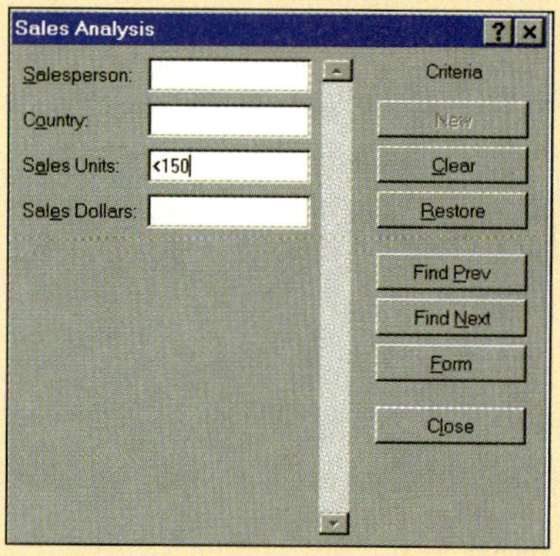

Using Multiple Comparison Operators

8. Click the **Criteria** command button to display the Criteria dialog box.
9. Click the **Clear** command button to clear the current criterion.
10. Type **Emry** in the **Salesperson** edit box and **<150** in the **Sales Units** edit box.

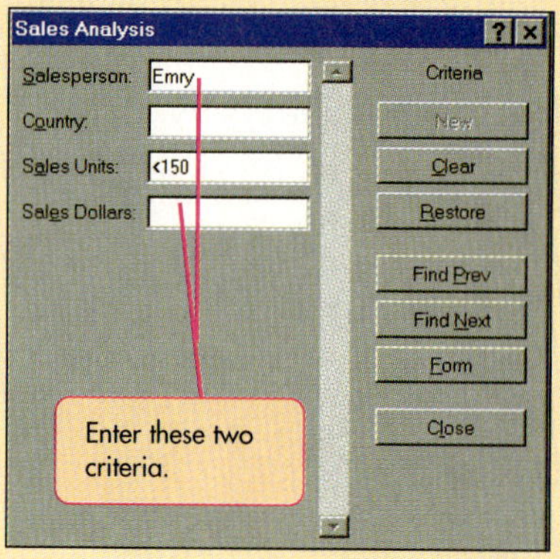

11. Click the **Find Next** or **Find Prev** command button to scroll through the records where Emry's unit sales are less than 150.

Finishing Up

12. Click the **Close** command button to close the data form dialog box.

13. Close the workbook without saving your changes.

6-5 FILTERING RECORDS

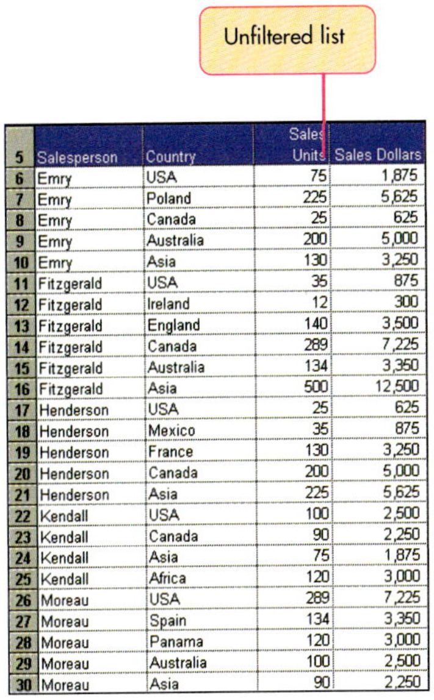

5	Salesperson	Country	Sales Units	Sales Dollars
6	Emry	USA	75	1,875
7	Emry	Poland	225	5,625
8	Emry	Canada	25	625
9	Emry	Australia	200	5,000
10	Emry	Asia	130	3,250
11	Fitzgerald	USA	35	875
12	Fitzgerald	Ireland	12	300
13	Fitzgerald	England	140	3,500
14	Fitzgerald	Canada	289	7,225
15	Fitzgerald	Australia	134	3,350
16	Fitzgerald	Asia	500	12,500
17	Henderson	USA	25	625
18	Henderson	Mexico	35	875
19	Henderson	France	130	3,250
20	Henderson	Canada	200	5,000
21	Henderson	Asia	225	5,625
22	Kendall	USA	100	2,500
23	Kendall	Canada	90	2,250
24	Kendall	Asia	75	1,875
25	Kendall	Africa	120	3,000
26	Moreau	USA	289	7,225
27	Moreau	Spain	134	3,350
28	Moreau	Panama	120	3,000
29	Moreau	Australia	100	2,500
30	Moreau	Asia	90	2,250

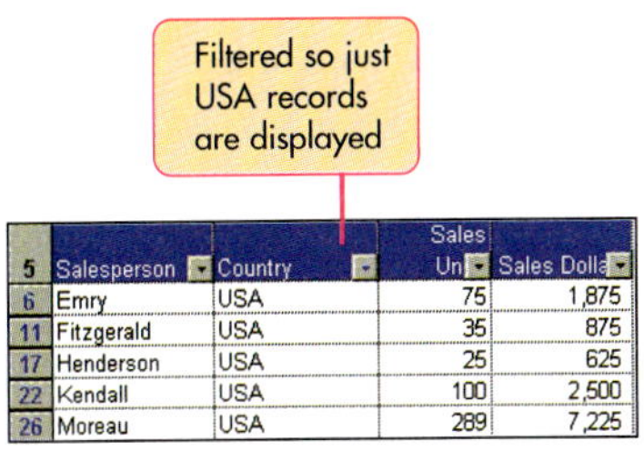

5	Salesperson	Country	Sales Un	Sales Dolla
6	Emry	USA	75	1,875
11	Fitzgerald	USA	35	875
17	Henderson	USA	25	625
22	Kendall	USA	100	2,500
26	Moreau	USA	289	7,225

There are times when only part of a list is of interest. For example, you may have a national membership list but only want to work with records for those members living in Lexington, Kentucky. Or you may want to know who are the top ten salespeople in a company. In cases such as these, you can hide the records of all other people by filtering the list. A filter screens all of the records and only those that match the criteria are displayed on the screen. Filtering does not rearrange the list as sorting does. Instead, it temporarily hides all records that do not match the criteria you specify.

To filter a list, you use Excel's AutoFilter command to look for exact matches or use comparison criteria just as you did to find records using the data form.

QUICKSTEPS

Filtering Records with AutoFilter

1. Select any cell in the list.
2. Pull down the **Data** menu and point to the **Filter** command to cascade the menu.
3. Click the **AutoFilter** command to add drop-down arrows (▾) to the column label of each column in the list.
4. Click the drop-down arrow (▾) for any column where you want to specify a criterion and select one of the filter criteria described in the box "Understanding AutoFilter Criteria." Immediately the program enters Filter mode, and records that do not match that criterion are hidden. (Repeat this step for other fields to filter the list even more.)
5. To display records again:
   - ▸ Click any blue drop-down arrow (▾) and click the *(All)* criterion at the top of the list to select it and turn off the filter for that column; or
   - ▸ Pull down the **Data** menu, point to the **Filter** command to cascade the menu, and click the **Show All** command.
6. To turn off Filter mode, pull down the **Data** menu, point to the **Filter** command to cascade the menu, and click the **AutoFilter** command to turn it off and remove the drop-down arrows (▾) from each column label in the list.

UNDERSTANDING
AutoFilter Criteria

When you are in Filter mode, you can click any of the drop-down arrows (▾) to specify a filter criterion for that column. When you do so, you have the following choices:

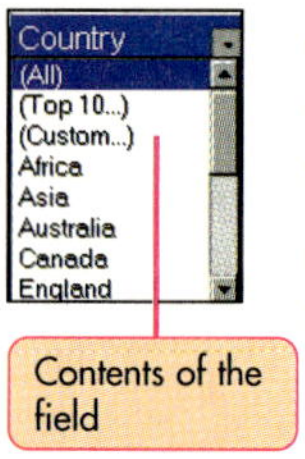

(All) turns filtering off for the column (and displays all records in the list provided the same has been done to all fields in the list).

(Top 10) displays a dialog box where you can specify which records are displayed. You can specify that they be from the top or bottom, how many, and whether to show items or percentages. For example, you can display the top or bottom 10 salespeople or the top or bottom 5% of salespeople.

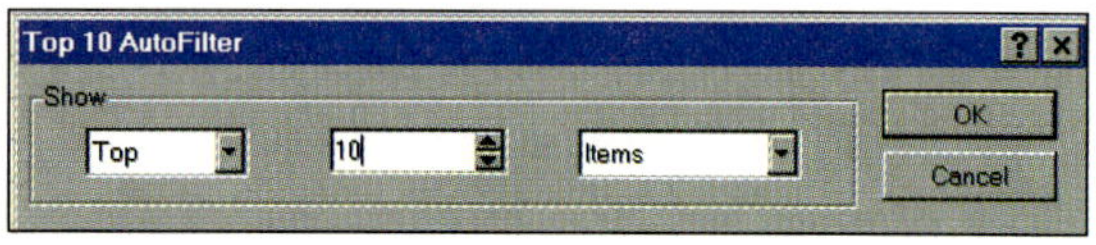

(Custom) displays the Custom AutoFilter dialog box. Using this box you can specify comparison criteria to display records that fall above or below a certain value or fall within a range. To do so, you use the drop-down arrows (▾) to specify a comparison operator (=, <, >, >=, <=, or <>) and a value.

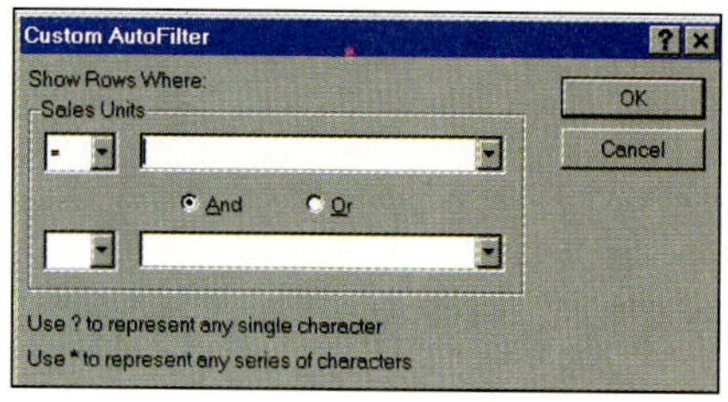

You can also use this dialog box to search for records that meet two or more criteria (an **And** criteria) or meet one of two or more criteria (an **Or** criteria). To do so, you click the **And** or **Or** option button (◉) and specify a second criterion.

- **And** criteria display only those records that match all of the criteria you specify. For example, if you enter **>100 And <500**, only records greater than 100 AND less than 500 are displayed. This is an ideal way to display only those records that fall within a range.
- **Or** criteria display all records that match one or more of the criteria you specify. For example, if you enter **<100 Or >500**, only records less than 100 OR greater than 500 are displayed. Or if you enter **=Ohio Or =California**, only records from those two states are listed. This is an ideal way to display only those records that fall below one value or above another or meet one of two criteria.

(Blanks) displays all records with no entries in the field.

(NonBlanks) displays all records with entries in the field.

TIP
Visual Cues When Filtering

When you filter a list, you may forget you've done so and assume that all of the records are displayed. To prevent this, Excel provides you with a number of visual cues that the list has been filtered and that the program is in Filter mode.

- The status bar indicates the number of records that match the criteria and the total number of records in the list.
- The drop-down arrow (▾) for the field where the filter criteria have been entered is blue.
- The row numbers for the filtered list are blue.

TUTORIAL

In this tutorial you filter a list so only those records that match your criteria are displayed. You create filters with a single criterion and filters that have two criteria where both (AND) must be met.

Getting Ready

1. Open the *Sales list 2* workbook stored in the *Tutorial Workbooks* folder on the *Excel Student Resource Disk.*

Filtering Records That Meet a Single Criterion

2. Select any cell in the list, then pull down the **Data** menu and point to the **Filter** command to cascade the menu.
3. Click the **AutoFilter** command to add drop-down arrows (▾) to the column label of each column in the list.

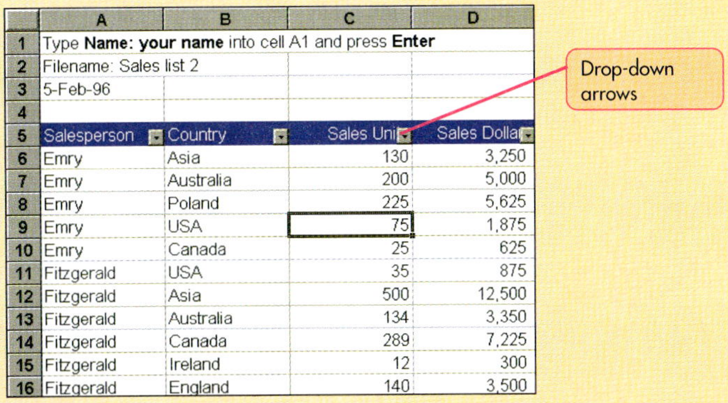

	A	B	C	D
1	Type **Name: your name** into cell A1 and press **Enter**			
2	Filename: Sales list 2			
3	5-Feb-96			
4				
5	Salesperson	Country	Sales Uni	Sales Dolla
6	Emry	Asia	130	3,250
7	Emry	Australia	200	5,000
8	Emry	Poland	225	5,625
9	Emry	USA	75	1,875
10	Emry	Canada	25	625
11	Fitzgerald	USA	35	875
12	Fitzgerald	Asia	500	12,500
13	Fitzgerald	Australia	134	3,350
14	Fitzgerald	Canada	289	7,225
15	Fitzgerald	Ireland	12	300
16	Fitzgerald	England	140	3,500

4. Click the *Salesperson* drop-down arrow (▾), and click *Kendall* to display just records with that name in the column (field). Notice how the drop-down arrow changes color so you know that records are filtered using that field.

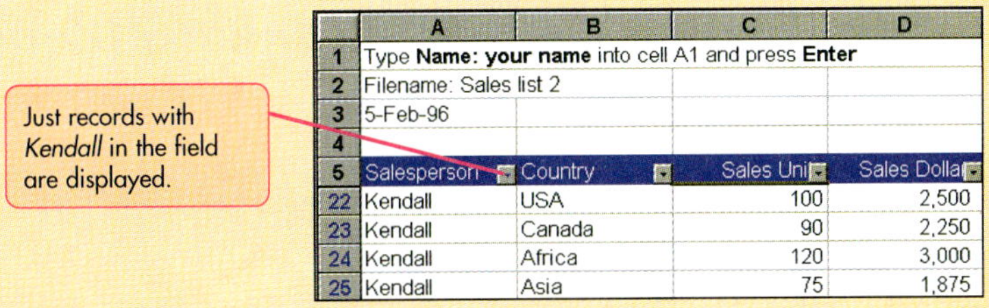

	A	B	C	D
1	Type **Name: your name** into cell A1 and press **Enter**			
2	Filename: Sales list 2			
3	5-Feb-96			
4				
5	Salesperson	Country	Sales Uni	Sales Dolla
22	Kendall	USA	100	2,500
23	Kendall	Canada	90	2,250
24	Kendall	Africa	120	3,000
25	Kendall	Asia	75	1,875

5. To display all records again, click the *Salesperson* drop-down arrow (▾), and click *(All)* at the top of the list. (You may have to scroll the list to see it.)
6. Click the *Country* drop-down arrow (▾), and click *Canada* to display just records with that country in the column.
7. To display all records again, click the *Country* drop-down arrow (▾), and click *(All)*.

Displaying the Top 10

8. Click the *Sales Units* drop-down arrow (▾), and click *(Top 10...)* to display the Top 10 AutoFilter dialog box. Click the **OK** button to display just the top 10 records in that column (field).
9. To display all records again, click the *Sales Units* drop-down arrow (▾), and click *(All)*.

Filtering Records That Meet Two Criteria in Separate Fields (AND)

10. Click the *Salesperson* drop-down arrow (▾), and click *Kendall* to display just records with that name in the column.

11. Click the *Country* drop-down arrow (▼), and click *Canada* to display just records for Kendall in Canada.

12. To display all records again, pull down the **Data** menu, point to the **Filter** command to cascade the menu, and click the **Show All** command.

Filtering Records That Meet Two Criteria in the Same Field (AND)

13. Click the *Sales Units* drop-down arrow (▼), and click (*Custom...*) to display the Custom AutoFilter dialog box. The first box contains an equal sign (=), and the insertion point is flashing in the text box to its right.

14. Click the drop-down arrow (▼) for the box containing the equal sign, and click the greater than operator (>) to select it.

15. Click the drop-down arrow (▼) for the text box to the right, and click 75 to select it.

16. The **And** option button on the row between the two criteria should be on (◉). If it isn't on, click it.

17. Click the drop-down arrow (▼) for the box below the one with the greater than sign, and click the less than operator (<) to select it.

18. Click the drop-down arrow (▼) for the text box to its right, and click *225* to select it. (You will have to scroll the list to see it.)

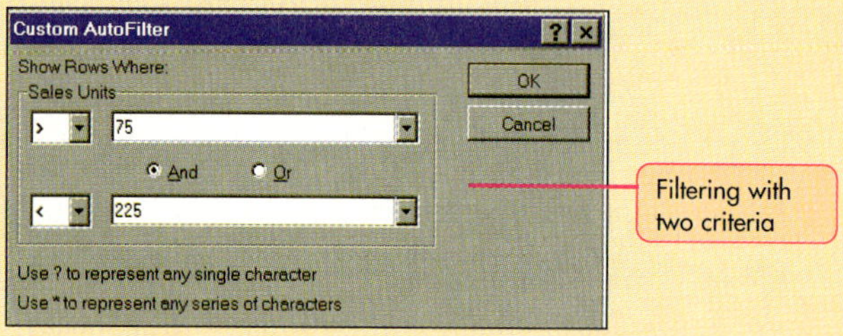

19. Click the **OK** command button to display all records with sales units of more than 75 and less than 225. Click in the *Sales Units* column and then click the **Sort Descending** button on the Standard toolbar to sort the list.

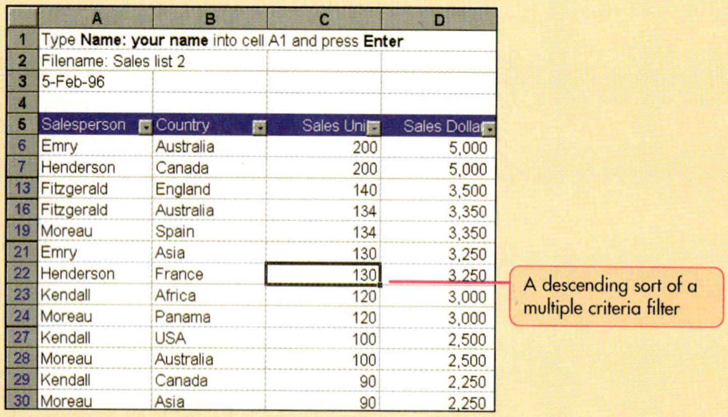

	A	B	C	D
1	Type **Name: your name** into cell A1 and press **Enter**			
2	Filename: Sales list 2			
3	5-Feb-96			
4				
5	Salesperson	Country	Sales Uni	Sales Dolla
6	Emry	Australia	200	5,000
7	Henderson	Canada	200	5,000
13	Fitzgerald	England	140	3,500
16	Fitzgerald	Australia	134	3,350
19	Moreau	Spain	134	3,350
21	Emry	Asia	130	3,250
22	Henderson	France	130	3,250
23	Kendall	Africa	120	3,000
24	Moreau	Panama	120	3,000
27	Kendall	USA	100	2,500
28	Moreau	Australia	100	2,500
29	Kendall	Canada	90	2,250
30	Moreau	Asia	90	2,250

20. To turn off Filter mode, pull down the **Data** menu, point to the **Filter** command to cascade the menu, and click the **AutoFilter** command to turn it off. This removes the drop-down arrows (▼) from each column in the list and displays all records.

Finishing Up

21. Close the workbook without saving your changes.

6-6 USING DATABASE FUNCTIONS

In PicTorial 4 we saw how to use functions. Excel has some special functions you can use to summarize data in lists. You use these functions, called *database functions*, when you want to summarize values that meet particular criteria. For instance, you can use the database function DSUM to total only sales from California and the database function DCOUNT to count the number of orders from Florida.

Let's look at an example based on the list we have been using in this PicTorial, *Sales list 2*. In this list, sales are broken down by salesperson, country, sales units, and sales dollars. We can use the DSUM function to summarize any aspect of this data.

To use regular functions, you specify arguments. Database functions have similar requirements, and take the form FUNCTION NAME(*database,field,criteria*). When reading this description, refer to the figure "Using Database Functions."

- The *database* is the address of the list you want checked, including the column labels. In our example, the database is the range A5:D30.
- The *field* is the address of the cell containing the column label of the data you want summarized. In our example, we will be summarizing sales dollars, and so we specify the field as the cell containing that column label, D5.
- To specify the criteria, you must create an area on the worksheet called a *criteria range* and enter into it the criteria to be used. The method in which you specify the criteria is important, and it is a little complicated.

In our example, we will use three separate criteria. We will summarize sales dollars by (1) salesperson, (2) country, and (3) salesperson by country. We will enter the criteria in three ranges, one of which overlaps the other two.

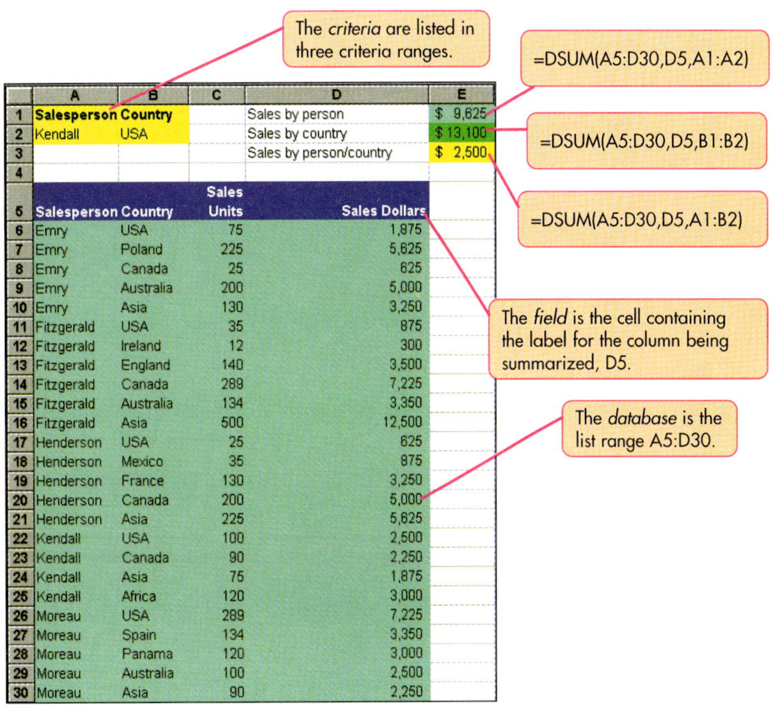

	A	B	C	D	E
1	Salesperson	Country		Sales by person	$ 9,625
2	Kendall	USA		Sales by country	$ 13,100
3				Sales by person/country	$ 2,500
4					
5	Salesperson	Country	Sales Units	Sales Dollars	
6	Emry	USA	75	1,875	
7	Emry	Poland	225	5,625	
8	Emry	Canada	25	625	
9	Emry	Australia	200	5,000	
10	Emry	Asia	130	3,250	
11	Fitzgerald	USA	35	875	
12	Fitzgerald	Ireland	12	300	
13	Fitzgerald	England	140	3,500	
14	Fitzgerald	Canada	289	7,225	
15	Fitzgerald	Australia	134	3,350	
16	Fitzgerald	Asia	500	12,500	
17	Henderson	USA	25	625	
18	Henderson	Mexico	35	875	
19	Henderson	France	130	3,250	
20	Henderson	Canada	200	5,000	
21	Henderson	Asia	225	5,625	
22	Kendall	USA	100	2,500	
23	Kendall	Canada	90	2,250	
24	Kendall	Asia	75	1,875	
25	Kendall	Africa	120	3,000	
26	Moreau	USA	289	7,225	
27	Moreau	Spain	134	3,350	
28	Moreau	Panama	120	3,000	
29	Moreau	Australia	100	2,500	
30	Moreau	Asia	90	2,250	

Using Database Functions

Both criteria on same row will find sales for Kendall in the USA.

	A	B	C	D
1	Salesperson	Country		
2	Kendall	USA		
3				
4				
5	Salesperson	Country	Sales Units	Sales Dollars
6	Kendall	USA	100	2,500

Criteria on different rows will find sales for Kendall or sales in the USA.

	A	B	C	D
1	Salesperson	Country		
2	Kendall			
3		USA		
4				
5	Salesperson	Country	Sales Units	Sales Dollars
6	Henderson	USA	25	625
7	Kendall	USA	100	2,500
8	Kendall	Canada	90	2,250

More than one column label will find sales for Kendall or Henderson.

	A	B	C	D
1	Salesperson	Salesperson		
2	Kendall	Henderson		
3				
4				
5	Salesperson	Country	Sales Units	Sales Dollars
6	Henderson	USA	25	625
7	Henderson	Canada	200	5,000
8	Kendall	USA	100	2,500
9	Kendall	Canada	90	2,250

(1) The criteria range A1:A2 tells the function to sum all entries for Kendall.

(2) The criteria range B1:B2 tells the function to sum all entries for the USA.

(3) The criteria range A1:B2 tells the function to summarize all entries for Kendall in the USA.

Since rows of the list can be hidden during certain operations, we place the range above or below the list, not to its left or right. Note that each criteria range contains at least one column label (*Salesperson* or *Country*) and one criterion (*Kendall* or *USA*) that filters the records to be summarized. The criteria range's labels must match the column labels in the list exactly. To make them match exactly, use the Copy or Paste commands to copy the labels from the list to the criteria range.

The shape and content of the criteria range vary slightly depending on your goal. You can find records that meet all of your criteria, one of your criteria, or any number of your criteria.

To find records that match all of your criteria (an AND criterion), enter the criteria on the same row. For example, to find records for Kendall in the USA, enter both on the same row.

To find records that match one of your criteria (an OR criterion), enter the criteria on different rows. For example, to find records for Kendall or records for the USA, enter them on different rows.

To find records that meet different criteria in the same column, use more than one of the column labels in the criteria range. For example, to find sales for Kendall or Henderson, enter the Salesperson column label for each.

TIP

Naming Ranges

When using database functions, it is easier if you assign names to the database range so that you can refer to it in the functions by name rather than by cell addresses.

QUICKSTEPS

Entering Database Functions

1. Select the cell in which you want to enter the function, and then click the **Function Wizard** button on the Standard toolbar.
2. Click *Database* in the **Function Category** list to select it and display database functions in the **Function Name** list.
3. Click the name of the desired function in the **Function Name** list to select it, and then click the **Next** command button to display the Function Wizard Step 2 of 2 dialog box.
4. Enter the database, field, and criteria in those text boxes, and then click the **OK** command button.

IN this tutorial you use database functions to calculate the sales by a salesperson, the sales in a country, or the sales by a salesperson in a specific country. When finished, your list should look like the one in the figure "The Database Functions."

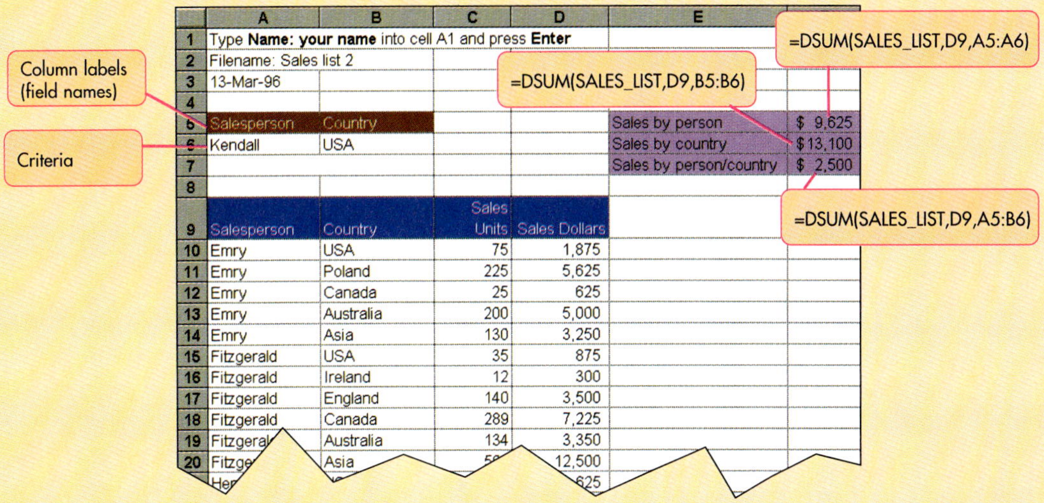

The Database Functions

Getting Ready

1. Open the *Sales list 2* workbook stored in the *Tutorial Workbooks* folder on the *Excel Student Resource Disk.*
2. Select rows 5 through 8 using the row headings, click the right mouse button in the selected area to display a shortcut menu, and click **Insert** to insert 4 blank rows above the list.

Entering a Criteria Range

3. Enter the labels for the criteria range by copying cells A9 and B9 (the column labels *Salesperson* and *Country*) and pasting them into cells A5 and B5.
4. Type the criteria *Kendall* into cell A6 and *USA* into cell B6.

Entering Database Functions

5. Select the range A9 through D34, click the Name box on the formula bar, type **Sales_List** to name the list, and press [Enter ↵]. Then click anywhere on the worksheet to remove the highlight from the selected range.
6. Enter the headings and functions shown in the range E5 through F7 in the figure "The Database Functions." Widen column E as necessary to fully display the descriptive labels for the functions, and format the function cells as currency with no decimal places. Notice how you identify the list by the name you assigned it rather than cell references. The numbers displayed in cells F5 through F7 are those for Kendall, for the USA, and Kendall's sales in the USA.

Filtering Records That Meet One Criterion

7. Delete *Kendall* from cell A6. The *sales by person* are now displayed for all sales people. The *sales by country* and *sales by person/country* are total USA sales.

8. Enter **Australia** in cell B6 in place of USA to calculate based on total Australian sales.

9. Type **Emry** into cell A6 to calculate based on total Emry's Australian sales.

Finishing Up

10. Save, print, and close the workbook.

6-7 CREATING AUTOMATIC SUBTOTALS

When you have a list containing identical entries in the same column, you can sort the list by that column to group identical entries together. You can then automatically subtotal other columns on the list based on those groupings. For example, you may have a list of sales by store, region, or country. Using Excel's Subtotals command, you can sort the list by any of these categories and then quickly add subtotals to compare them. This not only saves you time, but reduces the possibility of introducing errors.

UNDERSTANDING
The Subtotal Dialog Box

When you pull down the Data menu and click the **Subtotals** command, the Subtotal dialog box is displayed.

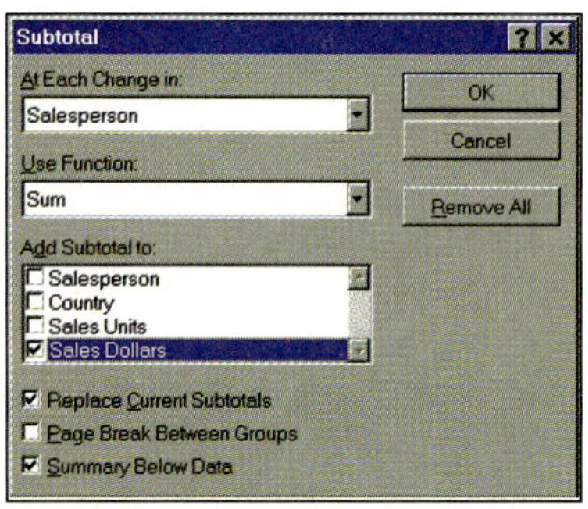

At Each Change In drop-down list displays a list of the columns in the list. Select the one that contains the grouping you want to subtotal.

Use Function drop-down list displays a list of subtotal functions you can specify. Your choices include:

- **Sum** totals the values in the subtotal group.
- **Count** counts the number of cells containing data in the subtotal group.
- **Average** averages the values in the subtotal group.
- **Max** finds the largest value in the subtotal group.
- **Min** finds the smallest value in the subtotal group.
- **Product** multiples all of the values in the subtotal group.
- **Count Nums** counts the number of records containing numeric data.
- **StdDev** estimates the standard deviation based on the subtotal group being a sample.
- **StdDevp** calculates the standard deviation based on the subtotal group being the entire population.
- **Var** estimates the variance based on the subtotal group being a sample.
- **Varp** calculates the variance based on the subtotal group being the entire population.

Add Subtotal to check boxes specify which columns will be subtotaled.

Replace Current Subtotals check box, when on (☑), replaces all current subtotals with new ones that you specify. When off, current subtotals are retained and new ones added.

Page Break Between Groups check box, when on, prints each group starting on a new page.

Summary Below Data check box, when on, places the summary rows and grand total row below the associated data. When off, they are placed above the associated data.

Remove All command button removes all automatic subtotals from the list.

QUICKSTEPS

Creating Automatic Subtotals

1. Sort the list using the field you want to group by as the Sort By column. (This is not the same column that you want to subtotal.)
2. Select any cell in the list, pull down the **Data** menu, and click the **Subtotals** command to display the Subtotal dialog box and automatically select the list. (If the list isn't selected correctly, click the **Cancel** command button, select the list manually, and then repeat this step.)
3. Enter responses into the dialog box as described in the box "Understanding the Subtotal Dialog Box."
4. Click the **OK** command button to add subtotals.

UNDERSTANDING

Outline Symbols

When you use the Subtotals command, outline symbols are displayed at the left side of the worksheet. These symbols include the *show detail* symbols, the *hide detail* symbols, the *outline level* symbols, and the *outline level*.

- *Row and column level symbols* (1, 2, 3) indicate the number of row and column levels in the outline. Click any one of these symbols to collapse or expand that level of the outline.
- *Show detail symbols* (+) indicate summary rows or columns with hidden detail rows or columns. Click the symbol to display the hidden detail.
- *Hide detail symbols* (-) indicate summary rows or columns with displayed detail rows or columns. Click the symbol to hide the detail data indicated by the column or row level bar.
- *Row and column level bars* appear when detail rows and columns are displayed. Click anywhere on these level bars to hide the detail rows or columns.

TUTORIAL

In this tutorial you create and remove automatic subtotals from a list. You also explore how you change the column used for determining which records are subtotaled.

Getting Ready

1. Open the *Sales list 2* workbook stored in the *Tutorial Workbooks* folder on the *Excel Student Resource Disk.*

Subtotals Based on Person

2. Click anywhere in column A of the list and then click the **Sort Ascending** button on the Standard toolbar.
3. Select any cell in the list, pull down the **Data** menu and click the **Subtotals** command to display the Subtotal dialog box and automatically select the list. The dialog box specifies that subtotals be added for each salesperson, that they be sums, and that the sums are to be added to the sales dollars column.
4. Click the *Sales Units* check box in the **Add Subtotal** to list to turn it on.

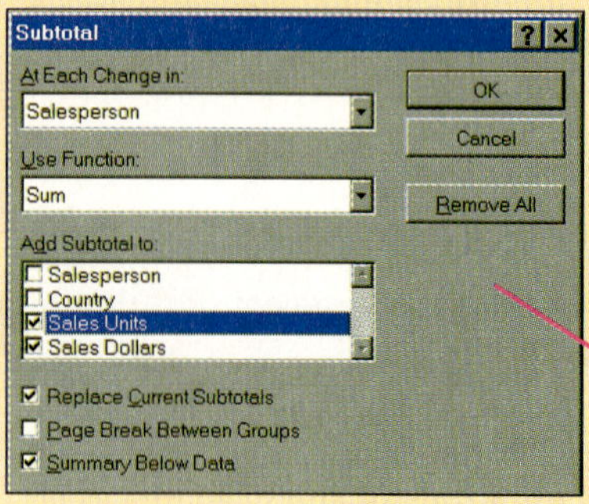

The Subtotal dialog box

5. Click the **OK** command button to add subtotals. Notice how new boldface "total" lines are inserted under each group of records with the same salesperson, and subtotals are added to the sales units and dollars columns. A grand total is displayed at the bottom of the list.

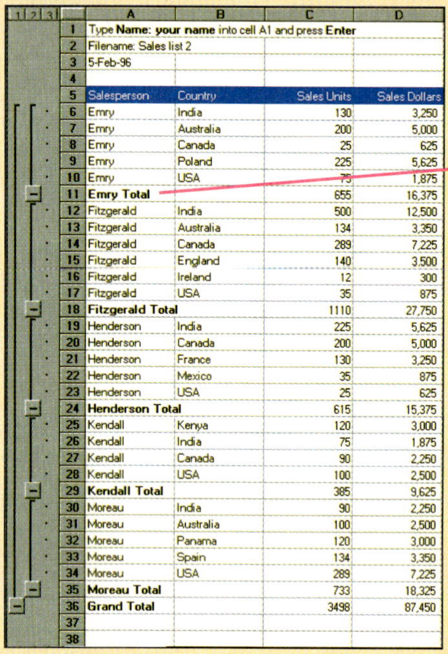

	A	B	C	D
1	Type **Name: your name** into cell A1 and press **Enter**			
2	Filename: Sales list 2			
3	5-Feb-96			
4				
5	Salesperson	Country	Sales Units	Sales Dollars
6	Emry	India	130	3,250
7	Emry	Australia	200	5,000
8	Emry	Canada	25	625
9	Emry	Poland	225	5,625
10	Emry	USA	75	1,875
11	**Emry Total**		655	16,375
12	Fitzgerald	India	500	12,500
13	Fitzgerald	Australia	134	3,350
14	Fitzgerald	Canada	289	7,225
15	Fitzgerald	England	140	3,500
16	Fitzgerald	Ireland	12	300
17	Fitzgerald	USA	35	875
18	**Fitzgerald Total**		1110	27,750
19	Henderson	India	225	5,625
20	Henderson	Canada	200	5,000
21	Henderson	France	130	3,250
22	Henderson	Mexico	35	875
23	Henderson	USA	25	625
24	**Henderson Total**		615	15,375
25	Kendall	Kenya	120	3,000
26	Kendall	India	75	1,875
27	Kendall	Canada	90	2,250
28	Kendall	USA	100	2,500
29	**Kendall Total**		385	9,625
30	Moreau	India	90	2,250
31	Moreau	Australia	100	2,500
32	Moreau	Panama	120	3,000
33	Moreau	Spain	134	3,350
34	Moreau	USA	289	7,225
35	**Moreau Total**		733	18,325
36	**Grand Total**		3498	87,450
37				
38				

Subtotals by salesperson

Removing Subtotals

6. Select any cell in the list, pull down the **Data** menu and click the **Subtotals** command to display the Subtotal dialog box and then click the **Remove All** command button.

Subtotals Based on Country

7. Click anywhere in column B of the list and then click the **Sort Ascending** button on the Standard toolbar.
8. Select any cell in the list, pull down the **Data** menu and click the **Subtotals** command to display the Subtotal dialog box and automatically select the list.
9. In the **At Each Change in** section, click the drop-down arrow (▾) to display the list of fields and click *Country* to select it.
10. In the **Use Function** section, click the drop-down arrow (▾) to display the list of functions and click *Average* to select it.

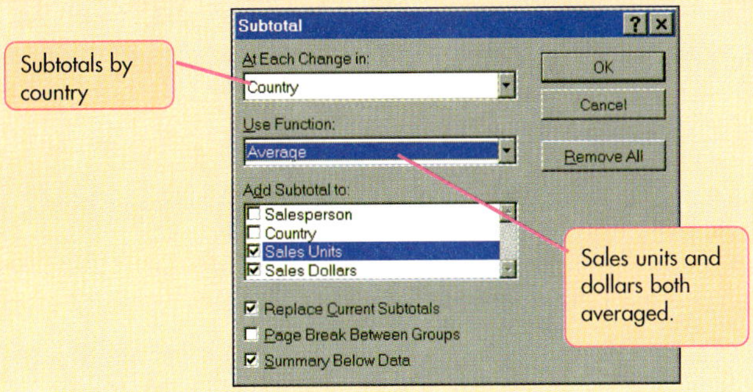

11. Click the **OK** command button to add subtotals based on the new settings. Notice how the subtotals average the number of units and dollars sold in each country.

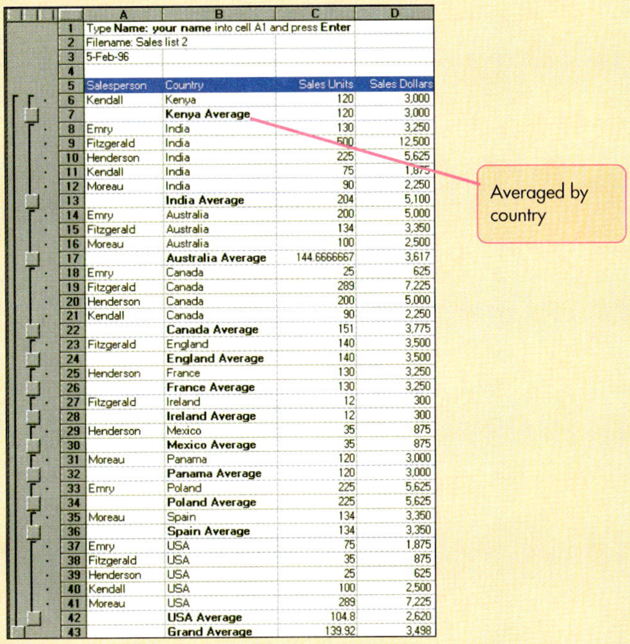

	A	B	C	D
1	Type **Name: your name** into cell A1 and press **Enter**			
2	Filename: Sales list 2			
3	5-Feb-96			
4				
5	Salesperson	Country	Sales Units	Sales Dollars
6	Kendall	Kenya	120	3,000
7		**Kenya Average**	120	3,000
8	Emry	India	130	3,250
9	Fitzgerald	India	500	12,500
10	Henderson	India	225	5,625
11	Kendall	India	75	1,875
12	Moreau	India	90	2,250
13		**India Average**	204	5,100
14	Emry	Australia	200	5,000
15	Fitzgerald	Australia	134	3,350
16	Moreau	Australia	100	2,500
17		**Australia Average**	144.6666667	3,617
18	Emry	Canada	25	625
19	Fitzgerald	Canada	289	7,225
20	Henderson	Canada	200	5,000
21	Kendall	Canada	90	2,250
22		**Canada Average**	151	3,775
23	Fitzgerald	England	140	3,500
24		**England Average**	140	3,500
25	Henderson	France	130	3,250
26		**France Average**	130	3,250
27	Fitzgerald	Ireland	12	300
28		**Ireland Average**	12	300
29	Henderson	Mexico	35	875
30		**Mexico Average**	35	875
31	Moreau	Panama	120	3,000
32		**Panama Average**	120	3,000
33	Emry	Poland	225	5,625
34		**Poland Average**	225	5,625
35	Moreau	Spain	134	3,350
36		**Spain Average**	134	3,350
37	Emry	USA	75	1,875
38	Fitzgerald	USA	35	875
39	Henderson	USA	25	625
40	Kendall	USA	100	2,500
41	Moreau	USA	289	7,225
42		**USA Average**	104.8	2,620
43		**Grand Average**	139.92	3,498

12. Click the **Print Preview** button on the Standard toolbar to see if the worksheet will print on one page. If it won't, click the **Setup** button to display the Page Setup dialog box, on the *Page* tab click the **Fit to** option button to turn it on, and then click the **OK** command button to return to the Print Preview window. Click the **Print** command button to print the worksheet.

Exploring the Hide and Show Detail Buttons

13. Explore clicking the [+] and [-] Show and Hide Detail symbols to see their effect.

14. Select any cell in the list, pull down the **Data** menu and click the **Subtotals** command to display the Subtotal dialog box, and then click the **Remove All** command button.

Finishing Up

15. Save and close the workbook.

REVIEW QUESTIONS

TRUE-FALSE

T F **1.** All text in a column should have the same format.

T F **2.** You can sort a list based on the contents of more than one field.

T F **3.** You can edit records using the data form.

T F **4.** You should have a blank row between column labels and records.

T F **5.** You can have as many lists on a worksheet as you desire.

T F **6.** It is recommended that column labels be formatted differently from the records below them.

T F **7.** When using a number as text, insert a double quotation mark before the number.

T F **8.** You cannot delete records using the data form.

T F **9.** A list should have the same type of data in each field.

T F **10.** You can find records using the data form.

MULTIPLE CHOICE

1. ________ are sets of related data.

a. Fields b. Lists

c. Records d. Cells

2. If using the criteria **=Gen**, the results would include ________.

a. General b. Generic

c. Gen d. All of the above

3. When entering numbers as text, type a(n) _________ as the first character.

a. Opening parenthesis b. Exclamation point

c. Quotation mark d. Apostrophe

4. When sorting, the ________ specifies the field on which the list is to be sorted.

a. Sort by column b. Then by column

c. Neither of the above d. Both of the above

5. The ________ must be entered as the first row of a list.

a. Fields b. Column labels

c. Records d. Cells

6. To use the asterisk or question mark in a text criteria without having it act as a wildcard, precede it with a(n) ________.

a. Tilde
b. Exclamation point
c. Quotation mark
d. Apostrophe

7. In the data form, edit boxes are labeled with a ______ name automatically taken from the list's column labels.

a. Row
b. Range
c. File
d. Field

8. ________ are columns of information that make up a record.

a. Fields
b. Lists
c. Column labels
d. Cells

9. When does Excel display the message *No headers detected. Assume top row is header row?*

a. When Excel recognizes that the disk is full
b. When Excel recognizes the file is full
c. When the labels on the header row have the same format as the records that follow.
d. When Excel finds data on the row above the first row of the list

10. When using the data form, to move between edit boxes, press ________.

a. Enter
b. Tab
c. Spacebar
d. Ctrl+Enter

FILL IN THE BLANK

1. Another name for column labels is ________.

2. The fastest way to locate a record in a long list is to use ________.

3. The term *database* is just another name for what Excel normally calls a(n) ________.

4. When working with a list, you can display it using a special dialog box called the ________.

5. When sorting in ________ order, text is organized from A to Z.

6. The row numbers for a filtered list are colored ________.

7. When sorting in ________ order, text is organized from Z to A.

8. When using AutoFilter, any records that do not match the criterion are ________.

9. The ________ indicates the number of records that match the criteria and the total number of records in the list.

10. When using AutoFilter, you can click any of the drop-down arrows to specify a filter criterion for that column. When you do so, you always have the following choices: ________, ________, ________, ________, and ________.

LAB ACTIVITIES

DRILLS

6-1 The Anatomy of a List

An Excel list is organized into fields (columns) and records (rows). Each field is named on the first row or the list. In this drill you create a simple list from scratch. When finished, your model should look like the figure "The Address List."

The Address List

5	LASTNAME	FIRSTNAME	STREET	CITY	STATE	ZIP	AREA	PHONE
6	Benjamin	Nancy	100 Elm Street	Cambridge	MA	01945	617	555-1000
7	Davis	John	300 Main Street	Alpine	NJ	07632	201	555-1001
8	Baxter	Michelle	46 Oak Avenue	San Francisco	CA	30255	415	555-1002
9	Jones	John	210001 3rd Street	Englewood Cliffs	NJ	07632	201	555-1003

1. Open the *Address list* workbook stored in the *Drill Workbooks* folder on the *Excel Student Resource Disk* and enter your name into cell A1.
2. Enter the column labels shown in the cells in row 5 in the figure "The Address List."
3. Use the **Color** and **Font Color** buttons on the Formatting toolbar to format the column labels so they have a black background and bold white text.
4. Enter the records shown in the cells in rows 6-9 in the figure "The Address List." (Remember to enter ZIP codes, area codes, and phone numbers as text by typing an apostrophe before typing each number. If you don't do this, ZIP codes beginning with a zero will not display the zero.)
5. Save, print, and close the workbook.

6-2 Entering and Editing Data Using a Data Form

In this drill you enter new records into an existing list using Excel's data form. When finished, your model should look like the figure "The Expanded Address List."

The Expanded Address List

	A	B	C	D	E	F	G	H
1	Type **Name: your name** into cell A1 and press **Enter**							
2	Filename: Address list							
3	5-Feb-96							
4								
5	LASTNAME	FIRSTNAME	STREET	CITY	STATE	ZIP	AREA	PHONE
6	Benjamin	Nancy	100 Elm Street	Cambridge	MA	01945	617	555-1000
7	Davis	John	300 Main Street	Alpine	NJ	07632	201	555-1001
8	Baxter	Michelle	46 Oak Avenue	San Francisco	CA	30255	415	555-1002
9	Jones	John	210001 3rd Street	Englewood Cliffs	NJ	07632	201	555-1003
10	Kendall	Liz	176 Midville Road	Chicago	IL	60615	312	555-1004
11	June	Gary	75 Howdy Blvd.	Tenafly	NJ	07632	201	555-1005
12	Henderson	Carolyn	Beach Lane	Red Bank	NJ	07631	201	555-3001
13	Sen	Kunal	1250 N. Lake Shore	Chicago	IL	60615	312	555-1007
14	Foley	Kim	25 Elm Street	Salem	MA	01955	508	555-2001

1. Open the *Address list* workbook stored in the *Drill Workbooks* folder on the *Excel Student Resource Disk*.
2. Use the **<u>D</u>ata**, **F<u>o</u>rm** command to display the list and enter the records shown in the cells in rows 10-14 in the figure "The Expanded Address List."

(Remember to enter ZIP codes, area codes, and phone numbers as text by typing an apostrophe before typing each number. If you don't do this, ZIP codes beginning with a zero will not display the zero.)

3. Save, print, and close the workbook.

6-3 Performing Simple Sorts

Sorting a list is the fastest way to see how the contents of fields are related. For example, you can sort text, numbers, or dates so they range from A to Z, smallest to largest, or earliest to latest. In this drill you practice sorting a list by a number of fields in ascending and descending orders.

1. Open the *Bugs Bunny films* workbook stored in the *Drill Workbooks* folder on the *Excel Student Resource Disk* and enter your name into cell A1.
2. Sort the list first in ascending and then descending order by release date. What were the dates of the first and last films?
3. Sort the list first in ascending and then descending order by title.
4. Sort the list first in ascending and then descending order by director's last name.
5. Sort the list by director's last name subsorted by date—both in ascending order.
6. Print the first page of the sheet, then save and close the workbook.

6-4 Understanding Criteria—Finding Records

When you have a large list, it can be difficult to find the record you want. To simplify the process you can use the data form's **Criteria** button to find a specific record. In this drill you find specific films based on dates, directors, and titles.

1. Open the *Bugs Bunny films* workbook stored in the *Drill Workbooks* folder on the *Excel Student Resource Disk.*
2. Use the **Data**, **Form** command to display the data form for the list.
3. Use the **Criteria** command button and the greater than symbol (>) to find all films released after *1-Jan-60*.
4. Use the **Criteria** command button to find all films directed by *Frank Tashlin.*
5. Use the **Criteria** command button to find the film titled *The Wacky Wabbit.*
6. Close the workbook without saving your changes.

6-5 Filtering Records

Instead of finding records, you can filter them so that only the records you want to see are displayed. In this drill you practice filtering the list of Bugs Bunny films.

1. Open the *Bugs Bunny films* workbook stored in the *Drill Workbooks* folder on the *Excel Student Resource Disk.*
2. Use the **Data**, **Filter**, **AutoFilter** commands to add drop-down arrows (▾) to the column label of each column in the list.
3. Click the drop-down arrow (▾) on the *Director, Last* field and filter the list so only films directed by *Jones* are displayed.
4. Click the drop-down arrow (▾) on the *Director, Last* field and filter the list so only films directed by *Freleng* are displayed. Use the **Data**, **Filter**, **Show All** commands to show all records.
5. Click the drop-down arrow (▾) on the *Release* field, select *(Custom...)* and filter the list so only films made on or before *20-Feb-43* are displayed (on or before is the same as *less than or equal to*).
6. Click the drop-down arrow (▾) on the *Release* field, select *(Custom...)* and

filter the list so only films made between *1-Jan-43* and *1-Jan-45* are displayed. Use the same drop-down arrow to show all records. (The two operators you use are *greater than or equal to* and *less than or equal to.*)

7. Click the drop-down arrow (▾) on the *Director, Last* and filter the list so only films directed by *Jones* are displayed. Then click the drop-down arrow (▾) on the *Release* field, select *(Custom...)* and filter the list so only films made by *Jones* on or before *1-Jan-46* are displayed.
8. Close the workbook without saving your changes.

6-6 Using Database Functions

In this drill you enter a database function that counts the number of films directed by the director that you enter in the criteria range. When finished, your model should look like the figure "The Bugs Database Function" shown in part.

	A	B	C	D	E	F	G
1	Type **Name: your name** into cell A1 and press **Enter**		Director, Last	Number			
2	Filename: Bugs Bunny films		Avery	4			
3	5-Feb-96						
4							
5	Films Starring Bugs Bunny						
6							
7	Release	Title	Studio	Director, First	Director, Last		
8	26-Aug-44	Buckaroo Bugs	Looney Tunes	Bob	Clampett		
9	11-Oct-45	Hare Conditioned	Looney Tunes	Chuck	Jones		
10	10-Nov-45	Hare Tonic	Looney Tunes	Chuck	Jones		

The Bugs Database Function

1. Open the *Bugs Bunny films* workbook stored in the *Drill Workbooks* folder on the *Excel Student Resource Disk.*
2. Enter a database function that counts the number of films made by any specific director. Into cell D2 enter **=DCOUNTA(A7:E176,E7,C1:C2)**. To ensure that you specify the criteria range successfully, copy the contents of cell E7 to cell C1. Use the Format Painter to format cell D1 to match cell C1.
3. Save the revised workbook, then print the page of the sheet with the database function on it.
4. Use the new function to find out how many films each were produced by *Jones, Avery, Freleng,* and *Clampett.* To do so, enter each of those names into cell C2 one after another.
5. Close the workbook.

6-7 Creating Automatic Subtotals

In this drill you use Excel's Subtotals command to count the number of films directed by each of the Warner Brothers directors. When finished, your model should look like the figure "Films Counted by Director" shown in part.

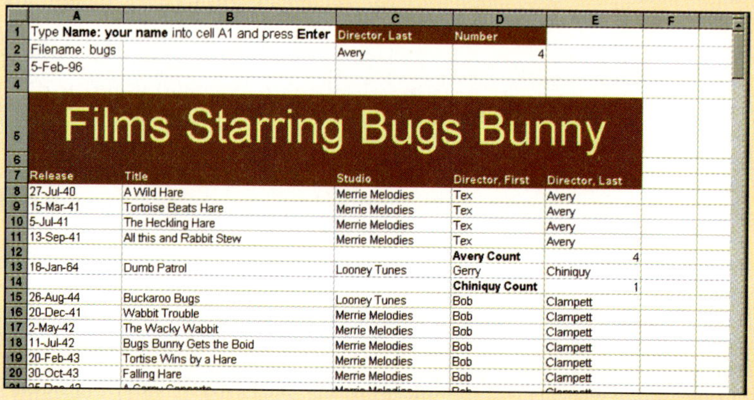

	A	B	C	D	E	F
1	Type **Name: your name** into cell A1 and press **Enter**		Director, Last	Number		
2	Filename: bugs		Avery	4		
3	5-Feb-96					
4						
5	Films Starring Bugs Bunny					
6						
7	Release	Title	Studio	Director, First	Director, Last	
8	27-Jul-40	A Wild Hare	Merrie Melodies	Tex	Avery	
9	15-Mar-41	Tortoise Beats Hare	Merrie Melodies	Tex	Avery	
10	5-Jul-41	The Heckling Hare	Merrie Melodies	Tex	Avery	
11	13-Sep-41	All this and Rabbit Stew	Merrie Melodies	Tex	Avery	
12				**Avery Count**	4	
13	18-Jan-64	Dumb Patrol	Looney Tunes	Gerry	Chiniquy	
14				**Chiniquy Count**	1	
15	26-Aug-44	Buckaroo Bugs	Looney Tunes	Bob	Clampett	
16	20-Dec-41	Wabbit Trouble	Merrie Melodies	Bob	Clampett	
17	2-May-42	The Wacky Wabbit	Merrie Melodies	Bob	Clampett	
18	11-Jul-42	Bugs Bunny Gets the Boid	Merrie Melodies	Bob	Clampett	
19	20-Feb-43	Tortise Wins by a Hare	Merrie Melodies	Bob	Clampett	
20	30-Oct-43	Falling Hare	Merrie Melodies	Bob	Clampett	

Films Counted by Director

1. Open the *Bugs Bunny films* workbook stored in the *Drill Workbooks* folder on the *Excel Student Resource Disk.*
2. Sort by the director's last name in ascending order.
3. Use the **Subtotals** command on the **Data** menu to count the number of films by each director. To do so, specify *Director, Last* as the field in the **At Each Change In** text box and select *Count* as the function from the **Use Function** list. Your results will look like those in the figure "Films Counted by Director."
4. Print the first page of the worksheet.
5. Sort by the *Studio* column in ascending order. When you do so, you will be warned that this will remove sorts and subtotals. Click the **OK** command button and the list is sorted.
6. Use the **Subtotals** command on the **Data** menu to count the number of films by each studio. To do so, change the field in the **At Each Change In** text box from *Director, Last* to *Studio.*
7. Close the workbook without saving your changes.

EXERCISES

6-1 Querying the Textbook Costs Database

One of the most widely used procedures in computing is using comparison operators to limit searches. In this drill you use comparison operators to locate specific groups of records in a small list.

1. Open the *Textbook costs* workbook stored in the *Exercise Workbooks* folder on the *Excel Student Resource Disk* and enter your name into cell A1.
2. Use the **Data, Filter, AutoFilter** commands to add drop-down arrows (▾) to the column label of each column in the list. Use the drop-down arrow (▾) on the % column and use the *(Custom)* choice to filter the list as follows:
   - Display only records with entries greater than 10%.
   - Display only records with entries less than 10%.
   - Display only records with entries less than or equal to 10.5%.
   - Display only records with entries greater than or equal to 10.5%.
3. Make a printout and then close the workbook without saving your changes.

6-2 Exploring the Congressional Database

When lists begin to get large, you can't tell much about them at a glance. However, using database procedures, you can analyze a list to see what organized information it contains. In this drill you analyze a relatively large database listing the members of the 103rd Congress of the United States. When finished, your model should look like the figure "The Members of 103rd Congress Database."

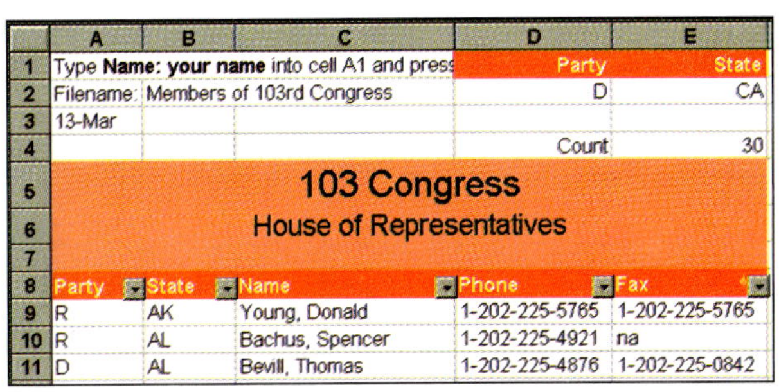

The Members of 103rd Congress Database

1. Open the *Members of 103rd Congress* workbook stored in the *Exercise Workbooks* folder on the *Excel Student Resource Disk* and enter your name into cell A1.
2. Use the **Data, Filter, AutoFilter** commands and use the drop-down arrows (▾) to filter the list as follows:
   - Filter the list so only members from California (CA) are listed.
   - Filter the list so only members from your own state are listed.
   - Filter the list so only Democrats from your own state are listed.
   - Filter the list so only Republicans from your own state are listed.
3. Use the **Data, Filter, Show All** commands to show all records.
4. Sort the list in ascending order by state, then use the **Data, Subtotals** command to count the number of members in each state.
5. Sort the list in ascending order by party, then use the **Data, Subtotals** command to count the number of members by party.
6. Use the **Data, Subtotals** command to remove subtotals from the list. Then use the **Data, Filter** command to turn off AutoFilter.
7. Enter the criteria range in cells shown in cells D1:E2 in the figure "The Congressional Database."
8. Select the following ranges and use the Name box on the formula bar to assign them the indicated names.
   - Assign the name **Table** to the range A8:E450.
   - Assign the name **Party** to cell A8.
   - Assign the name **Criteria** to the range D1:E2.
9. Type **Count** in cell D4 and enter the database function **=DCOUNTA (Table,Party,Criteria)** in cell E4 to count the number of members from any specified state as shown in the figure "The Members of 103rd Congress Database."
10. Use the database functions to fill in the counts in the table in the margin.
11. Make a printout of the first page and then close the workbook without saving your changes.

Party	State	Count
D	None	______
R	None	______
I	None	______
D	CA	______
R	CA	______
D	NY	______
R	NY	______
D	FL	______
R	FL	______

PROJECTS

6-1 Customer Analysis

Analyzing customer purchase patterns is a common practice in the retail business. Computers are used to see who buys what and who spends the most. This way, special promotions can be targeted at the right people. In this project, you open *Charge accounts* stored in the *Project Workbooks* folder of the *Excel Student Resource Disk.* This workbook contains a list like the one shown in the figure "Analysis of Customer Charges." You add the correct database functions to analyze the list. These functions should give the total charges, the average charges, and the number of charges for any customer you specify.

	A	B	C	D
1	Type **Name: your name** into cell A1 and press En			
2	Filename: Analysis of Customer Charges			
3	5-Feb-96			
4				
5	First Name	Last Name	Amount	
6	Martha	Smith	$8	
7	Allen	Smith	$10	
8	Avery	James	$12	
9	Zoro	Smith	$12	
10	John	Smith	$14	
11	Martha	Smith	$19	
12	Bob	James	$23	
13	John	James	$23	
14	Barbara	Smith	$25	
15	Zelda	James	$32	
16	John	Smith	$35	
17	Martha	Smith	$42	
18	Yaz	Smith	$75	
19	Raymond	Smith	$80	
20	John	Smith	$95	
21				
22	First Name	Last Name		
23	John	Smith		
24				
25				
26	Customer Analysis			
27	Sum	144		
28	Average	48		
29	Count	3		
30				

Analysis of Customer Charges

PicTorial

SEVEN

EXCHANGING DATA WITH OTHER APPLICATIONS

After completing this PicTorial, you will be able to:

- **Briefly describe the purpose of object linking and embedding (OLE)**
- **Understand the difference between linked and embedded objects**
- **Paste objects into Excel worksheets so they are linked or embedded**
- **Paste data into Excel worksheets and parse it so it fits into cells**
- **Insert new linked or embedded objects**
- **Insert linked or embedded objects created from existing files**
- **Edit linked and embedded objects**
- **Insert an Access database table into an Excel worksheet**

ONE of the recent trends in computing has been to make data, rather than applications, the focus of software design. Advances in design make it possible to include data in a document that has been created by other applications. For example, you can create a table in Access and then place it in an Excel worksheet. You can also use other types of applications to create and paste in line drawings, photographs, sounds, and even video.

Documents built from parts created with a number of different application programs are called *compound documents*. There is more than one technology used to create compound documents. One of the major ones is called *object linking and embedding*, or OLE—sometimes pronounced "olé," as if you were a bullfighter. OLE allows you to insert data from one application into another just as if it were copied. Compound documents created using OLE are called *OLE documents*.

Imagine how complicated a single program would have to be to edit all of these different components. Instead of one large program, you use many different programs, each dedicated to one task. For example, what if you wanted to send a worksheet discussing sales, and including a table, a chart, a spoken explanation, and an illustration? To do so with OLE, you would use a spreadsheet program to create the table and chart, a sound program to record and edit the comments, and a graphics program to create the illustration.

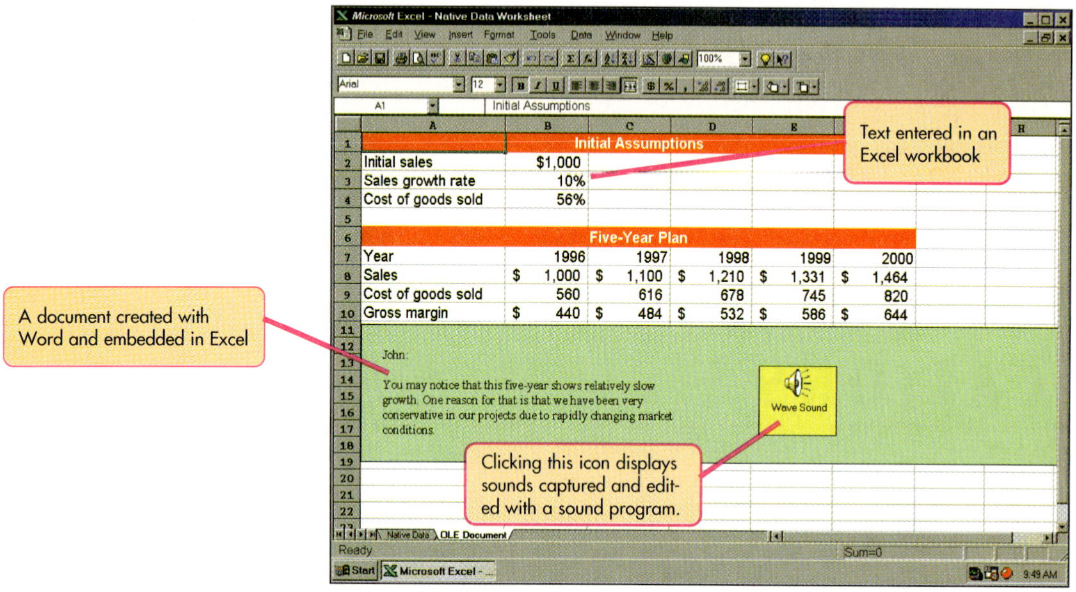

Compound documents are wonderful things. However, the big question is, "How do you get the data from one application into the other?" As you'll now see, Windows gives you more than one way to do so.

Copying Data Between Applications

One of the easiest ways to insert data from one application into another is to cut and paste it. To do so, you just copy some data from one application to the Windows Clipboard and then paste it into another application's document. You can even drag data from one application and drop it into another. It's as if you cut a picture out of a magazine and pasted it into a scrapbook.

As useful as copying data is, it has some drawbacks, the biggest one being that the copied data has no links to the application that created it. If you needed to update the data you pasted into a document, you couldn't do it from the document you copied it to. You'd have to open the application that created it, change the data, cut and paste it again—then delete the old version.

Concepts Behind Object Linking and Embedding

To overcome the shortcomings of copying data, most new Windows applications support OLE so you can insert data from one application into another. When data is placed in an OLE document, you can edit it within the document you placed it in. To better understand this, you have to understand a few new terms that identify the data being copied and the application programs being used.

- An *object* is the data you want to copy from one application into another. An object can be any type of data that is recognized by your system. It can include the data from a spreadsheet, paragraphs from a word processing document, a sound from a sound editing program, or a video clip. A *source file* or *source document* is the file on the disk that contains the object.
- An *OLE server application* is the application used to create the data that has been embedded. For example, if you paste some data from Word into Excel, Word is the server application.
- An *OLE container* (previously called a client) is an application that can contain objects or the document into which you paste an object. For example, if you paste some data from Word into Excel, the Word data is the object and the Excel document is the container.
- An *OLE document* (sometimes called a *container document* or *compound document*) is the document created with an OLE application into which objects have been pasted. For example, an Excel worksheet containing an object created with another application is an OLE document.

When using OLE, you can often choose between embedding and linking the object. These terms refer to the way the data pasted into an OLE document relates to the server application. Let's take a look at three ways data can be pasted into a container.

- *Native data* is the data created by the application into which an object is being pasted. For example, when you copy some data from Word into an Excel worksheet, any of the worksheet data that hasn't been pasted is Excel's native data. If you use the Clipboard to cut and paste data from one application into another, it is converted to native data and is neither linked nor embedded. For example, you can paste Word data into an Excel worksheet and it appears in Excel as a series of text labels. It has no links whatever to Word.

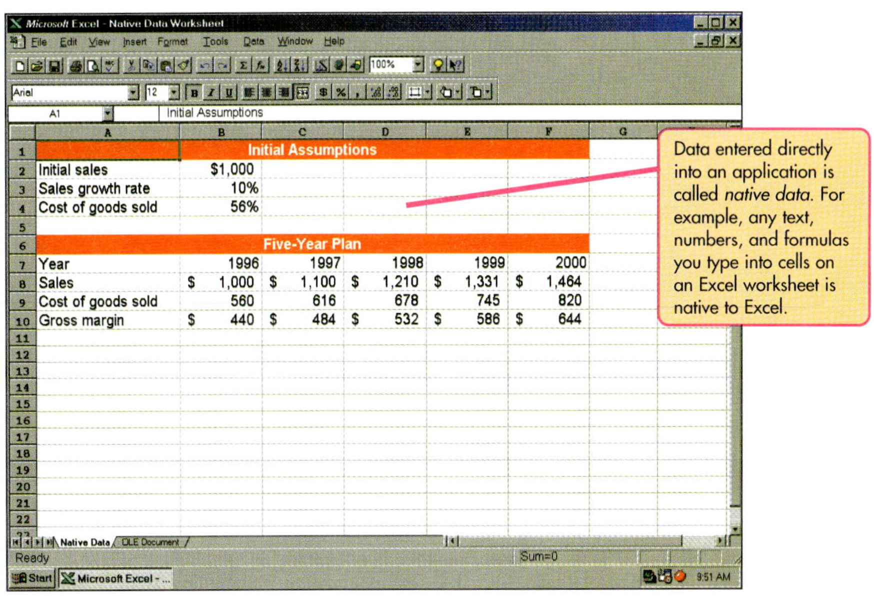

Data entered directly into an application is called *native data*. For example, any text, numbers, and formulas you type into cells on an Excel worksheet is native to Excel.

- An *OLE embedded object* is a copy of the data created by the OLE server application. When you embed an object, a copy of the data in the source document is placed in the OLE document just as if you had copied it. You can just double-click this copy to edit it in the context of its new document. When you do so, a number of things happen. The menu bar and toolbars change to reflect those used to edit the data in the *OLE server application.* In addition, any adornments such as row and column headings and scroll bars appear in the object's window. You can edit the data in the object just as if you had opened the *server application* to do so. However, any changes you make affect only the copy in the OLE document. The copy on the disk that you can open with the server application remains unchanged.

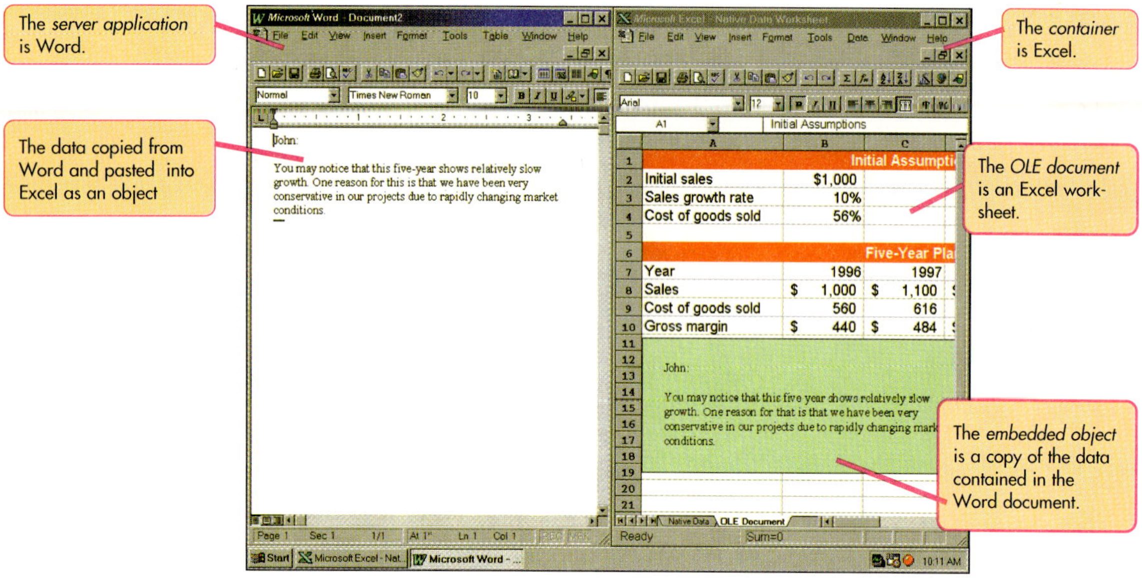

- A *linked object* is similar to an embedded object, but there are some differences. When you *link* an object, it isn't copied into the destination document—there is only one copy of the object, the original one. Instead, a link is established between the real object and an *image* of it in the OLE document. If you make any changes to the real object located elsewhere, those changes are carried through the link to the image of the object in the OLE document. If you double-click a linked object in a OLE document, the server application opens with the real object displayed. Any changes you make to this object are carried automatically to the object in the OLE document.

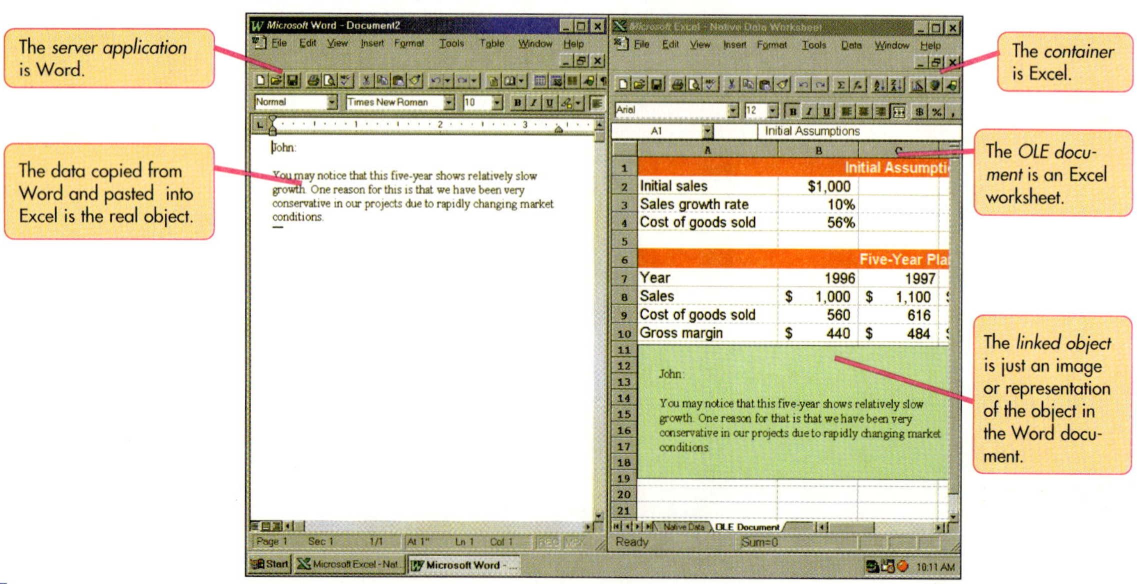

When to Embed and When to Link

When do you link and when do you embed? It depends on a number of issues.

It makes sense to use linking when the same object is used in a number of different OLE documents. With linking, if you edit the object, any changes are immediately reflected in all of the documents to which it is linked. For example, if you prepared a sales report in Excel, you could link the table and chart to a number of memos to different sales manager. Then, if you had to update the data, you would only have to do it once—the changes would be automatically reflected in all of the memos.

One reason to embed is to take advantage of visual editing (discussed in Section 7-3). This allows you to edit the object right in the document in which it's embedded. Linked objects don't offer this ability. Their objects must be edited with the separate application that created them. Another reason to embed is that you want to make changes in the OLE document's object that won't affect the original file the object is taken from. For example, if you embed an Excel table in a Word document, you can edit the copy in the Word document without affecting the copy created by Excel.

7-1 COPYING DATA INTO EXCEL

One of the easiest ways to move data from Word into Excel is just to cut and paste it. This works the same way as cutting and pasting with a document. You can even drag data from Word into Excel and drop it there.

QUICKSTEPS

Copying or Moving Text

1. Select the text in Word that you want to copy or move.
2. Do one of the following to copy or cut the selected text:
   - Click the **Cut** or **Copy** button on the toolbar.
   - Pull down the **Edit** menu and click the **Cut** or **Copy** command.
   - Click in the selected area with the right mouse button to display a shortcut menu and click the **Cut** or **Copy** command.
3. Make Excel the active application and click in the cell that you want to be the upper left corner of the new data's range.
4. Do one of the following to paste the cut or copied text:
   - Click the **Paste** button on the toolbar.
   - Pull down the **Edit** menu and click the **Paste** command.
   - Click the right mouse button to display a shortcut menu and click the **Paste** command.

If the data in Word is in the form of a table or separated by commas, it will automatically be inserted into individual cells. If the data is not broken up into columns in Word, you can break it up into columns after pasting it into Excel.

QUICKSTEPS

Breaking Text Into Columns

1. Select the column in which the text is actually entered (not those into which it overflows).
2. Pull down the **Data** menu and click the **Text to Columns** command to display the Convert Text to Columns Wizard.
3. Make any of the choices described in the box "Understanding the Text to Columns Wizard."

UNDERSTANDING

The Text to Columns Wizard

When you select text to break into columns, you use the Text to Columns Wizard. This wizard leads you through three steps. The first and third are the same for all kinds of text but the second step differs depending on which choice you make in the first.

Step 1 of 3

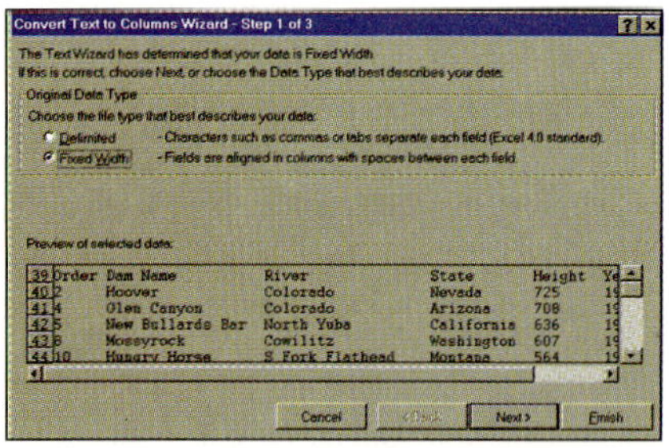

In this dialog box you specify whether the data is delimited or has a fixed width. Delimited data has tabs, commas, or other characters separating it to indicate where new columns start. Fixed width data is aligned in columns with spaces.

Step 2 of 3 for Delimited Data

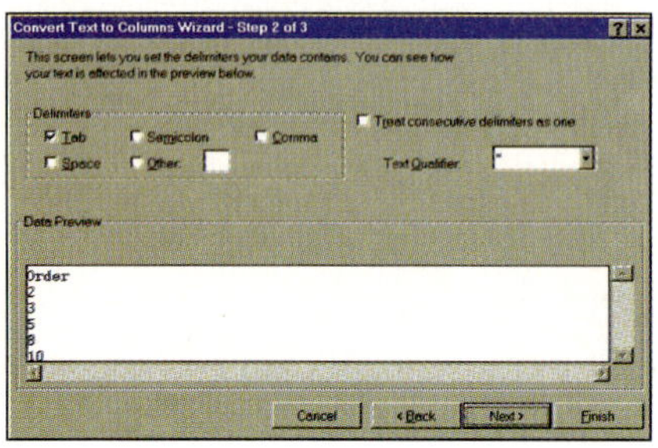

If you specified delimited data in Step 1, you use this dialog box to specify the delimiter being used.

Step 2 of 3 for Fixed Width Data

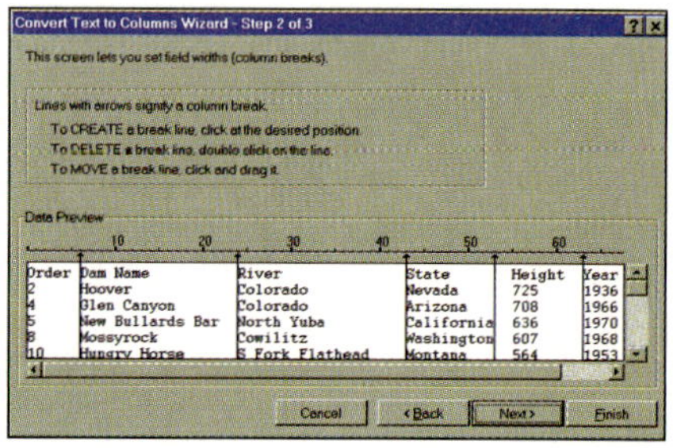

If you specify fixed width data in Step 1, here you see where Excel calculates each new column should begin. It does do with vertical lines. You can drag these lines, add new ones, or delete them to change Excel's guess.

Step 3 of 3

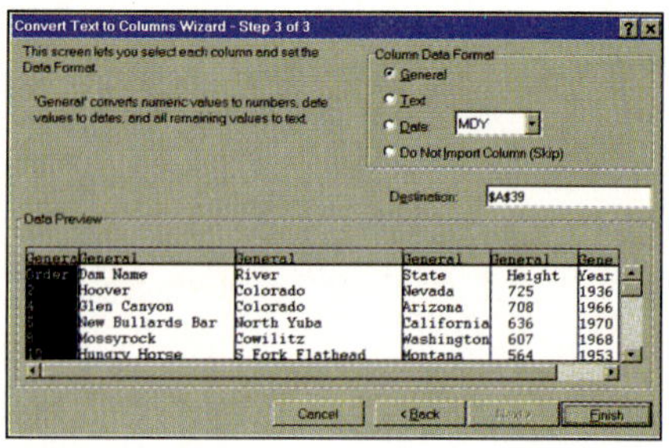

This dialog box allows you to select columns of data and specify certain formats. The Word data doesn't have date formats like Excel's, for instance, so here is where you specify them.

In this tutorial you paste data from Word into an Excel worksheet. In some cases, you then break it up into columns of cells.

Getting Ready

1. Start Excel and open the *Cut & Paste objects* workbook stored in the *OLE Files* folder of the *Excel Student Resource Disk*. Enter your name in cell A1 and maximize Excel's window.
2. Start Word and open the *Major U.S dams* document stored in the *OLE Files* folder of the *Excel Student Resource Disk*. (You open Word documents the same way you open Excel workbooks.) Maximize Word's window and notice how there are three versions of the same table, each in its own format.
3. Click the **Show/Hide ¶** button on Word's Standard toolbar to show paragraph marks. The first table has column separated by tabs and the last has them separated by spaces. The middle table is a Word table with entries in cells.

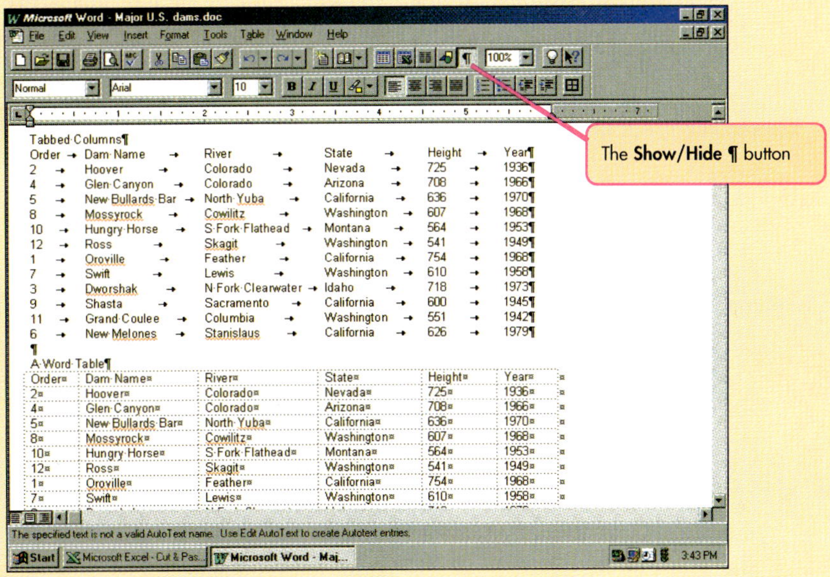

Cutting and Pasting Tabbed Columns

4. In the Word document, select the heading *Tabbed Columns* and the table below it, then click the **Copy** button on Word's Standard toolbar. (To select the table, click to the left of the word *Tabbed*, hold down the left mouse button and drag the highlight to cover the entire table.)

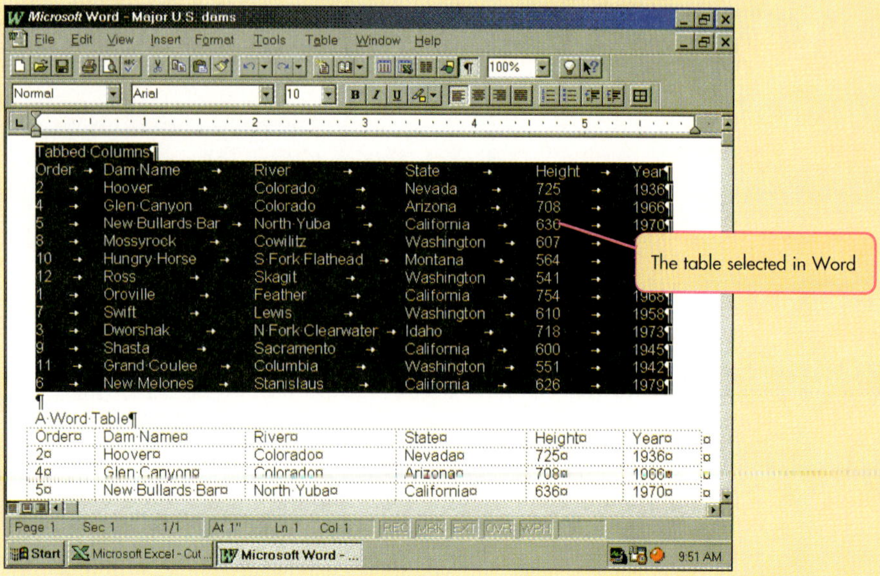

5. Click Excel's button on the taskbar to make it the active application, click cell A6, and click the **Paste** button on Excel's toolbar. The data is pasted in and broken up to form columns.

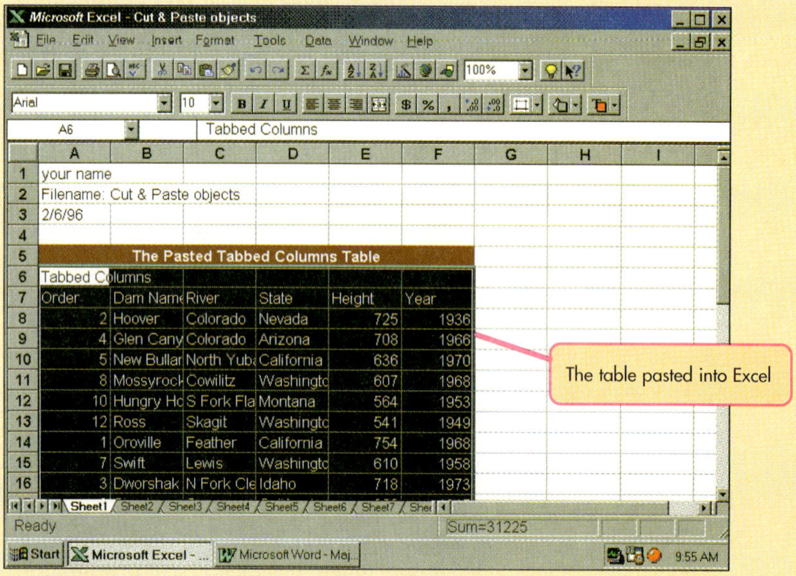

6. Use the column headings to select columns A through F, pull down the **Format** menu, point to the **Column** command to cascade the menu, then click **AutoFit Selection**. Narrow column A so there is just enough width for the column heading.

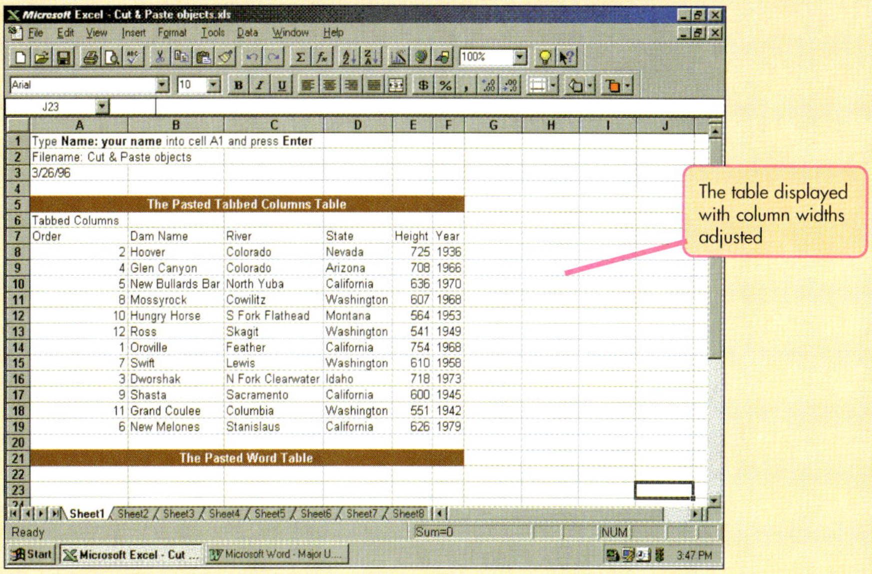

Cutting and Pasting a Word Table

7. Click the Microsoft Word button on Windows' taskbar to make it the active application, select the heading *A Word Table* and the table below it, then click the **Copy** button on Word's toolbar.

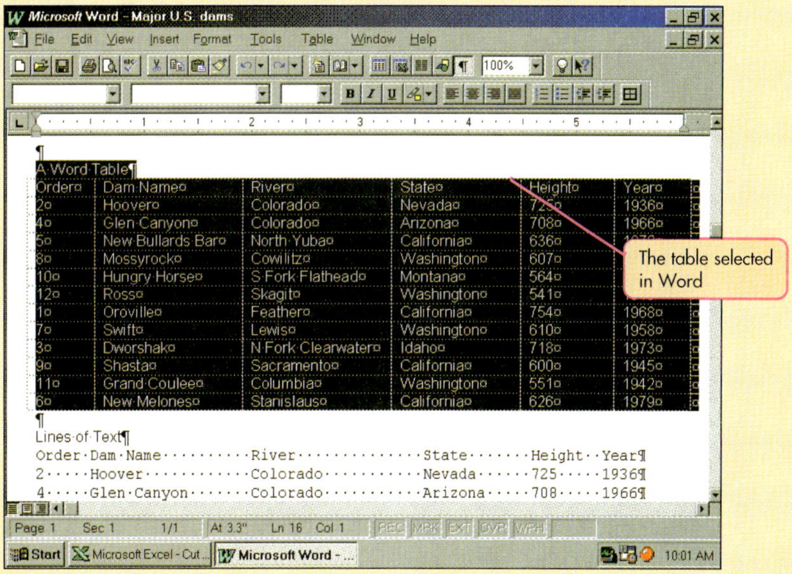

8. Click Excel's button on the taskbar to make it the active application, click cell A22, and click the **Paste** button on Excel's toolbar. Again the data is pasted in and broken up to form columns.

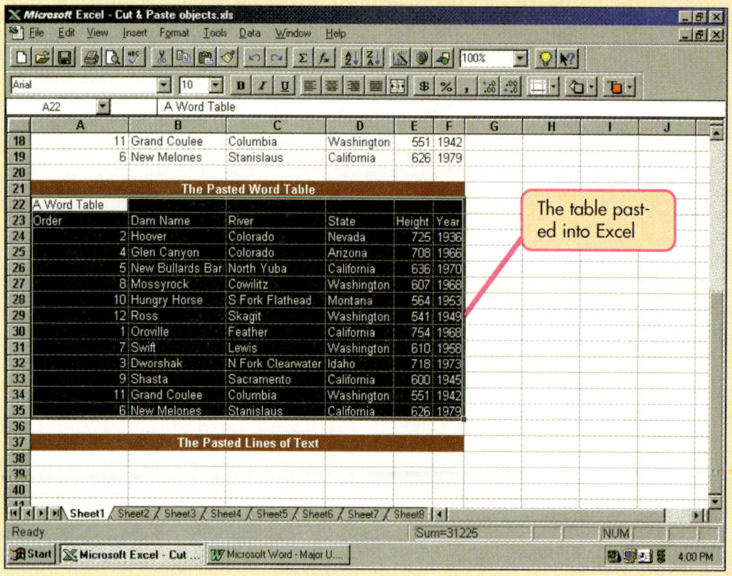

Cutting and Pasting Lines of text

9. Make Word the active application, select the heading *Lines of Text* and the table below it, then click the **Copy** button on Word's toolbar.

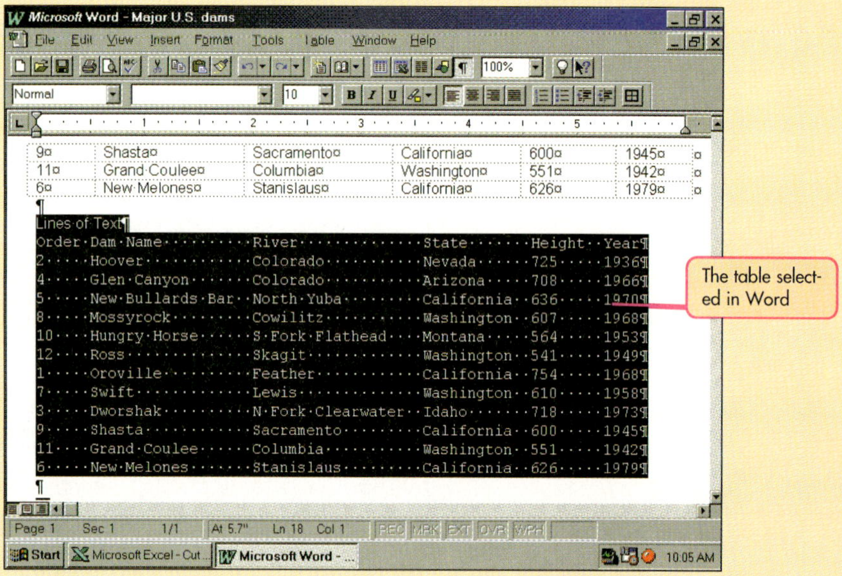

10. Click Excel's button on the taskbar to make it the active application, click cell A38, and click the **Paste** button on Excel's toolbar. Click in various cells in column A where you pasted the new table, and then look at the formula bar. You'll see that the entries are just long lines of text in the column. Click in any of the adjoining cells in columns B through F and you'll see they contain no data.

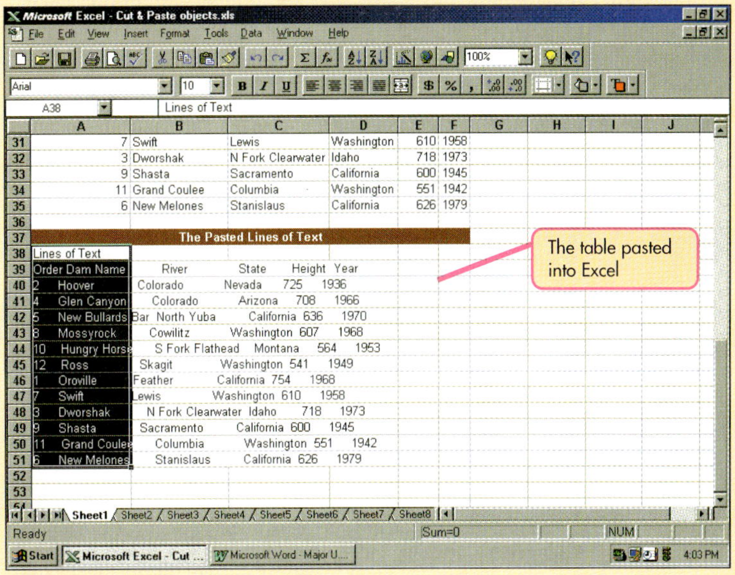

Breaking the Text into Columns

11. Select cells A39 through A51.

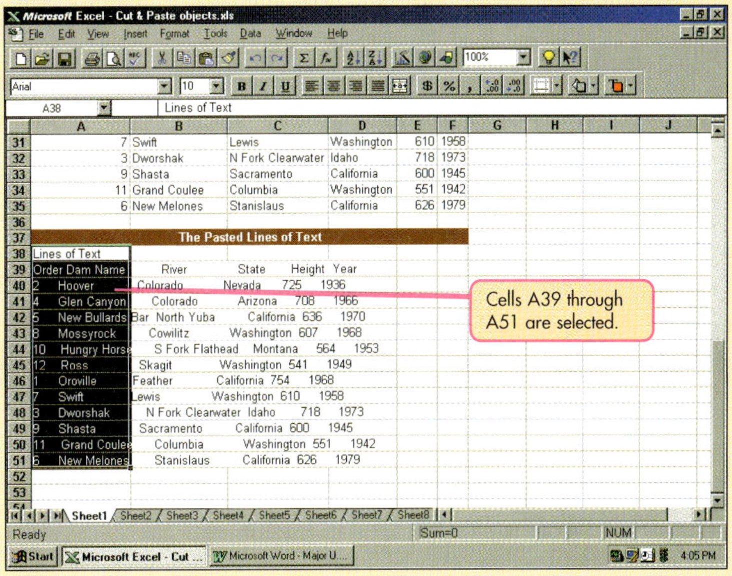

12. Pull down the **Data** menu and click the **Text to Columns** command to display the Convert Text to Columns Wizard. The dialog box has the **Fixed Width** option button on and displays how the table looks.

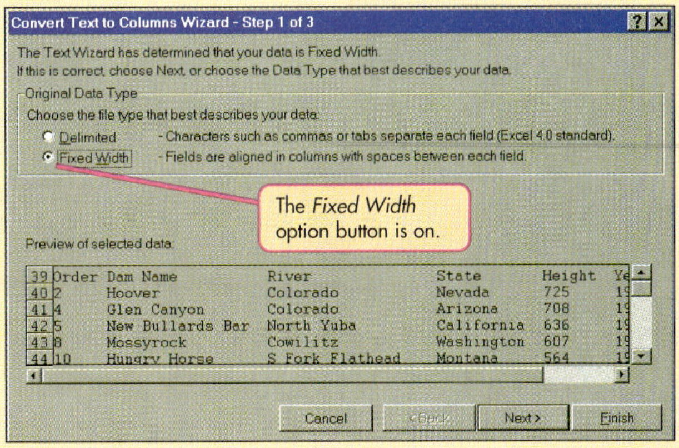

13. Click **Next** and see where Excel thinks each column should begin. In this case it has guessed correctly.

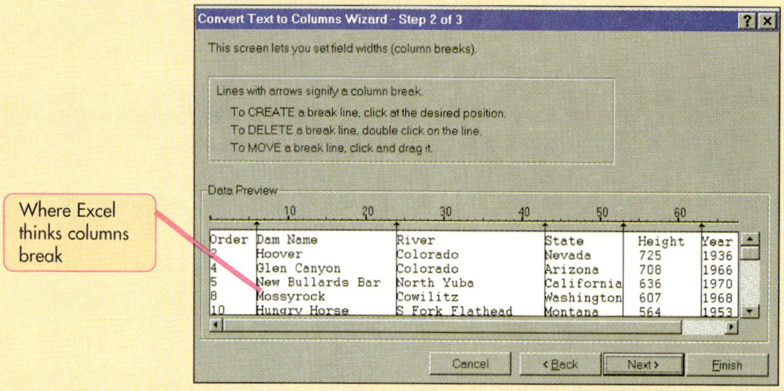

14. Click **Next** and see how Excel allows you to format columns of data.

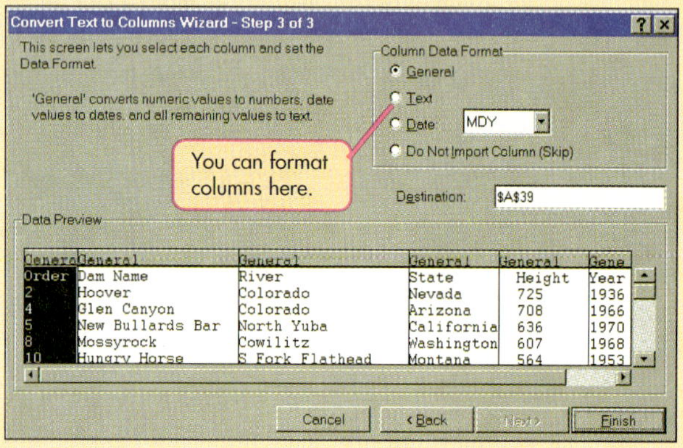

15. Click **Finish** and the data is broken into columns just like the two previous versions of the table.

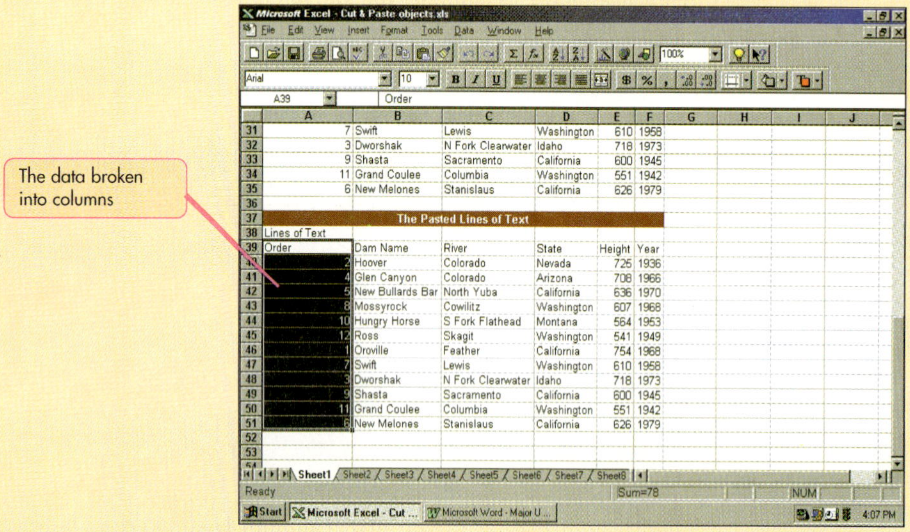

Finishing Up

16. Click the **Save** button and then the **Print** buttons on Excel's Standard toolbar.

17. Close all open applications or continue to the next section. If prompted to save any changes to the documents, click the **No** button.

7-2 PASTING OBJECTS INTO EXCEL WORKSHEETS

If you have already created data in one application that you want to link or embed into another, you can do so by cutting and pasting. Both embedded and linked objects float on top of the worksheet. You can easily drag them about and change their size or shape. Unlike native data, they do not occupy cells on the sheet.

QUICKSTEPS

Pasting Embedded or Linked Data in Excel

1. Cut or copy the data from the server application to place it on the Clipboard.
2. Make Excel the active application and select the cell in Excel where you want to paste the data. It won't be pasted in the cell, but the upper left corner of the object will be located there.
3. Pull down the **Edit** menu and click the **Paste Special** command to display the Paste Special dialog box.
4. Make one or more of the following settings:
   - To embed the object, click the option button for **Paste**; to link the object, click the **Paste Link** option button.
   - In the **As** list box, select the format in which you want to paste the data.
   - If the **Display as Icon** check box isn't dimmed, click it on if you want to display the data as an icon.
5. Click the **OK** command button to paste the data.

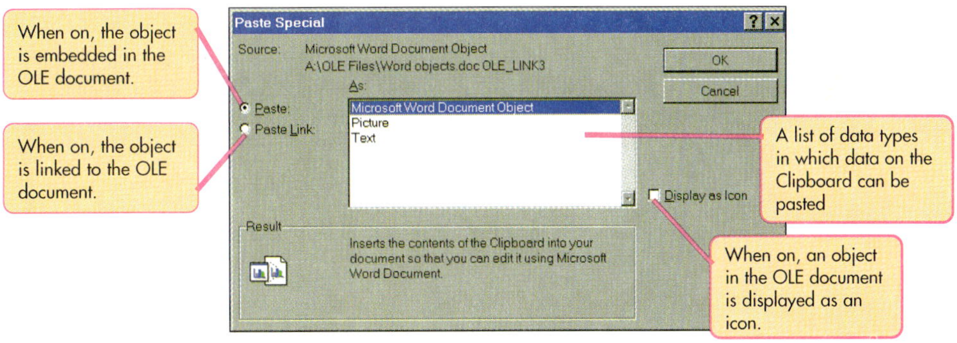

TUTORIAL

In this tutorial you embed and link Word objects into an Excel worksheet. The resulting worksheet becomes a compound document.

Getting Ready

1. Start Word and open the *Word objects* document stored in the *OLE Files* folder of the *Excel Student Resource Disk* and enter your name. Maximize the Word window if it isn't already maximized.
2. Click the **Show/Hide ¶** button on the standard toolbar to show paragraph marks if they are not already displayed.

3. Start Excel, open the *OLE Excel workbook* stored in the *OLE Files* folder of the *Excel Student Resource Disk,* and enter your name in cell A1. Maximnize Excel's window if it isn't already maximized.

4. Right-click a clear area of the taskbar, then click the shortcut menu's **Tile Vertically** command.

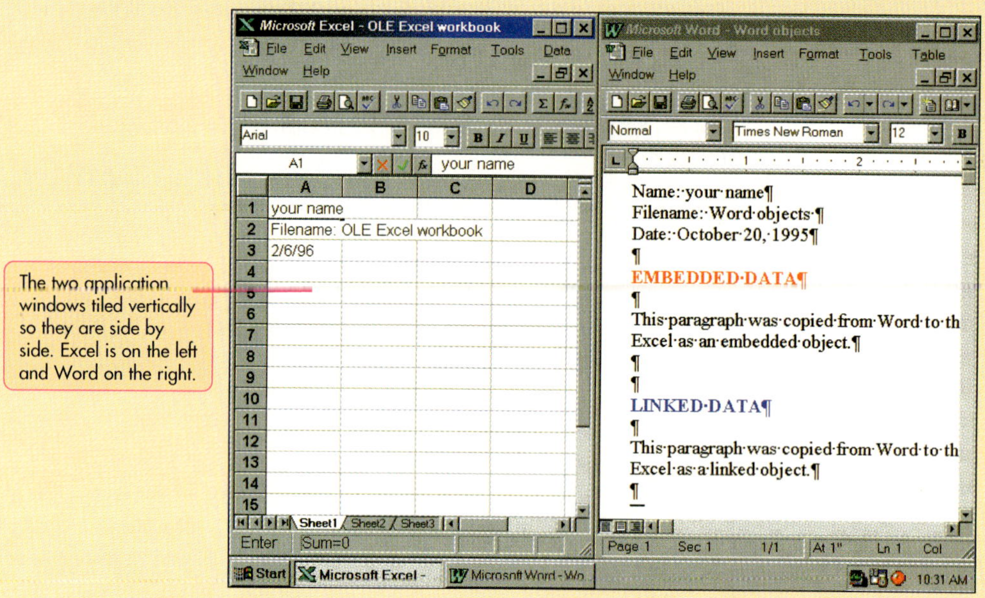

Copying Word Data to the Clipboard

5. Click in Word to make it the active application, then select the heading that reads *EMBEDDED DATA* and the paragraph that follows it including the paragraph mark (¶).

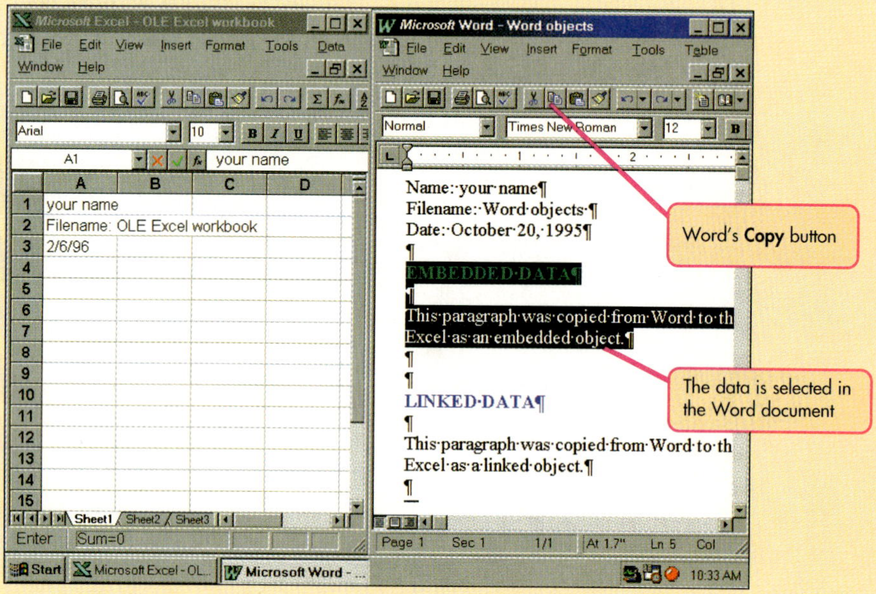

6. Click the **Copy** button on Word's Standard toolbar to copy the data to the Clipboard.

Embedding Word Data in the Excel Worksheet

7. Click in Excel to make it the active application, then click cell A5.

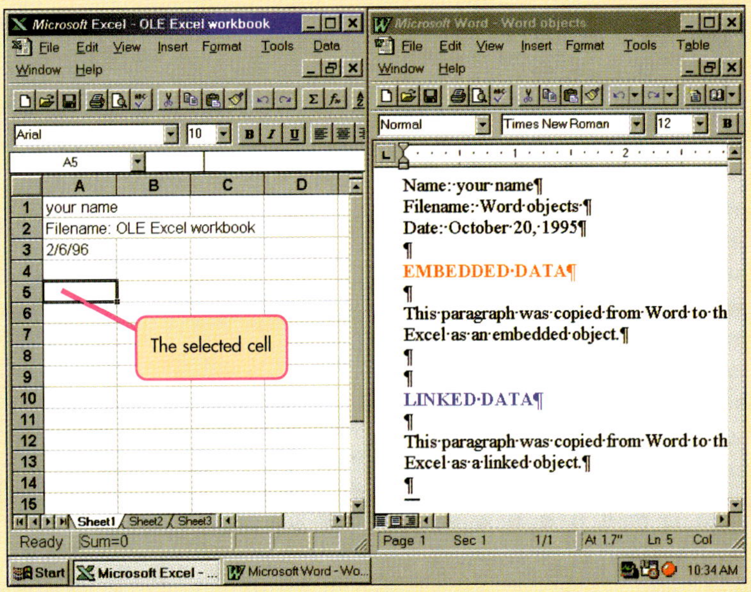

8. Pull down Excel's **Edit** menu and click the **Paste Special** command to display the Paste Special dialog box.
   - The **Paste** option button should be on.
   - On the **As** list box, the *Microsoft Word Document Object* should be selected.

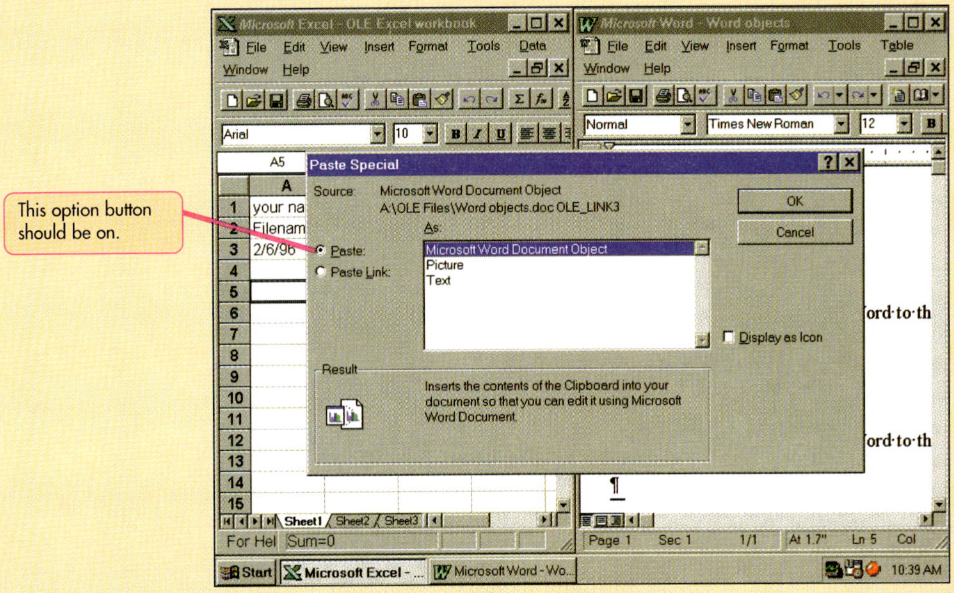

9. Click the **OK** button and the data copied from Word is embedded in Excel at the insertion point. It has selection handles, and it floats above the worksheet, covering the cells beneath it.

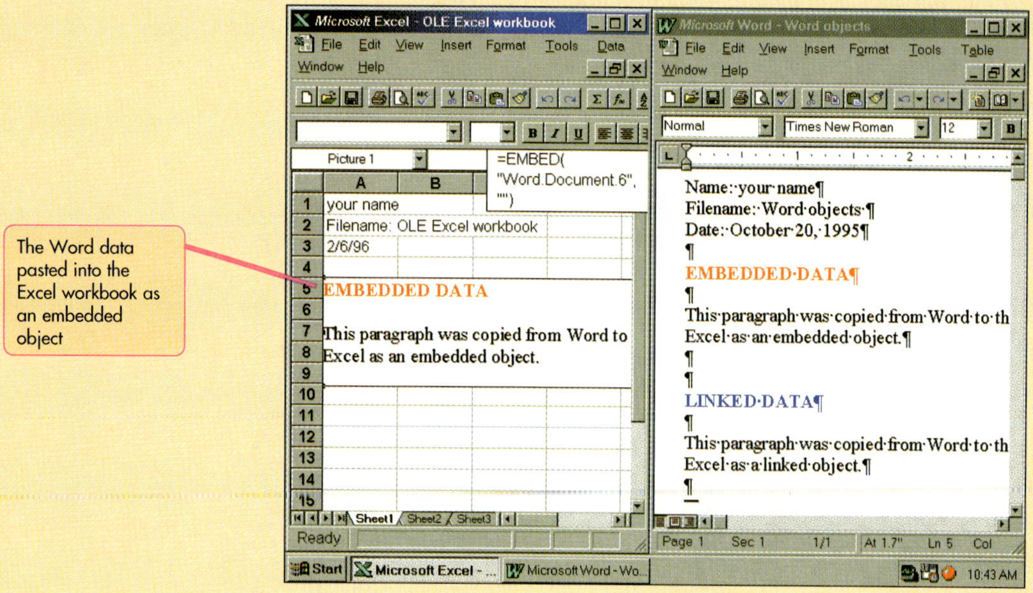

Copying Word Data to the Clipboard

10. Click in Word to make it the active application, then select the heading that reads *LINKED DATA* and the paragraph that follows it including the paragraph mark (¶).

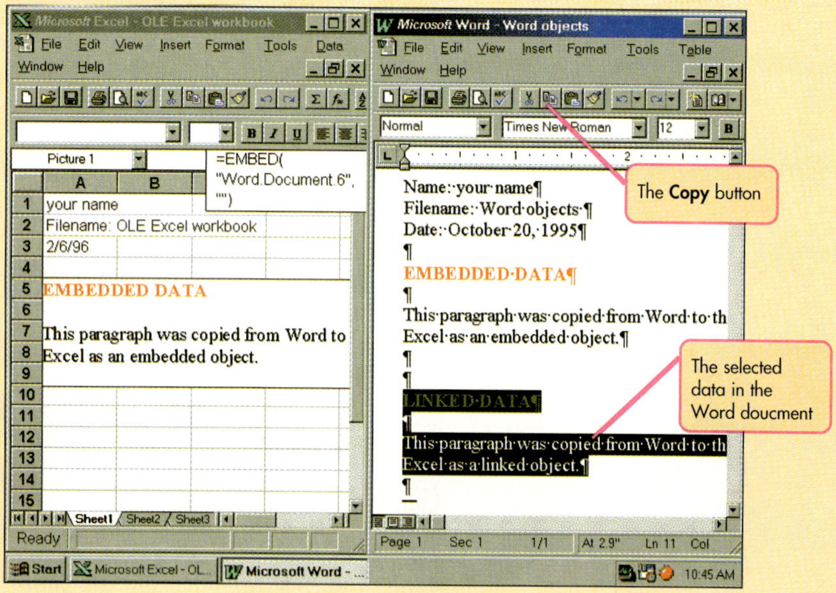

11. Click the **Copy** button on Word's toolbar to copy the data to the Clipboard.

Linking Excel Data to the Word Document

12. Click in Excel to make it the active application, then click cell A14.

13. Pull down Excel's **Edit** menu and click the **Paste Special** command to display the Paste Special dialog box.

- On the As list box, the *Microsoft Word Document Object* should be selected.
- The **Paste** option button should be on.

14. Click the **Paste Link** option button to turn it on.

Click this option button to turn it on.

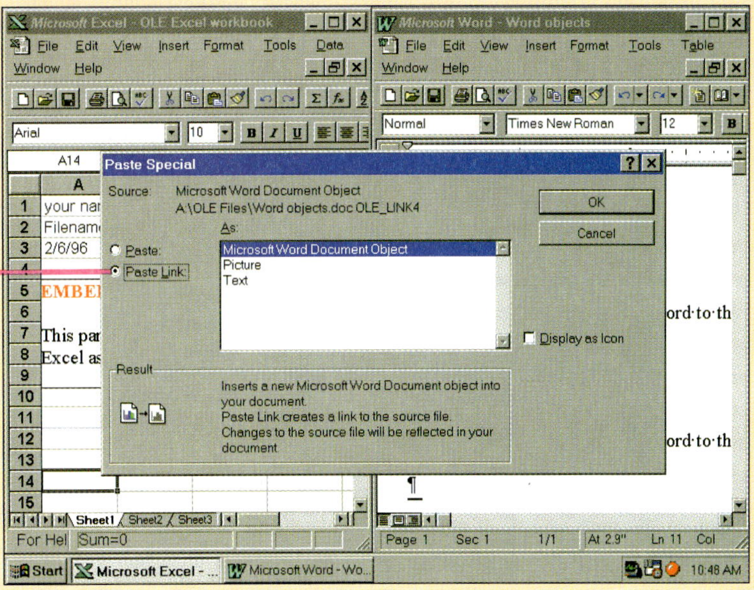

15. Click the **OK** button and the data from Excel is linked into the Word document at the insertion point. Like the embedded data, it has selection handles and floats above the spreadsheet, covering the cells beneath it. You'll see later, when editing the data, what makes the linked and embedded data different.

The linked object in the Excel workbook

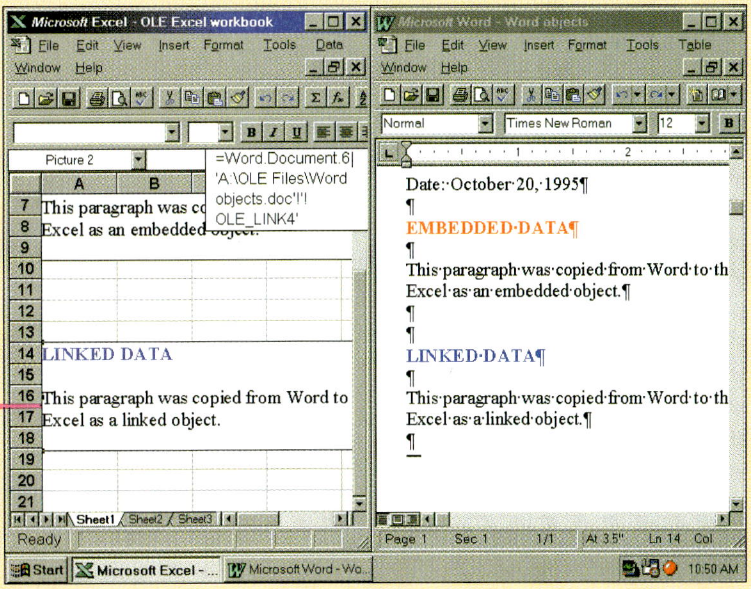

Finishing Up

16. Click Excel's **Save** button on the toolbar to save the revised document.

17. Close the Word application and Excel's workbook, and then continue to the next section, or close all open applications. If prompted to save any changes to the documents, click the **Yes** button.

7-3 INSERTING OBJECTS INTO EXCEL DOCUMENTS

If you want to insert a new object in an OLE document, you can do so. You can also insert an existing file on the disk as an object.

Inserting New Objects

When you insert a new object, it can only be embedded and not linked. This is because links can only be established to existing files.

When inserting a new object, you are given the opportunity of selecting an object type from a list. The list contains all OLE data types that are registered for your system. For example, if Word is on your system, you will be able to create a Word object. If Word isn't on your system, you won't be able to.

QUICKSTEPS

Inserting New Objects

1. Open the Excel worksheet where you want a new object inserted.
2. Pull down the **Insert** menu and click the **Object** command to display the Object dialog box.
3. On the **Create New** tab, select the type of object from the **Object Type** list, and click the **OK** button. The object you select will be embedded in the document.

Inserting Objects Created from Files

You needn't open a document to cut and paste an object in another application. You can create an object directly from an existing file on the disk. When you do so, you can choose between linking and embedding it.

QUICKSTEPS

Inserting Objects Created from Files

1. Open the Excel worksheet where you want to insert an object created from an existing file.
2. Pull down the **Insert** menu and click the **Object** command to display the Object dialog box.
3. Click the **Create from File** tab and enter the object's filename in the **File Name** text box or click the **Browse** button to search for it just as you would open an ordinary document. When you find it, click it to select it, then click the **Open** button. Click the **Link to File** check box if you want the object linked instead of embedded.
4. Click the **OK** button to insert the linked or embedded object.

TUTORIAL

In this tutorial you insert Word objects into an Excel worksheet. You first insert a new object, and then insert one from an existing file on the disk.

Getting Ready

1. Start Excel and open the *Insert objects* worksheet stored in the *OLE Files* folder of the *Excel Student Resource Disk*. If Excel isn't maximized, click its **Maximize** button. Enter your name in cell A1.

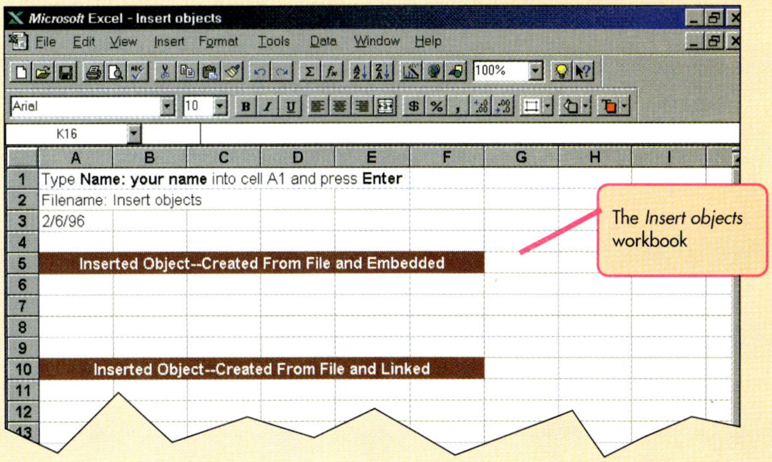

Opening a New Object

2. Click cell A6 below the heading *Inserted Object—Created From File and Embedded*.

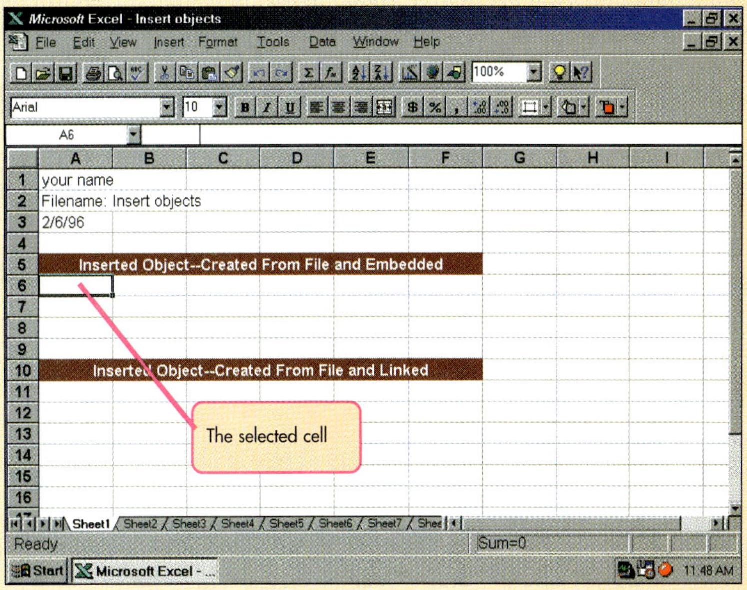

3. Pull down the **Insert** menu and click the **Object** command to display the Object dialog box.
4. With the **Create New** tab selected, select *Microsoft Word Document* from the **Object Type** list. (You may have to scroll the list to see it.)

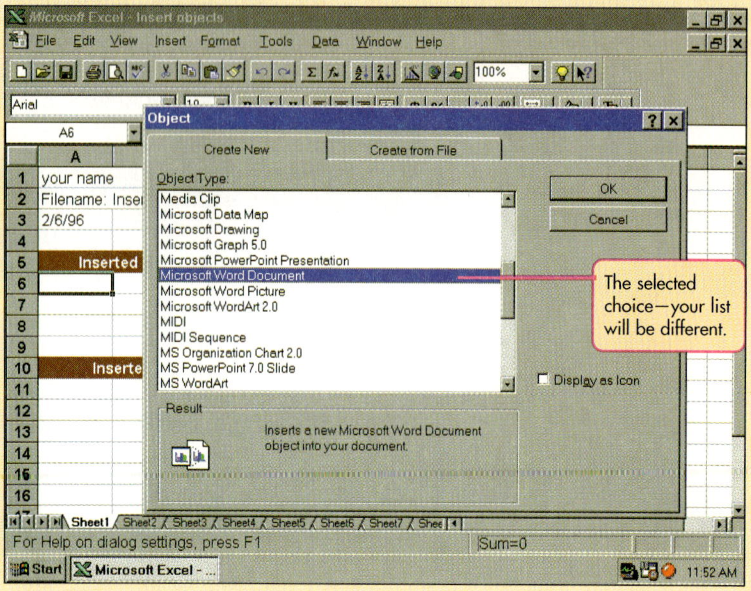

5. Click the **OK** button to insert the object. A Word document appears embedded as an object floating on top of the Excel worksheet. Type your name, then click anywhere outside of the object to deactivate it.

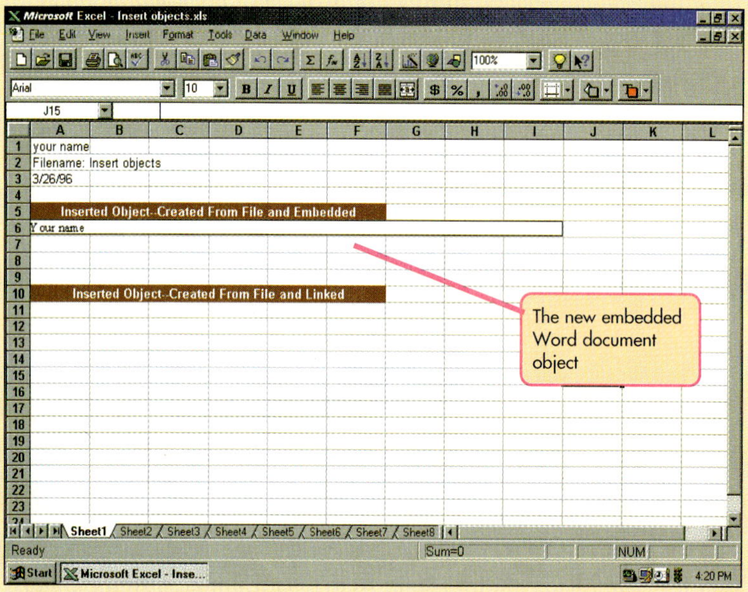

Creating a Linked Object from an Existing File

6. Click in cell A11 below the heading *Linked Word Object—Created from File and Linked* to select it.
7. Pull down the **Insert** menu and click the **Object** command to display the Object dialog box.
8. Click the dialog box's **Create from File** tab to display that tab.

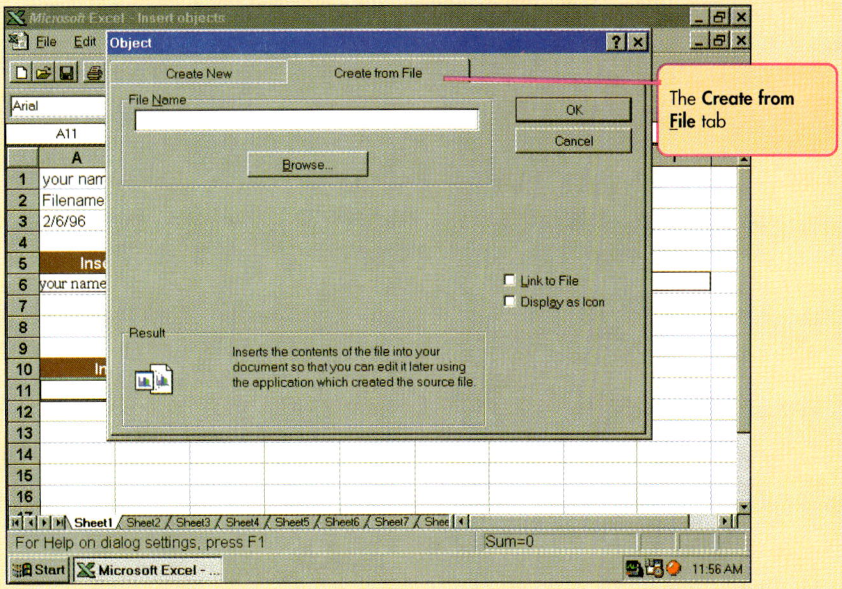

9. Click the **Browse** button and select the *Linked object* document stored in the *OLE Files* folder just as you would open an ordinary document, then click the **Insert** button.

10. Click the **Link to File** check box so the object is linked instead of embedded.

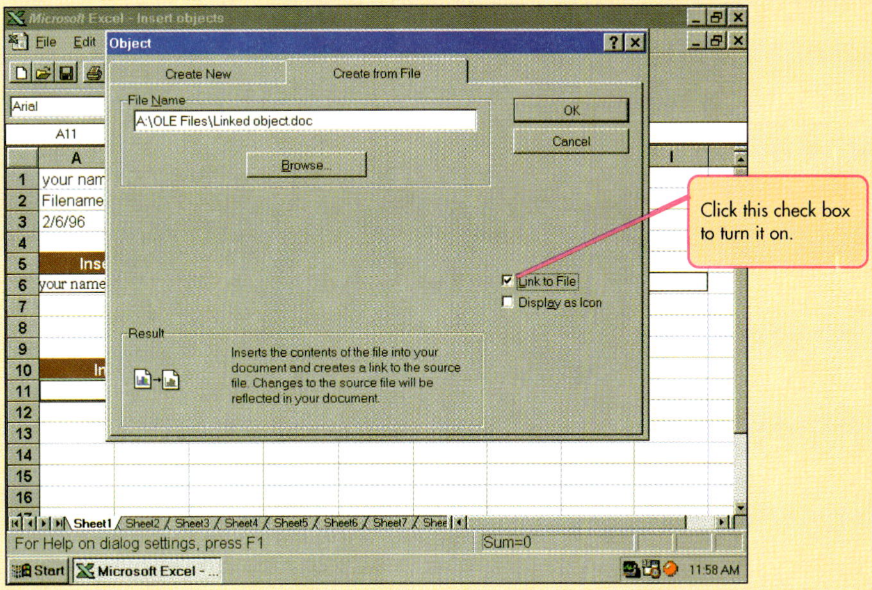

11. Click the **OK** button to insert the object, and the entire Word document appears in the Excel worksheet. Like the embedded object, it floats above the cells.

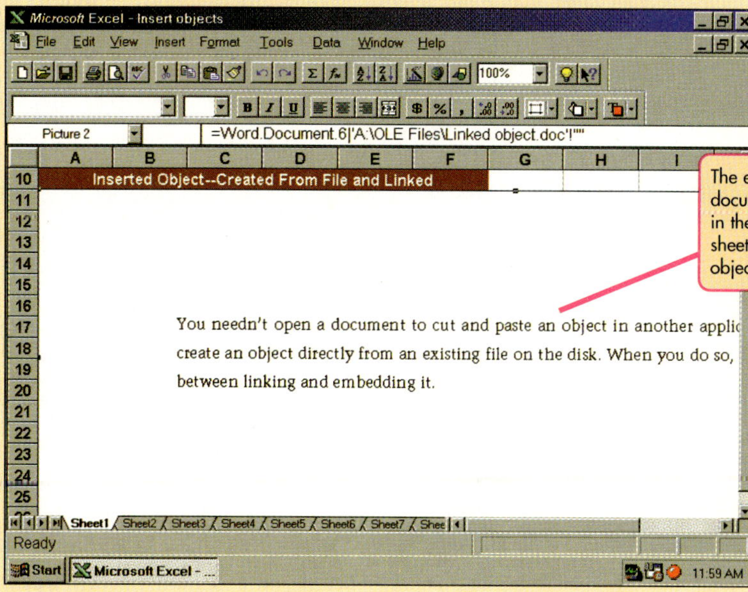

The entire Word document appears in the Excel worksheet as a linked object.

Finishing Up

12. Click Excel's **Save** button on the Standard toolbar to save the revised workbook.

13. Continue to the next section, or close all open applications.

7-4 EDITING LINKED AND EMBEDDED OBJECTS

After embedding or linking an object in a document, you can edit it without leaving the OLE document.

Selecting and Activating Objects

When an object in a document is linked or embedded, you can either select it or activate it. Normally you select an object to move or resize it, and activate it to edit it.

- To *select* a linked or embedded object in the OLE document, click it. A selected object displays eight handles that you can use to resize it, and the mouse pointer turns into a left-pointing arrow when over the object.

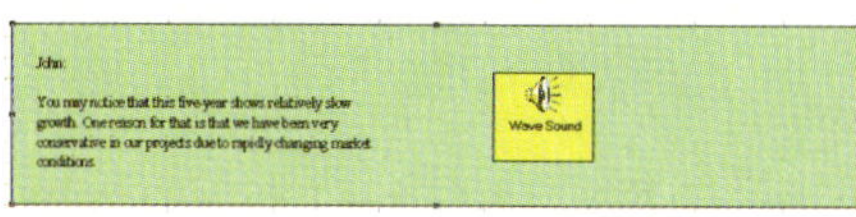

When you click an object to select it, sizing handles appear on the sides and corners.

- To *activate* a linked or embedded object in the OLE document, double-click it. What happens when you activate it depends on whether it is linked or embedded. If it is linked, the server application opens with the object displayed for editing or formatting. If it is embedded, the container application's menu bars and toolbars change to reflect those of the server application.

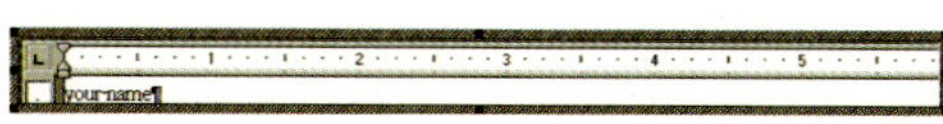

When you double-click an embedded object to activate it, it is surrounded by a hatched border.

In addition to selecting or activating an embedded object, you can also open it. This displays the object in a separate window so you can see more of the object. When an object is opened, it is displayed in the OLE document with an "open" hatched border that indicates it is open in another window. The easiest way to open an object is to right-click it and select the **Open** command from the shortcut menu's cascaded **Object** command. The window that appears is an alternate window onto the object and a separate application. Any changes you make are immediately and automatically reflected in the object in the OLE document. After making changes to the object, just click the object window's **Close** button to return to the OLE document.

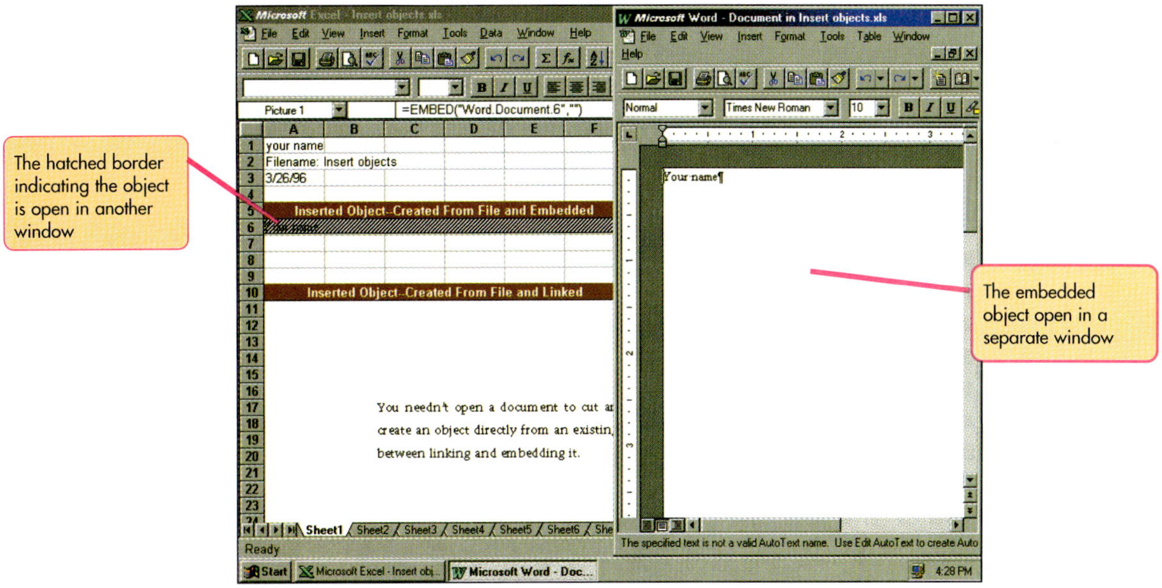

Editing Activated Objects

An object is most commonly activated to edit its contents in its current location.

- When you activate an embedded object, it displays a hatched border. This border indicates that the menu commands and toolbar buttons from the object's server application have temporarily taken the place of those normally displayed by the container application. In addition, the object displays its frame *adornments*, the name for such elements as row and column headings and scroll bars. This is called *OLE visual editing* because you edit the object in the visual context of the OLE document in which it is embedded.
- When you activate a linked object, the server application opens and displays the object for editing. This is necessary because the linked object is not a real object. It is only a stand-in that allows the source object to be displayed elsewhere, much like a reflection in a mirror. To change the object in the OLE document, you have to change the source object itself.

When you edit an embedded or linked object, the changes take place in the OLE document immediately and automatically. However, there is a difference in how changes affect the source file.

- Changes made to an embedded object affect only the copy of the object in the OLE document and are not carried to the original file on the disk.
- Changes made to a linked object are actually made in the source file and then automatically carried back to the image of the object in the OLE document.

QUICKSTEPS

Editing Embedded Objects

1. To activate the embedded object in the OLE document, do one of the following:
   - To edit the object in place, double-click the embedded object, or click it to select it, pull down the **Edit** menu, point to the **x Object** command (where x stands for the type of object) to cascade the menu, then click the **Edit** command.
   - To edit the object in a separate window, right-click it to display a shortcut menu, or click it to select it, then pull down the **Edit** menu. Point to the x **Object** command (where x stands for the type of object) to cascade the menu, and click the **Open** command.
2. Edit the object using the server application's menu commands and toolbar buttons that appear in the container application.
3. To deactivate the object, do one of the following:
   - If the object is activated within the OLE document, click anywhere else in the document but the object.
   - If the object is open in a separate window, click that window's **Close** button. Your changes are automatically saved.

QUICKSTEPS

Editing Linked Objects

1. To activate the linked object in the OLE document, do one of the following:
   - Double-click the object.
   - Click the object to select it, then pull down the **Edit** menu, point to the x **Object** command (where x stands for the type of object) to cascade the menu, and click the **Edit** command.
2. Edit the object using the server application.
3. Click the server application's **Save** button on the toolbar to save the changes, then click that application's **Close** button.

Managing Linked Objects

Linking objects keeps the OLE document's size smaller because the linked object is stored on the disk, not in the document. However, this can occasionally cause problems because the objects must retain links to the source file in which they are stored. (The object in the OLE document is just a visual representation, not the real object.)

If you move a linked object's file to another folder on the disk, Windows will keep track of its new location. However, if you delete a linked object's source file and then try to activate it, a message will tell you it can't be edited.

To transfer the OLE document to another system, you must also transfer the file containing the original object if you want to be able to edit it. (You need not do so if you are just going to view the object in the context of the OLE document on the new system.) Even if you include the object's file, then you may have to specify its new location. To do so, select the object, pull down the **Edit** menu, and click the **Links** command. Use the **Change Source** button to browse for the object's file.

Breaking Links

Sometimes you want to keep an embedded object from being edited. In these cases, you can break the link so double-clicking it no longer activates the server application. (Breaking links for linked objects makes the objects disappear.)

QUICKSTEPS

Breaking a Link

1. Select the embedded object whose link you want to break, and its link is displayed on the formula bar.
2. Select the entire text of the link on the formula bar and press Delete.

Deleting Objects

To delete an embedded or linked object from its OLE document, click it to select it and press Delete.

Resizing and Moving Linked and Embedded Data

After embedding or linking an object in a document, you can select it, then drag its sides or corners to change its size. You can also select it and drag it to a new location anywhere on the worksheet.

QUICKSTEPS

Resizing and Moving Linked and Embedded Objects

1. Click the object in the OLE document.
2. Do one of the following:
   - To resize the object, drag one of the eight handles.
   - To move the object, point to it, hold down the left mouse button, and drag the mouse pointer to where you want to object moved. When you release the mouse button, the object moves to the new position.

TUTORIAL

In this tutorial you edit both embedded and linked objects to see how the two procedures differ.

Getting Ready

1. Start Excel and open the *OLE Excel* workbook stored in the *OLE Files* folder of the *Excel Student Resource Disk*. A message box appears asking whether you want to re-establish links. Click the **Yes** button. Maximize the Excel window if it isn't already maximized.

Editing the Embedded Excel Data

2. Double-click the object with the heading *EMBEDDED DATA*. A hatched border appears around the object to indicate that the toolbars and menu bar have changed to those used by Word. Also, Word's ruler is displayed above the data.

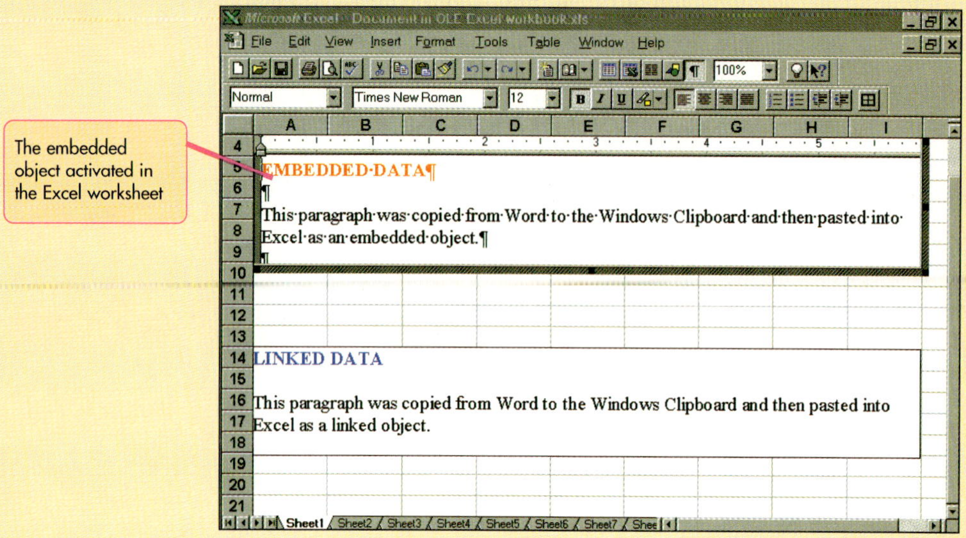

3. Click at the end of the first paragraph, press Spacebar, and type the new closing sentence **I can now edit the data within the Excel application.**

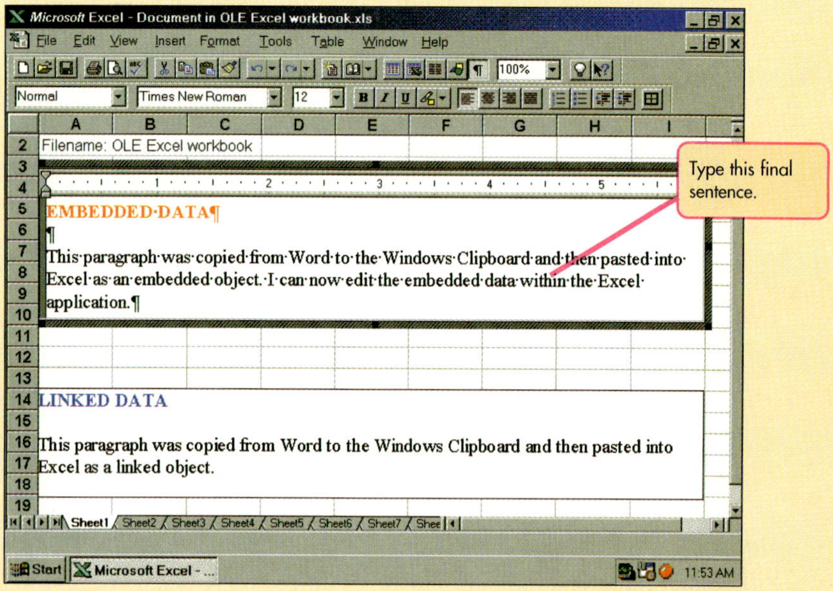

4. Click anywhere in the worksheet outside of the hatched border surrounding the Word data to deactivate the object. The ruler disappears, as do the Word toolbar buttons and menu names.

When you click outside of the object, it is no longer activated.

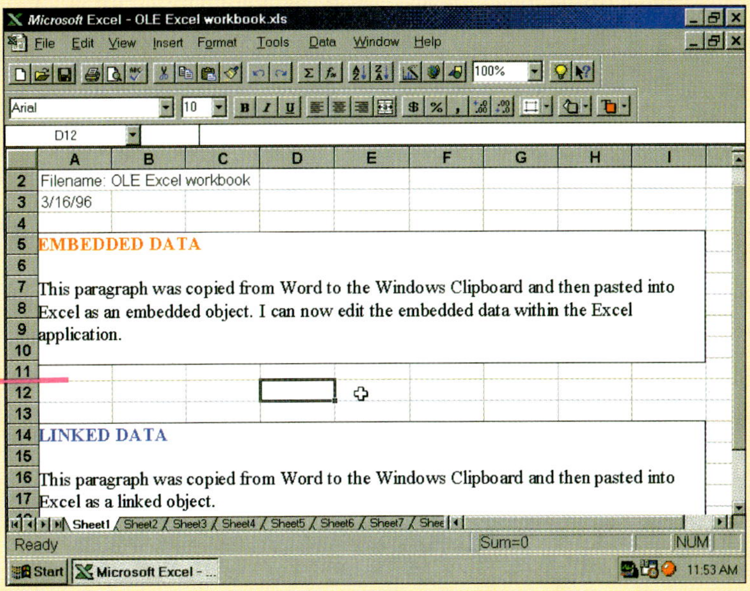

Editing the Linked Excel Data

5. Double-click the object with the heading *LINKED DATA*. The Word application opens with the original document displayed. Maximize the Word screen if it does not open maximized. Notice how the new sentence you added to the end of the paragraph under the *EMBEDDED DATA* heading has not been carried to the original document.

When you double-click the linked object, Word opens with the linked object displayed.

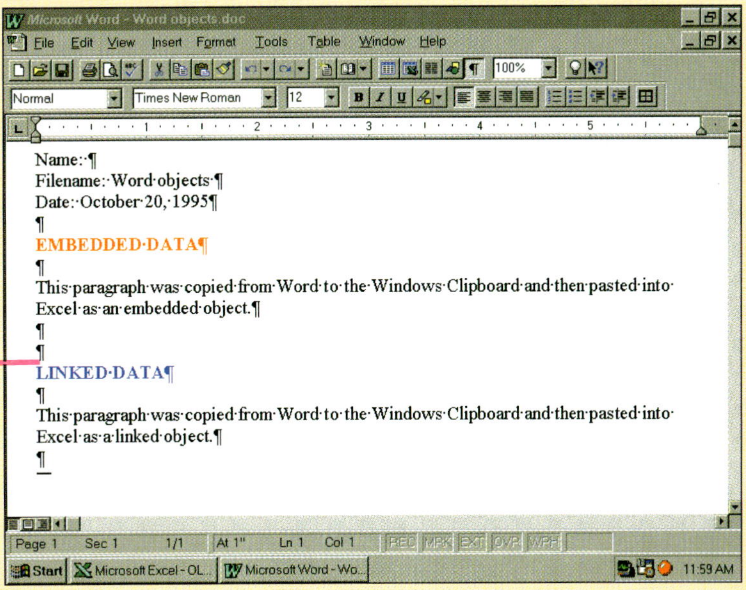

6. Click at the end of the paragraph under the heading *LINKED DATA*, press Spacebar, and type the new closing sentence **I can now edit the linked object using Word just by double-clicking it in Excel.**

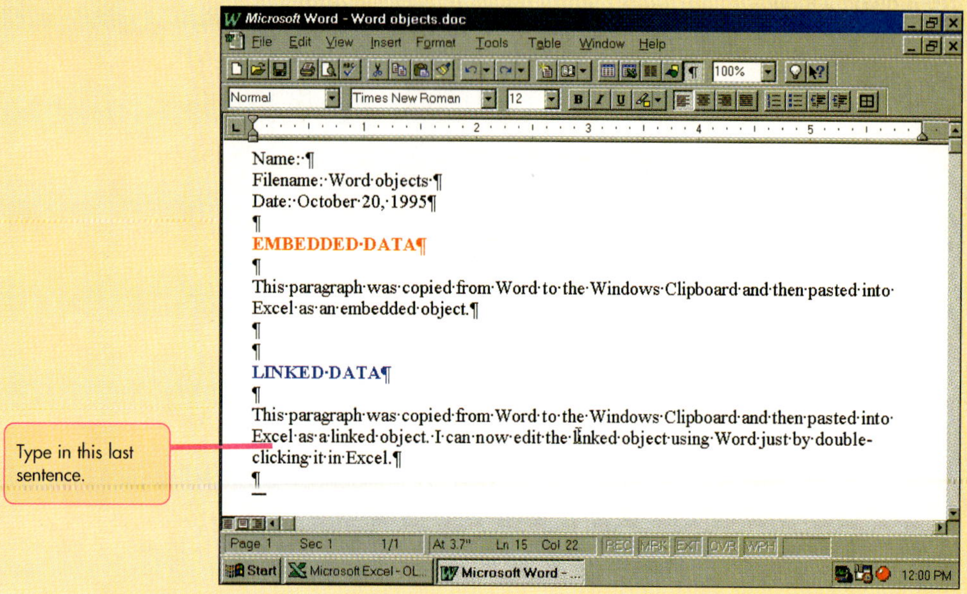

7. Click Word's **Save** button on the toolbar to save the revised document.
8. Click the Microsoft Excel button on Windows' taskbar to make it the active application.Notice how the sentence you added at the end of the paragraph under the heading *LINKED DATA* has been carried to the *OLE Excel workbook*.
9. Click Excel's **Save** button on the toolbar to save the revised document.

Finishing Up

10. Close all open applications without saving any of your changes to the documents.

REVIEW QUESTIONS

TRUE-FALSE

T F **1.** There is only one technology used to create compound documents, called *object linking and embedding*, or OLE.

T F **2.** Data copied using Copy and Paste commands retains links to the application that created it.

T F **3.** An object can be any type of data that is recognized by your system. It can even be a video clip.

T F **4.** When inserting a new object, you are given the opportunity of selecting an object type from a list of all OLE data types that are registered for your system.

T F **5.** Normally you select an object to move or resize it and activate it to edit it.

T F **6.** When you open an embedded object, the object is displayed in a separate window so you can see more of the object.

T F **7.** When you activate an embedded object, it displays a hatched border that indicates that the menu commands and toolbar buttons from the object's server application have temporarily taken the place of those normally displayed by the container application.

T F **8.** If you move a linked object's file to another folder on the disk, Windows will keep track of its new location.

T F **9.** To resize an object after selecting it, drag one of the eight handles.

T F **10.** To move an object after selecting it, just drag it to where you want to object moved and drop it.

MULTIPLE CHOICE

1. Documents built from parts created with a number of different application programs are called ________.

a. compound documents | b. OLE documents
c. Either a or b | d. Neither a nor b

2. An *object* is ________.

a. The data you copied from one application into another
b. The application that created the data that has been copied
c. The document into which the data has been pasted
d. None of the above

3. An *OLE server application* is ________.

a. The object you copied from one application into another
b. The application that created the object that has been copied
c. The document into which the object has been pasted
d. None of the above

4. An *OLE document* is ________.
   a. The object you copied from one application into another
   b. The application that created the object that has been copied
   c. The document into which the object has been pasted
   d. None of the above
5. Data that is in the same format as the data created by the application into which it has been pasted is called ________.
   a. Native data
   b. An embedded object
   c. A linked object
   d. None of the above
6. Data that you can visually edit in the context of the document into which it has been placed is called ________.
   a. Native data
   b. An embedded object
   c. A linked object
   d. None of the above
7. Data that you have placed in an OLE document that can only be edited with the server application is called ________.
   a. Native data
   b. An embedded object
   c. A linked object
   d. None of the above
8. When you edit the data in ________ object, the changes affect the original source file.
   a. An embedded object
   b. A linked object
   c. Either a or b
   d. Neither a nor b
9. When you edit the data in ________ object, the changes affect only the copy in the OLE document and not the original source file.
   a. An embedded object
   b. A linked object
   c. Either a or b
   d. Neither a nor b
10. To open a new Excel worksheet in an OLE document, you would begin by using the ________ command.
   a. **Edit** menu's **Paste Special** command
   b. **Edit** menu's **Paste** command
   c. **Insert** menu's **Object** command
   d. Any of the above

FILL IN THE BLANK

1. An __________ is the data you want to copy from one application into another.
2. When you edit an __________ object, the menu bar and toolbars change to reflect those used to edit the data in the OLE server application.
3. When you __________ an object, it isn't copied into the destination document—there is only one copy of the object, the original one.
4. If you double-click a __________ object in a OLE document, the server application opens with the real object displayed.
5. To paste linked or embedded data into the OLE document, pull down **Edit**

menu and click the _________ command to display the Paste Special dialog box.

6. When you insert a new object, it can only be _________ and not _________.
7. A _________ object displays eight handles that you can use to resize it and the mouse pointer turns into a left-pointing arrow when over the object.
8. To select a linked or embedded object in the OLE document, _________ it.
9. To activate a linked or embedded object in the OLE document, _________ it.
10. To delete an embedded or linked object from its OLE document, just click it to select it and press _________.

PicTorial 7

LAB ACTIVITIES

DRILLS

7-1 Copying Data into Excel

In this drill you copy a Word table into an Excel worksheet. Since the data is just lines of text, you then break it up into columns. The lines are already divided in the Word document by commas that indicate where each column begins. You use these commas, called delimiters, to tell Excel where each line of text should be broken.

1. Start Excel and open the *Text to Columns* workbook stored in the *OLE Files* folder of the *Excel Student Resource Disk* and enter your name into cell A1. Maximize Excel if it isn't already.
2. Start Word and open the *Bugs Bunny Delimited* document stored in the *OLE Files* folder of the *Excel Student Resource Disk*. Maximize Word if it isn't already. Each line of the table is divided into parts by commas—a typical delimiter.
3. Select all lines of the document (hold down Ctrl and press A), then click the **Copy** button on Word's toolbar.
4. Make Excel the active application, click cell A5, and then click the **Paste** button on Excel's toolbar.
5. Click in various cells in columns A through F and you'll see that the list is a series of long lines in column A.
6. Select cells A5:A171. (The fastest way to do so is to click cell A5, then hold down Shift while you press first End and then ↓.) Pull down the Data menu and click the Text to Columns command to display the Convert Text to Columns Wizard - Step 1 of 3 dialog box. Notice how the **Delimited** option button is on.

7. Click the **Next** button to display Step 2 of 3, click the **Tab** check box in the *Delimiters* section to turn it off, and click the **Comma** check box to turn it on.
8. Click the **Finish** button (you needn't complete Step 3 of 3). Use the **Format, Column, AutoFit Selection** command to widen columns B through E.
9. Scroll through the table and you'll see that Excel broke the lines up into cells using the commas as indicators of where new columns were to start. You'll also see where it made a few mistakes. In these situations, the entries themselves contained commas that Excel mistook for delimiters.
10. Save the workbook, print the first page of the worksheet, then close Excel and Word.

7-2 Pasting Objects into Excel Worksheets

If you have already created a file that you want to link or embed in another application's document as an object, you can copy and paste it in. In this drill you practice these procedures.

1. Start Excel and open the *Cut & Paste drill* workbook stored in the *OLE Files* folder of the *Excel Student Resource Disk*. Enter your name in cell A1. Maximize Excel if it isn't already.
2. Start Word and open the *Merge data document* stored in the *OLE Files* folder of the *Excel Student Resource Disk*. Maximize Word if it isn't already.
3. In Word, select all lines of the top table, including its heading *EMBEDDED MERGE DATA*, then click the **Copy** button on Word's Standard toolbar.
4. In Excel, click cell A6, the pull down the **Edit** menu and click the **Paste Special** command to display the Paste Special dialog box.
5. With the **Paste option** button on and *Microsoft Word Document Object* selected on the **As** list, click the **OK** command button to paste the data.
6. Return to Word and select all lines of the bottom table, including its heading *LINKED MERGE DATA*, then click the **Copy** button on Word's toolbar.
7. Return to Excel, click cell A22, then pull down the **Edit** menu and click the **Paste Special** command to display the Paste Special dialog box. *Microsoft Word Document Object* should be selected on the **As** list.
8. To link the object, click the **Paste Link** option button, then click the **OK** command button to paste the data.
9. Save and print the Excel workbook, then close both applications. If asked, don't save changes in the Word document or the data on the Clipboard.

7-3 Inserting Objects into Excel Worksheets

If you want to insert a new object or create an object from an existing file on the disk, you can do so. In this drill you practice the procedures used to embed and link objects created from existing files on the disk. Both objects that you insert are Word tables.

1. Start Excel and open the **Insert drill** workbook stored in the *OLE Files* folder of the *Excel Student Resource Disk*. Maximize Excel if it isn't already.
2. Click cell A6, pull down the **Insert** menu, and click the **Object** command to display the Object dialog box.
3. Click the **Create from File** tab and click the **Browse** button to select the *Embedded merge data* document stored in *OLE Files* folder on the *Excel Student Resource Disk*.

4. Click the **Insert** button to return to the Object dialog box, then click that dialog box's **OK** button to insert the embedded object into the worksheet.
5. Click cell A31, pull down the **Insert** menu and click the **Object** command to display the Object dialog box.
6. Click the **Create from File** tab and click the **Browse** button to select the *Linked merge data* document stored in *OLE Files* folder on the *Excel Student Resource Disk*.
7. Click the **Insert** button to return to the Object dialog box, then click the **Link to File** check box so the object will be linked instead of embedded.
8. Click the **OK** button to insert the linked object into the worksheet.
9. Save and print the Excel worksheet, then close the application.

7-4 Editing Linked and Embedded Objects

Once you have embedded or linked objects in a document, you can edit them in place. Here you practice the procedures you use to edit both embedded and linked objects.

1. Open Excel and use it to open the *Insert drill* worksheet stored in the *OLE Files* folder on the *Excel Student Resource Disk*. A message box asks you whether you want to re-establish links. Click the **Yes** button.
2. To edit the embedded object in place, double-click it to activate it. (It's the first object in the worksheet.)
3. Double-click the word *Liz* to select it and then type **Elizabeth** to replace it.
4. Click outside of the object so it is no longer activated.
5. To edit the same embedded object in a separate window, click it to select it, then pull down the **Edit** menu, point to the **Document Object** command to cascade the menu, and click the **Open** command.
6. Double-click the word *Elizabeth* to select it and then type **Liz** to replace it.
7. Click the document window's **Close** button to close it and you'll see the change is carried to the *Embedded Merge Data* table in the *Insert drills* worksheet.
8. To edit the linked object (it's the second object starting on row 31), double-click it to open it in a separate server application (Word) window.
9. Double-click the word *Liz* to select it and then type **Elizabeth** to replace it.
10. Click Word's **Save** button on the Standard toolbar to save the changes, then click Word's **Close** button. You'll see the change is carried to the *Linked Merge Data* table in the *Insert drills* worksheet.
11. Save the Excel worksheet, then close all applications.

EXERCISES

7-1 Embedding and Linking Objects

In this exercise, you explore embedding and linking objects on your own. You will work with the same objects you have been working with in tutorials and drills so they will be familiar to you.

1. Use Word to open the *Publisher list* document stored in the *OLE Files* folder on the *Excel Student Resource Disk*. Use Excel to open the *Publisher list* workbook stored in the same folder. Arrange the windows side by side.

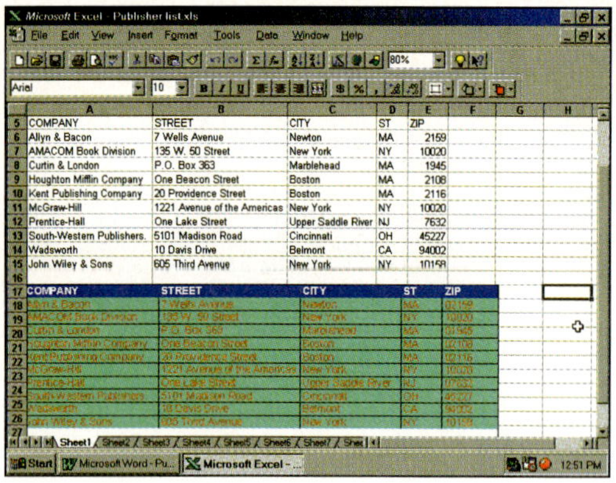

The Linked Publisher List

2. Copy the data in the table from Word to the Clipboard and then paste it into the Excel workbook below the 3-line heading.
4. Copy the data in the table from Word to the Clipboard again and paste it into the Excel worksheet below the first table. This time use the **Paste Special** command on the **Edit** menu and be sure to click the **Paste Link** option button so the object will be linked instead of embedded.
5. Size and position the linked object as shown in the figure "The Linked Publisher List."
6. Edit the linked object to change the name *Allyn & Bacon* to *Allyn & Bacon Publishers*.
7. Save and print the Excel worksheet, then close all applications.

PROJECTS

7-1 You're on Your Own

You have now come to the end of the text! At this point, demonstrate your skill with OLE by opening a new Excel worksheet and then linking and embedding objects into it in a variety of ways. Label each object and describe the procedure you used to link or embed it. You can use any of the objects that you find in the *OLE Files* folder on the *Excel Student Resource Disk*. If your system has sound capability, one in particular to embed is *John.avi*. This is a sound file commenting on a worksheet. It demonstrates how sound can be used to annotate reports.

INDEX